This enthralling book is much more than a history of Alaska. It is a detailed account of First Contact, good intentions and devious ones, a convergence of cultures on a grand scale, all sides fairly represented with vivid portraits; a valuable record of the complex fate of the last wilderness on earth.
PAUL THEROUX, *New York Times* bestselling author of *The Mosquito Coast, The Tao of Travel, Deep South, The Great Railway Bazaar,* and *Blinding Light*

The little-known meeting between the "Ice Chief" and the Tlingit guardians of Alaska's coast came at a moment of historic crisis and transition. Introducing an array of vivid characters, Daniel Henry deftly brings this hidden gem of a story to light, drawing on years of scholarly research, careful cultivation of local Native sources, and the author's deep knowledge of the physical Southeast Alaska landscape. Whether John Muir's appeals to brotherhood and altruism were justified—given the century of American rule that followed—is one of many glittering ambiguities that this story forces us to consider.
TOM KIZZIA, *New York Times* bestselling author of *Pilgrim's Wilderness* and *The Wake of the Unseen Object*

With Tlingit elders as narrative partners, Dan Henry has rendered a unique retelling of John Muir's encounters with Alaska's landscapes and people. Comprehensive and thoroughly sourced, *Shaman's River* is an essential book for those who seek fresh perspectives on the complexities of the Northern experience.
DEB VANASSE, author of *Wealth Woman: Kate Carmack and the Klondike Race for Gold* and *Cold Spell*

Henry is a gifted wordsmith and has written a convincing if complex narrative that begins with his own journey to Alaska in 1979 and backtracks one hundred years to John Muir's first trip of seven to the region. He has a gift parallel to Pulitzer Prize-winner John McPhee in taking a near-contemporary event and moving back and forth between historical events and modern issues, using oral history and testimony to reinforce documented events. The result is a well-crafted, cogent story of the contest to break the hegemony of Native chiefs.
WILLIAM SWAGERTY, PH.D., Professor of History; Director, John Muir Center for Environmental Studies, University of the Pacific author of *The Indianization of Lewis and Clark*

If you're looking for cheap amusement, dear reader, get another book. If you're looking for a new lens on history, a story both patient and provocative, scholarly yet stunning; illuminating and even radical, this is for you. This is the story of John Muir and the last hostile tribes of North America, the Chilkat Tlingits of Alaska. Not John Muir the naturalist or conservationist, but JM the pacifist and agent of Manifest Destiny, speaking on brotherhood and love. I devoured this great book.

KIM HEACOX, author of *Jimmy Bluefeather* and *John Muir and the Ice that Started a Fire*

Henry's book fills a gap in our understanding of Tlingit history and their relations with Europeans that no other study has attempted. Given that there is plenty of interest in the life and adventures of John Muir among environmentalists, there will be an equal number of Alaskan historians and students who will enjoy Henry's *Across the Shaman's River* and discuss the significance of its contents for decades to come.

REV. DR. MICHAEL JAMES OLEKSA, Russian Orthodox Archpriest of Alaska, ret., author of *Another Culture/Another World*

Across the Shaman's River is an elegantly written text, laced with novel insights that should attract a significant readership. Henry takes on a host of controversial issues; I doubt all of his readers will agree with his arguments. However, given the depth and quality of the research he has marshaled, critics will need to take his arguments seriously, and interrogate the original research he offers.

DAVID FRANK, PH.D., Professor of Rhetoric, University of Oregon, Eugene, OR, author of *Frames of Evil: The Holocaust as Horror in American Film*

Dan Henry tells a story about the history of Alaska in a way it has never been told before. This is a terrific read for both casual readers and nit-picky experts, a feat to celebrate and enjoy.

TERRENCE COLE, PH.D., Professor of History, University of Alaska, Fairbanks, AK, author of *Fighting for the Forty-Ninth Star: C.W. Snedden and the Crusade for Alaska Statehood* and *Banking on Alaska: The Story of the National Bank of Alaska*

ACROSS THE SHAMAN'S RIVER

Daniel Lee Henry

University of Alaska Press, Fairbanks

Across the Shaman's River

JOHN MUIR, THE TLINGIT STRONGHOLD,
AND THE OPENING OF THE NORTH

Text © 2017 University of Alaska Press

Published by
University of Alaska Press
P.O. Box 756240
Fairbanks, AK 99775-6240

Cover and interior design by Kristina Kachele Design, llc.

Cover digital artwork by Andy Romanoff; thanks to Taku Graphics.

Cover images: Main cover image of Favorite Passage, near Sentinel Island, photo by John Hyde for AlaskaStock (Image 019SE AJ0074D001); John Muir Portrait, circa 1875. MSS048. f23-1249.tif, John Muir Papers, Holt-Atherton Special Collections, University of the Pacific Library. © 1984 Muir-Hanna Trust.; Large Tlingit-style canoe in the Lynn Canal near Haines (paddled by Tlingits from Haines Mission), circa 1903, 1989.304.0005, courtesy of the Haines Sheldon Museum, Haines, Alaska.

Library of Congress Cataloging-in-Publication Data

Names: Henry, Daniel Lee, author.
Title: Across the shaman's river : John Muir, the Tlingit stronghold, and the opening of the north / Daniel Lee Henry.
Description: Fairbanks : University of Alaska Press, 2017. | Includes bibliographical references. |
Identifiers: LCCN 2016056624 (print) | LCCN 2017017857 (ebook) | ISBN 9781602233300 (e-book) | ISBN 9781602233294 (paperback : alkaline paper)
Subjects: LCSH: Tlingit Indians—Alaska—Lynn Canal Region—History—19th century. | Tlingit Indians—Cultural assimilation—Alaska—Lynn Canal Region—History—19th century. | Tlingit Indians—Missions—Alaska—Lynn Canal Region—History—19th century. | Muir, John, 1838–1914—Travel—Alaska—Lynn Canal Region. | Muir, John, 1838–1914—Diaries. | Naturalists—Alaska—Lynn Canal Region—History—19th century. | Shamans—Alaska—Lynn Canal Region—History—19th century. | Missionaries—Alaska—Lynn Canal Region—History—19th century. | Lynn Canal Region (Alaska)—Ethnic relations—History—19th century. | Lynn Canal Region (Alaska)—Description and travel. | BISAC: HISTORY / Native American.
Classification: LCC E99.T6 (ebook) | LCC E99.T6 H46 2017 (print) | DDC 979.8004/9727—dc23
LC record available at https://lccn.loc.gov/2016056624

To my teachers—Austin Hammond, Joe Hotch, and Rachel "Dixie" Johnson

I might say all my life I have never until now heard a white man speak. It has always seemed to me that while trying to talk to traders and those seeking gold-mines that it was like speaking to a person across a broad stream that was running fast over stones and making so loud a noise that scarce a single word could be heard. But now, for the first time, the Indian and the white man are on the same side of the river, eye to eye, heart to heart.

Karskarz (Kaa'shaax), shaman-headman of Chilkoot, to John Muir

Yandeist'akyé, Alaska NOVEMBER 7, 1879

Contents

Illustrations

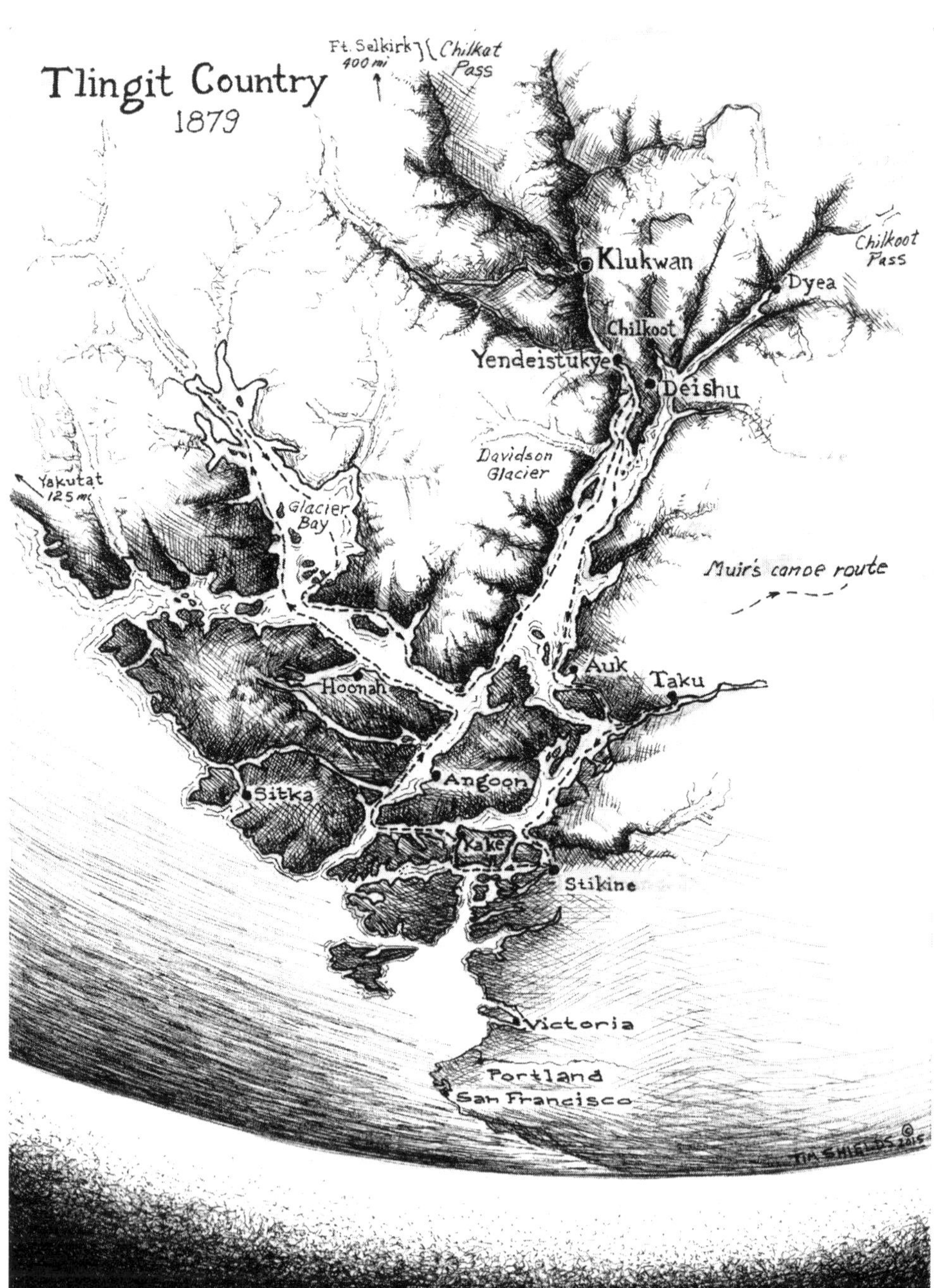

Tlingit Country
1879
Ft. Selkirk
400 mi
Chilkat Pass
Chilkoot Pass
Klukwan
Dyea
Chilkoot
Yendeistukye
Deishu
Davidson Glacier
Yakutat
125 mi
Glacier Bay
Muir's canoe route
Auk
Taku
Hoonah
Sitka
Angoon
Kake
Stikine
Victoria
Portland
San Francisco
TIM SHIELDS 2015

Foreword

:: CONNECTIONS MADE

This book is a remarkable achievement. Daniel Henry discerns, documents, and, with elegant and entertaining prose, connects people, events, and cultures that have always seemed unrelated. No one else has recognized this history. Taking a wider and deeper view, Henry has discovered the amazing relationship between the northern Tlingit clans, the American Presbyterian missionaries—particularly Rev. S. Hall Young—and pioneering environmentalist John Muir, and tells the fascinating tale of how their interactions opened the northern region of Alaska's Southeast Panhandle to global influences.

Cultures are ways of seeing the world. Certainly, all the main players in this saga had their own unique visions of reality. Indigenous peoples had discerned the inherent spiritual significance of their land, for they valued its resources and delighted in its scenic beauty. Their shaman leaders affirmed an ancient belief in the power of the invisible made manifest in the wonders of the natural world and brought into focus by the power and authority of those extraordinary spiritual visionaries who prophesied and healed them. Their faith was rooted in the land.

The American Protestant missionaries found God most especially in Holy Scripture, the Word of God as a Book, and considered people who venerated the earth at best misguided pagans, at worst hopeless barbarians. It was the preachers' task to convince Native people to abandon their ancient ways and become "civilized." To achieve this transformation, many missionaries, reformers, and Indian agents thought it would be necessary to eradicate much of the Natives' "primitive" culture and even suppress their tribal language. Later in his life, S. Hall Young insisted that the Tlingit language should be allowed to die in order to purge their "superstitions and lies," which, somehow, he intrinsically linked together. The sooner the old ways disappeared, the faster targeted populations could join the civilized world, albeit as laborers, miners, and fruit pickers. The Reverend Sheldon Jackson, Alaska's education commissioner and also a national leader of the Presbyterian Church, advised his subordinates to discourage and disparage the use of indigenous languages and customs, insist on the speaking of English alone, and to introduce or impose, if necessary, Anglo American cultural norms—the cutting of hair and wearing of starched shirts and of ties, coats, suits, and polished shoes. Civilized!

Another church official noted, "We have no higher calling than as missionaries to those who have not yet achieved the Anglo-Saxon frame of mind." One could hardly find two more diametrically opposed ways of seeing the world—two more opposite cultures—than those confronting each other in the prologue of this book.

The critical connecting link was the unlikely liaison, John Muir. His own upbringing was not unlike Reverend Young's, except that the doctrines of Muir's father, a preacher, were even more conservative and uncompromising. Nevertheless, Muir's evangelical Christian background provided him with a fundamental understanding of Young's convictions and commitment, thus enabling their friendship, as Henry shows in this book. Without this very human relationship, the events documented here could not have occurred.

What the author does is rather extraordinary insofar as he has appreciated and respected all the disparate elements of this drama and shown how, like the perfect congruence of planets on an astrological chart, these cultures and these people came together to enrich and inspire each other.

Muir understood very well the spiritual intuition of the Tlingit, but his own religious training prevented him from embracing it. He understood the positive motives of his new missionary friend as well but could not fully embrace his philosophy. Because he could empathize with both but accept neither, Muir became the bridge, the connection, capable in the end of bringing together conflicting, virtually opposite "ways of seeing the world" while forging another way.

Ironically, and perhaps even tragically, there already was another "way of seeing" available and already present in Southeast Alaska at this time. Introduced by Ioan Veniaminov, the Siberian Russian priest at Sitka, the Eastern Orthodox "way of seeing" affirmed the inherent spiritual value of the created world as basic to religious life. Byzantine theology discussed the Word of God as constantly seeking to be "embodied," and Saint Maximus the Confessor, in the seventh century, affirmed that the Word (Logos) had been "embodied" three times: in the whole cosmos, the created universe; in the Bible, the written Sacred Word; and finally in Jesus Christ, the Word Made Flesh.

In the twentieth century, Saint Nicolai Velmirovich went so far as to affirm that anyone who could not find God in the first embodiment, the visible creation, was unlikely to find Him in any book. "If you cannot find God in the wilderness," he explained, "the one crying in the wilderness will have nothing to say to you." How well this would have resonated with Muir's spiritual experience, a form of Christianity that celebrated and affirmed the inherent and eternal spiritual value of the natural world as blessed, sacred and even, as one ancient Orthodox writer stated, "God's Self-Portrait."

Veniaminov translated scriptural and liturgical texts into Tlingit, opened a school for the Tlingits to learn to read and translate texts into their own language, and built a chapel where worship was conducted in their language. The Great Blessing of Water, celebrated annually with processions from the church to the Pacific Ocean, renewed the original blessing that God Himself had bestowed, "in the Beginning," calling what He had made "very good." There are Orthodox rites for blessing land, houses, bread, flowers, salt, meat, fish, new wells, graves, and even beehives!

But neither Muir nor Young ever met the priests of Sitka. It was a potentially fruitful connection that was never made.

In this book, however, the author has discerned those connections that were made but have until now gone unnoticed. I hope all those who read these pages will be as delighted as I am to see how, despite all their limitations and differences, Native Americans, Anglo American missionaries, and one sensitive, brilliant, and visionary pioneer American environmentalist came together to create a new way of seeing for future generations.

Michael J. Oleksa, Th.D.
Very Reverend Archpriest, ret.,
Orthodox Church in America
Anchorage, Alaska OCTOBER 2016

Acknowledgments

I extend my profound gratitude to the hundreds of fine people whose comments and insights have contributed to this book over three decades and to the many kind friends who have cheerfully endured the details of this story.

My deep appreciation goes to the Chilkat and Chilkoot Tlingit people and other Southeast Alaska Natives who contributed to this research, especially Austin Hammond Sr., Rachel (Dixie) and Peter C. Johnson Sr., Nathan Jackson, Matilda and George Lewis, Mary and Richard King Sr., Maria Ackerman Miller, Tom Jimmie Jr., Wayne Price, Kimberly Strong, Elsie Spud, Sally and Val Burratin, Joe Hotch, Ed Warren Sr., Lani and Jones Hotch Jr., Marsha Hotch, Brian Willard, Al Morgan, David Andrews, Anne Keener, Jessie Morgan, David Strong, Glenda Robinson, Harriett Brouillette, Charles Brouillette Jr., David Light, Tim Ackerman, Jan Hill, Jay Miller, Charles Jimmie Sr., Ray Dennis, Jim Stevens, Carol Feller Brady, Rosita Worl, and Bob Sam, and to the Klukwan librarians, Genevieve Stevens and Jamie Katzeek. *Gunalchéesh* to friends and colleagues at the Tlingit Clan Conference.

My warm thanks also goes to those Chilkat Valley residents who volunteered to read drafts of this book and whose feedback proved invaluable: Lee Heinmiller, Cynthia (CJ) Jones, Joan Snyder, Alan Traut, Tony Tengs, Jay Proetto, Janine Allen, Beth Fenhauser, Harriett Brouillette, Scott Carey, Heidi Robichaux, Bruce Blake, Robin Grace, Nancy Berland, and Burl Sheldon. Members of my Klukwan creative writing class also reviewed early portions of this book. Additional thanks are extended to Lou Butera for volunteering to publish review drafts. In his enthusiasm, faith, and research, former Haines teacher and historian Norman Smith Sr., was an inspiration, along with my mentor and friend Ray Menaker.

I am indebted to the generosity of those scholars and writers who reviewed materials, listened to my questions, or offered guidance along the way: Nora and Richard Dauenhauer, Lani Hotch, David Frank, Holway Jones, Ronald Limbaugh, Kim Heacox, William Swagerty, Suzanne and Ron Scollon, Thomas Thornton, Stephen Langdon, Julie Cruikshank, Fr. Michael Oleksa, Peter Metcalfe, Dee Longenbaugh, M. J. Kirchoff, Kerri Edwards Eggleston, Carolyn Servid, Dorik Mechau, Sergei Kan, Jeff Harrison, Robin Kimmerer, Ron Arnold, Debbie Kellogg, Ken Waldman, Peggy Shumaker, Susan Carkin, Kathleen Dean Moore, John Straley, Ken Kesey, Wendell Berry, Bruce Merrell, and Gary Snyder.

These curators, historians, and archivists provided invaluable assistance with research: Cynthia (CJ) Jones, Jerrie Clarke, Helen Alten, Nancy Nash, Aly Zeiger, Andrea Nelson, Madeline Witek, Michael Wurtz, Trish Richards, Zach Jones, Rosita Worl, Cynthia Von Halle, Karl Guerke, and Judy Munz. For his keen eye, knowledge, and generosity of spirit, I am indebted to Durwood Ball of the University of New Mexico. For their willingness to walk with me on the long path to publication, I am grateful to the editors of University of Alaska Press, James Engelhardt, Amy Simpson, and Krista West, and to the members of the Press' Advisory Board. Thanks to Katrina Woolford of Taku Graphics and to Andy Romanoff for additional cover digital artwork. Tim Shields made the map; Rob Goldberg supplied wisdom.

To "Buckwheat" Donahue, Jeff Brady, Katrina Woolford, and the writers and supporters of the North Words Writers Symposium in Skagway, Alaska—dreams come true.

For institutional support I am indebted to the Holt-Atherton Reserves/ John Muir Archives, University of Alaska Southeast, Alaska Humanities Forum, Sealaska Heritage Institute, University of Alaska Press, Tlingit Readers, Inc., Haines Sheldon Museum and Cultural Center, and Lane Community College.

For decades of music and honest interest in this story, I am grateful to Barry Sless, Pete Sears, John Molo, Anne and Roger McNamee, and Big Steve Parish.

This book exists in large part because my wife, Robin Grace, dedicated herself fully to my passion for this story and scrutinized every word. Thank you, my love. To our son Charlie Skyhawk Henry, my parents JoAn and Bob Henry, and brother Ken Henry—thanks for your patience and support.

ACROSS THE SHAMAN'S RIVER

Introduction: *To Tell the Story*

A hundred years after John Muir first stepped into Alaska mud in deep drizzle, my Alaska Airlines flight touched down on Juneau tarmac under an ice-
blue sky in June 1979.

As the coach of a successful college debate program, I was drawn north by
passionate arguments surrounding the bill that Pres. Jimmy Carter would
sign as the Alaska National Interest Lands Conservation Act. Red-faced and
scolding, environmentalists and loggers locked horns at every turn in the
claustrophobic state capitol. From there I gravitated a hundred miles north
into Lynn Canal, the fjord-riven land called Jil̲káat aaní (Chilkat territory or
domain) by its Tlingit inhabitants, where I sought clues about a man who, a
century earlier, had changed the course of the world through his dedication
to wildness. In an event all but ignored by his biographers, the wilderness
prophet transformed one of America's last enclaves of "heathen savages" in
ways that are difficult to reconcile with Muir's legendary status. I needed to
know how Nature's foremost American champion might also have been an
agent of Manifest Destiny.

Most curious to me was how John Muir could reconcile his vision of wilderness with the people who had previously inhabited his hallowed landscapes. As far as I could tell, the fashionable blend of suspicion and pity he
held for Native Americans seemed to be the one that shaped their rhetorical
role in the twentieth-century wilderness debate.

Writers and filmmakers in the 1970s and 1980s popularized Chiefs Seattle, Joseph, and Sitting Bull for their articulate elegies to a vanishing way of life. That was the problem, my inner debate coach insisted. I distrusted metaphorical paeans to a noble end when the evidence seemed plain that most Native Americans experienced cultural and physical trauma. Rhetoric—persuasive communication—implies a society in which a rhetor's audience is allowed to choose freely among ideas. Violence, disease, and poverty deny that choice.

For nearly a century the United States waged a declared war against Indians. Rather than firepower or ultimatums, however, in Alaska John Muir transformed Native listeners with words and his character, or *ethos.* For the rest of his life, he promulgated policies that dispossessed tribes of their land and that deemed it preserved forever as unpeopled or uninhabited wilderness. Muir's ethos turned the popular understanding of wilderness from a dangerous enemy to be vanquished into a divine gift to be revered, studied, and left alone. In the long run, I wondered, was rhetorical capitulation a means for peace or just another battle in the war?

When he arrived in Alaska in 1879, Muir was in his ascendance. He was a self-taught naturalist in pursuit of glaciers, a published writer, and a popular lecturer. Prior to the journey, Muir had dismissed Native Americans as degraded specimens of a people once self-sustaining and "wild." As did most educated white people of his era, he pitied and feared the remnant populations sequestered on the reservations and in the rural backwaters of a diminished frontier. However, a few months among the Tlingits challenged Muir's assumptions. Abundant natural resources and limited contact with Euro-Americans left much of their original culture intact. Muir observed that Alaska Indians were keen to the economic and educational advantages of whites yet still retained their cultural integrity. The northern Tlingits—Chilkats and Chilkoots—resisted altogether the changes that accompanied white immigration. With a fierceness resembling "Macedonians," Muir wrote, "these savages [are] warlike and inflexible in their opposition to the entrance of miners into their mountains."[1] Moreover, they were among the last Native Americans touched by missionaries and a target for Presbyterian forerunners dedicated to spreading the gospel in the nation's newest territorial acquisition.

Accompanied by his missionary friend, S. Hall Young, and a crew of four Tlingits, Muir embarked in poor weather on a canoe voyage that eventually brought him to the doorstep of the Chilkat-Chilkoot fortress. And by the strength of the only religious sermon Muir was ever known to deliver, the legendary tribes laid down their arms. Once jealous guardians of secret trade routes into the Yukon, northern Tlingits subsequently acceded their "money trails" to white men seeking gold in unmapped lands. In a letter written six weeks after his speech and published in the *Daily Evening Bulletin* of San Francisco, Muir confirmed that the previously "hostile" Chilkats were now prepared to guide miners to the mother lode.[2] The trickle of adventurers drawn by the report became a flood in the late 1890s as news of the Klondike gold strike electrified the nation.

A century after John Muir unlocked the last Tlingit stronghold, a survivor of the flood assured me that despite the stream of prospectors and soul-savers, Tlingit traditions remained vital among the treasures of his people. Within minutes of our first meeting at his culture camp in 1983, Chilkoot traditional leader Austin Hammond Sr. showed me a grand weaving that, he claimed, was the deed to traditional lands. "Some people ask me where is your history," Hammond said. "I'll tell you. We're wearin' our history."

As the seventy-four-year-old headman rose to his feet in the fire circle, a large *xaq'naakein* (Chilkat blanket or robe) unfurled from his shoulders revealing an intricate design woven in mountain goat wool. Slowly he pivoted, extending his arms for full display. "Raven showed us why we're gonna own everything," Hammond said as he began a story about the unique relationship between the Lukaax̱.ádi Tlingit people and Sockeye Point on Chilkoot Lake and explained how his people can be whole only when they occupy their home again.

"My grandfather told me to dress this way when we're in trouble," Hammond said. Raised by his mother's parents, Jim and Martha David, Hammond bore the name of his great-grandfather, Daanawáaḵ, once headman of Yandeist'aḵyé and friend to John Muir. In 1982, as Raven House *hit-saati,* or headman, Austin Hammond, also Daanawáaḵ, displayed the robe to Haines, Alaska, magistrate Carl Heinmiller, who accepted the woven proof of land ownership. The following summer, Lukaax̱.ádi clansmen and supporters pioneered the Chilkoot Culture Camp, one of the first Native culture camps in Alaska and an important step toward reclaiming home.[3]

Over the next three seasons of kids and elders, brown bears and dry-fish, Hammond's culture camp drew me, first as a print and radio journalist, then as oral historian and volunteer. In time, relationships with elders grew into projects and friendships. Once a week for three years, Maria Miller and Rachel "Dixie" Johnson trudged arm-in-arm up a long flight of stairs to meet me in the studio of our lone radio station, KHNS, for live episodes of "Tlingit Words and Songs." For fifteen minutes a week they spoke and sang in Tlingit, encouraging the white guy's awkward attempts to speak, sometimes responding with giggles. Dixie would ask me to repeat a phrase until she'd cut in with a knowing "Aaaaah." Pause. "Now you're talking like an Indian." Niece and auntie cackled like birds at low tide.

The women contributed to another radio project called *Yeil Koo'klak: Raven Stories* featuring Miller, Dixie and Pete Johnson Sr., Austin Hammond Sr., Matilda and George Lewis, Mary and Richard King, David Andrews, Ann Keener, Charlie Jimmie Sr., and Tommy Jimmie Jr.—mostly from the L̲koot ḵwáan (Chilkoot village). Five men hefted Hammond's brother Horace Marks in his wheelchair up and down twenty-eight stair-steps to the studio. Over several winter nights in 1986, people squeezed into glass radio booths to sing songs and tell stories from time immemorial.

In the next decade I spent many evenings in local living rooms listening to life histories. Following one such session, Dixie said: "I'm gonna give you an Indian name. Might as well, you know too much already." Stoowukaa. Idea man. "Now you're in cahoots with a lot of big people," she said. "Kaagwaantaan—the whole kit and caboodle."

At times I ached knowing how much more I could do for my adopted clan, but didn't. Memorial potlatches missed, fish not shared, conversations unspoken. I felt guilty for my name, that I should do more to earn it. By recording oral histories in ensuing years, however, I began to understand my role as memory keeper.

Like blankets and berry patches, Tlingit people own their clan stories, so it is not my place to repeat the Sockeye Point narrative told to me by Austin Hammond. Nor, for that matter, is it proper for me to relay the clan stories of more than thirty elders interviewed since the early 1980s. Tlingit anthropologist Nora Dauenhauer says that traditional Tlingit law allows retelling stories without direct permission but the "oral copyright" requires source attribution, respect, and accuracy. Those stories are for others to tell; this book is warmed by the heat of cross-cultural engagement, much of which is public record. On the other hand, access to local Tlingit history is perhaps best gained through relationships—and patience. Researching this story the white-man way only took me so far; I had to earn the trust of a people recovering from generations of outsiders like myself.

In my early years as a local journalist, some Native leaders were clearly more accessible than others. Concerns about traditional ownership and use of their lands drew vocal Chilkoots to mediagenic projects. Three seasons of my involvement with Hammond's culture camp was enough to elicit warm smiles, handshakes, and free-range opinions. Folks in Klukwan, a Chilkat village, were more evasive. News from the Chilkats spread along clannish lines, rarely surfacing in public. Several times, I drove the forty-mile round trip for an interview only to find empty houses. I took it as a sign to back off, so satisfied myself with the longer route—basketball games and cultural celebrations, funerals and graduations. Gradually, eye contact increased, then came the ribbing, jokes, and laughter.

After a quarter century of teaching Chilkat kids, recording Chilkat elders, and broadcasting Chilkat culture, our stories wove us together. In 2005 I produced "Tlingit Time," a fifty-two–part radio program featuring Tlingit-language instructor, Marsha Hotch. Two years later, I taught a semester-long public-speaking course to village administrators through the University of Alaska. Rather than open the first week's class with Aristotle, I reviewed two hundred years of rhetorical encounters between Chilkats and white men.

"Are these stories okay for me to tell?" I asked the class at the beginning of the lecture. Characteristic silence filled the room, the sound of minds working, mouths waiting. Council president Kim Strong cleared her throat and smiled like a well-prepared student. Heads nodded once, acknowledging what was to come. White-man history is different than clan stories, she explained. "Your people's history is your business, but for our stories, you get permission and you give credit."[4]

This book offers my best effort to find stories that may answer these questions: Did John Muir, as he suggested in *Travels in Alaska,* play a significant role in the conversion of the Chilkat and Chilkoot Tlingit tribes from shamanism to Christianity? If so, did he light the fires or fan the flames of change? What were the effects of this moment of cross-cultural contact on Muir and his Native brethren? How do tribal descendants respond today? What does the story reveal about American attitudes and policies toward Native people? What rhetorical factors influenced the change? We know that Muir and the northern Tlingits were irrevocably changed by their encounter. This book suggests that the history of Alaska and the nation was altered by the moment.

Neither ethnography nor biography, this book blends aspects of each into a rhetorical history of events leading up to Muir's watershed moment with the northern Tlingit and of consequences unspooling in the aftermath. Part 1, Jilḵáat Aaní, chronicles cross-cultural encounters in Chilkat Country prior to Muir's 1879 visit, beginning with interclan relationships that arose during early Tlingit migration and then moving onto white contact. Part 2, Dleit Aankáawu, follows Muir's life as he grew into a spokesperson of the national lands preservation movement, examining the evolution of his communication style, religious views, and relationship with Native Americans, especially as it built toward his pivotal week among the Chilkat-Chilkoot

Tlingit. Chapter 11 and the epilogue show how the experience affected Muir and his Native hosts and discuss the greater cultural consequences of their encounter.

Quotations of letters, journals, diaries, and other primary sources include idiosyncrasies and errors in spelling, punctuation, and grammar, thus eliminating the pesky *"sic."* As they first appear on the page, most Tlingit names and words are represented with both the common usage and modern orthography. Common historical spellings of names, such as Glate Ankow and Koh'klux, determine their spelling thereafter. A glossary of Tlingit terms is provided in the appendices. The community of Wrangell has also been called Fort Wrangel, Wrangel, and Fort Wrangell, but appears here as the earlier Fort Wrangell and then, simply, Wrangell. I am grateful for the sharp eyes and editorial grace of linguist Keri Edwards, the lead author of *Dictionary of Tlingit*, and assume full responsibility for any spelling or orthographic errors in the text.

The racialized use of *chief* persisted in Muir's lectures and in articles about him, although the actual meaning of Dleit Aankáawu is different. Rather than mainstream society's conception of *chief*, explicit Tlingit leadership roles fell to clan leaders, generally called headmen. A headman might rise to *sháade háni*, which some likened to a corporate board chair, but never with the implied autonomy of a chief. Since *dleit* means snow, ice, or white, and *aank̲*áawu suggests wise leader, ambassador, or lord, Tlingit linguist Marsha Hotch suggested Muir's name might have meant "Best White Man." Others have interpreted the phrase as "White Aristocrat." *Glate Ankow* is used here when considered from the perspective of Muir or other non-Natives; Dleit Aank̲áawu when referenced by the Tlingit.[5]

Seven generations since the Chilkat and Chilkoot headmen identified the site of a Presbyterian mission for Muir and his companions, the indigenous people of my adopted home still claim ownership. No treaties were ever signed; no battles were lost. Conservative and wary, the northern Tlingits first approached white newcomers as intruders, then as business associates, and finally as brothers.

"Our roots are together, no matter what color we are," Austin Hammond (Daanawáak̲) said to members of our fire circle. "You are my family, every one of you. Raven put us together from all the way down."[6]

Flames played in the headman's aviator glasses. The weight of his mission spread across a face as brown and whorled as a walnut. A smile flickered when I asked Hammond about his birthday. He was born on Alaska Day, October 18, 1910, in a clan house at Taiyasanki Harbor, the only sheltered cove in the narrow fjord between Haines and Skagway. That makes me a "real Alaska man," he joked. His birth father was a man named Tom Phillips (Neechku.oowú) of the Kaagwaantaan clan from the Killer Whale House in Klukwan; his mother was Jennie Marks (Kultuyax Sée) of the Lukaax.ádi at Chilkoot.

When Hammond was two, his father and Joe Wright found a canoe in the fjord that contained the murdered bodies of a man, woman, and children. They tied the boat to their canoe and paddled to Haines. A court determined their guilt and sent them to federal prison at McNeil Island in Washington. When the charges were dropped the next year, the men returned to Haines. Shortly afterward, Phillips succumbed to complications from a prison injury. His mother remarried Willis Hammond from Hoonah, but Austin lived with his grandparents. Shocked by the lost traditions since his return to Haines, Joe Wright composed a traditional song to show his sorrow for a withering homeland. In 1989 Austin Hammond gave permission for the song to be used as the Tlingit national anthem.[7]

Renowned basketball player, fisherman, and father, Hammond aspired to the life of a successful "Twentieth Century man." A heart attack in 1975 compelled him to confront his mortality, so he "asked God to give me my life back so I can tell my children the Story." In a dream he found a letter in his mailbox announcing in golden script that he would be widely known for a crusade that enlisted all races to preserve Tlingit culture. "That's why I'm not afraid to tell my white brothers the Story," he explained.

He caught my gaze and held it. "I'm tellin' you the Story so you can tell it later. You got to tell the Story."

A pitch glob sizzled and snapped. In the flare, a brown hand tentatively emerged and grasped a corner of the Sockeye Robe. Twin tears tracked Eva Davis's ruddy, round cheeks as she recalled her grandfather telling her that one day she would be the last in the family to tell their stories. "I'm not talkin' about myself, I need to save all my gran'chirdren!" Gently, her hand tugged at the robe with the cadence of her speech. "Now all our people are scared to use this blanket. I'm not afraid to protect all my people, all the way down."[8]

Davis clung to the Chilkat robe as her words sunk in. River voices filled the long silence. A raven chortled in the darkness. Austin raised his face, eyes closed, then spoke in prayerful tones of tumbling water and birdcall.

He began to tell the Story.

Gratitude to the elders, historians, and storytellers who nourish this work.

Gratitude to you, the reader, for holding this. Through the words of witnesses and descendants of witnesses, I mean to tell a nearly forgotten story.

To you whose ancestral memory contradicts this research, forgive me.

For doubts provoked about cherished beliefs and myths, forgive me.

Different versions of these stories are told, many of which are acknowledged here.

Forgive my assumptions and omissions.

I am a student. Many Native elders witnessed their truths to me, believing my capacity to convey a fair account. "You. You have to tell the story," they said.

I am an educator. As a high school/college teacher in Haines, Alaska, I was concerned that students were unaware of their community's greatest story, so stood before classrooms vowing to write it down.

Thirty years after receiving my homework assignment, this is the story.

—DANIEL HENRY

Prologue

Beacon

Sideways rain turns to sleet, encasing the six men huddled against the blast. All day, the white preacher and five Tlingits waited in their tents for Glate Ankow (Dleit Aank̲áawu)—Muir's translation was "Ice Chief"—to emerge from the tempest. He arose before light and set off on a glacial traverse from which he has not returned.

"He may be a witch," declares the wizened headman, To'watte (Taawyaat). "Why else would a *gunuk* (white man) choose to tramp alone across the ice-giants on a day like this?"[1]

Another man, largest in the group, heaves onto the signal fire an Ice Age stump recently disgorged by a retreating glacier. Constellations of sparks shoot into the wind, streaking the dark. The elder's words voice his thoughts: "This is a bad-luck place. No protection in the storm. Though rolling icebergs may eat our canoe, I say get out now, before our will is gone."

The Tlingits lapse into a silence scoured by wind. During the stormy week in Glacier Bay, their frustration was compounded as they learned the breadth of Glate Ankow's utter disregard for safety. To'watte dreaded navigating his canoe between the gigantic ice bergs, which might disintegrate at any moment, yet Glate Ankow insisted they push on. The barren, rocky landscape depressed the men, who waited as Glate Ankow traipsed across the very ice rivers Natives traditionally avoided. No sane person would endure such agony.

Anxious and unsettled, To'watte enlisted the youngest crew member, Sitka Charley, to help him haul pitch torches and firewood to a high point, where they lit a signal fire. Darkness smothered any clue of their comrade's whereabouts.

Near midnight, when all traces of day are compressed to black despair, the men hear a faint crunch of boots. A few dozen footsteps later, Glate Ankow materializes. Sopping wool clings to the man's slender frame, meltwater runnels pour from his saturated cap. Runoff collects in his unruly red beard and drains onto his chest. Firelight spills from his eyes. Embarrassed and angry, the Tlingits stare at the ground as their "God's Man," missionary Hall Young, rises to shake hands with the hiker.

"Ah!" sighs Glate Ankow. "I'm lucky to be in camp, the glacier almost got me this time. If not for old To'watte's blazing beacon, I might have had to spend the night on the ice. I was progressing further into the glacier when I caught the flash of light."

The Native crew feared him lost, says Young. Although he assures them that John Muir walks with God's blessing, the men take little comfort and insist on decamping.

To'watte lifts a flickering gaze to his God's Man. "My heart is not strong. We need my canoe to get out of this ice-prison, but I fear it's too late, and wind will smash us into the icebergs."

A sudden gust moans its reply, straining the guy-lines of the two canvas tents.

The big man, a Hoonah seal hunter, pushes his face a few inches from Muir's. "If you like danger so much, we will leave you with all the danger you want. Do you know why my people never come here this time of year? We want to live a little longer."

The bearded adventurer clucks once before he squats in the lee of the tent. One by one, the others hunch around him. Young hands him a plate of hot food, which Muir ignores as he speaks through the interpreter, Stickeen Johnny. In a bold tongue powered by fervor for the natural world, Muir assures his companions that for ten years in California he "wandered alone in the mountains and storms, and good luck always followed me; that with me you need fear nothing. The storm will soon cease and the sun will shine to show us the way we should go, for God cares for us and guides us as long as we are trustful and brave, therefore all childish fear must be put away."

The men pause to consider the authority of Muir's speech. The preacher reiterates the value of faith and the purpose of their mission. Minutes pass before Kadachan (Káadashaan'), a gregarious man, brightens and says he likes to travel with "good-luck people." To'watte adds that Muir's talk makes his heart strong again and that he no longer fears the canoe breaking up, for he will go to heaven in good company.

Buoyed by the certitude of Glate Ankow, crew members drift back to their tents as he unfurls a full account to Young. Crawling under a glacier's blue belly, Muir discovered "a thousand rooms of God's crystal temple . . . a thousand feet down in the crevasses, with matchless domes and sculpted figures and carved ice-work all around me. . . . I was tempted to stay there and feast my soul, and softly freeze until I would become part of the glacier. What a great death that would be!" Muir's fervid monologue lasts three or four hours.

When the wind changes two days later, the paddlers catch the ebb tide out of Glacier Bay back into an island kingdom of forests and bears and people. Despite repeated warnings of alcohol-fired "Hooch Wars," the crew heads north into Chilkat Country with news of a Presbyterian God for one of the last enclaves of "wild savages" in the United States.

At forty-one, John Muir was still honing the voice that would shape modern American ecological conscience. Years of exploring Yosemite's wild Sierras had earned him regional celebrity as a scientist, but on his voyage to Alaska in 1879, the nature enthusiast was not yet enshrined as a wilderness crusader. Vigorous international debate spurred Muir's first visit to Alaska to prove that glaciers—not catastrophic floods and earthquakes—had carved California's "Range of Light." The zeal that sent Muir deeply into the High Sierras delivered him to the North—he sailed to Alaska as an acolyte and returned to San Francisco, a prophet.

The stormy week of negotiating ice and "new birthed" land answered questions the geologist would integrate into modern theories accepted by scientists since his time in Alaska. But more than academic study, glaciology was a spiritual crusade for Muir. Raised in an ultraconservative Protestant household, the adult Muir rejected his father's ironclad fundamentalism for the transcendental purity of God's creation. Nature was church; Muir was no less evangelistic than his father, whose righteous harangue drifted from the windows of homes and meeting halls while his sons plowed the fields. Rather than worshipping the Old Testament God of his father, the younger Muir devoted his passion to saving Eden, his vision of wilderness in North America.

Muir was often shy or awkward prior to speaking, but once the prophet-bearded scientist took the podium, his stories and theories captivated audiences, usually for hours. Muir's first public lecture was delivered just three years before his Alaska voyage, so his speeches to the Tlingit were formative. Despite his burning spirituality, Muir rarely spoke about religion. However, the sermon he delivered a week after his "discovery" of Glacier Bay forever changed the course of Tlingit friends whom he judged to be far ahead of the same class of any people in Europe and further shaped his sense of identity and message to the world.[2]

Most histories of Native–non-Native contact since Columbus involve seven general stages (not necessarily in this order): initial meeting, disease, resource capture, population pressure, military intervention, religious conversion, and homeland dispossession. By 1879, Native America had endured most or all of these civilizing strategies. In the United States' new northern possession, a century of Russian military, economic, and religious influence had profoundly affected most indigenous residents. Proximity to Sitka, capital of Russian America, familiarized Tlingit people with European ways as did trade with British, French, and U.S. sailing ships.

Only the northern Tlingit stronghold, Jilḵáat aaní, posed a real or imagined threat to white people, so most left it alone. Protected by geographic isolation and a fierce reputation, the Chilkoot and Chilkat Tlingits of northern Southeast Alaska governed themselves in a realm of steep fjords and salmon-rich rivers. Last keepers of the Old Ways, the Chilkoot-Chilkat alliance forbade white settlement, maintained a thousand fierce warriors, and supported a powerful shaman who opposed any occupation of their traditional lands.

Enter John Muir, who with Reverend S. Hall Young and his Native crew, cemented the destiny of the last and largest group of unassimilated Indians in the nation. Muir approached his hosts without fear and spoke to them from his heart. At the end of his brief sermon, the oldest shaman stood before the gathering and announced the whole-cloth conversion of his people.

Through his Tlingit encounters, Muir was forced to re-examine his understanding of humanity—wild and civilized—as he witnessed the fortitude of an unconquered people. His role as an agent of Manifest Destiny led Tlingit listeners to a cultural divide, provoking a chain of remarkable events that not only resonates among Alaska Natives today but for anyone who discovers this unexpected story.

PART I
Jil<u>k</u>áat Aaní

1 :: Sojourners

From a ridgetop above John Muir's last Glacier Bay camp of 1879, a bald eagle launches. Its eight-foot wingspan taut, the adult male slices east over an arm of Muir Glacier (now Muir Inlet) between a pair of seven-thousand-foot rock castles yoked by a frozen cape, then rides a williwaw over Davidson Glacier into the grand canyon of Lynn Canal, the largest fjord in North America. The bird rockets over the fanned toe of Davidson Glacier and next over two miles of seawater to the tip of the peninsula that divides Lynn Canal into two narrow inlets, Chilkat and Chilkoot. Just off land's end, five steppingstone islands drift southward down the middle of the sea-filled canyon. Veering north, the eagle hitches a draft over the Chilkat Peninsula's fifteen-mile-long spine to a summit nearly two thousand feet between sinuous coastlines. The bird slows to scan muskeg meadows for ground squirrels or grouse. An unconcerned porcupine waddles over the saturated moss carpet. Still hungry, the feathered predator descends to the narrow isthmus where the peninsula joins other mountain ranges hunching toward a vast northern Interior. The eagle alights on a limb of an old-growth spruce overlooking a cove that someday will serve as a harbor for the town of Haines, a community that sustains about two thousand humans in the early twenty-first century.

On this slate-sky October day, however, the eagle's stereoscopic gaze scours a crescent beach devoid of humanity and guarded on the uplands by a phalanx of shaggy spruce and hemlock. From the shore, seawater stretches across Chilkoot Inlet three miles east to the Coast Range, a glacier-draped wall abutting eight hundred ragged miles of Pacific edge. The eagle scans the point where the Inlet bifurcates. The eastern branch, a narrow, cliff-sided corridor, leads to the seasonal village of Dyea at the grassy terminus fifteen miles due north; its western finger hooks back to the mouth of the Chilkoot River and the larger village of Lkoot (without a cache). Twice daily, seawater from an ocean a hundred miles away flushes the fjord with twenty-foot tides. North Pacific brine pours into a chasm deeper than the Grand Canyon to mix with the silty discharge of hundreds of glacial streams and waterfalls, producing a pale turquoise dilution that teems with marine populations. The eagle scans the water for supper.

Moon-washed tides propel rafts of bladder wrack, bull kelp, and sea-hair into Lynn Canal, a skein through which herring, needlefish, capelin, sculpin, and smelt burst into iridescent galaxies. In April, a glinting run of eulachon ("hooligan")—a fish so oily it can be set ablaze—wriggle up the Canal pursued by anything big enough to eat them. Sea lions, seals, and sharks chase the greasy morsels by water; clouds of gulls, crows, plovers, godwits, and curlews thicken and dive. Like ornaments on Christmas trees, ravens and eagles adorn the limbs, ready to swoop when food flashes below. Diners scatter in the presence of whales pursuing fish flesh: famished humpbacks just in from Hawaii; and killer whales ravenous for anything that bleeds. Sixty-pound king salmon arrive in May, harbingers of huge runs of sockeye, chum, pink, and coho driven by genetic destiny to spawn and die in the rivers that pour into each inlet tucked in respective corners of the Canal's terminus.

On this gray November day, the eagle is roused only by a half-dozen ravens standing like deacons around a black carcass curled into beach boulders. He plunges from his perch and scatters the protesting ravens by landing on the shoulder of a fermenting harbor seal. With its thick beak, the eagle tears away a few scraps of belly fat, then returns to an upper branch of the big spruce. He needs hardly extend a wing to the afternoon's freshening sou'easter to ascend from the treetop and soar northwest over the narrow isthmus called Deishú and up the Chilkat River valley.

A tailwind propels the eagle over twenty miles of interwoven river channels, dark braids separated by ribs of sand. Near the river mouth, smoke curls from lodge fires in a cluster of log buildings called Yandeist'akyé (Yawn-dace-stuck-yeh) by Tlingit residents. Low water exposes rotting

Chilkat Valley. Photograph by author.

salmon carcasses, but the high-flying predator passes. Even this late in the season, the river boils with fish, hence the human name Jilḵáat (salmon cache). A half-mile away, a brown bear and two cubs trot across the valley bottom, unencumbered by the deeper river passages into which they plunge, muzzles pointing skyward as they swim. The eagle flies on.

Moments later, the bird traces a right angle in the valley and plummets toward a broad plain fashioned by the confluence of four streams. From this lofty perspective, dendritic channels unravel, then gather at the narrowing river bend. Closer, a piercing chorus of four thousand fellow eagles becomes audible. The outsized bird alights on an overhanging branch of a big cottonwood to survey the muscular current below, milky with glacial flour, and the delta expanse where the rivers meet. Stationed six or seven to a tree, perched on every driftlog or rootwad, even crouched on stream banks, eagles scan for fish.

The last salmon run of the year draws these bald eagles to a raucous feast at the "Council Grounds." Although freezing temperatures have sealed most northern rivers by November, the Chilkat stays open from warm upwellings flushed by convergent waters. Joining the raptors for the autumnal banquet are wolves, coyotes, marten, wolverines, and the occasional brown bear willing to delay hibernation for a last meal. Resting four miles apart on banks facing the flats, two Tlingit villages attest to the rich resources in this spot. Most people live in Klukwan, sometimes called the "mother village," which, at the time of Muir's 1879 voyage, was one of the largest permanent Native American communities on the continent.

With one shrill, descending whistle, the eagle flaps several long, steady beats across the flats, angles over Klukwan, and rides the thermals upriver twenty miles north to Turtle Rock. Below its wings, the upper Chilkat twists northeast and stair-steps into cloud-hemmed peaks toward its origins in Yukon ice only ten miles from the head of the Yukon River, where water travels two thousand miles to the Bering Sea. Instead of following the stream past the tree line, the bird rises over a pass in the Takshanuk Mountains, angles east, and drops into the head of another river valley hemmed by another granitic range. From its thousand-foot vantage, the eagle scrutinizes the deep forest of the upper Chilkoot watershed as it tumbles through an uninhabited valley to Chilkoot Lake. Opposite its mouth on the south side of the lake, the valley narrows to a few hundred yards where the Chilkoot River leaves the lake for its last mile to the sea.

The powerful bird descends to inspect the river more closely, a misty corridor flanked by old-growth spruce. Just after the river leaves the lake, another Tlingit village hugs the shore. Slab-board platforms, from which villagers spear passing salmon, extend into the river. The eagle glides a halfmile downstream until he spies his mate hunched atop a coho carcass on a grassy bank. The new arrival pipes a shrill acknowledgment and lands on a nearby house-sized rock seamed with moss and blueberry. Bramble around the outsized boulder is pressed flat to the ground, evidence of the scores of humans who recently gathered around Deer Rock for a peacemaking ceremony between former disputants. The eagle sees only the rotting salmon in his mate's talons. He half-unfolds his wings and hops clumsily toward his lifelong companion. She delivers a piercing admonition and returns to her meal. He sulks back to the rock.

In the lazy, late morning that it takes to wing from Glacier Bay to the lower Chilkoot River, the eagle soared over much of a 2.6-million-acre homeland once considered the property of Chilkat and Chilkoot people. They claim it today.

Despite the popular misconception that communal property dominated Native American society, the Tlingits of Southeast Alaska possessed a keen sense of ownership, especially for *at.oow* (clan treasure), which included

Austin Hammond Sr. Photograph by author.

artwork, regalia, and weapons as well as landscape—lakes, stream mouths, berry patches, beaches—even stars. As custodians of two coveted passes into interior lands, northern Tlingits historically required that visitors ask permission and likely pay for use of their *aaní* (territory).

In the centuries before John Muir's visit to Jilḵáat aaní (Chilkat country), traditional conflicts usually ignited around rights of entry, resource use, or personal affront. In his 1927 memoir, S. Hall Young, Muir's missionary friend, held that Tlingits derived from ancient Hebrews because of their "ready acceptance of the doctrine of blood-atonement."[1] Tlingit law dictated that wrongs be avenged with swift force, often resulting in prolonged tensions between village and clan groups.[2] In his book, the missionary neglected to note the custom of establishing "peace rocks" where embattled local parties resolved grievances and recommitted themselves to unity. Young offered a more-righteous path to peace: "Boston men" expected Natives to resolve their conflicts in a different, civilized way: signing a paper before armed soldiers, sometimes consummating the exchange with ceremonial alcohol and always ending with prayer.

:: "ALWAYS BEEN A COMMUNITY"

According to Lukaax̱.ádi headman Austin Hammond, the story of the northern Tlingit began with the Flood. Hammond wasn't sure when it happened, but he retained key details from repeated tellings by his grandfather, Joe Whiskers of the House That Came Down from the Sky.

An abrupt rise in water level off the tip of Chilkat Peninsula sent fishermen back to Ḻkoot to warn villagers. The community responded immediately. Men felled trees that they lashed together in huge rafts. Women and children wrapped food and possessions in hides secured to the logs. Barking dogs kept bears from clambering aboard, so wild animals rode out the Flood on other logs.

The water rose over four thousand feet until the rafts reached the rock spires of Kashagnak, a steep mountain whose walls plummet to the western shore of Chilkoot Lake. Villagers tied their canoes to the spires, sometimes called "Noah's Posts," but the flood currents tore them loose. The wayward vessels carried castaways past the Coast Range into the Interior where they were found by the G̱unanaa (Different People).

The bands of Athabaskans who roamed the Yukon–Rocky Mountain region assimilated the newcomers, but Tlingit elders warned their children against settling: "This isn't our land. This isn't our land. Don't get crazy here. Our land is way on the other side of the mountain."[3]

When the children were grown, Hammond said, they longed for their homeland, so groups paddled down from the Interior plateaus on the great rivers of the Northwest Coast—the Taku, Stikine, and Nass. Upon reaching the coast, clan groups dispersed throughout the island empire that white men later called Alexander Archipelago. Modern scholars suggest that the mass migration more likely occurred about ten thousand years ago, but most agree on the settlement patterns. Those Tlingits who navigated the Nass River settled in the southern portions of the region, including Tongass (Ketchikan-Saxman), and on Prince of Wales Island at Klawock. Most Stikine (Shtax̱ héen) clansmen congregated at a large village near the mouth of the river, but some ventured as far as Sitka on the outer coast and in the area that eventually became Glacier Bay. Taku people settled closer to their salmon-rich river near present-day Juneau. After venturing down the Nass, the people of Hammond's mother built a village in Duncan Canal, a sheltered inlet that nearly pinches Kupreanof Island in half. They called it Lukaax̱ and themselves the Lukaax̱.ádi.[4]

Since Tlingits resided near year-round subsistence resources, food tied people together. For purposes related to food and social balance, villages and seasonal camps were established throughout each claimed territory. Domestic conflict is a reason for residents to move away from their aaní, which may have happened with the Lukaax̱.ádi.[5]

"We were sojourners here," said Hammond—wanderers in search of a home.[6] As they paddled north, the Lukaax̱.ádi scouted for unoccupied territory but encountered only lands claimed before them, so they moved on. They continued to the head of Lynn Canal, where they discovered in the eastern arm a thriving salmon stream apparently unclaimed by another group. Before long, Tlingits arrived in canoes from a big village up the fjord's western arm. They claimed the river but permitted the Lukaax̱.ádi to establish a community called Lk̲oot.

For their village site, the immigrants chose a river bend just below the lake outlet. From there, the river muscles through a mile of old-growth spruce and huge boulders until it spills into Lutak Inlet. Its name derives from the cooling shade of the narrow valley, which made fortified sheds unnecessary to overwinter salmon stores. Expansive and sunny, the river in the western valley was called Jilk̲áat (with a cache) because food preservation required the protection of log structures. Runoff from six glaciers keep Jilk̲áat waters opaque. The Lk̲oot runs clear.[7]

Exactly when the Lukaax̱.ádi settled at Lk̲oot is hard to say. Fish-trap remnants found at the Chilkoot River mouth in 2002 were carbon-dated to twenty-one hundred years ago.[8] Some Native peoples, possibly Lk̲oot, lived there then, but their precise identities remain a mystery.

The narrative in these pages might differ from what Austin Hammond and other elders envisioned in the 1980s when they urged me to "tell the story," but it is one a white student can tell. Other than as contextual reference, I leave the legends and clan stories to their owners. Instead, these chapters view a century of Chilkat-Anglo interface through a rhetorical lens and tell a story of indigenous people using persuasive strategies with white people (especially Muir) and each other, and relate the effects over time. This work borrows from anthropologists, linguists, historians and culture bearers, but aspires neither to retrace their steps nor affirm their theories.

Rather, the intent here is to convey the breathtaking story of the northern Tlingit people, who attempted through various persuasive means to sustain a venerable culture while attempting to ride the white wave.

Consider Aristotle's view of rhetoric as the "art" used for "discovering in the particular case the available means of persuasion."[9] The keen observer of humanity understands the process. First, the exigency arises—a moment that demands a response, like threats to life, land, or freedoms. Second, the rhetor considers "the nature of the soul" she wishes to persuade. Third, based on an assessment of the audience, she selects a strategy and conveys messages by verbal and nonverbal means. Since a rhetorical act is "judged by its effect on someone," the outcomes of historic encounters reveal clues to the persuasive powers at play.[10] Moved, swayed, turned, blocked—we often talk about the effects of rhetoric in physical terms. Sometimes violence is mistaken for persuasion. Absent audience choice, violence for its own sake is not rhetorical, but the *threat* of violence sustains exigencies from which clans or nations may construct entire diplomatic relations.

Chilkat reputation depended on it.[11]

This book also parts with Austin Hammond's perceptions of time. According to anthropologists Frederica de Laguna and Catherine McClellan, the Tlingit mind conceives of time within these frameworks: Early Mythic Time, Raven Myths, Legendary Time, and Historical Time. The first three time frames connect Tlingit people of today with their ancestors—myths set origin themes; Raven grafts the mortal with the divine; clan legends reinforce affiliation. The Tlingit sense of time allows myth to arise even today; old stories are still considered clan property to the modern Tlingit. Those stories are best told by clan members or by those authorized to do so.[12]

These pages focus on northern Tlingit encounters with non-Natives in the decades leading up to and including their meeting with John Muir. A second book will trace the effects of Muir on the next seven generations of Chilkat and Chilkoot people, featuring a longstanding conflict over some of the most-valuable Native artifacts in the United States. Woven into a narrative built from authoritative texts and documents are the voices of contemporary Tlingit elders whose forebears were transformed by the Ice Chief. Although sometimes vague, contradictory, or incomplete, Native oral histories offer cultural insights not available in the diaries and reports of Euro-Americans. Beyond infrequent archeological discoveries on the Northwest Coast, precontact activities are primarily known by legend or hearsay. Anyone seeking clues to the past must consider—or at least listen to—the context of memory. For example, northern Tlingit elders agree that while the Lukaax̱.ádi were the first permanent inhabitants of Chilkoot and Taiya Inlets in the eastern half of the aaní, they also suggest that the G̱aanax̱teidí controlled the entire area long before the sojourners' arrival. The "first family" saw the advantage of an alliance, so they formed partnerships with the latecomers. Elders are less certain about the Great Flood, which nineteenth-century biblical scholars claimed occurred around 1650 b.c.

Five days' paddle south from Chilkoot, signs of human settlement at Groundhog Bay (near the mouth of Glacier Bay) establish a residency of ten thousand years. But until knowledge of the Lḵoot fish-traps, archeologists lacked evidence of habitation in the huge northern fjord farther back than the sixteenth century. Had he known about the fish-traps before his death in 1994, Austin Hammond would probably say that they belonged to the Old Ones, whose log rafts washed away in the Great Flood.

G̱aanax̱teidí canoes landed in Glacier Bay perhaps a thousand years ago, before glaciers formed in the Little Ice Age began creeping closer to the villages. Clan members sought a new homeland, where they could lay claim to salmon streams and berry patches, which they would pass on to untold generations.

They were exiles from the Henya ḵwáan ten days' paddle south, kicked out over a domestic dispute involving a woman's relationship with an enormous woodworm. The large clan abandoned its village on Prince of Wales Island at the southern end of the Tlingit domain and set out to build a new community. Fifty-foot war canoes delivered the G̱aanax̱teidí to places already occupied by other tribes, so they pushed on. In the northernmost reaches, back in the hydra-headed terminus of Lynn Canal they discovered an unoccupied region of mountains and rivers, the largest of which hosted all six species of Pacific salmon. From the mouth of the Chilkat River (Jilḵáat Héeni) flowing into the western arm of Lynn Canal, the explorers paddled a full day against a rushing current to a south-facing embankment they called Kuthwultu. It seemed a fine site for a village until the men discovered a spring two miles upriver where the water tasted sweeter. The clan agreed with the advanced guard and built the first log clan house a few feet from the rushing current, where tribal members would forever feast and dance and live by the water that gave them life. According to Klukwan elder Sally Burratin, the newcomers found at least one old clan house built by people who had migrated down from the Interior long before, so the G̱aanax̱teidí called their new home Klukwan (Tlákw Aan), or "always been a community."[13]

They knew nothing of white people. The G̱aanax̱teidí probably settled in the "mother village" around the time Viking and Danish ships were pillaging the northern coasts of Britain. In the aftermath of a devastating plague, millions of Eurasians were embroiled in bloody battles over land and souls. In its protected hideaway on the other side of the world, Klukwan thrived.[14]

The warm centuries that drew back the ice cover from the Northwest Coast briefly reversed during the Little Ice Age between 1400 and 1800 a.d. Just over the icy crown in Klukwan's south viewshed, a massive glacier at the base of fifteen-thousand-foot Mount Fairweather gushed mineralized meltwater into streams that veined a ten-mile-wide delta plain sloping to Icy Strait and the Pacific Ocean. Along the sockeye-rich river on the plain's eastern edge, several hundred Tlingit lived in Klem'sha'shakeen (Sandhill Town). A smaller village flanked the mouth of Chookanheeni, or Grassy Creek, at the western corner of the outwash. The cooling trend leading to the Little Ice Age fed the ice giant, later called Muir Glacier, whose freezing force likely killed salmon stocks first, then a generation or two later crushed the village itself. The glacial mass pushed as far as Icy Strait, furrowing the sand plains under its weight. Then the weather changed again. As the ice mass retreated the sea rushed in to form Glacier Bay. Today, the Muir Glacier has pulled back more than fifty miles from its apogee in the 1700s.

About the time Glacier Bay refugees dispersed in canoes to new homes, Spanish galleons half a world away were testing the secrets of a great ocean. Three or four centuries later, the queen's ships would bear the first whites into a region unknown to Europeans and into a majestic fjord controlled by fierce Natives.

The advance of Muir Glacier forced some to resettle on the opposite shores of Icy Strait in a community they called Xunaa (Hoonah). According to Klukwan headman Joe Hotch, remaining members of the Kaagwaantaan escaped in two directions. One group followed the rugged outer Pacific coast south to Sheet ká (Sitka), where Kiks.ádi residents permitted the immigrants to stay. Others paddled east through Icy Strait, a waterway up to eight miles wide that twice daily flushes the northern arteries of the archipelago. A clan house was erected at Point Couverden where the strait meets the southernmost extent of Lynn Canal, but most kinsmen turned north into the grand fjord. The ocean passage narrowed between sheer mountain walls as the canoes pushed on. Finally they reached the large river in the western arm where they encountered the G̲aanax̲teidí, who welcomed the Kaagwaantaan as valued cohorts.[15]

Group members likely knew of each other and perhaps even consorted at memorial ceremonies called *ku.éex'*(potlatches), which drew celebrants from afar. The Kaagwaantaan had a penchant for war and wealth, but their greatest value to the G̲aanax̲teidí lay in the rigid Tlingit social system. Tlingit society recognizes two cultural camps partitioned as Eagle and

Raven moieties dictated by maternal lines. Until recent years, same-moiety marriage was considered taboo. Committing to one's opposite moiety evolved into a complex system dependent on "in-laws" for house construction and funeral arrangements. The Kaagwaantaan arrived just when the G̲aanax̲teidí needed them most.[16]

The meeting of the two clans on the riverbank presaged a long-lived reign.

The visitors maintained a majestic air in addressing their hosts; the G̲aanax̲teidí spoke likewise, anticipating a profitable merger. Every word counts when two parties commit to a long-term relationship. Cautious language engenders respect. "It's just like carrying a long pole," Joe Hotch recalls elders saying. "If you're talking any old way, you never know who that pole will hit."[17]

Careless words and deeds are blamed on historic conflicts between Chilkat and Chilkoot kin. Some say that insertion of a labret into a Tlingit woman's lower lip began as a means to curb gossip, later evolving into a fashion ornament. Replaced with larger versions through one's life, the lip plug made speech quieter, slower. Thus encumbered, the matriarchy nonetheless retained social control.[18]

Together, G̲aanax̲teidí, Kaagwaantaan, and Lukaax̲.ádi combined forces to defend the Jilk̲áat aaní against unwanted intrusion. Generally, power-sharing among Tlingit clans required highly regulated discourse—in Chilkat even more so. For centuries, Chilkat/Chilkoot warriors raided groups along the Northwest Coast with legendary boldness, appropriating slaves and valuables as they desired. Grudges might fester between clans or communities for generations, occasionally to erupt in deadly skirmishes. While aggressive behavior on "away games" was a point of regional pride, at home it amplified tensions between families and clans, sometimes with fractious results. Klukwan was known for interclan entanglements that sometimes threatened to tear the village apart. Chilkat anthropologist Louis Shotridge despaired that his people lacked a more harmonious temperament: "How bad it must have been on our ancestor for his offspring only to be the antagonist to another man."[19]

In old times, brutal reciprocity was the mortal consequence of certain crimes like murder, witchcraft, or facial disfigurement, but in some cases, when traditional law led to years of revenge and retaliation, clan leaders turned to ritual.

Details of the peace ceremony varied from place to place, but the idea was the same: Members of one clan visited the home of their adversary, where they engaged in formalities leading to a mock battle to be resolved by exchanging "hostages," usually clan leaders. Through a period of prayer and song, the hostages transformed into *guwakaan* (deer), the most peaceful animal in the forest. In Chilkoot, guwakaan maneuvered around Deer Rock, a house-sized boulder on an upper riverbank carpeted with chocolate lily, Nootka rose, and marsh globe. Following the ceremonial selection, each hostage resided as an esteemed guest of his former enemy—sometimes for years—until the dispute was fully settled.[20]

"We were all one Chilkat," Joe Hotch says at a Klukwan history talk in April 2009. At eighty-one, Hotch emanates stability. Crowned by a shock of white butch-cut hair, the Kaagwaantaan clan leader holds his stocky body like a wrestler-prince. Like Austin Hammond, who died in 1994, Hotch was raised by grandparents who strove to keep the culture alive in their grandson. In a culture without designated village chiefs, Hotch is widely recognized as the traditional spokesperson. His voice is calm, assured.

"We only got divided because non-Natives started to infringe all over our land." All of this—Hotch waves his hand in a broad arc—"it still belongs to us. No one signed a paper to take it away. Two-point-six-million acres. I'm a Tlingit and I'm rich—I'm overflowing because nothing was given away."[21]

Twenty miles upriver from the Chilkat mouth, the mother village hugs south-facing shores, protected from frigid north winds by Iron Mountain at its back. In Klukwan's viewshed, the confluence of three rivers creates an open expanse called the Council Grounds with enough late-run salmon in the braided channels to attract a convergence of eagles and wildlife before winter's door shuts tight. On the horizon ten miles south, the Takhinsha Range rises into a serrated glacial crown that tilts ice rivers southward into Glacier Bay's ocean fingers.

Shielded from weather and white men, Klukwan people believed then and now that they lived in the best place on earth. No other coastal Tlingit village boasted access to teeming fish and wildlife resources so far out of the range of gunboats. Ample subsistence stocks and a singular commitment to place left leisure time enough for a proliferation of traditional arts—carving, weaving, dance, oratory. The "last old-time Tlingit village," Klukwan became a repository for cultural treasure.[22]

Along with abundant local resources, village location assured Chilkat control of the Grease Trail, a steady source of income for centuries. Named for the highly valued oil of the eulachon, the trading route started at tideline near present-day Haines, crossed Deishú isthmus to Yandeist'akyé,

Joe Hotch. Photograph by author.

and followed a narrow cut-bank along the Chilkat River to Klukwan. At the village, gear was stowed in canoes for a twenty-mile upriver paddle to trailheads off the Klehini or upper Chilkat.

Then the real work began. Men strapped on packs that weighed up to 160 pounds, 80 percent of which was trade goods. Each trail led up the coastal mountains until tall trees were replaced by waist-high alders and alpine meadows, then over thirty-four-hundred-foot Chilkat Pass and north across tundra. In trains of twenty or more packers, Chilkats trekked northward hundreds of miles to locate their Athabaskan trade partners; similar-sized crews paddled south in war canoes to partners and relatives in coastal communities.[23]

The earliest Chilkat forays beyond the Pass likely involved a day's hike west to a pass near Samuel Glacier. Travelers crossed the glacier's crevassed surface into the O'Connor River drainage, then walked two days through the crumbling glacial canyons that spill into the Tatshenshini-Alsek watershed, a swift-water passage to the Gulf of Alaska. The earliest Tlingit explorers may have walked beside the river to the sea, but in later times they rode cottonwood canoes on cement-hued currents to the ocean.

Close to the convergence of the Tatshenshini and the larger Alsek Rivers, a few Chilkat families lived at a seasonal outpost called Nukva'ik, a halfway house built to maintain closer ties with coastal partners. Only a speck in the panorama of rock and ice, the outpost offered little respite for residents accustomed to lush lowlands and intertidal zones. Touched by the breath of glaciers, transplanted residents subsisted on salmon speared in glacial torrents and berries gathered from an occasional patch of tundra. All other victuals—seal meat, eulachon oil, dried seaweed, potatoes—were at least a three-day journey away. Though a testament to Chilkat economic verve, Nukva'ik is barely remembered today.[24]

Steering a cottonwood canoe down the substantial currents of the Alsek brought traders to a small village at Dry Bay, a sheltered haven on the exposed North Pacific coastline. A number of Chilkat Valley Tlingit today still claim a family connection with the long-abandoned coastal community. From Dry Bay, a three-day hike westward on North Pacific beaches brought travelers to relatives and trading partners in Yakutat, which remains a thriving Tlingit village of about six hundred residents.

Wood chips floating down the Alsek alerted Nukva'ik residents to the existence of humans upriver, said Annie Ned, a southern Tutchone elder. Several days of tracing the Tatshenshini toward its headwaters brought a Chilkat party to Neskataheen, the southernmost Athabaskan village in the Yukon Basin. Ned said that the Tlingits found people upstream dressed in thick, decorative furs that were much warmer than their coastal "ground-hog clothes." Soon they were trading eulachon oil for Athabaskan attire.[25]

A well-known Chilkat story proposes otherwise, naming K̲haakeix'wti of Glacier Bay as the first coastal man to cross the barrier mountains and make contact with Southern Tutchone. Joe Hotch tells of a time when Klukwan villagers spotted unfamiliar people on Chilkat Pass. The newcomers were so shy that the Chilkats called them G̲unanaa. Villagers left gifts of salmon and eulachon oil on rocks in the high country, a generous practice that eventually won over the newcomers. In generations to come, Chilkats engaged Interior Athabaskans in trading and familial relationships that evolved into a regional cartel enforced by Tlingit claims of exclusive trading privileges.[26]

In 1999, Canadian hunters found the half-thawed remains of a man in the mud near a melting crevasse into which he fell while crossing a glacier. His close proximity to the Grease Trail suggested that the twenty-two-year-old was on the Alsek River route to Dry Bay and Yakutat. DNA testing put the fatal journey around 1450 A.D., about the time Spanish wool merchants became parents of Christopher Columbus and Henry VI ruled with terror and madness.

A bear or wolverine likely made off with the man's head, but the body was intact. His effects included a finely woven cap, squirrel-skin robe, small

Al Morgan. Photograph by author.

bow, and pouch containing dried salmon. Forensic examiners announced in 2004 that Kwaday Dan Ts'inchi (Long Ago Man) lived most of his life on the coast and had eaten a meal of shellfish and beach asparagus a day or two before his death. The absence of a pack points to a motive beyond economics and more likely, say some, courtship.[27]

Genetic investigation identified Kwaday Dan Ts'inchi's blood relatives among Tlingits and Tutchones living today. The announcement spurred several events celebrating regional ties, but at least one descendant was unimpressed. At a public discussion in 2008, Haines elder Al Morgan groused that despite flaunting his genetic ties to archeological celebrity, he still couldn't find a girlfriend in town.[28]

2 :: Power Plays

The luminous midsummer night beckons. Three men in a cottonwood canoe slice across mirroring water at evening slack tide when gulls are silent and sea currents hesitate. The usual breeze is dead; each man fore and aft lifts his paddle. The craft glides a long time before it pauses at the entrance of Chilkat Inlet, where the ice-blue walls of Sit-ky'a (Davidson Glacier) fill the starboard view. Whenever the ice walls collapse, house-sized chunks explode, splash into Lynn Canal, and are sucked away by currents, becoming obstacles to safe passage. Cross-legged in the center, the old man straightens his back and touches the amulets that hang from his neck. Rising from a mass of dreadlocks is an ornate *shakee.át* (ceremonial hat) draped with winter-white ermine pelts; sea-lion whiskers sprout from the crown like exclamation points. The carved head of Raven protrudes just above eyes that roll inward as the íx̱t' communicates with the unseen.

He prepares to dive.

In a dream only days before, spirit helpers—*yéik*—warned the íx̱t' of invaders approaching. Residents needed to be on their guard. After a four-day fast, the old man commanded his nephews to transport him to the inlet mouth where Sit-ky'a met tidewater. Now they tie a twenty-fathom line around their uncle's chest. He grasps the amulets hanging from his neck—bear claws, eagle talons, killer whale tooth—and begins to sing. The nephews lift their uncle out of the canoe while he shakes a rattle in one hand, holding eagle down in the other. They lower him to the sea floor.

Sometime later the nephews feel a tug on the line. When the íxt' resurfaces, he still holds the rattle and dry feathers. Three ships will arrive on the next tide, he predicts.

The next day, some say, three boats belonging to Capt. George Vancouver sailed into Chilkat Inlet. Lt. Joseph Whidbey's subsequent confrontation marked the tenor of Chilkat encounters to come and reflected the passion locals felt for their homeland.[1]

This chapter illustrates the rhetorical nature of Native–non-Native interaction in the northern Lynn Canal region—Jilḵáat aaní—from 1794 to 1852. The selected situations described here cast light on persuasive strategies employed by each set of rhetors and demonstrate outcomes. Rather than compare relative "truths," my goal is to present each perception as a strand in a larger conversation about the destiny of an indigenous homeland.

Twenty years before Vancouver, the search for the fabled Northwest Passage lured Spanish ships into Lynn Canal. Seeking the Northwest Passage, galleons sailed into the grand fjord, but finding only steep rock walls and assertive Natives, likely never landed.[2] Local Natives today mention the Spanish only to accuse them of introducing disease. From first contact with Tlingits in 1774, Spanish galleons from Mexico and California probably introduced the initial round of pathogens that ravaged villages for a decade or so. As the only coastal Tlingit village not built on tidewater, the "Mother Village" of Klukwan withstood early assaults of pestilence.

The earliest report of smallpox among the Tlingit came from English explorer Nathaniel Portlock, who interviewed pockmarked survivors on the outer coast of Chichigof Island in 1787. Villagers had made contact with the viral carrier at least ten years earlier, so Portlock determined the ship to be Spanish. A later Russian report confirmed that the epidemic was probably introduced from the 1775 expedition of the *Santiago,* which dispensed death from Stikine to Sitka but not to the northern aaní.[3]

"Klukwan people knew the value of the quarantine," lifelong resident Judson Brown told an oral historian in 1983, although villagers were less successful with future bouts.[4]

Early Chilkat-European interface occurred away from Klukwan in sister communities or seaward passages when hand-hewn war canoes encountered great ships. Long sea voyages were routine, including the two-hundred-mile paddle from Klukwan to their trading partners in Yakutat located on the rugged, outer coast of the Gulf of Alaska. It was here that Chilkat people first engaged with non-Natives in a distinctly rhetorical way.

When navigators Dmitrii Bocharov and Gerasim Izmailov sailed the *Three Saints* into Yakutat Bay on June 11, 1788, several canoes containing amicable "Koloshes" guided the Russian vessel out of the open surf and behind a cluster of sheltering islands. The canoeists led the navigators on a village tour that concluded with a group of subchiefs, members of a ruling class the Russians called "toen." When the Russians inquired about a top headman, the Yakutat toen all deferred to Yeil.xaax, a visiting Chilkat leader.

The *sháade háni* was with a large group of his people on their annual visit to see relatives and trading partners by way of reasserting Chilkat hegemony. Although the navigators observed some squabbling among their hosts, "all without exception" obeyed the Klukwan headman.

A few days later, Yeil.xaax boarded the *Three Saints* and asked about the Russian royal portraits displayed in the ship's quarters; the navigators assured him of the great power and beneficence of the Russian empire. To certify his allegiance to Russia, Bocharov and Izmailov presented the Jilḵáat headman with a copper crest on which was etched the double-eagle, and told him to display it to all foreigners. Yeil.xaax returned the next day with the shield sewn into his cape and asked for a portrait of the Great Heir of Russia. He received it with "exaltation and shouts," then repaid the favor with a piece of iron shaped like a raven's beak, a woven grass bag, and six sea otter skins.[5]

:: "EVERYTHING FROM AFAR DRIFTS ASHORE"

As trade expanded, so did Klukwan. Intermarriage and wealth especially benefited the two most-prominent clans, G̲aanax̲teidí and Kaagwaantaan. Joe Hotch says up to three thousand people lived in the village at the time of first white contact. An Aleut slave released to Russians in 1802 reported over two thousand men at Chilkat; adding family members more than doubles the estimate, making Klukwan one of the largest permanent indigenous settlements on the continent.[6] Whatever the village size, Klukwan always *seemed* formidable, the appearance stemming from a reputation that enabled privilege through sustained threat. Yeil.xaax's proprietary mind-set—and his deferential subjects—came from long relationships borne from the lingering mists of war.

Twenty miles downstream at the mouth of the Chilkat River, Yandeist'aḵyé guarded the border between Jilḵáat and Lḵoot realms. Although village leadership was traditionally Lukaax̲.ádi, the G̲aanax̲teidí and Kaagwaantaan each maintained a clan house in the "gateway" village and participated in daily affairs.[7] Clustered along a bank where the deepest

Chilkat channel meets an intertidal estuary, Yandeist'akyé was the only one of five Chilkat/Chilkoot villages in plain view of the sea. As a place of outside contact and interclan convergence, Yandeist'akyé was the front line for the Chilkat Valley, a checkpoint for upriver travelers. Villagers served as welcoming committee or security force, depending on visitors' intentions. If travelers paid their respects to the Yandeist'akyé headman, they might advance up the valley. For those who tried to pass the village without permission: death—blood smeared on four-mile cliff face near the river was a warning.[8]

Yandeist'akyé overlooked the jagged seams where mountains fall into ocean. As many as two hundred residents maintained tight control of valley access from the place whose name meant "everything from afar drifts ashore."[9] From their vantage, villagers monitored the Chilkat side of Lynn Canal. Sentinels posted at intervals on Chilkat Peninsula shores relayed any news of visitors, such as the arrival of John Muir and S. Hall Young in 1879.[10] Yandeist'akyé residents likely were participants in the first regional confrontations with non-Tlingits.

On July 13, 1794, a cutter and two yawls commanded by Capt. George Vancouver's Lt. Joseph Whidbey sailed the length of Chilkat Inlet and landed on a sandy shore near the river mouth. From their camp, they spied smoke rising from Yandeist'akyé five or six miles distant. They gazed across the water a mile away at a treeless island rising like a canine tooth where a glacial river meets an olivine sea and, on the opposite bank, spied the towering Takhinsha Mountains. Concerned about their proximity to "savages," sailors demonstrated their firepower with several rounds of musket shot and were undisturbed through the dusky midsummer night.

What happened next depends on which version one chooses to believe. Vancouver's log entry (likely written by Whidbey) describes the encounter in terms of a strategic reconnaissance in hostile territory. Journal entries from ship's surgeon Archibald Menzies convey a bemused awareness of a threat. Klukwan headman Joe Hotch recounts a much darker crime suppressed by the British.

Early the next morning, several canoes landed near the campsite. The occupants emerged singing in a style that Menzies felt reflected the "solitary gloom" of the "deep narrow vale" in which he was confined.[11] The song was a greeting. Whenever Tlingit residents approached an unfamiliar group it was common to sing a trade song to identify social connections and motives.[12]

As the crew advanced upriver toward Yandeist'akyé, more locals approached, entreating the white men to stay for a few days to meet

"Gincaat," probably the Jilḵáat headman from Klukwan. Inquiries about the territory prompted maps drawn in the sand that showed passes at the heads of each inlet, over which trails led to lakes and rivers into the Interior. The Tlingits were eager to trade and promised to return with the finest furs and "trinkets." Disappointed to learn that the sea passage did not lead to open ocean, the Englishmen turned south. The trio of small boats sailed the fifteen-mile length of Chilkat Peninsula, then past the five stepping-stone islands into the middle of Lynn Canal.

Joe Hotch will tell you that at least one of Whidbey's boats tarried at land's end. Smoke from a cooking fire near the peninsula's point spurred the sailors to investigate. They found a lone Tlingit woman tending camp for her husband and other seal hunters.

"Five men," says Joe Hotch. "They raped the woman and left her on the beach."[13]

As they sailed south, the white men were overtaken by a large canoe gliding out from behind an island. On a box amid thwarts stood Klukwan headman Gincaat "dressed more gorgeously and tastefully than any other chief on the Northwest Coast." Snowy ermine furs flowed from the shakee. át atop the headman's head. Two Chilkat blankets hung from his tall frame, "curiously wrought & diversified with a great variety of black emblematical figures." The sailors were "astonished" by the sháade háni's unrestrained capers, wrote Menzies, especially his dexterous spinning of an ornate rattle. The white men demanded an encore performance after which they made for the nearest island to prepare supper. Gincaat presented Whidbey with sea otter pelts to which the officer responded with several small gifts. Eased by the warm welcome and calm seas, the sailors lingered through the long twilight of midsummer.[14]

Good weather held to the early morning launch, but the mood soured. The ships' log shows five war canoes bearing on Whidbey, "steered and conducted (by) five principal ladies," who, with thirty or more warriors apiece, seemed bent on plunder. The women were Kaagwaantaan, according to Joe Hotch, respected for their strength and courage. The headman says the appearance of unexpected reinforcements indicates motives beyond last-minute shopping: they desired to avenge their kinswoman.

Whidbey estimated that more than two hundred Natives gathered around the sailors; Menzies counted half as many. The numbers were enough, however, for the watchman to rouse comrades whose first sight of the day was the headman's large canoe alongside Whidbey's pinnace. Menzies reported Gincaat leaping aboard to pass items back to his men; Vancouver's log describes "Indians in all directions" seizing anything that wasn't nailed down. When a sailor aimed a musket at his craft, Gincaat "very coolly took up his blunderbuss" and prepared to return fire. Whidbey ordered ships to weigh anchor and to display weapons. Encircled by five war canoes, the flotilla slowly drifted south.

Through his brass megaphone, Gincaat spoke in conciliatory tones, appearing "exceedingly anxious" to make peace and resume trading. Whidbey refused. According to Vancouver, the headman became aggressive, interrupting his speeches to peer into a spyglass or aim his blunderbuss. Though well armed, the warriors refrained from violence as the British prepared for battle. Commands in Tlingit and English rang across calm waters.

After a few hours of tailing the intruders, the canoes faded back into the northern recesses of the great fjord that Vancouver would name for the English district where he spent his youth. The captain named the tip of Chilkat Peninsula Seduction Point to commemorate the "artful character of the Indians" who ushered his sailors out of the aaní. For some Tlingits today, the rocky point's English name still evokes anger.[15]

Besides the alleged attack, another surviving impression of the Whidbey encounter is the strategic leadership of Kaagwaantaan women. In Klukwan today, Lani Hotch attributes some formative military successes to her kinswomen's' "take charge" attitude. Her research suggests that Yanwaa Sháa (tough women) reinforcements may have tipped the outcomes of battles against several European and American ships.[16]

Tlingit educator Agnes Bellinger held that the Yanwaa Sháa tradition began with the appearance of a Dutch (some say Danish) ship—the first they had ever seen—that resulted in the deaths of three Kaagwaantaan men. As the foreign vessel sailed out of Chilkat Inlet, a squad of female warriors trailed far behind in a war canoe. Hours later, the Chilkats found the ship anchored in William Henry Bay, so landed and hid their canoe in the woods. Concealed in a narrow strip of Sitka spruce that paralleled high tide, the warriors followed the shoreline under deep cover until they heard sailors' voices.

Among other weapons, each Tlingit likely carried one of the large copper daggers for which Klukwan was known, more than eighty of which are said to be forged by the same woman.[17] Judging one Kaagwaantaan life to be worth three white men, the women killed eight sailors and released one to relive the horror to his mates. Not long afterward, Kaagwaantaan women began wearing sailor hats at special occasions. Their story was made public when Alaska district governor John Brady granted Tlingit women permission to wear sailor hats at a big 1904 potlatch in Klukwan. Some Chilkat women still wear them at potlatches and cultural events.[18]

Lani Hotch. Photograph by author.

The foundations of reciprocity eroded among the minority of residents of Sitka and Fort Wrangell who became close to the Russians, but in remote Tlingit villages the old law prevailed.[19] While virtually all of the region's inhabitants had been touched by non-Native diseases, religion, economics, or other influences, Chilkats were perceived as masters of their fjord fortress, protectors of the Old Ways. Even today, Tlingits sometimes refer to Klukwan as "Old Town," a bastion of deep tradition where slavery lingered long after the American Civil War and the traditional law of reciprocity (eye for an eye) was applied into the twentieth century.[20]

In the first half-century of Chilkat contact, however, European and American sailors observed little of local culture beyond what they saw from the deck of a ship: well-dressed Tlingits in war canoes, who offered luxurious Interior pelts at premium prices. A fearsome reputation and remote location kept most white traders at bay until later when the Russian occupiers agreed to lease trading rights to the British.

A year after Whidbey's encounter, Russian-American Company manager Aleksandr Baranov sailed into Chilkat Inlet, where he placed Orthodox crosses at prominent landmarks near the river mouth.[21] Canoe loads of Natives approached the ship and offered to trade their furs for Russian goods. Baranov engaged them but quickly realized that his ship was tracking the gradual retreat of Tlingit canoes into a narrow passage that, by the looks of the gathering forces, portended an ambush. The governor's ship backtracked down Lynn Canal and returned to Kodiak.

One of the earliest American ships to enter Jilkáat aaní was the *Dragon* under twenty-six-year-old captain Richard Cleveland.[22] With a crew of English, Irish, and American refugees from the India trade, Cleveland set sail from Canton, China, on January 10, 1799, in a fifty-ton English cutter carrying ten four-pound brass cannons. The winter crossing was brutal, but by spring Cleveland had piloted the *Dragon* to the sodden Northwest Coast and sailed into the head of Chilkat Inlet on May 6. The absolute stillness of the next morning was offset by five hundred well-armed warriors in nearly thirty canoes surrounding the ship.

"It will be perceived that our situation was now one of great danger," Cleveland wrote in his memoirs. Dead calm rendered the ship immobile. The day dragged on as the crew of sixteen stood statue-like, guns aimed at warriors and lit matches hovering at cannon fuses. From the closest canoes Chilkats held up furs and expressed their eagerness to trade. Each man on the *Dragon* remained at his post, unmoved by the sales pitch. As evening shadows filled the fjord, sailors were relieved to see the warriors return to shore. The Tlingits made no threat through the night but loudly mocked each half-hour call by the ship's watch.

A brisk north breeze in the morning lifted flaccid sails and spirits as the ship pulled away from the gathering flotilla. As the *Dragon* re-entered the main body of Lynn Canal, Sit-ky'a's icy walls loomed at starboard; portside, two war canoes sped toward the ship. Cleveland paused long enough to buy four furs, then left behind what he suspected were reinforcements for a war party that never materialized. With "great disappointment" in their faces, locals watched the white men get away.

In a later meeting with Captain Beck of the British ship *Cheerful,* Cleveland learned that the northern Tlingit forces were likely seeking revenge for an earlier incident. About a month before the *Dragon*'s encounter, the *Cheerful* ran aground on a sand bank near the mouth of the Chilkat. When the captain saw scores of Natives approaching the vulnerable ship, he ordered warning shots overhead, but the paddlers closed in. The captain instructed his men to shoot directly into the amassing canoes, stirring enough confusion to permit Beck's hasty retreat. The subsequent appearance of the *Dragon* presented an opportunity for reciprocity.

In the same year, Aleksandr Baranov sailed again from Kodiak to Sheet'ká at the edge of the eastern North Pacific. With little Native resistance, he established the community of New Archangel on a beach about two miles away from a Kiks.ádi log fort on the large island that bears his name today.

On a solemn October day, Baranov conducted an elaborate ceremony to certify the supremacy of God and the sovereignty of Czar Pavel Petrovich. Following Baranov's burial of a copper possession plate, prayer and proclamation were punctuated by frequent gunfire. The ceremony culminated with songs and a "circle of fire" in which everyone present formed a circle around the barracks and fired volleys while cannons shot into the ocean. Natives were then led into the barracks and served a "common feast" followed by an evening of Russian songs and ballroom dancing.[23]

Despite Baranov's demonstrations, Tlingit-Russian relationships deteriorated. In a letter dated April 7, 1800, Baranov reported generally good Native relations, "except that one has to be careful of the Chilkats," subjects of rampant rumors among the Tlingit.[24] As news of the Russian occupation traveled through tribal networks, dissent became apparent. After a trip north to attend a Klukwan ḵu.éex', a Kiks.ádi man returned home bent from the shame that his Kaagwaantaan opposites had heaped on him for allowing the white men to build homes on Tlingit land. Even from afar, the Chilkats' mocking anger is credited in part with igniting the "fighting spirit" that fueled the 1802 ouster of the Russians from Old Sitka.[25]

Oaths to God and Mother Russia sent Baranov back to Sheet'ká in 1804, where he rekindled the ire of Tlingit warriors who fought at a furious pitch until a night when the entire village slipped into the forest. This time, the Russians built a fort on the old village site at Castle Hill and relocated Natives in the "Ranche" behind a fortified log fence.

The Chilkat high command responded with reinforcements.

A thousand Tlingit warriors from villages throughout the region converged offshore in the winter of 1806–1807. The sight of so many fighting men in war canoes unnerved Russian commander Ivan Kuskov and compelled him to call a meeting with a visiting Chilkat headman. Forty men accompanied their leader to meet Kuskov, who wrote that he "was kind to these guests, and gave them gifts." Rumors were out, Kuskov confided with the leader, that the Chilkats "always had a friendly face, but evil intentions." The Russian judged the rumor to be untrue and convinced the Chilkats to preserve the peace and their honor by leaving the Ranche. Pleased by Kuskov's acknowledgment of his special status, the headman withdrew his forces. Leaderless, inter-ḵwáan (community) unity dissolved, and the Russians gained ground.[26]

The uneasy truce between northern Tlingits and whites unraveled the following summer when seventy Chilkats were killed as they raided an American trading brig in Lynn Canal. The incident kindled a hatred of Americans in Klukwan, amassing debts payable in blood.[27]

For Chilkat headman Xet-su-wu, white intruders were of no more concern than the demographic shift he saw in Klukwan. Perhaps as early as 1800 the aging G̲aana̲xteidí sháade háni worried about the purity of his Raven bloodline, holding that marriage to lower-caste Tlingits endangered the social order. Living among founding families in the sixty or more clan houses of Old Town were immigrants from Sitka, Stikine, Hoonah, and the Interior whose intermarriage threatened to dilute the near-royal status of the G̲aana̲xteidí clan. The headman had heard of a great Boston tyee (great white leader) who governed his nation from a magisterial White House; why not assert the authority of the "first family" by building a Tlingit White House? To honor a long-held clan symbol, Xet-su-wu named it Yáay Hít (Whale House). Beyond its prominent size, the clan house would contain the finest at.óow (treasured objects) designed to tell the G̲aana̲xteidí story to the ages.[28]

For an artist worthy of his vision, Xet-su-wu sent a delegation on the week-long paddle to Stikine to summon Kadjisdu.axtc, sometimes called the "Michelangelo" of the Tlingit art world. In his youth, the Stikine nobleman studied with Haida master carvers; around 1775, the middle-aged carver established a regional reputation by contributing to a fabled array of art pieces for the great Chief Shakes House in Stikine, later called Wrangell. When Xet-su-wu made his offer more than thirty years later, Kadjisdu.axtc was near the close of a long career, but accepted the invitation and brought his family to Klukwan.[29]

Four nine-foot house posts, a rain screen, and a fourteen-foot Woodworm Bowl comprise Kadjisdu.axtc's primary work in the Whale House. It is likely that the Stikine master and his family created a number of smaller works purchased by other households, some held in esteem today, like the Mother Basket. Another key piece of the collection is an iconic rainscreen on which a later Klukwan leader painted more than a hundred ancestors' faces.[30] Kadjisdu.axtc's level of technique and design far exceeded any Tlingit standard of the time and is still unparalleled. Art critic Barry Herem effused that the Klukwan artifacts "transcend what we term beauty. Electrifying, monumental, they combine equally the undying primal energy of myth and the unique spark of individual genius."[31] More than a year of carving earned Kadjisdu.axtc ten slaves, fifty dressed moose skins, and many stacks of blankets.

Whale House Interior. Photograph by Winter and Pond, 1895; image, 1982.303.0047, Haines Sheldon Museum, Alaska.

The Stikine artist's creations invigorated the G̲aana̲xteidí, who completed the timber-framed Whale House in time to shelter their at.óow. "It represented the best type of Tlingit architecture," wrote ethnographer George Thornton Emmons at the end of the nineteenth century, "a broad, low building of heavy hewn spruce timbers, carefully united through groove, tenon, and mortise, to support each other without extraneous fastening." Set vertically, hewn boards four to six inches thick formed the walls of the fifty-by-fifty-three-foot house to be used for storing treasure and lodging guests.[32]

The first Europeans likely to set foot in Klukwan sailed into Chilkat Inlet on the schooner *Chilkat* in May 1834. Sent by the Russian-American Company's Aleksandr Baranov, Lt. Fedor Kuznetsof sought talks with Xet-su-wu and his successor, Annahootz, to determine the source of the Chilkats' luxurious Interior pelts.[33] The crew likely inspected the big clan houses, feasted with villagers, and listened to speeches that recognized ancestors and honored their relationship with Russia. Surely, Xet-su-wu displayed the symbols of his allegiance including various papers, crosses, and the copper crest presented to Yeil.xaax in Yakutat. Two generations later, another Chilkat headman named Yeil.xaax lost several papers and a silver cross when his canoe capsized in the fjord en route to a formal event in Juneau.[34]

Vigorous entrepreneurs, the Chilkats hoped that a stronger relationship with Russia would bring more goods to be packed to Interior trading partners. A procession of Klukwan packers followed the Grease Trail a few times a year to trade with Southern Tutchone groups two to four weeks away. The average pack of an overland trader weighed a hundred pounds, three-quarters of it retail goods.[35] The highest-valued trade item produced by northern Tlingits was Chilkat blankets, cinched into northbound packs along with hides and eulachon oil. According to Athabaskan elder Annie Ned, Tlingits also introduced alcohol, guns, and sugar to Interior bands.[36]

Even more deadly, trade goods sometimes spread disease. Geographic isolation helped Klukwan evade the initial Northwest Coast smallpox epidemic of the 1770s, but the virus returned with a vengeance to coastal Tlingits in the late 1830s. The village of Lḵoot was nearly wiped out; perhaps a third survived in Klukwan. Such die-offs among North American indigenes often hastened cultural disintegration, but Klukwan stood firm. The Grease Trail allowed Chilkats to escape from sources of infection and maintain a steady income. It seems that coastal traders transmitted diseases to Interior Natives, many of whom perished about the same time. Isolated from other white communities, Klukwan survived the ravages.[37]

But white people didn't go away. Prompted by a bid from the Hudson's Bay Company (HBC) to lease trading rights in her waters, in 1838 Russia dispatched a survey team headed by a German pilot named Lindenberg. The crew landed at Glacier Point, then hiked along the thin strip of beach between tide and the hundred-foot wall of Sit-ky'a. Thirty years later the glacier would be named Davidson; its Tlingit name almost forgotten.[38]

Once past the glacier, the surveyors hiked the steep, irregular coastline of Chilkat Inlet to the river mouth. The men kept to the shore opposite Yandeist'aḵyé lookouts posted three miles across the delta. Upriver in Klukwan the surveyors encountered a village struck by smallpox. A pall hung over nearly every house. Some families were completely gone.

Lindenberg hired several healthy men to accompany his crew on the two-day journey by paddle and foot to an alpine pass on the trade route. When they reached the high divide, the surveyors scribbled instrument readings while their Native guides lifted a one-ton table rock upon two upended slabs to denote the margins of the Tlingit domain. In the ensuing century, the Stone House became an important marker along the Grease Trail. The rock roof slid off one support but today still leans on the other. The bearing signified a topographical point for Russians who were accustomed to drawing lines around conquered lands and people, but for Chilkat men, Stone House marked the gateway to an inland trading empire controlled by the Jilḵáat and Lḵoot people, stewards and defenders of a 2.6-million-acre homeland, Jilḵáat aaní.

Whatever the claims of absentee landlords, locals were certain of their control of the land and resources that sustained them. The Russians largely ignored the northern tribes, so ḵwáan residents retained their perception of sovereignty—and enforced it—even when the Americans took charge.

An 1840 leasing agreement gave HBC access to various Alaska ports, which opened new markets for the enterprising Tlingits. Among available trade items, the British most highly valued the super-insulating furs offered by tribes like the Stikines and Chilkats, who were supplied by Interior trade partners over the Coast Range in British America.

For several springs, three HBC ships appeared at Labouchere, a pocket of deep water in the western corner of the Chilkat River mouth, known later as Pyramid Harbor.[39] As local Natives learned the needs of their white customers, their palaver sharpened, product line deepened, and bottom line stuck. Despite an agreement with the Russians to do otherwise, British traders routinely used alcohol as a bargaining lubricant. Unfettered by government ethics, the HBC tapped thirsty markets among Native clients.

With economic expansion among the northern Tlingits came a growing sense of propriety. By the 1840s, generations of Interior trade engendered a monopolistic attitude. "The Stick Indians were our money," Agnes Bellinger said at an elders meeting in Klukwan.[40] Trade with Southern Tutchone introduced Chilkats to Athabaskan handiwork and, by degrees, to the work of Inupiaq people living on the Arctic Ocean. Strengthened also by business connections down the West Coast, Klukwan grew as a major indigenous trading center but one counterbalanced by its culture and geographical isolation.

Competition arrived in June 1848 when HBC manager Robert Campbell built Fort Selkirk at the confluence of the Pelly and Yukon Rivers, four hundred miles north of Klukwan. In August, a Chilkat trading party arrived to exchange goods with the HBC steamer *Beaver* but instead found Campbell and his dozen men at the new fort. Chilkat expectations of seasonal trade with white men did not include long-term residency. The durable Scot complained about the "villainous" attitude of the coastal Natives who conveyed their ire with hideous noises and mock attacks.[41] The HBC remained. Determined to squeeze out the interlopers, Tlingit traders attempted to wrest control of the fort three years later but were chased off by Indians loyal to Campbell.

"We warned them twice," Joe Hotch said one morning in April 2009. An outbreak of smiles creased the faces of a mostly Native audience in the Klukwan school library. "Then we had to do something."[42]

In 1852, Klukwan sháade háni Koh'klux (Kalaaxch') enlisted twenty-seven men—including brothers Skandoo'o the shaman and Yen-da-yonk the guide—for the thirty-day trek to Selkirk. When they reached the Yukon, the Chilkats made five rafts and floated a few miles to Fort Selkirk. On August 19, Campbell spotted the war party bearing on his shore. Compromised by the absence of a hunting party, Campbell ordered all others inside the forthouse. According to Hotch, when the Tlingits arrived at the post, "Koh'klux told Hudson's Bay that they needed to go," but Campbell refused. He wrote that though he "used every conciliatory appearance to soothe them they were like a volcano, every moment ready to burst out." Through that day and the next, Tlingits strolled the fort grounds with loaded rifles, keeping their prisoners indoors. Two women and a man sneaked away in the night, leaving the fort, according to Campbell's notes written under siege, "entirely in their power."

Arrival of hunters and traders in three boats the next morning inflamed the Tlingits. "No one who has not seen it can imagine," Campbell began a scene that described Chilkats in their "wildest fury." Screaming like "a fiend let loose from pandemonium," the raiders descended upon the river party, which fled. Campbell ran after them. Vicious attacks on Athabaskan employees drew the fort founder directly into the arms of the raiders. "They were already our masters," Campbell wrote of his assailants, who stripped him of weapons, carried him to the river bank, and left him "stunned with vexation." No one was seriously hurt during the ordeal, but the Company's inventory was "smashed into a thousand atoms."

Koh'klux led his men into the hills behind the fort where, in the twilight of a northern summer night, they set huge, smoky fires. When they returned the next morning, the Tlingits found the fort abandoned. They burned it to the ground, then tramped back to Klukwan loaded with booty for a "big celebration."[43]

Even today, Tlingits, Athabaskans, and European descendants occasionally gather on the banks of the Yukon to remember the siege at Fort Selkirk.

Robert Campbell retreated, as did the Hudson's Bay Company, which waited eighty-seven years to build another post on the Yukon.

3 :: Moving Heaven and Earth in Klukwan

Minutes before 10 p.m. on April 14, 1865, lamplights were lowered at the colonial house on Lafayette Square in Washington, D.C. Upstairs, Sec. of State William Henry Seward was nearly asleep in his bed, trussed in a neck brace necessitated by a carriage accident nine days earlier. At his bedside sat daughter Fannie; a male nurse, George Robinson, stood by the door. They did not hear the commotion erupting at Ford's Theatre a few blocks distant where actor John Wilkes Booth had shot Pres. Abraham Lincoln during the performance of a play and escaped on foot. Audience members poured into the streets in a frenzied dash to capture the assailant.

Fannie knew nothing of the chaos beyond her walls, but a noise at the front door piqued the twenty-year-old's curiosity. From the second floor landing she watched her brother Frederick argue with a brawny young man claiming to be the doctor's assistant come to administer a dose of new medicine to the elder Seward. Forcibly denied entrance, Lewis Powell aimed a revolver at Frederick's head and pulled the trigger. The gun misfired and the struggle continued until Powell smashed Frederick's skull with the weapon and left him in a heap as he dashed upstairs.

Robinson, a thirty-two-year-old Union soldier assigned as Seward's guard while he healed from his own battle wounds, grappled with Powell at the bedroom door. With a great effort, William Seward rose to interpose himself between his daughter and the assailant, who repeatedly plunged his Bowie knife into the secretary's face, neck and chest. Seward collapsed onto the bed. As a dark stain spread across his victim's nightshirt, Powell dashed through the door, down the stairs, and into a night unlike any other in American history.[1]

Seward survived his mortal wounds, saved by the metal frame and webbing of his neck brace. Lincoln died at seven o'clock the next morning. Within a year of the bloody night, Seward lost his wife and daughter to illness and trauma derived from the violence. He remained secretary of state under Lincoln's successor, Pres. Andrew Johnson, and, aided by his son, Asst. Sec. Frederick Seward, committed his final years to acquiring the crown jewels of America's Manifest Destiny.

The secretary's consummate passion to expand the empire linked his name indelibly to Alaska. For more than a decade, negotiations to purchase Russian America had languished under the weight of war; when the Russians reopened dialogue in early 1867, they found Secretary Seward most agreeable. The U.S. Congress was less so. Bearing the scars of his assailant's knife, Seward regularly held forth in the Capitol chambers on the wisdom of annexing the vast northern territory. The balance of opinion eventually tipped when Massachusetts Republican senator Charles Sumner delivered a stirring three-hour speech about the territory he proposed to call Alaska, meaning "great land" in Aleut. The United States flag was raised in Sitka on October 18, 1867.

Two years later, seventy-one-year-old William Seward and his son Frederick toured the nation's newest possession. Their trip included a rendezvous with scientist George Davidson and territorial governor Bvt. Maj. Gen. Jefferson C. Davis to observe a total eclipse in Klukwan, Alaska. Though widely feared and respected, Chilkat headman Koh'klux welcomed the high-stationed visitors, whose powers were magnified by their apparent control over the sun. Thus did events place the famed abolitionist onstage with the one of the last slaveholders in the "slaveless" United States of America.

This chapter depicts events and persons in the Klukwan area during the week of the total eclipse on August 7, 1869. The stories are derived, in part, from recent research by John Cloud of the U.S. Geological Survey and by the author's investigation of the George Davidson archives at the University of California in Berkeley. Also, a close reading of the eyewitness report of Frederick Seward as well as his father's speeches lend clarity to an occasion shrouded in myth and inaccuracy.

Viewing the incident through a rhetorical lens brings into focus the message construction and persuasive effect of the principal players. Koh'klux and Secretary Seward met as statesmen who, as rhetorician Kenneth Burke suggests, desired to "induce action" in the other. The extraordinary circumstances of the eclipse added elements of Burke's "primitive magic," in which rhetorical strategies are believed to "induce motion in things."[2] Celestial powers at work or not, Koh'klux perceived the white men's authority and responded with traditional Tlingit diplomacy. Whatever prior distrust existed between the "saucy and turbulent" Chilkats and their new landlords dissipated—at least temporarily—when Koh'klux pledged his friendship and opened the aaní for business.[3]

:: "DO NOT HIT A SHARK ON THE HEAD"

William Henry Seward, a New Yorker, devoted most of his political career to the abolition of southern slavery. In 1846, he defended William Freeman, an African American man accused of murder. Seward and his wife, Frances, paid the bills for former slave Frederick Douglass to print *The North Star*, an abolitionist newspaper. The Sewards deeded a home on seven acres to the Underground Railroad conductor, Harriet Tubman. With Frances Seward as the voice of abolition in her husband's ear, William became the conscience of the moderate Republican president, Abraham Lincoln, when he took office in March 1861.[4]

Abolition became a reality with the close of the Civil War, so the secretary turned his powerful gaze westward. Twenty-three months after the attacks on his family, Seward engaged in a three-week parley with Russian minister Eduard de Stoeckl that ended with a 4 a.m. signing of the treaty that authorized purchase of Alaska. Pen-strokes on parchment drew the starting line for another six months of political wrangling before the czar wholesaled a northern territory twice the size of Texas. Its forty-four-thousand-mile coastline more than tripled the extent of the nation's former coastal property.

Before the United States agreed to pay Russia $7.2 million, or about two cents an acre, Congress dispatched a trustee to assess the value of a place many deemed worthless. From their search for a dedicated scientist-appraiser, solons chose the western chief of the U.S. Coast Survey, George Davidson, to lead the first federal survey of southern Alaska's convoluted shores.

As a young man, British-born Davidson studied among Philadelphia astronomers and later with a mentor who led him to a career of surveying the coast. Davidson was a teen when he began working with the U.S. Coast

Survey (now the National Oceanic and Atmospheric Administration) charting the East Coast and twenty-five years old when he relocated with his wife, Elinor, to San Francisco in 1850 to chart the California coast.[5]

Davidson's job with the Coastal Survey turned strategic when the first battle of the Civil War erupted in 1861 at Fort Sumter on the South Carolina coast. Though a civilian office, the Coast Survey remained a unit in the Union government, reassigning Davidson to the East and Gulf Coasts to draw secret charts for the War Department.[6] After the war, Secretary of State Seward, aware of Davidson's work approved of him as surveyor for the new territory of Alaska. The congressionally sanctioned investigation sent Davidson back to San Francisco in the summer of 1867, where he recruited a crew and set sail for Alaska on the U.S. revenue steamer *Lincoln*.[7]

From August through October Capt. W. A. Howard piloted his cutter into the farthest reaches of Alaska's Inside Passage as the surveyors assessed the value of trackless forests, mineral peaks, and the mouths of silty rivers.[8] The archipelago Russia called "Great" became "Alexander" after Davidson's mentor and former U.S. Coast Survey superintendent Alexander Dallas Bache.[9] Davidson's *California Coast Pilot* was already an essential nautical reference south to Mexico. The charts Davidson produced from his 1867 and 1869 investigations became the *Coast Pilot of Alaska,* for decades a seminal guide to northern waters. Much of the narrative in the first edition promoted the wealth of resources including timber, water, minerals, fur-bearers, and fish—spoils of a frontier treasure chest. Davidson noted that the "most important discovery" was a seam of coal near Sitka, but an undoubted personal highlight was installing marker number one at the northernmost point of the West Coast survey.[10]

By midautumn the Purchase of Alaska was complete except formal ceremonies in Sitka on October 18. Now near the end of his last tour of the season, Davidson gazed from aboard the *Lincoln* as it entered Lynn Canal, a spectacular canyon flooded by seawater two thousand feet deep contained by sheer granite walls rising six and seven thousand feet to glacier-caped summits. Midway up the sixty-mile fjord, a long, narrow peninsula divides the waters into Chilkat and Chilkoot Inlets; Captain Howard steered left into the western arm and guided his steamer to a tiny island, an incisor protruding at the mouth of the Chilkat River.

The deeper water on the south side of Labouchere Island (sometimes called God's Island) served as an anchorage for the three-masted ships of the HBC and Russian-American Companies, whose crews sought Interior furs from the Tlingit middlemen. In 1838, a German surveyor christened the barren island Pestchani, or Farewell, but U.S. possession changed that. On a breezy day in mid-October 1867, Davidson pounded into the wind-scoured summit of "Sandy Island" the prime benchmark for a survey that connected the West Coast to the tip of Baja, Mexico.

Davidson also installed an astronomical station from which he predicted the area to be ideal for viewing a total eclipse due in August 1869.[11] As part of a cross-continental team of Coast Survey eclipse observers, Davidson established the site of the northernmost field station. For years, he had debated the popular mythology of eclipse phenomena and intended to disprove such "rubbish" as "Bailey's beads" and the colored star reputed to hang on the "moon's bright disk." The best viewing, Davidson surmised, would be from the village of Klukwan twenty miles up the Chilkat River.[12] He knew the fierce reputation of the locals, but a desire to watch the eclipse outweighed any misgivings. Even after an intimidating encounter during his inaugural visit, Davidson was resolute.

When the *Lincoln* first approached Sandy Island, a dozen canoes appeared on the horizon, then sliced through the pale turquoise seawater to the ship's side. Howard had long anticipated the scenario. He stood at the rail, flanked by men armed against the worst circumstances. The five surveyors were likely ordered to the wheelhouse or below-decks. Davidson wrote little about the rendezvous in his report to the Coast Survey beyond noting his incredulity at the quantity of furs sold by Chilkats to HBC traders that year. European ships traded with Tlingit communities throughout the archipelago, but the remote location of the Chilkat fortress and the hostile reputation of its residents reduced incentives for trade and settlement. Few white men dared venture in the Jilkáat áani, but the captain was charged with conveying the authority of the U.S. government over every corner of its new possession. He invited the sháade háni and his entourage aboard.

Called "chief" by white men who assumed a Western hierarchy, the Tlingit leader, or sháade háni, was actually a clan spokesperson who might represent many houses, even a consensus of the village, but generally not the opposite moiety. Facing Captain Howard on the deck of the *Lincoln* was Daanawáak, leader of Yandeist'akye, a small village set slightly upriver from the Chilkat River mouth. His people were Lkoot, called Chilkoot by white men, with perhaps four hundred residents in a few small villages located in the eastern arm of Lynn Canal. Following introductions, Captain Howard distributed gifts, then inquired about Koh'klux, the Chilkat sháade háni. Daanawáak's mood darkened, and he declared that his current war with Klukwan made the upriver journey impossible. The Yandeist'akye headman wished to be treated as the United States' liaison with the kwáan, but Howard declined. Gifts of tobacco, bread, and molasses offended Daanawáak, who demanded whiskey. Again, the captain refused and, upon the party's leave, dispatched a runner to Klukwan.[13]

The next afternoon, five war canoes pulled alongside the revenue cutter, one flying a HBC flag. Captain Howard's first impression of Koh'klux was of a "very quarrelsome Indian," especially when denied whiskey. Broad-chested, six feet tall, and ornately attired, Koh'klux presented a threatening figure to the uniformed white men.[14] Deep scars on both cheeks were reminders of the act that had earned him the name meaning "do not hit a shark on the head" or "hard to kill." Different stories are told about his scars, but in 1881 travel writer Eliza Scidmore interviewed Koh'klux familiars who said the sháade háni once scoffed at a rival who held a revolver to the Chilkat's head. When the rival pulled the trigger, the wet powder hardly fired, but the bullet pierced one cheek and exited the other. Koh'klux swallowed his teeth and responded: "You cannot hurt me. See!"[15]

Such was the man to whom Captain Howard attempted to explain the sovereignty of the United States. Unlike British and Yankee traders who routinely flaunted the law, a federal agent could not dispense spirits to Natives.

"If I have no presents," the headman growled, "why come? Talk without whiskey is nothing; s'pose plenty whiskey and presents, then talk good."

Eventually, Howard convinced Koh'klux that he was not a trader, but a representative of the great Tyees in Washington, D.C. The Tyees prohibited him from distributing alcohol and guns, but if the Chilkats were good citizens, Howard guaranteed future rewards from a beneficent government. The headman departed "much better disposed" when presented with an American flag and a red military coat trimmed in gold braid. Captain Howard reported that the Union Jack flying off a stern mast was replaced by the Old Glory, which snapped in the breeze as the sháade háni paddled upriver. In his private journal, Professor Davidson was less celebratory, decrying the "farce" of Howard "giving [an] American flag to [a] filthy Indian who stuck it in canoe [as] another canoe raise[d] English flag and both went off."[16]

On the morning of the eighteenth, soldiers hoisted the flag at "Chilcate" within a few minutes of the colors flying at Sitka. Moved by ceremony, mutual respect, and free trade, Koh'klux determined to tout the American Way to his people.[17]

At a regional council of Tlingit leaders months later, the Chilkat sháade háni urged cooperation with the latest wave of white men. The United States proved itself a superior force, he said, "able to purchase the interests of the Russians and drive away King George's Men whom we know to be strong."[18] The Klukwan sháade háni acknowledged the greater authority of their new trading partner but ceded nothing. Other communities might make different arrangements, but Chilkats fully controlled their homeland—monitored for intruders, owned overland access, and sustained a large, defensible village protected by satellite settlements and camps on every salmon-bearing river in the region. Two-point-six-million acres.

The coming eclipse would confirm Koh'klux's opinions about Boston strength, to which he responded in a traditional Tlingit manner—by revealing to the white men the extent of his own power.

In the months leading up to Davidson's return in 1869, Gen. Jefferson C. Davis, commander of the Department of Alaska military district, had several run-ins with Chilkat men, which led him to call them the "most formidable and hostile" of all Alaska Natives. Davis was sent to Sitka at the end of a long, checkered career in which mishaps overshadowed his accomplishments. First, Davis held the dubious distinction of not being *the* Jefferson Davis, former president of the Confederate State of America, but a brevet major general in the Union Army. He was also the only U.S. general in history to kill another U.S. general on American soil. After a heated argument in a Louisville hotel lobby, Davis shot General William "Bull" Nelson in the chest, which earned him a manslaughter indictment. His case languished, however, and the accused officer was eventually released to lead a battalion on Maj. Gen. William T. Sherman's destructive March to the Sea. Davis's infamy spread when he destroyed a bridge meant to aid African American refugees rescued by and following Union troops, leaving stranded slaves to be slaughtered by vengeful Confederate soldiers on the opposite bank. In 1867, after the Civil War, Davis was reassigned as the first administrator of the District and later Department of Alaska in Sitka. He immediately set the tone by ordering all Russian residents out of homes to be reoccupied by Americans. Public military exercises seemed to quell local Native residents, but the Chilkats remained a vexation.[19]

General Davis was encouraged in May 1868 when a delegation of Chilkat leaders paddled to Sitka to apologize for past conflicts with white men. The ambassadors insisted that the general visit their homeland to taste the hospitality of the Chilkats. Knowing them to be "very wealthy Indians," Davis was intrigued. He knew the rumors of secret trade routes controlled by Chilkats from the Lynn Canal tide-line far into the Yukon Basin.[20] Generations-long trading relationships between Chilkat and Interior Athabaskan partners assured a steady supply of the highly-valued thick pelts to European and American markets. In 1867 alone, white traders reported that at least twenty-three hundred marten and sable pelts were obtained from Chilkat-Chilkoot fur-brokers.[21]

Davis made an appearance in midsummer at the mouth of the Chilkat River, where he learned more about the "Grease Trail" over which Tlingits carried the precious eulachon oil to trade with Interior tribes for beautiful, thick, valuable pelts. Davis reported that the welcoming committee "seemed quite earnest in their desire to have us come among them and trade with them."[22] According to his informants, Chilkats had convinced a white ex-soldier to live among them, so he could show them how to prospect for gold. Davis reported that, if funds were authorized, the Chilkats were willing to escort an official exploration party on the Grease Trail as early as the next spring.

In the final weeks of 1868 another Chilkat delegation came to Sitka, but the atmosphere was fouled, Davis reported, by Colchika, one of the "principal chiefs" from Klukwan. Davis was bothered by the "very haughty and imperious" manner of the Chilkat headman, whose sense of entitlement, he feared, would infect the pacified locals. In a letter to his superior officer, Davis labelled Colchika "the most powerful and vindictive" Tlingit leader of all, along with Koh'klux whose ill will "toward the Americans showed itself very conspicuously on many occasions." What Davis omitted from his report was his own role in an uprising that nearly pitched the Tlingit population into war with white Sitka.[23]

When Colchika, Sitka Jack, and another leader (probably Koh'klux) paid a New Year's Day visit to General Davis, he celebrated their friendship with a toast of hard liquor, then sent each along with a bottle of "apple toddy." Once outside, the clan leaders sat on the Custom House steps and consumed their gifts. Colchika grabbed a sentry's rifle, but the soldier refused to let go, so the Chilkat dragged him several hundred feet. Soldiers apprehended and briefly jailed Colchika before he escaped into the Native part of Sitka known as "the Ranche." That night Davis imposed a lockdown on the Ranche; the next morning, two gunboats lay offshore, each capable of wiping out large sections of the community. Davis demanded that Colchika be brought to him "dead or alive," or he would "blow the Indian village to pieces."[24]

Sometimes called "forest diplomacy," the practice of obliterating villages was a strategy employed by the U.S. military in the early era of U.S. sovereignty in Alaska. The policy justified bombings of Angoon, Stikine, Kake, and Yakutat, memories of which have been passed down many generations. Because Klukwan was twenty miles up the Chilkat River, the "mother village" was beyond cannon range, a factor some felt led to its villagers' apparent disregard for military might.

Throughout the Sitka standoff, Colchika refused to surrender. Unwilling to risk a massacre, Davis eventually rowed to the Ranche shore, accompanied only by an interpreter to craft an agreement with the leaders. All instigators were jailed; Koh'klux vowed to keep the peace and was released ten days later. A council of peaceable Sitka headmen signed on, but others, like the Kakes, were dissatisfied. An army bullet had killed a Kake man, so his relatives sought independent reparations, preferably the death of a soldier. No one in Sitka openly supported the family's traditional demand for blood atonement. Moreover, Davis included the Kakes in the curfew, adding to their frustration; they slipped out of the Ranche to do their work elsewhere. On an Admiralty Island beach, the Kakes found and introduced themselves to two white men, whom they promptly killed.[25]

General Davis and naval commander Richard Meade Jr. decided that the time had come for forest diplomacy. The Sitka military authorities dispatched the gunboat USS *Saginaw* off the northern shores of Kupreanof Island where it cannonaded three Kake villages to rubble.

:: "THE GREAT SPIRIT GENERALLY DOES
WHATEVER THE BOSTON MEN WANT HIM TO"

When George Davidson returned to Sitka in July 1869, much of Native America was at war to defend itself against the national government. The 1868 Constitutional Amendment that guaranteed equal protection and due process to former African American slaves denied Native Americans most citizenship rights. The Fourteenth Amendment made it possible for Maj. Gen. Phillip Sheridan to declare that "the only good Indian is a dead Indian" to justify deploying U.S. Army troops that year to subdue and remove Cheyennes, Comanches, Kiowas, Sioux, and Arapahoes. On the Northern Plains, treaties proved useless against white encroachment, provoking skirmishes with Sioux, Nez Perce, and Shoshones. The installation of a Civil War general as president in early 1869 guaranteed armed retaliation. While praised for his Peace Policy on the reservations, Pres. Ulysses S. Grant pursued a war policy aimed at further sanitizing the nation's remaining frontiers, including Alaska.[26]

In Alaska, relations with Tlingits were somewhat better. Rather than defend white Sitkans from attack, the five hundred troops under General Davis's command were more likely dispatched to stem interclan war and punish bootleggers. Since the U.S. Purchase, access to alcohol deepened the severity and length of internecine conflicts. "Hooch" was produced by rising numbers of stills in the villages, supplemented by an "immense quantity of beer" shipped out of a Sitka brewery, one of the first successful businesses after the U.S. flag was raised.[27]

From Davis's perspective, relations with Chilkats remained on edge. In the year following the Purchase, he targeted northern tribes as most likely deserving "summary punishment." In the first months of 1869, three Chilkat men were shot and killed in the Ranche, so soldiers were on alert. Nonetheless, the general sent an invitation for Koh'klux to meet Professor Davidson in Sitka and serve as his host for the duration of the mission in Klukwan. Davis had "little doubt," he assured the surveyor, that Koh'klux would make "all the arrangements you desire." The general also offered a military escort to transport the astronomers to Chilkat Country, but Davidson turned him down, prompting at least one of his companions to call him "reckless."[28] Unfazed by the tensions with Natives, as one colleague observed, Davidson appeared "less anxious about the Indians than about the weather." One of the astronomer's biggest fears was the possibility of cloud-cover on the day of the eclipse.[29]

Koh'klux "was certainly not in a friendly mood" when Davidson met him in a Sitka jail cell. Along with several Klukwan men, the Kaagwaantaan sháade háni had been charged with "some petty offense." The mood lightened when General Davis promised their freedom if the "the greatest warrior and diplomat of all the tribes north and west of the Stak-heen" would escort the Americans. Koh'klux agreed.[30]

On his departure from Sitka, Davidson left word for William Seward, who, with his son Frederick was finally seeing the territory on which he had staked his career. If their schedule allowed, the astronomer invited the former secretary of state and his party to join them for the eclipse in Klukwan.

Because Davidson refused an armed transport, General Davis could only offer him a wooden rowboat big enough to accommodate the surveyors and three journalists. Instead of the normal week's passage to the upper Lynn Canal, blustery weather demanded eleven days of deadening labor from an unseasoned crew. A war canoe powered by Koh'klux and company carried the expedition's supplies, including an array of delicate astronomical instruments. Each evening the Chilkats set up camp and attended to their guests.[31]

A day from Klukwan, Davidson revisited the three-mile-wide glacier that bears his name. Although he recorded the Tlingit name as Sit-ky'a, his supervisor, Alexander Bache, renamed it Davidson Glacier on published charts. Expedition accounts and pictures spread knowledge of the glacier to a public hungry for Alaskan images—including John Muir of Yosemite, who yearned to witness for himself the glacier "grandly descending" into Lynn Canal. Sketches from the initial investigation show ice cliffs a few dozen feet from the tide-line. In the two years since the surveyor had last seen his

Davidson Glacier,
ca. 1890. Photograph,
69 1976.006.0009,
Haines Sheldon
Museum, Alaska.

glacial namesake, the ice had substantially withdrawn, allowing growth of a more-established forest on the terminal moraine between ice and tide.[32]

By their entry into the Chilkat River on July 26, the oarsmen lagged far behind the war canoe as they wrestled up the final stretch: twenty-one miles of swollen meltwater to Klukwan. Gunshots erupted along three points of the river, but Davidson assured his crew that it was celebratory and forbade them from returning fire. By the time they reached Klukwan, the sháade háni had prepared the visitors' lodging in one of his treasure houses. Davidson lauded Koh'klux for treatment that "fulfilled in spirit and letter every promise, and our every wish was attended to." Despite their load of valuable equipment, he added, "We never lost a single article during our stay at his strong village."[33]

In the week and a half leading up to the eclipse, the Americans savored Chilkat hospitality, including ample quantities of "fish and fowl" at every meal.[34] Through his investigations, Davidson judged Chilkat Valley climate and soil to promise greater agricultural productivity than anywhere else in the Alexander Archipelago. Behind Klukwan, the scientist determined, stood an entire mountain of iron in extraordinary concentrations, and close proximity to the sea made the resource an especially valuable asset to the new owner-nation. Within the week, one of the country's most esteemed leaders, William Seward, would personally inspect it.[35]

With the election of President Grant, Secretary of State Seward stepped down from a post he held for eight years. The assassination attempt and family deaths had taken a toll on the lifelong politician. He yearned to travel as a civilian and see the nation to which he had devoted his adult life. With his middle-aged son, Frederick, the former secretary set out on a tour of the United States in 1869 with close inspections of the Rocky Mountains and Far West. While in San Francisco, Seward "expressed a wish" to see Alaska;

within days he was northbound aboard the private steamer *Active*, which was equipped with such luxury that a "sovereign, visiting a distant province, in a royal yacht, could hardly have made his journey more commodious and comfortable."[36]

Following a scenic cruise along the Northwest Coast, Seward's party arrived in Sitka on July 30. Their tour of Alaska's principal city included the harbor, brewery, and sawmill, but of special interest to Frederick Seward was the "fantastic savagery" he saw in the stylized forms carved into masks and totem poles. He marveled at the array of creatures who kept watch with "great staring eyes" and served as heraldic symbols similar to the family crests of Europe.

William Seward's party soon headed north again on the *Active,* this time with General Davis and a few soldiers. A remarkably accessible frontier slipped by as the *Active* probed to the northernmost point of its voyage. Through the maze of forested islands and fish-filled streams, the Sewards marveled "that a place so temperate and healthful, so rich in resources or industry and commerce, so long had prevailed untenanted by civilized man." Frederick recalled Davis "laughingly" inviting his father to assist with Chilkat negotiations. This was an opportunity, General Davis reminded the elder statesman, to "civilize" one of the last "wild" tribes in the nation. Upon receiving assurances of peace from Koh'klux in Sitka, Davis had promised to reciprocate, he told Seward, by bringing to Klukwan the "Great Tyee" who purchased Alaska. Humored and honored, the chief diplomat accepted.

On August 5, the steamer hove in sight of the sandy knob at the mouth of the Chilkat, which by 1869 was called Pyramid Island. Several Tlingit canoes approached the *Active* and agreed to send a message upriver to Davidson. The next day, the canoes reappeared bearing an invitation to join Davidson's crew in the sháade háni's palatial quarters. Koh'klux sent additional canoes to transport the guests, but soldiers escorted Davis and the Sewards in a boat from the steamer. The oarsmen pulled ahead while far behind the *Active* slowly nosed up channels cloudy with glacial silt. After several hours, the rowboat landed just below Klukwan on a sandbar where Davidson and Koh'klux waited. The headman assigned Seward's party to another of his clan houses where they passed the night warmly, wrapped in bearskins and blankets amidst "semi-civilized, semi-savage surroundings."[37]

When the sun turned "sick" on the appointed day, Davidson's crew members were posted at various stations, each man armed with a camera, chronometer, sextant, telescope, or notebook, focused on the sky, and encircled by curious villagers. As the landscape darkened in the shadow of the eclipse, one Sitka journalist described horrified Klukwan residents fleeing to their homes and refusing to emerge until the sun came back. This view has been reinforced in scholarly and popular work for decades, with some interpretations casting the eclipse in the role of the cavalry saving white men from Indian attack.[38]

In his father's biography published in 1891, eyewitness Frederick Seward conveyed a wholly different scene. As light faded, Seward saw mounting anxiety in the faces of the Chilkat people who, instead of running, pressed closer to the astronomers. Birdsong ceased, insects faded. Hushed tones and rapid exchanges between Davidson and the surveyors led villagers to believe the scientist was "personally conducting the exhibition." Clouds, the surveyors' bane, had obscured most of the sky that day but began to dissipate just before the celestial event. A signal fire from a post on the mountainside a mile away confirmed a second clear view.

As the moon's silhouette half-obscured the sun, a local man broke the silence. He was "convinced of the 'Boston men's' skill," the interpreter said, and "feared bad consequences" if the display continued. Crew members ignored him.

At the apogee of the eclipse, visiting Sitka Tlingits dropped to their knees as trained by Russian priests and began to recite the Lord's Prayer. Unfamiliar with Christian practices, Klukwan residents could only stand shoulder to shoulder, watching the white men adjust sextants and scribble calculations. Light's return brought relieved shouts from villagers. It was apparent to them, Frederick wrote, that the Boston men were moving the moon off the sun, "as skillfully and methodically as they had put it on."

When the dramatic display was done, Koh'klux invited the white men to his house, where they took up matters of state. The sháade háni sat with his visitors near the firepit in the center of the lodge, surrounded by "grave, passive rows" of up to three hundred "chiefs," warriors, and women. When all were assembled, Koh'klux stood and spoke emphatically, translated by a Native interpreter: "Some time ago, the Kolosh (Sitka Tlingits) killed three of the Chilcats. Now the Great Tyee has come, we have gathered to ask him—What is he going to do about it?"

The compact statesman with the prominent nose was intrigued by the direct appeal and responded with cautious authority.

"When did this killing take place?"

Through the "Indian fashion" of calculating solar and lunar cycles, Koh'klux confirmed that the crime occurred nine or ten years earlier.

"Then it happened when this country belonged to the Emperor of Russia," William Seward replied, "long before it became the property of the United States." He urged Koh'klux to seek reparations from the czar, which, after translation, prompted vigorous discussion among the headmen. Eventually, the Tlingit leader answered:

"We did appeal to the Emperor of Russia, but he gave us no redress. Perhaps he was too poor. We know he was poor because he had to sell his land to the great 'Tyee.' But now the great 'Tyee' himself is here, in his stead. And we want to know what he is going to do about it?"

Within the dim recesses of the packed Tlingit clan house, the sháade háni and the statesman stood only a few feet apart, so each likely noticed the prominent facial scars of the other. Wearing his own mask of power, Koh'klux would consider the knife wounds in Seward's neck and face to be evidence of the Tyee's strength. The secretary consulted with the general, then turned back to the headman and asked about appropriate redress. Upon translation, Frederick Seward observed visible enthusiasm in the crowd. The elders again engaged, and Koh'klux responded:

"A life for a life is the Indian law and always has been, but as these three Chilcats were of the chief's family, we reckon each of their lives to be equal to the lives of three common Indians. What we want then, is the great 'Tyee's' permission to send our warriors down to kill nine of the Koloshes to avenge the death of the Chilcats."

Absolutely not, Seward returned. Blood atonement was out of the question. What about another form of restitution? Chilkat faces, wrote Seward, "beamed with satisfaction when this was translated to them. It began to look like business." The headmen regrouped for further discussion, then Koh'klux announced terms.

"We know that the Boston men are averse to any killing, except by their own soldiers. So we have sometimes consented to take pay in blankets. We think that the life of each Indian is worth about four blankets. Nine times four blankets, if the great 'Tyee' chooses to give them to us, would be full redress, and make our hearts glad; and we would henceforth regard the Kolosh as our friends and brothers."

Seward turned to Davis. "Well, General, there you have the conclusion of the case. I think we can afford to give them thirty-six blankets to make peace between the tribes."

Along with his hearty endorsement, General Davis declared an end to the "last of the Indian disputes" in Alaska. To show the gravity of the commitment, the general required that several Chilkat commissioners be appointed to travel to Sitka for a public peace ceremony between clans. Koh'klux and company readily agreed.

Celebration broke out among the Chilkats, many of whom had relatives in Sitka. Peace meant they could again visit family unencumbered by revenge or reprisal. The festive mood grew when Seward's party invited clan leaders to dine with them that evening aboard the *Active* anchored downriver from Klukwan.

A flotilla of brightly decorated canoes arrived at the appointed time, but only the main six *hitsaati* (clan house keepers) could fit in the cabin with their esteemed hosts. The elders were attired in their best Boston clothes, and Frederick Seward thought Koh'klux especially handsome in his "neat suit of black broadcloth." A "bewildering" variety of dishes served in "lavish" portions were served to cabin diners, then passed out to clan members crowded on the decks of the steamer. Following victuals and conversation, Secretary Seward asked the clan leaders if they had any further questions of him. As before, the men conferred, then delivered an answer: They wished for the great Tyee to explain the eclipse. Seward responded by holding an apple and an orange before a cabin light and showing the effect of their alignment. Through the translator, he explained the process in the simplest terms, asking if they understood.

The elders deliberated before their answer.

"The chiefs have understood much, though not all, the great Tyee has told them. They understand him as saying that the eclipse was caused by the Great Spirit, and not by man. Since he says so, they will believe it. They have noticed, however, that the Great Spirit generally does whatever the 'Boston men' want him to."[39]

While the Chilkat respected Seward for his rank, they regarded George Davidson as a divine. "I had the reputation of a great medicine man," he wrote, a status that earned him the confidence of Koh'klux. Unsolicited, the headman offered to draw a map of the 1852 expedition he led to destroy Fort Selkirk. For days Koh'klux bent over the floor tracing the route on the backs of ship's charts, often pausing to confer with his two wives. Though he had never before used paper and pencil, the sháade háni sketched a topographic corridor between Seduction Point and the fort in a "corkscrew spiral" four hundred miles long. With over a hundred Tlingit place names, the map filled in details of a vast landscape previously unknown to outsiders.[40]

On a pattern board otherwise used for Tlingit design preparation, Davidson returned the gesture by rendering in red and black the moment of eclipse totality as he saw it through the telescope. A similar image appeared in Davidson's article about the map published thirty-two years after Koh'klux presented it to him. Worried that the news might precipitate a stampede, the professor waited until the Klondike Gold Rush of 1897–1899 subsided before publishing an article in *Mazama,* a small West Coast climbing magazine, in 1901. The "Koh'klux Map" resides today in the Bancroft

Archives at the University California; Davidson's painting is said to remain in Klukwan, but the exact location is disputed.[41]

:: "MULTIFARIOUS POPULATION"

Five days after the eclipse, Secretary Seward stood before hundreds of Sitkans to deliver an hour-long speech that broadly praised the new territory for its weather, land, resources, and, above all, potential development. During his campaign for northern expansion, Seward sustained a missionary zeal against the vocal skeptics, and now he could extol the wisdom of the Purchase. Incentives to attract settlers, he told the crowd, were needed to balance a "multifarious population" still in need of civilizing. The abolitionist decried the Native victims of long-running clan wars who were condemned to a state of "perpetual slavery" now anathema in post–Civil War America.

Despite pockets of resistance, the secretary's faith derived from the integrity he saw in even the least reconstructed of "savages." For instance, he had faced the most "feared" Indian in the territory and found "Kla-kautch" to be an intelligent, hospitable leader whose resources were considerable. Behind his village rose a thirty-mile mountain range comprised of concentrated iron ore. More importantly, Seward announced, the renowned "chief" unveiled to him the Chilkat route to wealth. Beyond the coastal mountains stretched a gentle land "very fertile, in a genial climate, and . . . of boundless extent," a northern extension of the "rich and habitable valley lands" of the Pacific Northwest.

The promotional passions of the Great Tyee mitigated whatever restraint Davidson gained by delaying map publication. To Seward, the Grease Trail was emblematic of the limitless fortunes promised in the gospel of Manifest Destiny. He called his mostly white audience the "advance guard" of a civilizing force soon to reach Alaska's shores, then joined Davidson on the *Active* for their return to the States.[42]

National expansion was essential to the survival of the Union, Seward reiterated to a Salem, Oregon, audience a few weeks later, and with its "inexhaustible" supply of timber, minerals, fish, and furs, Alaska offered the next great economic contribution to America's destiny. A "successful republic," however, must never be built on "human bondage." Free enterprise required free men.[43]

A few days after Seward's and Davidson's departure from Klukwan, Koh'klux led a group of miners into the Interior. According to one prospector, the Chilkat headman was "as interested in the gold, silver, copper or coal as we are" and eager to show them the country. The relationship cooled, however, when Chilkats asserted their interest in profit sharing. When miners admitted the possibility of building houses in the Chilkat Valley, some Tlingits became so angry they threatened to decapitate General Davis. The widely publicized threats stifled regional enthusiasm about the route to riches, drawing further calls for a military presence in the northern aaní.[44]

But unrest between Chilkats and whites did not erode the friendship William Seward felt toward Koh'klux. Months after his visit to Klukwan, Seward sent the Chilkat sháade háni a large yellow chinchilla blanket bearing the inscription, "To Chief Shathitch, from his friend William H. Seward." The secretary died two years after his meeting with the esteemed Tlingit leader, but in the last two decades of his life, Koh'klux wore the gift as a "robe of state," which bolstered his legend and redeemed him in the eyes of military officials.[45]

That he tattooed Seward's name on his arm further demonstrates Koh'klux's faith in the Tyee's word, so much that he finally freed his own slaves in 1883, twenty-one years after President Lincoln signed the Emancipation Proclamation.[46]

4 :: Eagles in the Heart

:: "SOMETIMES HE MAKES A LOT OF NOISE,
   THAT'S WHEN HE GETS THE POWER"

In Yandeist'akye, a chief is dying.

Accompanied by his slave, Usha, Kood-wot was hunting goats in the thin spaces near the summit of G̲eisán, whose massive rock face darkens the sky behind the village.[1] Not far from the summit, Kood-wot slipped on a crumbling outcrop and fell. Usha found his master broken, vomiting blood. After comforting Kood-wot, the slave slid down three thousand vertical feet of steep ravines to the village, where he roused a rescue party. Clansmen ran up the mountain until they found their sháade háni and bore him home to a bed arranged in a prominent place in the clan house.

Aloft in thick layers of goat cape and bearskin, an unconscious Kood-wot retains a regal pose. He wears the clan tunic, its story woven in goat wool by women three generations gone. Brown bear claws curve upward from a necklace on his chest. Snowy ermine skins drape his head from a shakee.át crowned by sea lion whiskers bristling at the spirit world.

To signify the power of clan at.óow, Chilkat blankets and regalia hang from the crossbeams over the large, central room of the house, enclosing two hundred mourners. Box-drum cadence booms from a shadowed corner. A final, authoritative thump signals the shaman's entrance.

Yealh-neddy is "hideous in the extreme," Presbyterian missionary Caroline Willard wrote in her fiction novel, *Kin-da-Shon's Wife,* originally published in 1892. The author and her husband, the Reverend Eugene Willard, were missionaries and among the first white people allowed to live in Jilḵáat aaní. Caroline was the first white woman to encounter the local medicine man, her model for Yealh-neddy, whom she described with lurid fascination: "bony and nude, except that girdling chest and loins are strings of teeth from the carcasses of sharks and beavers, with the claws of bears, talons of eagles, and bones of various kinds."

Anticipation clutches the room—every breath held, every child hushed.

More than his freakish apparel, Mrs. Willard feared the shaman's face "with its uncanny, snakish power . . . the gaping mouth, the wide, thin lips, the sunken cheeks, the vulture-like nose . . . but the mystery of the face is in the eyes, felt, not seen . . . deep-set in shadowy hollows and overhung by matted hair, they seem to emit flame." In Yealh-neddy, Willard exposed gaslight-era Americans to a barbaric force in their midst, evil to the bone, a Presbyterian archetype of Satan on earth.

Hardly louder than a heartbeat, the drum resumes. The shaman sways with the rhythm, breathing like a file rasp. Breath becomes a mutter, then a chant. Transfixed, the crowd leans in. His wide eyes roll back as if to peer within, snapping back to focus with an otherworldly gaze that sweeps the room, "throwing light lurid as from hell." Drumbeat quickens. Invisible forces tug his shoulders and elbows, yanking the man into a dance "moved by infernal machinery." Each spidery hand grips an ornate wooden rattle shaken with rising urgency until Yealh-neddy freezes at the last resounding beat.

"With the cry and spring of a panther," the shaman lands at Kood-wot's bedside. His shrieks pierce the dense drum pulse, poun-ding, poun-ding, bone and cartilage hiss from sinew strings that twist around the writhing form. He leaps over the bed once, twice, again, often casting glares at nearby onlookers and dashes at the dying man "as if he were about to tear him to pieces." He clutches and claws the air, leaps again, then sinks into a tight coil. "Moved by irresistible power," Yealh-neddy lurches again toward the bed for an epic battle with unseen spirits. At his most frenzied pitch, two men have to restrain the shaman "from eating his own flesh."

After a long pause, Yealh-neddy crawls into the audience, sniffing, muttering, searching for the witch that caused this fall. As minutes pass, his quest grows more animated, sending ripples of paranoia through the crowd. Spasms wrack the shaman's body. He mutters like a man trying to awaken from a nightmare. In a coarse whisper he declares that the "spirit of the

Studio Portrait of Skondoo with Rattles. Photograph by Winter and Pond, 1894, Haines Sheldon Museum, Alaska.

great chief must pass before us ere the setting sun." People strain to catch his next word. "Sha-he-he." It is the name of a young woman of a lower caste and new to town. The crowd turns on her, binds her feet and hands, and proceeds to torture her in ways that surely startled, perhaps outraged, Mrs. Willard's readers.

Following magic-lantern depictions of brutal savagery, Mrs. Willard's mob tethers Sha-he-he to a stake until she confesses to witchcraft. The frenzy hits its peak with the sacrificial beheading of ten slaves, including faithful old Usha. Their spirits are expected to accompany Kood-wot into the next world. Clansmen cremate their fallen leader and scatter the slaves' remains in the forest as offerings to bears and ravens. Mrs. Willard fades to black as "the unwonted night of pitchy darkness falls over the land of Chilkat."[2]

Four New York editions of *Kin-da-Shon's Wife* in 1892 tapped into popular curiosity about the United States' indigenous heritage, by then largely resculpted into passion plays from an already-mythic frontier legacy. Throughout the book, Mrs. Eugene S. Willard (her pen name) cast her principal players in a dramatic chiaroscuro of shadow and fire. Unveiled in these pages are the last, violent throes of a collapsing culture reconstructed by one of its would-be saviors. Murder, theft, vengeance, greed, and betrayal enmesh Native villagers, whose lives are shattered by successions of alcohol-fueled violence often associated with one shaman or another. The only light that pierces Willard's literary gloom are individual acts of compassion, like star points in a glacier night sky.

The accused witch, Sha-he-he, eventually escapes her tormentors, whose fury swerves the next day to a middle-aged slave accused of using witchcraft to kill an infant. Men drag the woman to a low tide sandbar where they lash her to a stake and leave her to watch for hours as the tide creeps in and covers her. She is saved at the last possible instant by Kotch-kul-ah, daughter of the deceased chief, Kood-wot. She needs the slave to guard against the shaman's advances. Kotch-kul-ah names the woman Usha, in memory of her father's longtime servant, and the plot follows their crusade against darkness toward the light of holy redemption.

Skewed as it is toward her religious mission, Mrs. Willard's portrayal of the relationship between the two women opened a portal through which her readers explored the complexities of Tlingit society. Among *hitsaati,* or house leaders, men displayed power in a public way—as speakers, warriors, shamans, or diplomats—while women managed the internal activities of the house, each containing multiple families. Clan membership among the Tlingit flows through matrilineal relationships, granting women the final word on anything of value. So much clan power, in Willard's view, distracted from their duties as mothers.

As their children approached puberty, parents relinquished more responsibility to the tribe. Boys lived with uncles who taught them to hunt, fish, and carve clan legends in wood. To toughen their nephews, uncles drove them into salt water by the crack of their hemlock whips. Mothers and aunties instructed girls in food preparation, clan songs, and Chilkat weaving. At the first signs of menses, aunties sequestered nieces for two months or more, usually under the floor or in an outlying hovel. Passage into adulthood was celebrated with feasting, dance, and speeches. In addition to strengthening clan ties, such ceremonies allowed members to pay debts and acquire status. In Mrs. Willard's eyes, potlatch hosts who gave away all their wealth perpetuated poverty and jealousy. K̲u.éex' traditions flew in the face of what she judged as proper American capitalism.

Set in the years leading up to John Muir's pivotal encounter in Chilkat Country, *Kin-da-shon's Wife* charts the brutal decline of a heroic people at the mercy of a despotic shaman. The rising presence of white bootleggers and unscrupulous traders compound the sins of the antagonist, who enslaves his victims in an alcoholic stupor. Only Mrs. Willard's God can save

Studio Portrait of Eugene and Caroline Willard. Photograph, 83 B5 no. 001,
Haines Sheldon Museum, Alaska (ca 1890).

the villagers from annihilation but not until they open their hearts to the light. A man of peace will come. Until that time, k̲wáan residents moil in the shadow of Yealh-neddy, Child of Raven.

Trickster, prophet, or pest—Raven of the Northwest Coast is a mischief-maker, a source of phenomenological change and human insight. Foremost, Raven is the bringer of light. Although the Tlingit story varies by region or teller, most versions agree that the world was once covered in darkness, when humans saw light only in the flicker of cook fires. Once, when Raven was flying near the Nass River, just below Alaska's southernmost border with British Columbia, he fell in love with a young woman and disguised himself as a hemlock needle. She swallowed him while drinking water and soon became pregnant. Infant Raven was always in trouble for his insatiable curiosity, so of course when he heard about the valuables stored in his grandfather's treasure chest he pried open the lid. Out popped the sun, stars, and moon, which drifted to the ceiling and through the smoke-hole. Raven followed, flinging light across a world that had only known darkness.[3]

But Raven's achievement clashed directly with the source of Presbyterian light, and the íx̲t' became an obvious missionary target.

As the ebony bird bridged mythic and clan ties, so the shaman acted as an intermediary between spirit and mortal realms. Some peculiarity or ancestral resemblance usually marked the íx̲t' at an early age, such as "copper" (red) hair among Chilkat and Chilkoot. When the prospective íx̲t' came of age, elders oversaw months-long training that included a solo quest for a *yéik*, or personal spirit-messenger. All things in nature contained a yéik, Tlingits believed, including humans, water, rocks, animals, plants, mountains and glaciers. Some were beneficial, others insidious. The reputation of an íx̱t' was based on the success rate of his own yéik to mollify or banish evil spirits. If the yéik killed the patient, assigning blame to a "witch" was another duty of the íx̱t', whose accusations often resulted in torture, sometimes death.[4]

A life dedicated to communicating with the unseen placed the íx̱t' in a position of power and complicity with village leaders. The íx̱t' was never far from the ear of his leader. A sháade háni relied on his shaman to know the future, predict battle outcomes, and communicate telepathically with others in faraway villages. When someone was stricken by illness or accident, the family commissioned a shaman to oust the malevolent yéik.

Dressed in skins and amulets, the íx̱t' labored beside the patient's bed, hands gripping rattles, howling through the mouth-hole of a large, carved mask. Stringy dreadlocks sprayed the air with sweat. The Tlingit shaman could lance an infection or apply a poultice, but was not an herbalist in vocation. The potency of the cure depended on the strength of the performance. Sessions might continue for weeks until the subject showed improvement. If a patient died, the íx̱t' paid the family a full refund.

"Before the white people came around we had the shaman," Chilkoot leader Austin Hammond told me in 1985. "He cures everything. Sometimes he makes a lot of noise, that's when he gets the power."[5] Mock ferocity deepened the leathery creases in Hammond's face, then he relaxed, chuckling.

Perhaps the old sháade háni was thinking of his son, Charlie Jimmie Sr., whose thousands of public performances as an íx̱t' had made him a familiar face in Alaska for nearly half a century. Brochures, posters, and magazines feature a barrel-chested brown man wearing a dreadlock wig, beaded dance-smock, large silver nose-ring, and broad smile.

In his seventies, the big belly and nose-ring are gone, leaving a gaunt, gray-bearded man in his recliner who loves to talk about being raised by his uncles and aunties. Jimmie reels out narratives in conversational English, but when he recalls his uncles' stern voices, the words boom in Tlingit. Jimmie remembers being seven and fishing in the Chilkoot River when elders called him over to their firepit. For the first time, instead of calling out orders they welcomed him into their circle. In a few years the clan would need a song leader, they said, a role that required knowledge of traditional songs, dances, drumming, and stories. His loud voice and self-confidence made Charlie the chosen one. Elders warned him repeatedly that if he didn't

Charles Jimmie Sr.
Photograph by author.

take his Tlingit education seriously, his people "just won't have nothin.'"
The youngster began his apprenticeship that day.

The precocious first-grader attracted the attention of Anna Soboleff, lead teacher at a Native boarding school in Wrangell where Charlie attended in the 1940s. Devoted pastor's wife and mother to an influential clergyman, Soboleff was nonetheless dedicated to her Native upbringing in Killisnoo, a traditional village on Admiralty Island. She saw in young Charlie an old-time spirit that even her Christian mission could not repress. One day, she held Charlie's shoulders, captured his gaze, and asked in a quiet, deliberate voice if he wanted to learn how to act like a medicine man just for "fun."

By saying yes, the boy entered a "whole different world" in which Christian values intersected with those of his pagan ancestors. While Mrs. Soboleff continued teaching Sunday school to the children of Wrangell Institute, during the week she mentored Charlie in the performance art of the íxt', promising that if he was good enough, he could perform with the school's dance group. Even though some associated the íx̱t' with the devil, Mrs. Soboleff reminded him Tlingits knew shamanism was a practice, not a religion. The medicine man's role was to "do everything to wake up everybody," then proceed with the check-up "just like a regular doctor would."

Her guidance steered two years of performances in Wrangell and inaugurated nearly five decades of his shaman act for the Chilkat Dancers of Haines. "I'm the only one that's done it as far as I know," said Jimmie at home in 2009.

Given his renowned Christian teacher and steady church involvement, I ask Charlie how he views Presbyterian attitudes against the íx̱t'. His usual amiable demeanor darkens. He looks away and mumbles a few words in Tlingit before he pauses and regains eye contact.

"People don't like to talk about it." More Tlingit words, louder. "It's not good that way, you know."[6]

As I pivot away from the topic, I remember how Charlie Jimmie's father, Austin Hammond, responded twenty-four years earlier. The Salvation Army sergeant major preached an Old Time Gospel that borrowed openly from his culture. Hammond's grandfather, Jim David, told him to "respect the power of Raven" and "try to pass it on to the Christian people." The parallels were everywhere, Hammond said, starting with the Great Flood and extending to the Holy Trinity: "Big Raven, White Raven, and the virgin birth—Raven the Son."

Talking in private or speaking before large groups, the Chilkoot leader stressed commonalities between cultures, his Brotherhood of Man.

"Our roots are together, no matter what color we are. You are my family, every one of you. Raven put us together from all the way down. The story fills me up. We know the story, how to respect everything."[7]

:: "DEVILS IN WHITE SKINS"

Where the íx̱t' prevailed, white men trod lightly. Even gold lost its allure when argonauts added hostile traditionalists to the usual isolation, bad weather, bugs, and scarce supplies.[8]

In the decade following the Alaska Purchase, the Chilkats' reputation discouraged the meager white population of Sitka from northward exploration and expansion. Fewer than a hundred non-Natives lived in the Alaska capitol (later moved to Juneau) in the mid-1870s, and in an era of despotic and often absent U.S. military leadership, settlers lived in fear of Native uprisings. Bvt. Maj. Gen. General George Custer's defeat by Sioux and Northern Cheyenne forces at the Little Bighorn in June 1876 terrified a white

Sitka population guarded at the time by only thirty soldiers. Emboldened Tlingits tore open a hole in the high fence that separated the Ranche from town, broke into the stockade and stripped the old Russian fort of ornate casements and doors. Instead of a violent takeover, however, fence-crossers merely desired easier access to goods and employment.[9]

As more Kiks.ádi and Kaagwaantaan kin adapted to the American lifestyle in Sitka, outlying villages sought similar ties. Despite their isolationist reputation, most Klukwan residents desired innovation and advantage, but were constrained by geography, intertribal politics, and a deeply protective attitude. Weeks after George Davidson and William Seward visited Klukwan in August 1869, one early prospector's geological questions stirred in Koh'klux a clear "interest in the gold, silver, copper or coal."[10] The headman personally guided a few groups to the summit of Chilkat Pass, a five-day round trip by pack and paddle. Once guardian of a secret trail network, Koh'klux now shone light on his people's pathway to wealth, attracting further attention from white men. Chilkat locals expected work from the prospectors but turned hostile at any suggestion of building a town in their precinct and vowed blood retaliation for white settlement, including beheading the military governor of Alaska, General Davis.[11]

Although William Seward's 1869 negotiation in Klukwan cooled their dispute with the Kiks.ádi, Chilkats still held against the Stikine people a long-standing grudge that for decades had disrupted familial and economic connections. When a Stikine leader requested intervention into his tribe's old dispute with Klukwan, Rear Adm. Alexander M. Pennock sailed a warship to Chilkat, then upriver in a smaller boat to Klukwan, where he met with Koh'klux in summer 1873. Pennock's report to the secretary of the navy declared the infamous headman "ready to bury the hatchet."[12]

On the Chilkoot side, a white man paid Daanawáak to authorize passage on the tribe's "money trail," a route previously guarded with "jealousy bordering on fanaticism."[13] The next July, Chilkoot Jack and two Native slaves escorted George Holt on their private route into the rumored goldfields. Although the prospector produced little pay dirt, he returned to Sitka with two nuggets purchased from Interior Natives as proof of a northern Eldorado. Before he publicly identified the source, however, two "Alaska Indians" murdered Holt, delaying further exploration.

Four years after Holt's expedition, twenty miners and a federal marshal landed on the same beach near Dyea, a seasonal village of one hundred to two hundred residents near the mouth of the Taiya River. Protected by a U.S. Navy gunboat, the miners disembarked onto the Taiya River delta, an expanse of intertidal meadow locked between sheer mountainsides. They were met by several dozen Tlingit residents including clan leaders wearing beaded tunics and Chilkat blankets.[14]

A thousand years of salmon runs brought Chilkoot families each summer to this northernmost saltwater shore of the Inside Passage. Tlingit forays up the glacial valley revealed an icy pass separating thirty miles of coastal watershed from two thousand miles of Yukon River flow. Like their Chilkat kinsmen to the west, Chilkoots traveled over a divide that would eventually distinguish the United States from Canada, a gateway into a lonely land of rivers and extreme temperatures. On the banks of unmapped rivers and lakes, Chilkoot men encountered bands of Southern Tutchone and Inland Tlingit, whose mutual interests converged as trading partners and in-laws. Increasing numbers of brigs, barks, and schooners placed more pressure on Coastal Tlingits to procure Interior furs, feeding a rise in the number of packer trains along the trail. Although Klukwan residents had led whites to Chilkat Pass forty years earlier, the reputation of the icy ledge known as Chilkoot Pass far exceeded it, transformed into a symbol of hope and desperation by a single Klondike gold rush image: a solid line of prospectors crawling up a snowy mountainside on their way to untold fortunes.

Through an interpreter, a naval officer greeted the assembly and directed a leader to stand forth. Koh'klux, the widely feared "Chief Hole-in-the-Face," happened to be visiting; he stepped before the officer. The Great Tyee in Washington, D.C., wanted American lands open for all his people, said the uniformed white man, so all would benefit, including cooperative Native packers. The officer punctuated his sincerity with rounds fired from a Gatling gun. Koh'klux consented. No doubt the leader spoke further, but whatever else he may have added about the use of the trail or their land was left out of the final report.

Sporadic army patrols had ceased entirely in 1877 when newly elected U.S. president Rutherford B. Hayes squelched nearly all federal funds to Alaska in order to fortify western communities against the threat of Custer-inspired Indian uprisings. Fresh troops arrived in southeast Alaska the following spring of 1878, but instead of munitions, they carried the Good Word.

Most church-going Natives in Alaska in the 1870s were Russian Orthodox, an exotic vestige that American missionaries aimed to eradicate. Foremost among evangelical advocates was Sheldon Jackson, superintendent of the Rocky Mountain Presbytery. Bearded, bespectacled, and barely five feet tall, Jackson was a tireless promoter whose efforts built hundreds of churches across the American West. In Alaska, Jackson saw a vast wilderness containing the last communities on the continent without Protestant missionaries—an outright mandate to extend his Presbyterian empire.

When Jackson and Amanda McFarland walked off the gangplank at Fort Wrangell in May 1877, they entered one of the roughest outposts remaining on the American frontier. The army had withdrawn all troops from Alaska earlier that spring, leaving only two small U.S. Treasury revenue cutters and a handful of Marines on the aging warship USS *Jamestown* in Sitka. With neither police nor clergy present in Stikine, social control was left to clan leadership among the Tlingit, and vigilante justice prevailed among white miners. For the ensuing two years, absence of military authority spurred illegal alcohol production and use, along with unprecedented and unchecked violence.

Within hours of landing in the muddy village, Jackson and McFarland recognized the same debilitating effects of liquor and violence they knew from other western outposts—only worse. Between white bootleggers, child slavery, and home distilleries, the missionaries watched the community dissolving in plain view. Lacking a tradition of moderation, entire Tlingit clans were rendered helpless by the sudden availability of alcohol in massive quantities. One early army officer observed that Tlingits became so "fond of ardent spirits" that they would "sacrifice everything in their possession" to purchase or secure it.[15] To start the civilizing process, the missionaries knew, drunkenness and debauchery must end.[16]

Before the United States bought Russian America, Yankee traders openly flouted the Russian-British agreement that forbade the sale or distribution of alcohol to Tlingits, thus uncorking competitive ambitions along the coast.[17] Commensurate with impulsive behavior, Americans learned that Natives also would pay top prices for a single drink. Business boomed. Prior to the U.S. Purchase, alcohol was a trading commodity imported on ships to the villages in limited stocks. In months following U.S. occupation, a brewery became one of Sitka's most prosperous businesses, fortified by shipping "very large quantities" to the villages.[18] But beer alone did not quench Native thirst. Most likely, a Civil War veteran was responsible for teaching residents of Hutsnuwu (Xutsnoowú) how to distill molasses into a strong alcoholic brew popularly known as hooch.[19] Stills soon appeared in every community; Mrs. Willard reported violent conflict over operations in the Chilkat Valley in the 1880s. Hooch became an integral element in <u>k</u>u.éex' memorials—liquor dulled the grief as it eroded the elaborate traditions of the ceremonial gatherings.[20]

For residents of Willard's literary <u>k</u>wáan, ascendance of the shaman, Yealh-neddy, fueled the bitter interclan "Hooch Wars" waged in the late 1870s and early 1880s. The shaman of *Kin-da-shon's Wife* controls the chief's daughter, Kotch-kul-ah, by dissolving her will in "alcoholic servitude." Her melodramatic descent follows hooch-fired eruptions that destroy the delicate balance of Tlingit tradition: parents neglect to feed families; house groups quarrel; violence begets greater violence. Her future mother-in-law condemns all whites, including missionaries, for introducing the "blood-of-witches" to Chilkat. "They are devils in white skins," she snaps. "I want to see none of them in this country."[21]

From his Presbyterian base in Fort Wrangell, where up to half the houses contained stills, Sheldon Jackson intended to wield the Word like a mighty sword to smite the godless, drunken north.[22] The old Russian fort at the mouth of the Stikine River was the northernmost steamship port on the Pacific West Coast mainland. British Columbia gold strikes in 1873–1874 attracted hordes of prospectors to Fort Wrangell as a gateway town before steaming three hundred miles upriver to the Cassiar gold-fields. Even after the rush peaked, scheduled steamers still discharged strangers at the wharf, some looking for gold, some for trouble.

To stem the tide of sin, Jackson would first erect a girls school, with a righteous woman sitting as director.

While stopping in Portland, Oregon, to expedite his northern mission, Jackson reunited with his "old missionary friend," Amanda McFarland, whose rock-solid faith and "two hundred pounds of good nature" were "exactly fitted" to impose Christian order on wide-open Alaska. Jackson knew her as the wife of the Reverend David McFarland, who ended three centuries of Catholic hegemony in the Territory of New Mexico by founding the first Protestant church in Santa Fe. A year into regular church services, the reverend experienced health problems and cholera took the McFarlands's only child. Jackson also knew Amanda's reputation for keeping up to a dozen foster children at once. The McFarlands moved to Kamiah, Idaho, in 1873 to work among the Nez Perce at the first American Indian Presbyterian church in the country. When failing health turned fatal for Reverend McFarland in 1876, his forty-four-year-old widow steamed down the Columbia River to Portland, where she assured the Reverend Aaron Lindsley of the First Presbyterian Church that she was prepared to carry on the Lord's work.

As Alaska's first Protestant missionary, McFarland was charged to recruit Native girls—considered more reliable and obedient than boys—from their newly converted families to a boarding school where they would abandon Tlingit attire, speech, and beliefs for a mainstream white-American makeover. Successful acculturation depended on a strategy of isolating students from the community, denying most visits with family and friends, and barring participation in potlatches, subsistence activities, and other cultural

Mrs. Amanda R. McFarland. Illustration from Sheldon Jackson, *Alaska, and Missions on the North Pacific Coast* (New York: Dodd, Mead and Company, 1880).

events. Some parents were eager to release their daughters, but McFarland literally recruited others by tearing them from the arms of abusive white miners. Stories of the brave widow protecting her ladies from prospectors and shamans were standard fare in Jackson's fundraising speeches to Christian women's groups in the Lower Forty-eight.[23]

During his short visit to Wrangell, Jackson depended on his oldest and most-fervent Stikine convert, To'watte (T'aawyaat), to sustain local interest. The eighty-year-old elder's role as sháade háni guaranteed a core group of adherents to the white man's religion; in-laws cast a wider net. Known regionally as a peacemaker, To'watte convinced enough key clan headmen to condone a mission, although some remained skeptical. In particular, the village íxt' complained loudly as former clients rejected their services in favor of To'watte and his "church Indians." To To'watte's repeated pleas for a minister, Jackson promised to send a God's Man the next spring. In the meantime, he urged the elder to continue McFarland's Sunday services in his tribal house.[24]

While Jackson awaited a southbound steamer, a Chilkoot war canoe arrived from the north, captained by Daanawáak's second chief, Lunaat, a "shaman chief," and a dozen "wild Chilcat savages." The thirty-five-foot craft contained bundles of furs hauled from the Interior over their "money trail" bound for a HBC post in Fort Simpson. Even though the travel was longer, the price paid by British traders made up for low American returns in Sitka. Also aboard the canoe were six Tsimshian carvers returning home after months of producing commissioned canoes, bowls, hats, and totems for their northern clients. When the canoe landed at the Stikine village, the crew was a week into a thousand-mile voyage.

Midway through *Kin-da-shon's Wife,* Caroline Willard describes the encounter between the heathen northerners and the newly converted Stikines. Upon meeting the fresh Christians, the shaman Yealh-neddy rears back when a Wrangell resident mentions their new God's Man.

"Yours?" Yealh-neddy exclaimed.

"Yes, *ours*—high chief Chilkat! You are slow of hearing, if this is the first you know of it. We have a school, too, and are getting the white man's tongue. The Stickeens are a long step ahead of the Chilkats—for all of you carry so many eagles in your heart."

"No more eagles than we've talons for, let me tell you."[25]

Despite his suspicions, the shaman consents to transporting the diminutive reverend, who offers to pay for passage in silver. As Jackson wrote later, language differences kept him from preaching to his hosts during the voyage, but when they reached Fort Simpson, Lunaat and another headman approached him with an interpreter. They wished to "give up the old way and learn the new," so Jackson promised to send a missionary as soon as possible.[26]

:: "SHAMAN OF SHAMANS"

Two-and-a-half years of tides rose and fell before a missionary paddled into Yandeist'akyé with his crew of Tlingit converts and a red-bearded glacier-walker they called Dleit Aankáawu.

In the thirty months before Jackson's pledge was fulfilled, the shaman dramatized in Mrs. Willard's book conducted a campaign of intimidation and violence that touched all corners of the region. The character Yealh-neddy was likely based on Skandoo'o, the principal shaman of Yandeist'akyé, whose resistance to church and state stretched into the 1890s. Tlingit shamans in outlying villages sustained limited practices through the turn of the century, but Skandoo'o was more dramatic, flying in the face of all that the missionaries represented. Presbyterians were a threat to Tlingit tradition—and his job—so the shaman mounted legendary resistance remembered today only by his name.

For soldiers and lawmen on his trail, the renegade íxt' was the slippery "Scum Doo."[27] For Christian memoirists Mrs. Willard, Sheldon Jackson, and S. Hall Young, Skandoo'o embodied evil incarnate—he was the devil in detail. Reverend Young complained that the shaman disrupted the mission's civilizing influence by refusing to cease "making medicines . . . and collecting blankets on foolish charges from those he accused of witchcraft."[28]

A member of the Shangukeidí (Daghisdinaa) clan of the eagle moiety living in Yandeist'akyé, Skandoo'o is also said to be closely related to Chilkat headman Koh'klux of the Cinnamon Bear House.[29] Some accounts refer to Skandoo'o as his son, but a decade difference in their ages makes it more likely that the sháade háni was the shaman's uncle or clan father. The shaman's name, Skandoo'o, meaning "one who is enraged at him," first appears in historical record of the 1852 raid on Fort Selkirk.[30] Among the warriors were Skandoo'o and his brothers Yen-da-yonk and Karskarz (Kaa'shaax). The latter, whom white men called "Monkey Man," was born with a spinal deformity and may have been a Chilkoot village leader and shaman. Brother Skandoo'o was widely feared as a "cruel" persecutor sporting copper dreadlocks that sprouted from double cowlicks. As a strategic advisor, Skandoo'o could see over time and distance, powers that were essential to the successful assault on Fort Selkirk. The third brother, Yen-da-yonk, was esteemed as a packer and guide who later led white explorers into unmapped territory in the region. For the quarter century after the burning of Selkirk, few non-Natives ventured into Jilkáat aaní, so while Christians routed shamans in other villages, Skandoo'o retained his dominance as the íxt' of Yandeist'akyé.[31]

Unlike the Russians, whose displays of white-man "magic" were designed to overawe and subdue Native doctors, Yankees targeted shamans as superstitious holdouts whose witch hunts often culminated in the torture or death of their victims. For the first two decades of military administration in Alaska Territory, no fewer than twenty commanders implemented policy, much of it directed at subduing the íxt'.[32]

Once the offender was in custody, reform started with a haircut. Since the shaman's long, unkempt dreadlocks were considered integral to his supernatural strength, the military pursued a policy of shaving heads. Most fought wildly against capture, yielding only to overwhelming physical restraint. Under Capt. Lester A. Beardslee, shamans were shaved, transported to Sitka, and led into a Russian steam bath, "thus cleansing their spirits."[33] Captain E. C. Merriman burned the hair to add shame to the shave, then sent the íxt' into a roaring mob. Thus emasculated, a medicine man lost his magic along with identity and tribal status.

A few evaded capture. When the "Taquedi Shaman" refused to leave his home in Yakutat, he defied his tormentors with hair that broke scissors.[34]

In Angoon, Klee-a-keet used hideous dramatics to turn locals against non-Natives. Whenever U.S. gunboats appeared in Lynn Canal to roust out Skandoo'o, the "red-haired Chilkoot doctor" simply vanished, fueling a celebrity status that led author Jack London to crown his fictitious version as the "shaman of shamans."[35]

Beyond guile and stubbornness, Skandoo'o was especially maddening to white settlers through his association with another prominent rebel. The shaman's protest of American occupation was amplified by aggression from Sitka Jack, whose counter-insurgency further bedeviled the transition of sovereignty.[36] Tied to powerful clan members in Sitka, Angoon, and Klukwan, Sitka Jack declared his resistance region-wide with roving bands of renegades in war canoes, íx̲t' cruising at his side. The "Chief of Sitka" opposed Boston restrictions on firearms and alcohol, and advocated renewing ties with the HBC.[37] To celebrate building his "white man's house" in Sitka, the unreconstructed Sitka Jack hosted a grand k̲u.éex' in 1877, at which he publicly refused to free his slaves and threatened to lead a thousand men in an insurrection against the government. Marriage to a sister of Koh'klux obligated Sitka Jack to travel often to Klukwan for visits with in-laws.[38]

With U.S. authority in flux, intimidation by malcontents like Sitka Jack and Skandoo'o set the white minority on edge.[39] The meager military presence promoted instability, asserted Reverend Jackson, creating a vacuum best filled with Presbyterian doctrine. "I never before saw a people so hungry for the word of God," he wrote after his initial reconnaissance in Fort Wrangell. Jackson may have similarly reassured McFarland as he embarked on a voyage with his L̲koot hosts, leaving her behind to fend off the "sorcerers" whose "devil-worship" ravaged the community.[40]

:: "WHEN THE TIME COMES I'LL HIT
   THAT THING—*AND HIT IT HARD!*"

On a fundraising tour to the East in the following months, Jackson pled the case of "thirty-five thousand heathens" in Alaska, whose darkened lives he called "a reproach to civilization." A speech delivered around Christmas at Western Theological Seminary in Pittsburgh fell on the ears of a thirty-year-old student whose destiny was soon intertwined with the "stubby, little, sawed-off man with a grizzled beard."[41]

Heir to a long line of "stern, inflexible and intolerant" Calvinists, Samuel Hall Young—he went by Hall—likewise thirsted to spread the Word. One of eight children raised in Butler, Pennsylvania, Hall Young was a minister's sickly son who dutifully attended church and memorized the Bible by age ten. Home-schooled by his mother, sermonized by his minister father, Hall came of age barely knowing the world beyond a tight-knit home life tucked in the Allegheny Valley.[42]

By his own reckoning, three events set Hall Young on the trail to Alaska.

When the Civil War erupted in his fourteenth year, his sheltered world abruptly expanded. An ardent Republican, Hall's father voted for Lincoln, preached against slavery, and watched four sons take up arms for the Union. Late one night, his youngest son awakened and wandered into the kitchen to discover a family of runaway slaves staring at him in horror. With a hand placed gently on Hall's shoulder, the minister explained the plight of the black family and the necessity for absolute silence. The longer Hall carried the secret, the deeper his hatred for slavery grew, until he finally revealed the incident late in life.[43]

Young's religious passion subsided briefly in his teens as he absorbed Thomas Paine and the Greeks, and fantasized about becoming a lawyer. Secular ambitions dissipated when a conversion in his early twenties recalibrated all his energies toward missionary work. Only the darkest corner of the United States would suit the youthful zealot, who said he was lured to the frontier pulpit by "danger . . . and the possibility of martyrdom."[44] A few years of teaching and preaching in rural Pennsylvania led to study at the Princeton and Western Theological Seminaries. Young was nearly through his senior year when Sheldon Jackson triggered a third epiphany.

After hearing a rousing oratory affirming the dire need in the Far North, Hall Young and a classmate approached the Presbyterian publicist and plied him with questions about Alaska. Men of exceptional faith were needed to do the Lord's work among the Tlingit, Jackson confirmed, as well as endure harsh winters and great loneliness. That Young was unmarried was a liability—bachelor clergy could be tempted by Indian women and prostitutes. The slender divinity student held firm.

Frequent correspondence from Amanda McFarland in Fort Wrangell that winter elicited "frantic appeals" for innocent Tlingit girls exposed to immoral and unsanitary conditions, slavery, and shamanism. Stories of witchcraft and slavery were like nectar to Young's Protestant appetites. Into the heart of heathendom he must march, carrying the word of the Father capable of saving them from themselves. Fueled by "pictures of sordid and disgusting shadows" from Jackson and McFarland, and by the letters of A. L. Lindsley, "Father of Alaska Missions," Young divined his life's purpose.[45]

On July 10, 1878, sporting a new suit and full Franz Josef whiskers, Hall Young boarded a train from Pennsylvania to Portland, where he met Pastor

Lindsley for his final instructions and prayer. Two more days of rail and ferry landed Young in Victoria, British Columbia, the southern port for the Alaska-bound steamer *California.* Skirting a thousand miles of somber forests and island mazes brought the ship to its northernmost port, Fort Wrangell, with two remaining passengers, Young and a HBC manager named McKay. As they neared shore, McKay offered Young "the most valuable piece of advice" of his life: *"Don't become an Indian."* His boundaries thus fortified, the minister resolved to lead the "battle of Christian civilization" shielded by a bulwark of immutable moral standards.[46]

Reverend Young's crusade began with a policy mandating "English *only*" in church and school.

What most disturbed the new missionary in his first weeks was the "confusion of tongues" that he heard from all corners of his adopted community. Just before his arrival, the Cassiar gold rush had drawn throngs of European and American prospectors, five hundred of whom overwintered among the Stikine in Young's first year. Speakers overcame linguistic differences by weaving threads of a common trade language into conversations otherwise clothed in French, Norwegian, Tlingit, or Haida. Young railed against the use of Native languages, which he felt were "ridiculously inadequate" to convey civilized ideas. Despite directions from Sheldon Jackson to translate the Bible into Tlingit and other Alaska languages, Young refused to uphold a Presbyterian policy that promoted "superstition and sin." Natives must come to the King James Bible; the Word should not go to them.[47]

The success of the policy depended on an adept translator who was capable of walking Young's narrow path of righteousness. Reverend Jackson resolved his need the previous summer when he met Mrs. Sarah Dickinson, a Tongass Tlingit woman known for her "great personality and devotion." Educated by the Reverend William Duncan among the Tsimpsian at Metlakatla, Dickinson spoke three regional Native languages as well as impeccable English. The woman who became Young's primary translator was the wife of white fur trader George Dickinson and mother of two children, Billy and Sarah. Service with McFarland during her first year prepared Mrs. Sarah Dickinson for the often-complex task of interpreter—she called herself an "interrupter"—but under the new minister, her work demanded more-direct confrontation with local residents, Natives and non-Natives alike, than she had experienced.[48]

Flanked by teachers Dickinson and McFarland, the Fort Wrangell God's Man applied vigorous English education, Bible studies, and work programs to those he judged "peculiarly susceptible" to a Western education. Missionary practice held that new Native converts, though "naughty, wayward, and careless," should be "pitied, loved, borne with and patiently tended as *children.*" As students adjusted to school routines and church membership grew, Reverend Young refocused his energies on the community at large, where he intended to "replace anarchy with law." With or without a military presence, Young trusted in the power of religion to "transform and civilize" his children into adult Americans. In defense of his growing flock, Young declared war on the *"conscious frauds"* whose "false beliefs" led to the "diabolical persecution" of innocents accused of witchcraft. Superstition, he wrote decades later, "is hydra-headed and dies hard," conquered only by an "uncompromising attitude."[49]

Success for Young depended on no less than complete annihilation of the íxt'. Among the most dreaded medicine men were Klee-a-keet of Angoon and Skandoo'o of Yandeist'akyé, figures whose provocations made them obvious targets. Each occasionally visited the Stikine on clan voyages for trade or a ku.éex'; each defied the God's Man with open dissent. When in Fort Wrangell, Skandoo'o would pester Young to no end with the "mocking call of the laughing gull" outside his window at night. Removal of the brazen íxt' would signal a real shift in power, Young reckoned, and hasten the end of a long, dark reign.[50]

Problems arose shortly after the minister's arrival when a Stikine shaman singled out a church-going Tlingit wife of a white miner-merchant because one of his kinsmen dreamed she was a witch. Clan members seized the mother of two, bound her into a painful contortion, and left her under the floorboards where the shaman forced the victim to drink saltwater and whipped her with thorny devil's club branches. Such tactics, said Young, usually produced confessions and the names of accomplices, thus feeding a frenzy akin to another infamous American witch hunt nearly two centuries earlier.

The drama grew until ten victims—including five women, two elderly men, and three children—were shoved into the dark hole. McFarland protested each case with "tears and entreaties," but even her most-devoted Native Christians shrunk from the íxt'. Upon returning from an outing, the first victim's husband discovered the predicament, set the captives free, and shoved his pistol into the clan leader's mouth threatening to "blow his head off" if the witch hunt continued.

Community tensions subsided briefly, so Young, Dickinson, and McFarland proceeded with a plan for "house calls" throughout the village. Often with the aid of relatives and clan members, the three forcibly entered dozens of houses bent on smashing stills and extracting so-called "orphans" from their families. Excitement swirled among the Stikines in late summer when the renowned shaman, Klee-a-keet, arrived from Angoon to cure a wealthy Taku headman of tuberculosis. Eager to see the íx̱t' in action, Reverend Young joined hundreds of onlookers who crowded into a clan house to witness the event, which opened with twelve drummers filing inside and down to the central firepit. At the last thundering thump of moosehide drumsticks, an eerie, wavering loon cry emanated from the darkened doorway. After an unnerving silence, Klee-a-keet screamed and rushed into the audience, often jumping over heads toward the firepit. His helpers prevented him from falling into the flames.

Nude but for his uncut hair and heavy necklaces of amulets and shells, Klee-a-keet roared, leapt, and communicated with six individual masked yéik for a two-hour session that climaxed in physical collapse and a frozen trance for another two hours. Upon awakening, the íx̱t' announced that he had just returned from the "spirit world," where he discovered information leading to the identity of the witch behind the patient's ailment. He launched another performance, even more wild and intimidating, that led through all corners of the audience until he came to a cowering cluster of slaves.

"It is he! It is he!" Klee-a-keet cried as he fell and writhed on the floor planks.

When spectators grabbed an elder slave, a knot of church-going Tlingits physically restrained their God's Man from entering the fray. Young gaped in horror as friends of the ailing Taku chief ripped clothing from the accused witch and pressed live coals onto his skin. The minister was forcibly escorted away as the slave was bound and tossed under the floorboards.[51]

In the sleepless night that ensued, Young considered his hero, Abraham Lincoln. He could not imagine his martyred president standing by while God's children were enslaved and tortured. Shocked that no one had yet enforced antislavery laws in the community, the minister added it to his campaign, echoing Lincoln's stance on slavery: "When the time comes I'll hit that thing—*and hit it hard!*"[52]

Native and Anglo community members responded to Young's righteous stance by advising him to stay far away from shamans and clan politics. Northwest Trading Company manager John Vanderbilt advised him "above all, not to interfere with the medicine-men." It would only risk his life and inflame the locals, the Portland businessman argued. His employee, George Dickinson, had enough to worry about without the missionary pushing his wife, Sarah, in harm's way.

But Young was determined to destroy the íx̱t' whom he accused of acting entirely out of self-interest, encouraging tribal members to defend their society. He organized a village council of elders including Chief Shakes to

Monkey John (Karskarz), Skondoo (Skando'o), and Schwatka (Schwatki, Yen-da-yonk) in Tlingit Regalia, ca. 1907. Photograph, A7 no. 51, Haines Sheldon Museum, Alaska.

sign an anti-shaman pledge to which Klee-a-keet responded by redoubling his dramatic performances. Young prepared for a confrontation. When the brother of Chief Shakes took ill, his powerful sibling employed the Angoon shaman. Even church members kept the event a secret from their minister until Young deduced it from the arrival of two war canoes carrying a hundred tribal members in full regalia and bearing ornately carved masks, drums, hats, and boxes packed with blankets. When the drumming began the next day, Young took a stroll on the muddy paths to the clan house. Along the way he accosted a white man named Charley Jones, whom he promised would "see some fun" if he came along.

The white men entered a room packed with Native onlookers, all focused on the shaman's theatrical methods. Eyes shifted as Reverend Young elbowed a route to the firepit. The íx̲t' and his drummers froze. The surprise in Chief Shakes's eyes heated to an indignant boil.

"Why did you come into my house and disturb us?" he thundered.

"Why have you lied to me?" returned the minister. If the sháade háni were an honorable man, his pledge would be firm. "You have broken your word. Now I demand that this man be turned out, with all his people."

Klee-a-keet refused to leave; Shakes insisted on continuing. Young and Jones gathered the shaman's paraphernalia and carried it to the parsonage for storage. By morning, the minister had a strategy: Shakes's brother seemed very close to death, so Young negotiated a position: If the patient lived, old-style healing practices could remain in the village; if he died, the shaman was banished forever. Chief Shakes assented.

Hundreds of locals attended an evening ceremony that reached new heights, producing a din heard in all corners of the settlement. In the aftermath of a performance marked by hours of "snarls and screams," the minister strolled to the clan house, where Klee-a-keet assured him that the patient would survive. Shakes's brother died the next morning. After demanding and receiving full reimbursement, family members of the deceased escorted the shaman and his entourage to the beach, where they lingered until the Angoon party paddled out of sight.[53]

Tensions arising from Young's frequent face-offs over the winter led most whites and Natives to expect his swift departure by summer. Parishioners were relieved in December, however, when their pastor steamed to Sitka to marry missionary Fannie Kellogg, and returned to Fort Wrangell to set up housekeeping. The flood of northern light that returned to the Stikine in spring 1879 corresponded with lightened spirits in the nascent Presbyterian community of Fort Wrangell. Reduced shamanic activity and alcohol production encouraged church members, who felt that a "new order" was soon to follow, though their minister reflexively warned them about battles yet to fight against multifamily houses, interclan warfare, and maltreatment of girls.[54]

Moreover, no Tlingit would be truly free, Young held, until all villages broke the grip of the shaman. In the dozen or so major Native communities stretching across four hundred miles of islands and fjords, missionaries had conducted services in all but the most remote—in Chilkat country. Skandoo'o's "mocking" laugh fortified Young's vow to transform the last heathen enclave in Alaska.

PART 2

Dleit Aankáawu

5 :: True Believers

Klukwan confronted its first—and perhaps worst—epidemic in 1838, the year John Muir was born in Dunbar, Scotland.

Tlingit villages that missed the withering effects of smallpox a generation earlier were especially vulnerable that year. Since the horrific die-offs from Spanish infection in the 1770s, southern groups like the Haida and Nootka received regular vaccinations from HBC doctors. Outlying communities such as Klukwan tended to shun preventative treatment, a fear promulgated by shamans who viewed inoculation as a form of enslavement.

Records show the ship that introduced smallpox to Klukwan was likely the Russian-American Company's supply ship *Sitka*, which sailed in 1836 from Fort Ross on the northern California coast to the Arctic Ocean. An American trading vessel is also suspect. Contact with Chilkats likely occurred in Sitka, from which the carriers paddled their plague back home. Ships' calls at infection hubs like Fort Vancouver and Victoria helped spread death throughout Pacific Northwest tribes. Of eight thousand Kalapuyan Natives estimated in Oregon's Willamette Valley, the epidemic killed at least seventy percent. In the same period a witness calculated ten thousand deaths among Chinook tribes near the mouth of the Columbia and Willapa Bay. Farther up the coast, some Salish villages suffered ninety percent mortality. A thousand miles north, HBC captain James Douglas counted 2,400

Chilkats in 1835, a tally that dropped to 598 when his ships traded with survivors seven years later.[1]

Neither had Dunbar escaped pestilence. The coastal town's four thousand residents remembered well the Great Cholera Epidemic that spread from India in 1825 until it seeped into Scottish water in 1832. Within twenty months, entire clans became ghosts. John Muir was born at the cusp of recovery and change, when the Lowland Scots of Dunbar still clung with raw-knuckled tenacity to a barren scrap of coastline defended by generations of tribal warriors. For the love of a home, stubborn Lowlanders withstood poverty, disease, and bad weather to eke out a hard-fought destiny. In the decade to come, however, millions would abandon the clan ghosts and sail away.

Below the Scottish borderlands, Londoners of 1838 devoured tales of class disparity portrayed in Charles Dickens's bestsellers *Oliver Twist* and *Nicholas Nickelby*. The books reflected growing concerns about child labor and education in Britain, and about the Crown's responsibility to its most impoverished subjects. The human rights movement coalesced in London that year around the People's Charter, a watershed document declaring universal suffrage for British citizens.[2]

Across the Atlantic, a newer, similarly principled government was at the height of a campaign to relocate its indigenous wards to the hinterlands. Since the Indian Removal Act of 1830, U.S. president Andrew Jackson's scorched-earth policy pushed tens of thousands of Native evacuees onto the Trail of Tears. The year 1838 was the apex for relocating Cherokee and Chickasaw families from homes in Georgia and Tennessee to uncertain futures in an alien land west of the Mississippi River. Prolonged intergenerational trauma fractured the southern Natives' traditional means of coping, so they spiraled into alcohol, domestic abuse, and poverty.[3] Enter religion. Survivors rebuilt lives structured by Christian missionaries who preached salvation through English literacy, sanitation, and industry. Methodist and Congregational missions sprouted among reformed tribes on the American frontier in 1838. The Presbyterian Missionary Society, founded in 1837, would stretch far into the heathen lands, eventually establishing hundreds of outposts in the West and Alaska.[4]

In Dunbar, young John Muir studied the same Bible and faced the same harsh consequences if he didn't memorize it.

An entrenched social network and promise of redemption kept the Church of Scotland apace with Dunbar's fifty-three pubs, boisterous waterfront, and seedy vice district. Calvin's theology of suffering resonated with a congregation comprised mostly of businessmen and professionals, more than a few of whom came to the Lord after a go-round or two with sin. The daily realities of self-denial and hard work nourished the skinflint Protestantism pervasive in the Lowlands.

Daniel Muir scorned what he saw as secular self-interest in the Church, so he quit the mainstream to join Secessionists. With silent wife Anne and seven children trailing him into the sanctuary every Sunday, Muir was a cornerstone of the Dunbar Secessionist Church. A substantial tithing bolstered the prosperous merchant's status, so the congregation was scandalized when Muir led others to quit over a policy of hiring ministers from the landed gentry. A fiery sermon by Alexander Campbell convinced Daniel Muir to trust his intuitive faith with the Disciples of Christ over the bureaucratic Church of Scotland. Enthralled by the budding evangelical movement in America, the businessman abruptly sold his store and joined three hundred thousand other Scots who fled their broken homeland in 1849.[5] Into the frontier margins of the New World, wrote historian Frederick Jackson Turner, Scottish immigrants carried a "true democratic germ" that spread freedom's contagion into every corner, one nation under God.[6]

In the wilds of south-central Wisconsin a man could worship as he wanted and harness Satan's wilderness to serve God's chosen people.

Third born after sisters Margaret and Sarah, John Muir received an upbringing befitting his father's Abrahamic code. Two brothers and three more sisters (the youngest born in America) arrived in short succession, but none felt the wrath of Daniel Muir as keenly as his oldest son. Throughout his youth, John submitted to thrashings "that would try anybody but an American Indian," whose serene repose he emulated to disguise inner agony. Any disobedience or forgetfulness earned whippings, Muir recalled, to shame him into working harder. The only factor that limited Daniel Muir's righteous parenting was a supply of "the right kind of switches."[7]

On the backs of children, Fountain Lake Farm emerged from wilderness in Wisconsin. Workdays for the Muirs began as early as 4:00 a.m. and rarely ended before 9:00 in the evening. Daniel Muir turned in at seven o'clock after dinner and prayers, then arose for a coldwater bath before seeing the family to bed. Ample rest restored their bodies for another day of fighting Satan.[8] Hacking, burning, and hauling prepared the land for its divine purpose, which, for Daniel, was wheat. Agriculture sustained a larger population than had Indian land use, thus proving to disciples God's blessing upon the Europeans. After eight years of developing Fountain Lake, Daniel bought a half-section nearby and directed his family to "begin all over again to clear and fence and break up other fields." John resented his indentured servitude in the building of Hickory Hill farm yet remained impassive as he wielded the crosscut saw and plow.

Only on the Sabbath could the Muir children luxuriate in play. Sundays after church were devoted to exploration, pranks, and imaginary battles. Free from Father Muir's doctrine, the eldest son exulted in his "baptism in Nature's warm heart—how utterly happy it made us!" Unlike the roads and ruins of Scotland, the New World offered unimagined abundance. The young Scot shared a profound kinship with whippoorwills, bullbats, copperheads, and lightning bugs. Through his thirst for scientific knowledge John sustained a spiritual bond linking him to all organisms through which the "current of the Universal Being circulate(d)."[9] Old Testament imperatives held no sway in a democracy of snapping turtles and windflowers.[10]

As Muir's connection between nature and spirit matured, one aspect of God's wilderness remained enigmatic to him, even threatening: Indians. Forced off their lands by federal troops in 1840, scattered bands of Winnebagos and Menominees still roamed the countryside when the Muirs arrived. Natives sometimes visited Fountain Lake Farm to sharpen their knives on the grindstone or beg for food while John and his brothers posted themselves to prevent livestock theft. The boys marveled at the Natives' hunting skills, though John always cheered for the prey. In his memoirs, Indians appear in sparse vignettes detailing the swift dispatch of wildlife. Amid numinous descriptions of pond life and meadow ecology, Natives pass through the pages as ghosts, in focus only as they stalk a deer or spear a "poor beaver rat."

By his mid-teens, Muir's discomfort with Native Americans reflected feelings common among immigrants who settled near subjugated peoples: guilt, fear, and disgust rolled into the romance of a vanishing culture.[11] How did Natives view him? From the eastern seaboard to Oregon Territory, memories of an old society dimmed as conquerors poured into the cleansed frontier. Many Natives regarded the mass immigration as a harbinger of their end, an opinion articulated by Duwamish chief Sealth (Seattle) in an 1854 speech. He told the Seattle audience about "a time when our people covered the whole land as the waves of a wind-ruffled sea covered its shell-paved floor. But that time has long since passed away with the greatness of tribes now almost forgotten. I will not mourn over our untimely decay."[12]

Landscape devoid of Natives enabled John Muir to conceive of a Promised Land more sacred than his father's own heaven. Set against idealized standards for perfect wildness, Indians disappointed Muir. His references to Wisconsin Natives as "cruel" and "blackmailing" did not exclude them from his sympathies but revealed his own pain at witnessing "degraded" specimens of what was once wild. Muir mourned the decline of Natives but rejoiced in his access to freshly uninhabited Creation.[13]

For all other subjects, however, John's curiosity outpaced the few books allowed in the house, so neighbors loaned him volumes that he read in secret. Typical of bright young men, Muir used authors as springboards for withering debates with his father, who accused him of being a "contumacious quibbler too fond of disputation." Household harmony vanished whenever father and son locked horns, especially when the issue boiled down to The Good Book versus a good book. Tensions finally climaxed in a spat over John's desire to read Plutarch's *Lives* in the house. The younger Muir argued the validity of the Greek historian's biographical profiles, but the elder condemned the "old pagan" as a purveyor of false philosophy and ordered the book returned to its owner. Muir sneaked it later, as he would Shakespeare, Milton, Humboldt, and others.

Five minutes of candle-lit reading absorbed the oldest son each evening while the family bedded down. Peeved that John routinely required an additional request to snuff the light, Daniel insisted that he cease nightly readings. An argument ensued. Possibly because John was reading a biblical history that evening, his father grumbled that if he turned in with the family, he could get up as early as he wished. For the remainder of the winter John arose at the "same gloriously early hour" of one o'clock. In addition to his books, Muir devoted many predawn hours in an unheated cellar workshop, tinkering by the light of a single candle. His efforts produced a self-setting sawmill, water wheels, automatic horse-feeder, and other labor-saving devices, as well as a variety of clocks, thermometers, and hygrometers. Best known among Muir's inventions was the "early-rising machine," which was run by cogs, coils, and pulleys that raised the sleeper upright at the appointed hour. The bed caught the attention of neighbors who encouraged John to enter his inventions at the Wisconsin State Fair in Madison.

Blinkered against his father's disparagement, twenty-two-year-old John Muir set off for the state capital with his tools and inventions. Forty miles was farther from home than John had ventured since his arrival in America; the buckboard and train trek to Madison spanned an even greater cultural distance. Although strangers might be put off by the farm boy's awkward behavior, his complex inventions warmed them to a steaming intellect. The devices attracted large crowds, a ten-dollar award, and regional acclaim. Lest he succumb to vanity, the young Scot avoided praise and shunned positive newspaper accounts.[14]

Amid the smoke and tumult of the Civil War, Muir attended the University of Wisconsin in Madison in March 1861. His enrollment was financed by sales of a few early-rising beds and an unexpected check from his father. In two-and-a-half years of study, Muir's reputation as an independent thinker grew among a network of influential friends and mentors. Foremost among his supporters were science professor Ezra Carr and his wife, Jeanne, mother of four boys and spiritual mentor to Muir. Professor Carr introduced Muir to the sciences, including geology; Jeanne helped Muir build a bridge between his genius and humanity. Society was a mystery to the farm-boy in his bedraggled beard and threadbare work clothes, but the next four decades of correspondence with Jeanne Carr supplied the inspiration he required to actualize the passions of a remarkable life.

"How warlike it is here," Muir observed to his sister Sarah after the first term of college.[15] A Wisconsin National Guard regiment mustered downhill from the school, puncturing the air with drills, shouts, and rifle fire. Muir avoided the encampment, unmoved by pageantry that he thought masked the "hideousness" of war.

His adopted nation teetered on the brink of destruction. In the fragile year since Lincoln's election, the end of slavery loomed closer while war raged on. The Republican victory in late 1860 had spurred South Carolina's secession in December followed by a failed Peace Conference in January. In his most important speech to U.S. Congress, Sen. William Seward, Lincoln's nominee for secretary of state, threatened a "perpetual civil war" unless southern states acknowledged the "vast calamities" they reaped by secession. He urged solemn diplomacy.

A day after the March 4 inauguration, President Lincoln received word that Confederate troops were poised to capture U.S. troops at Fort Sumter in Charleston Harbor. To Seward's dismay, Lincoln ordered reinforcements. On April 13, after an intense Confederate bombardment from shore, the fort's commanding officer surrendered, igniting the deadly struggle the secretary predicted. In Baltimore six days later, the first blood spilled when a secessionist mob attacked Union troops en route to defend Washington. Bull Run, Fredericksburg, Vicksburg, Gettysburg, Petersburg followed over four years—the death toll climbed.[16]

As drumbeats resounded across the land, John Muir felt "tormented with soul hunger" that kept him from heeding counsel to settle, marry, and put his talents to work. His brother-in-law David Galloway urged him to "help mankind" by inventing labor-saving devices; his oldest sister, Sarah, counseled marriage. Instead, he meandered like his idealized Indians along rivers and hardwood ridgetops—not for food, but to collect plant specimens and study the earth.[17]

Overlooked in a federal draft round, Muir lit out March 1, 1864, on a "planless route" into a Canadian wilderness he hoped would satisfy his gnawing appetites. Powered by a diet of little more than bread, Muir tramped the broad-leaved forests and limestone escarpments of southern Ontario, plant specimens filling pockets and hands, a small bag of personal items slung over his shoulder. Fortune sometimes provided food and shelter, but the lone traveler mostly slept outdoors in his clothes. His greatest joys came from botanical encounters like the dismal swamp where he found a calypso orchid in full bloom, an event that restored the enervated botanist "as if never more to feel any mortal care."

John was broke when he joined brother Dan at Niagara Falls in September, where they found employment devising inventions for a tool-handle manufacturer. John and Dan moved in with the Scottish owners, devotees of the Disciples of Christ, who treated the brothers as family. John's mechanical acumen produced handles for thirty thousand brooms and twelve thousand rakes by February 1866, with Sabbaths available for Muir to lead outdoor Sunday school rambles. Preaching in an ecstatic style that the owners' children never forgot, Muir wove Bible stories with his passion for the natural world, exhorting students to keep herbariums and map the night skies.

In March, the factory burned to the ground. When the owners proposed that their mechanic become a partner in a new plant, Muir refused, saying he "loved nature too well to spend my life in a work that involves the destruction of God's forests." He accepted two hundred dollars for wages, then caught a train for Indianapolis where he found employment at a large factory producing carriage parts.[18]

The United States Muir re-entered was a nation transformed by war and death, although his profound disinterest in current events probably prevented his noticing. The blood-soaked conflict between brothers ended in a Union rout that forced the penultimate Confederate surrender in Shreveport, Louisiana, in May 1865. At a cost of six hundred thousand lives, the thirty-three re-United States drew closer to the Founders' intent that all citizens were equal and due the same rights. Muir's journals and letters reflected little of the war but focused on the natural world, which occasionally included the rural folk living at the margins.

Two months after the Civil War ended, the pursuit of tribal rights impelled Sioux leadership to confront U.S. troops assigned to build a fort in Wyoming Territory where the grassy eastern flank of the Bighorn Mountains rises from the Powder River. The Sioux opposed a wagon road from Laramie to Bozeman, which would expose prime buffalo territory to settlers' houses, cows, and guns. Incensed by Cheyenne concessions to allow white passage, Red Cloud and Sitting Bull led hundreds of Sioux warriors into the first of a series of wars that climaxed eleven years later when troops fighting with General George A. Custer met their end at the Battle of Little Bighorn.

After more than a year of guerrilla warfare, the road stayed open and some Sioux relocated onto reservations. Red Cloud told his fellow Oglala that it was "our misfortune to welcome the white man." As he prepared to lead warriors into the ongoing fray, he implored his people to stand firm against the intruders: "Shall the glittering trinkets of this rich man, his deceitful drink that overcomes the mind, shall these things tempt us to give up our homes, our hunting grounds, and the honorable teaching of our old men?"

Congress answered Red Cloud's rhetorical question on April 1, 1866, with a Civil Rights Act that guaranteed equal rights for all Americans except Indians.[19]

New to Indianapolis, one immigrant Scotsman paid no attention to his civil rights but devoted six days a week to improving the production of carriage parts, with Sundays off for rambles in nearby woods and meadows. A letter of introduction from a Madison professor led John Muir to the doorstep of the Merrill family, where he met Miss Catherine Merrill, her sister, and a nephew, ten-year-old Merrill Moores. Later in his life, Moores remembered their visitor with Scottish accent and humble attire as "the handsomest man I had ever met." Muir entranced his audience for hours as he narrated his five-hundred mile "pilgrimage" in search of the calypso orchid.

The next time Merrill Moores came into contact with the newcomer was in March the following year when a neighbor girl told him that Muir had punctured his eye and was confined to a dark room. The accident occurred at the carriage factory while Muir was attempting to loosen stitching on a belt drive. The point of the sharpening file slipped and jabbed a corner of his right eye, spilling the aqueous humor into his hand. The eye "closed forever to all of God's beauty"; the other followed from sympathetic shock.

Alarmed by the news, Moores, his mother, and six female cousins hurried to the afflicted man's bedside. The girls offered to bring flowers, which elicited a swift retort from the bandaged victim that compared domesticated blossoms with artificial. Instead, Muir encouraged them to seek "God's posies" growing on the margins of the city. While the maidens gathered wildflowers, young Moores visited daily to read Washington Irving's Knickerbocker Tales, a favorite of the invalid. As sight gradually returned to both eyes, Moores watched a certain passion rise in the man. The boy read

First View of the Pacific Ocean from Mount Tamalpais. Photograph by author.

less aloud as the carriage engineer spoke more about a new vision for his life.[20] Previously attracted to machines by their marvelous efficiency, Muir now regarded his accident as a divine warning to seek the purity of nature.[21]

"God has to nearly kill us sometimes, to teach us lessons," Muir wrote of his transformation from machinist into a student of the wild.[22]

:: "WALKING IN THE PATHS OF THE DEEVIL"

Muir and Moores strolled out of Indianapolis on their shared birthday, April 21, bound for Muir's Wisconsin home before he embarked on a botanizing excursion to the Gulf of Mexico. Muir was twenty-nine; Moores eleven. Wearisome days ended with the hikers on their knees, Muir praying that the Almighty forgive their sins and guide them safely. The boy often nodded off during the windy entreaties, provoking "stern rebukes" throughout the prayer until Muir carried him to bed at last.

Amid bucolic descriptions of Wisconsin countryside, Moores's recollections of Daniel Muir's "narrow and bigoted fundamentalism" stand out. Joined by his "pious wife," the elder Muir pestered his son constantly about the wickedness of geology and botany, yet never spoke to the substance of his son's ideas. Tensions at Hickory Hill farm boiled over when Daniel condemned John for "walking in the paths of the Deevil," to which the son countered that he felt closer to God on rambles than his father's severe faith ever allowed.

The ferocity and duration of father-son altercations startled young Moores, but he was more shocked by Daniel's foolishness. For example, he thought it bizarre that the elder Muir should cut down a patch of white oaks, then plant skinny Lombardy poplars for shade. On warm days Daniel copied a prayer book while sitting in a shady stripe that rotated like a sun-dial, forcing him to shift his chair every fifteen minutes. When Merrill asked why he omitted so much text from his transcriptions, Muir's father replied, "Aboot a half of the buke is in Layton, and I dinna ken Layton and the words would be of small use to me."

As summer slid by, Muir and Moores often escaped the farm on forays into the central Wisconsin countryside. Upon hearing of a rare, fragrant fern, the two took a train thirty miles to Wisconsin Dells, where they located a specimen that exuded an odor Muir deemed "entrancing." Below the scenic rapids of the Wisconsin River, they assembled drift logs into a raft that they rode all the way back to Portage. Writing seventy years on, Moores judged the day one of his best in his life.[23]

While the two were saying farewells to the Muir family in August, Daniel fired a parting shot by asking his son to pay room and board. John betrayed little emotion as he produced a gold piece from his wallet but spoke as he surrendered it: "Father, you asked me to come home for a visit, I thought I was welcome. You may be very sure it will be a long time before I come again." Later in life Muir visited his mother and siblings, but saw his father just once more.

Muir escorted young Moores to his family in Indianapolis, then set off to fulfill his core desires on the "wildest, leafiest, and least trodden way" possible. From early September to January 1868, he hiked back roads and trails across lands surrendered by indigenous people to wealthy landowners who fled during the Civil War and reinhabited by survivors: small farmers, black freedmen, common bootleggers. Muir sauntered past the unending agriculture and "dreary" townsites of Kentucky and Tennessee, impressed by the verdant countryside but eager for mountains and jungles ahead. Only as he straddled the Appalachian spine did the botanist begin to realize his imagined wilderness.

Some nights, the hiker broke a promise to his mother by sleeping under bushes, but mostly he found refuge in the households of poor people—white and black. In the thinnest days of his lifelong "bread diet" regime, a dipperful of milk or a mess of greens sustained John for another ten miles. As he grew accustomed to the kindnesses of black folk, Muir found their interest in botany far surpassed whites, who usually regarded his avocation with suspicion. Likewise the issue of slavery. The Scotch pacifist saw no point in it but learned that speaking his views at white dinner tables usually drew silence.[24]

Among encounters described in his trip journal, Muir never mentioned Native Americans. His only nod to the previous inhabitants was to name the tribe on a visit to a Cherokee impoundment site along the Trail of Tears.[25] All visible signs of Natives along Muir's route were scrubbed away first by the dogged ambuscades of Gen. Andrew Jackson and later by the Confederate troops who forced thousands of evacuees to Indian Territory in Oklahoma. The end of the Civil War allowed the U.S. Army to refocus its firepower on the remaining hostile strongholds on the western frontier: the southern road through Ute and Apache land, and the central and northern routes incising Sioux, Cheyenne, and Nez Perce territories.

Two years after Red Cloud voiced his concerns about white encroachment in Wyoming, his warriors massacred Capt. William Fetterman and eighty soldiers on the north-south Bozeman Road. The bloodbath froze all movement on the road, halting wagon trains and ratcheting tensions. U.S. military operations paused as politicians debated. One camp led by Maj. Gen. William Tecumseh Sherman advocated the immediate and "vindictive" annihilation of all hostile Native Americans; Congress shuffled with caution.

While John Muir gathered botanical specimens in newly depopulated areas of the South, the Taylor Peace Commission engaged Native American tribes in the West to negotiate their imminent relocation to reservations. Cherokee, Creek, and Seminole people were herded off portions of their lands to accommodate new roads, railroads, and settlements in the south, and the fate of Oglala, Blackfoot, and Shoshone in the north seemed certain. The progeny of farmers and merchants who had displaced eastern tribes three decades ago now poured onto western tribal lands. Papers were signed, compensation was promised. The details of reservations and treaties escaped Muir at the time, although in the years ahead he would lead campaigns to establish reservations for landscapes.[26]

On a trail of charred buildings and broken lives, John Muir strolled past the remnants of General Sherman's "vindictive" force dealt three years earlier. From Savannah, Muir secured passage to Florida and walked west to the Gulf and Cedar Keys. Delighted with his new, verdant environs, Muir nonetheless suffered a malarial infection that laid him down for weeks. After an interminable stretch of delirium, a growing lucidity allowed him to take stock of his fortunes. Whither true wilderness? Though illness might thwart his original plan to follow the trail of Alexander von Humboldt to South America, Muir remained resolute in his quest to seek the wild.

While tramping through Cuba, Muir spied a newspaper ad that led him to consider California, a land in some ways as exotic as the Amazon. The luxuriant tropical life that lured Muir south also seethed with disease, which worried him. California offered good weather and wilderness enough for a man to immerse himself completely. Systematic exterminations of Natives by volunteer militia troops in the 1850s left the Sierra Nevada range in a "pure" state, where indigenous voices no longer intersected with those of water, wind, and birdsong. California was free of disease and savages—safe.

Muir booked passage to San Francisco.

6 :: Crossed Paths

"Short, bewhiskered and bespectacled," Sheldon Jackson thrilled audiences with tales of an America where shamans still reigned and slaves were ritually beheaded. Whether in Boston or Boise, the reverend never tired of describing in lurid detail the primitive acts, according to the *San Francisco Daily Evening Bulletin,* of America's last "wild" tribes. Tens of thousands of breathless listeners grimaced in their pews at the "hardships of every kind" endured by Reverend Young and Mrs. McFarland as they strove to save Tlingit souls. As with other tribes before them, Jackson noted, the teachings of Christ were starting to take root. In clothing, sanitation, language, and faith, Tlingits were beginning to withdraw from the darkness of a heathen past. Good Christians could not allow victory to slip away just as God's light dawned on Alaska.[1]

A year of barnstorming the country with Alaska stories raised twelve thousand dollars for the Wrangell Mission. So effective were the Presbyterian firebrand's recruiting appeals that some listeners surprised themselves and their families by abruptly enlisting for duty in that faraway realm.

On the morning of June 8, 1879, Jackson lamented the state of Native Alaskan culture to an overflowing crowd in the newly completed Yosemite Chapel. Standing on a riser behind the pulpit, the diminutive preacher grew in proportion to the stentorian urgency with which he advocated reforms.

The nation wept for the plight of her newest "citizens." Since withdrawal of U.S. troops two years earlier, Alaska had lapsed into a state of near anarchy, so Christians were duty-bound to rescue their fellow Americans, the Tlingit.

Jackson spoke as a guest of the National Assembly of Sunday Schools, whose minions descended upon the California landmark for a week-long chautauqua featuring sermons, lectures, a minstrel show, campfire programs, and scheduled excursions to waterfalls and viewpoints. Topping the extensive lineup of speakers was the Reverend Joseph Cook, a volcanic orator known widely for his commanding presence and Old Testament expertise. The man Karl Marx once called "very badly informed" was considered by others to be "greater than Daniel Webster." Whatever the topic, Cook spoke with unassailable conviction.[2]

A chartered train carrying 350 conventioneers pulled out of Omaha June 1 bound for California with a stopover in Salt Lake City. Curiosity drew most of the Protestant travelers to a service at the Mormon Tabernacle, but the "exhibition of silliness, bigotry, and fanaticism" confirmed their prejudices and deepened their opposition to Utah statehood. The following day, the assembly gathered in the city's downtown Methodist Church to listen to Reverend Cook's fierce denunciation of the "Latter Day Swindle." Several Mormon leaders sat expressionless through the thundering excoriation.[3]

Three days later, conference goers offloaded in Merced where stage coaches transported them on the last eighty-five miles to Yosemite Valley. Many attendees were drawn to the California state park by newspaper engravings of unearthly scenery, but all were unprepared for the grandeur of sheer granite walls plunging thousands of feet to the narrow valley floor. They gawked, marveled, prayed. Never had so many tourists landed in the valley at once, filling to capacity every room, cabin, and woodshed. Three hundred listeners jammed into the new chapel; more stood outside, trying to catch phrases flung from open windows and doors. Sheldon Jackson's lecture on Alaska drew a large crowd. The next speaker was a seemingly shy man in rumpled clothes and a tangled red beard.[4]

All ears strained to John Muir's moderate inflections as he built a case for the glacial hands that shaped the central Sierra. Medium height and slender build concealed the strength that sustained the speaker for weeks at a time alone in the mountain kingdom. He described rocks and waterfalls like close friends. From a single seep or snow-patch, the Scotsman revealed webs of connections with the entire Sierra Nevada range. "Fortified with a background of diagrams," Muir's rhetorical passions grew as he assailed the audience with his theory. He scoffed at the "official" geological interpretation published by Harvard professor and California state geologist

　　　　　　　　　　　　　　　　　　　　　　DLEIT AAN<u>K</u>ÁAWU

Josiah Whitney, who argued that the Sierras were shaped by "subsidence" or the combined forces of earthquakes and erosion. Whitney posited that Yosemite Valley was the product of cataclysmic forces during which the mountains cracked apart and disgorged mudslides carrying mega-tons of debris. In his *Yosemite Guide-Book,* the professor pooh-poohed the presence of ice: "There is no reason to suppose or at least no proof, that glaciers have ever occupied the Valley or any portion of it. This theory, based on entire ignorance of the whole subject, should be dropped without wasting any more time upon it."[5]

Muir's decade of tramping the mountains had convinced him otherwise. He applied another Harvard professor's observations of glaciation in the Swiss Alps to suggest that the Sierras were once covered by a sheet of ice, which gradually carved the dramatic mountain range from its granitic mass. With scientist Louis Agassiz in his camp, Muir argued that Yosemite was less a product of earthquakes and erosion than millenia of glacial grinding. Among the slate of presenters, the *Sunday School Journal* judged Muir to have given "a most captivating talk." The ice prophet enchanted hundreds more the next evening in a lecture billed as "Mountain Sculpture."

Back at the hotel, a freshly converted glacier believer attempted to explain Muir's theory to Reverend Cook, whose expansive back stiffened and chest swelled with resolve. After studying *Yosemite Guide-Book* on the train, he said, the truth was obvious: "I stand with Whitney!"

The debate peaked on the evening of June 12 when Cook proclaimed his geological orthodoxy to an overflowing audience. With his broad forehead, prophet's beard, and piercing gaze, the formidable orator resembled another contemporary evangelist: Brigham Young. The congregation was rapt as Cook lumbered across the platform and pounded the pulpit to underscore his agreement with the state geologist.

Applause acknowledged the celebrity's stature but died as heads turned toward a man in the audience rising from his seat. An expectant silence dampened the room as Muir calmly strode to the podium. Although naturally gregarious, the wooly upstart was a reluctant public speaker. In a packed Sacramento Congregational church just three years earlier, Muir had opened his first public talk by admitting that "he ventured upon the lecture with trepidation, he had never lectured, was not gifted in delivery, and was not certain that he should not utterly fail." As soon as the speaker broached his glacial infatuation, however, his manner became "so simple, fresh and artless" that the audience was entranced to the end. So it was at the Yosemite conference where a reporter characterized Muir's style as the "calm after the storm." In a lilting brogue, he praised Cook's oratorical prowess, which he admitted towered over his own rusticity and proceeded to illustrate through observation and experience the empirical certainty of glaciers in the Sierras.

Muir's conclusion triggered an ovation that rose in waves within the valley's fortress walls. Ample face frozen in astonishment, Reverend Cook retreated without comment.[6] He reappeared at a trailhead the next morning to join hikers led by Muir to find signs of glaciation. Free of the formal constraints of the previous night, Muir's monologues were even more animated and personal. As the group strolled to Vernal Falls, the naturalist chatted nonstop about the trees, flowers, and critters inhabiting a verdant canyon once filled with ice thousands of feet thick. After a rest at Vernal, hikers draggled behind Muir up dozens of narrow switchbacks to a high overlook of Nevada Falls. At every stop Muir pointed out telltale signs of glaciers: house-sized erratics, deep scratches on every wall, granite polished by centuries of lapidary. A bedazzled Joseph Cook saw the country with new eyes but wasn't nimble enough to avert slipping on a slick rock and falling on his wrist. Muir escorted his newest convert down the narrow trail to the valley floor, delivering the "Glacier Gospel" up close and personal.[7] For the rest of the chautauqua Cook thumped the pulpit with his good hand as he boomed his allegiance to Muir, whom he called the "Hugh Miller of the Pacific Coast" as tribute to the famed Scottish geographer.[8]

For Muir, the Sunday school convention was the culmination of a decade of studying California's grand cordillera and interpreting his findings to others. Since his first visit to Yosemite in April 1868, Muir evolved into the champion of a place he deemed "unrivaled in height and breadth and flawless strength." Seasonal jobs as a sheep-herder, sawyer, and guide for his four-year residency in Yosemite Valley allowed time for long solo "tramps" in places seen by very few white men. With little more than a crust of bread in his coat pocket, the bearded aesthete rambled deeply into the "Range of Light" on a quest for greater intimacy with saxifrage, water ouzels, and the remnant glaciers, from which he gradually coaxed great secrets. Emblematic of the sublime landscapes Muir considered "perfect and harmonious as any in heaven" were waterfalls plummeting from stone palisades that seemed to "glow with life." Higher yet, in the company of peaks and snowfields, Muir pored over stories etched in "rocks of the glorious temples" to divine the origins of their sculpting. More than a scientific theory, the glacial story was scrawled upon the pages of John's Bible.[9]

In the past hundred years, eloquent voices have reimagined and reiterated Muir's wilderness relationship to fresh generations of students, who continue to produce much notable scholarship and literature. Rather than focus on Muir's legacy as a scientist, adventurer, or advocate, however, a rhetorical view sees message-making as a way to create perception, in this case Muir's evolving views about his own species as part of his beloved wilderness. What concerns us are the people and events leading to the pivotal 1879 meetings in the "Country of the Chilkats," and the impact on ensuing generations Tlingit, white, or otherwise. So we ask: What was Muir's relationship with Native Americans before Alaska? How was he transformed? How did the obsessive recluse gain a voice and a message strong enough to transform a tribe, let alone a nation?

The answers could fill a book.

Entries written in Muir's journals during his first eleven years in California mention Indians almost exclusively as place names. The land is alive with the play of light on Tissiak's (Half Dome) mighty "brow" or with sunset rays "rosily touching the highest pines" above Indian Canyon. A small effort is made to touch on Native American legends, but references seem penned to appease readers rather than ignite passion. Not until his first day in Fort Wrangell in July 1879 did Muir write about Indians as more than myth, victim, or foe.[10]

Rather than seek the collective knowledge of human generations, Muir gathered news of the natural world by bending close to mosses or clinging to high-hanging boulders.

In a realm swept of its indigenous inhabitants, every hike reaped new discoveries, every view felt virginal. But Muir was not the first person to apprehend the Sierran Eden. Less than a generation before he set foot in Yosemite, the Ahwahneechee band of Miwok Indians inhabited the valley, as had their ancestors for perhaps six millennia. The sheer walls around the settlement formed a natural citadel seven miles long and a half-mile wide, easily defensible from competing Miwok bands to the west, with Mono Lake Paiutes partitioned away on the mountains' eastern slopes. Embraced by hidden Yosemite, generations of Ahwahneechee summered in the shade of granitic buttresses where they collected acorns from groves of black oak, hunted deer, and dug for lily bulbs in the sprawling lower meadows. Although cloistered by their environs, the "people of the gaping mouth" maintained traditional ties with cohorts, trading with Miwok and Pomo people in western valleys and regularly traversing the Sierra to parley with their Mono Lake Paiute trading partners.[11]

Gold, as usual, changed everything. The color that flashed in the pans of John Sutter and James Marshall in 1848 opened the sluice gates to California for a hundred thousand settlers in little more than a year. After Sutter's strike on the South Fork of American River, white residents of what is now greater Sacramento expanded into potential goldfields along the entire western slope of the Sierras. To groom those last unsecured valleys for civilization, Maj. James Savage led the Mariposa Battalion on a campaign to remove all Indians to lowland reservations. Through spring of 1851 two hundred soldiers combed every watershed up to its head, including the upper Merced after captive Miwoks told them about the Ahwahneechee, whom they called "johemite" (some of them are killers).[12]

In May, Ahwahneechee leader Tenaya appeared alone before Maj. Savage, who declared an ultimatum—surrender or be destroyed. Tenaya's response was quoted by Muir decades later: "My people do not want anything from the Great Father you tell me about. The Great Spirit is our father and he has always supplied us with all we need. We do not want anything from white men. Our women are able to do our work. Go, then, let us remain in the mountains where we were born, where the ashes of our fathers have been given to the wind."

Savage accused young Ahwahneechee men of murdering soldiers and burning homes. The chief must decide—the troops awaited their orders. The elderly tribal leader argued further, but the Major was steadfast. After a long silence, Tenaya responded: "It is useless to talk to you about who destroyed your property and killed your people. I am old and you can kill me if you will, but it is useless to lie to you who know more than all the Indians." He promised to return with his band. Three days later, Savage was infuriated when Tenaya appeared with some seventy women, children, and elders, but none of the accused. Troops galloped up the Merced into Yosemite Valley to find only the ashes of a former village.[13]

On paths trod by ancestors, able-bodied tribal members had stolen away over the mountains. Only trails remained as evidence of former human use, the same routes used by Muir to follow his wild desires. Up a favorite trail, Muir declared that Tenaya Lake felt like "one of the most perfectly and richly spiritual places in the mountains."[14] A generation earlier, people remembered mostly by their leader's name hurried on the lakeshore trail toward refuge from white soldiers. Muir called them Diggers, a name derived from white perceptions of their subsistence activities. Though considered racist today, the term was commonly used by westerners and even bestselling authors such as Bret Harte and Mark Twain. Muir thought of these western Indians, like the Winnebago of his Wisconsin youth, as people "fallen" from a higher, wilder state of grace. Although he developed a "shy respect" for one Native farmhand, the Scottish immigrant subscribed to the dominant Anglo view that the conquered Indians were "dirty," "lazy," and "superstitious." Muir especially balked at Natives' squalid living conditions, which he believed imprisoned them in a purgatory neither civilized nor wild.[15]

Thirteen years after the Mariposa Battalion began its campaign to cleanse Yosemite of Miwoks and other Natives, President Abraham Lincoln authorized a land grant that allowed California to create the first state park in the country. In its inaugural year the park drew barely a hundred visitors up the steep, rutted track through the Canyon of the Merced to the valley. By the early 1870s, however, over a thousand tourists annually endured the trek on horse or mule. For those who sought Muir's guiding services or found him cradling wildflower bouquets in the meadows near their lodge, his tales of the grand, grinding landscape inspired new ways to look at the frontier. A few Ahwahneechee women and their children lingered nearby, sullen vendors of baskets and trinkets whom Muir said "had no place in the landscape."[16] Without fear of attack by animals or Indians, wild land metamorphosed into a place for renewal and contemplation. When mountains became temples and bare ground a featherbed, an increasingly urban America could begin to conceive of coming home to wilderness.

A rising tide of tourists carried notables like Ralph Waldo Emerson, Phineas T. Barnum, and Vicountess Therese Yelverton to the margins of Muir's granite Xanadu. Newspaper images and articles sharpened public interest in the sublime landscapes of Yosemite. Readers of the New York *Tribune* in 1872 learned about the park from a new writer whose ecstatic renderings of wild landscapes were tempered by a keen, scientific sensibility. Like the soaring lectures he dispensed to hiking companions, Muir's luminous writing left readers breathless. Inspired by the man and his landscape, Vicountess Yelverton published a novel titled *Zanita* in which the leading lady meets the reclusive "lunatic," Kenmuir, scampering across sheer edges with his "head thrown back as if swimming, and long, brown hair falling wildly around his face and neck." As she gazes into his glacial blue eyes, the protagonist sees a Christ figure whose feet hardly touch the trail. In fiction and life, the author/heroine drank in Muir's narrative flights like she did the alpine melt-water to which he led her. Until her death at age forty-five, Yelverton sent requests for Muir's company, but he never took her up.[17]

Lesser known among the hardy few to force a pack animal over the "narrow and torturous" path to Yosemite was Muir's former walking partner,

Merrill Moores, now sixteen years old. Prompted by a letter from his mentor, the young man traveled by rail from Indianapolis to San Francisco, where thirty-five dollars bought a horse and saddle for the four-day jaunt to the Valley. From May through October 1871, Moores and Muir tramped together in the high country, searching for the ice the elder thought once cloaked the shoulders of the Sierras. The younger man aided with measurements and procedures that made possible the discovery of a "living glacier" lying below the summit of Mount Lyell and supplying the proof needed to advance Muir's nascent theory.

Atop Lyell, Moores prepared to turn back for the long hike to the Valley, so said his goodbyes to Muir and Prof. Joseph LeConte, both continuing east. LeConte wished him a safe journey home. Muir clasped his right hand and said: "Weel, Merrill, ye may possibly become a great mon, and t'would nae mickle astonish me an ye do it; but I assure ye, ye'll nae ever make an eminent naturalist and I wad ye'd so tell your mither."[18]

The wilderness prophet was spot on: Moores eschewed science for a life of public service. He attended Yale, became an attorney, and served five terms as a U.S. congressman from Indiana. But Muir's parting shot also reveals elements that inform his evolution as a persuader—colorful speech, rugged enthusiasm, searing honesty. For these and other qualities, friends and advisors urged him to write a book. Muir acquiesced in late 1873 by trading the candescent grandeur of Yosemite for a window view in Oakland.

Close scrapes and landscapes filled Muir's frequent letters during his tenure at the "University of the Wilderness," but the flow of correspondence sputtered as he relocated to a desk in the city.[19] Sequestered for nine months in the home of Oakland school superintendent Joseph B. McChesney, the scraggly-bearded visionary climbed walls instead of peaks as he labored over the language to replicate Yosemite's splendor for the *Overland Monthly,* a respected San Francisco magazine.

Months before Muir moved to the Bay, the *Monthly*'s first editor, Bret Harte, had resigned in a fog of economic woe and salacious rumor. Celebrated for stories like "The Luck of Roaring Camp" and "The Outcasts of Poker Flat," Harte had endeavored to pin California on the American literary map with an ambitious journal that featured the young state's finest authors. Publication of Mark Twain's work propelled the *Overland Monthly* into popular notice, but Harte was unable to disentangle business from his personal failings, so he bowed out.[20]

His successor was Benjamin P. Avery, a New Yorker transplanted by Sutter's strike and sustained by two decades of California newspapering. The new editor veered from the coarse gold-rush vignettes of Harte toward nature, science, and the arts. Avery contributed Delphic paens to California's premier mountain range in the January and February editions of 1874 . Rapturous prose gushed from his pen to extol Yosemite, where "Nature seems to re-assert herself as in the time of her unbroken solitude, when the trees grew, and the flowers bloomed, and the birds caroled, when the bright cataracts leaped in song, and the lazy canyon walls rose in softened grandeur. . . ." While the essay reflected the luminist leanings of the Hudson River School painters—perhaps an Albert Bierstadt or a Thomas Cole—it failed to touch the Earth.[21]

Conversely, an esteemed scientist in the January issue firmly advanced his argument for glacial gouging. Months before Muir asserted his theories in the same publication, George Davidson reasoned that tectonic uplift was only part of the story behind formation of the continent's West Coast. Enough was now known about "present local glacial action," wrote the U.S. Coastal Survey chief and University of California astronomy professor, to convince him that the deep abrasions on seaward mountain slopes were carved by the "action of ice, moving slowly but surely as a great planing or molding machine."[22] Davidson's concurrence with Muir's recent *Tribune* articles was based on twenty-five years of charting the coastline from Baja to Chilkat—a reputation Josiah Whitney dared not dispute. Backed by the findings of Harvard's Louis Agassiz and University of California geology professor Joseph LeConte, Davidson publicly embraced the "campfire science" of Muir.[23]

One by one, key figures warmed to Muir's insights, but the man whose approval he most desired condemned his writing. About the time "The Wild Sheep of California" appeared in the April *Overland Monthly,* Muir received a letter from Wisconsin urging him to retreat from the "cold, icy-topped mountains" or face eternal damnation. Muir had not seen his father for seven years, since the day Daniel Muir demanded payment for lodging during a family visit. Ensuing years sent Daniel throughout central Wisconsin, evangelizing wherever he was welcomed. Woe to an errant son who would divert good Christians from "God's work" by enchanting his flocks with worldly scenery. It was even worse that travelers might mistake sunsets or rock piles for the Divine! Father Muir closed the letter with advice meant to last a lifetime: "The best and soonest way of getting quit of the writing and publishing your book is to burn it, and then it will do no more harm either to you or others." Fifteen years passed before Muir's first book was published, an event his father did not live to see.[24]

A dozen books and over a century of international recognition contradict Daniel Muir's dire caution, but what of his eldest son's soul? How did John reconcile his spiritual evolution with an Old Testament upbringing? Merrill Moore's boyhood memory of Muir's long-winded prayers confirmed a religious routine that persisted at least through his twenties. Dropped to his knees, hands clasped, Muir had beseeched the Lord in a manner instilled by his father's raw-boned Calvinist pedagogy.

Never one to seek an organized congregation (another feature of his father's itinerant faith), Muir worshipped alone in the company of redwoods, water ouzels, and stars. Meeting Ralph Waldo Emerson in Yosemite catalyzed the thirty-three-year-old's interest in Transcendentalism, the radical American spiritual philosophy that apprehended the faculty of cognition, rather than belief, to witness a Higher Power. Muir's brief, vigorous conversations with the Boston Brahmin, America's most-distinguished living man of letters, were augmented by correspondence from Jeanne Carr, now living in Berkeley with her family. The professor's wife introduced him to the works of other Transcendentalist authors such as Henry Thoreau, whose "holy and heroic" view of nature tapped into Muir's deepest instincts. Emerson proposed poetry and science as conduits to the "Oversoul;" Thoreau found it through experience and scrutiny of the ordinary. In the purity of wildness, Muir peered through the lenses of each for his personal view of the Divine.[25]

But even as the son sang hosannas to the God he found in Nature, something of Daniel Muir lingered. Behind Muir's brimming notebooks and armloads of plant specimens was a man dispensing moral canons that applied equally to oaks and humans. Earth-maker, gardener, steward—God's touch was evident in all Creation. Immersion in nature permitted Muir to translate the divine laws he saw written in the mountains and convey them with an evangelistic fervor reminiscent of his father. Unlike Daniel who praised distant angelic choirs, John rejoiced in the songs of crickets and chickadees heard now in the natural world.[26]

While John Muir might drop a scriptural reference into casual chat, God rarely came up. So "unaffectedly religious" was his manner that only close friends understood the mountaineer's deepest convictions. Prominent conservationist Henry Fairfield Osborn remembered Muir as "the most devout theist I have ever known. His attitude toward God was that of the Psalmist, of the prophets, and of the Book of Job. His kindliness toward his fellow men was like that of Christ, yet he rarely, if ever, attended religious services." The Reverend Hall Young, pious reformer of the Tlingit, agreed that despite little "outward display" of his beliefs, Muir was the "most intensely religious man" he knew. For Muir the deity was implicit—his missionary fervor focused on imparting the spiritual value of the natural world to a growing congregation of urban Americans.[27]

The beatific sheen Muir applied to Yosemite in the six *Overland Monthly* articles during 1873–1874 derived more from Emerson than Jesus, but at least one lifelong bias remained despite the transformation. In his essay, "By-Ways of Yosemite Travel," the author exulted in the "ineffable tenderness" of Nature in places "where the world seemed wholly new" as flower fields and granite temples gleamed in radiant sunlight. From a high overlook, however, Muir's ecstasy evaporated when he spied a party of Mono Indians traversing an ancient route to Yosemite Valley for the annual acorn harvest. Revulsion welled as he watched the "boneless wallowing motion" of the band passing below, members' faces "abraded . . . ugly; some altogether hideous." His disgust dissipated only after the Native travelers became "mere dirt specks in the landscape." In the next paragraph Muir proclaimed the "universal love" he discerned in the faces of wildflowers lifted up to a divine light.[28]

Muir's impatience with humanity went farther than Indians. Just as conquered tribes marred Muir's vision of Eden on earth, so too did Christian teachers, those "ecclesiastical slave-drivers" who forced all that was wild from their Native American students.[29] Best to avoid both, he surmised.

The "eternal grind" of writing wore at the naturalist like the glacial action he strove to depict. Rumors about the *Overland Monthly*'s uncertain future led him to suspend work for the magazine (in later years he wrote twelve more *Overland* articles), but the reprieve from "scribbling" was short-lived; Muir accepted an offer to write regular dispatches about the Sierra Nevada for the San Francisco *Daily Evening Bulletin*.[30]

Until he moved to Oakland, Muir's conversation and writing reflected a realm insulated from civilization and hardly ruffled by the vagaries of frontier society. His essays transported readers to glowing landscapes made whole by the absence of humanity. Journal entries recorded scientific observations and particular adventures. The naturalist's sphere was well contained and self-affirming, but city life forced him to engage with humanity.

Boarding with Superintendent McChesney and his family meant suppers with people who expressed informed opinions about current events gleaned from the Oakland *Daily Tribune,* a free daily newspaper launched in February 1874. By that summer, western newspapers announced that Bvt. Maj. Gen. George Armstrong Custer's troops had discovered gold in the Black Hills of South Dakota. Custer's publicity all but nullified a six-year-old treaty affirming Lakota Sioux ownership of the Black Hills. The usual wave of drifters and dreamers poured onto ground held sacred by five major tribes.

The story was the same all over the West—a patch of paradise drowsed in obscurity until someone found gold or silver and triggered a rush. The gold discovery in early 1848 turned the world's attention to California which, like other states, systematically prepared lands for extraction and settlement. Foremost to development was eliminating all risks to safety and security. In a generation wolves and bears were gone from the state, as were all Indian groups outside reservations. By 1874 only one regional band still resisted removal, so the public was transfixed by any news of the Modoc War. As the drama played out in the *Daily Tribune,* Muir heard about it at the McChesney dinner table and likely chimed in.

In the remote, northeast corner of California, a band of Modoc warriors held off U.S. troops for five months. The armed dispute struck terror in every rural community within five hundred miles. In the fertile wetlands east of Mount Shasta, increasing numbers of settlers provoked frequent confrontations with Modoc groups who, unlike other Californian tribes, refused to yield their homeland. Government efforts to relocate the defiant Indians resulted in the deaths of an army officer and twelve settlers. Negotiations by Modoc leader Kintpuash (Kei-in-to-poses) were undercut by rival factions seeking retribution for two dozen Indian deaths. Called "Captain Jack" by white men, Kintpuash was forced to retreat with his men into the lava fields at the base of Mount Shasta. The Modocs' intimate knowledge of the forbidden landscape kept U.S. regulars at bay from late January to mid-April, when a parley was arranged. In the council tent, three peace commissioners accompanied Bvt. Maj. Gen. Edward R. S. Canby, a seasoned Indian negotiator. Frustration grew in both parties as the General turned down Kintpuash's repeated requests for a reservation in his homeland. A skirmish broke out resulting in the point-blank shootings of Canby and a commissioner.[31]

The killing of a general summoned a thunderous response from government forces. "The Indians have murdered their best friend," rued Interior Secretary Columbus Delano over the esteemed Canby's death. "I hope they will be punished severely, and shall ask for no mercy for them."[32]

Three days later, over a thousand soldiers surged into the volcanic battlements. Their around-the-clock shelling and sniping eventually forced

　　　　　　　　　　　　　　　　　　　　DLEIT AAN<u>K</u>ÁAWU

a Modoc retreat into the plain. For days the fugitives moved unseen while Kintpuash argued strategy with other warriors. Unable to reconcile differences, Jack's rivals and their followers broke away and eventually surrendered to the soldiers. The defectors negotiated directly with Canby's replacement, former commander of Alaska Territory, Bvt. Maj. Gen. Jefferson C. Davis, who agreed to protect them if they led his troops to Captain Jack.

The story skids to a predictable halt, with a grisly twist.

After a dramatic confrontation and capture, Kintpuash faced a military tribunal without counsel. In his defense he reminded the court of his efforts to seek peace while kinsmen betrayed him with violence: "You white people conquered me not; my own men did." Newspaper readers across the United States sighed in relief when Captain Jack and three codefendants were hanged in October 1873. One hundred and fifty-three Modoc men, women, and children were deported to Oklahoma. A few months later, Captain Jack's embalmed corpse surfaced on the carnival circuit. Coast to coast, gawkers paid a dime to stare without fear into the face of infinite Modoc heartbreak.[33]

Just as the chapter closed on one of California's last insurgent tribes, John Muir's thoughts drifted north to the broad tule marshes, lava beds, and "white Shasta cone sweeping high into the cloudless blue." A year after the Modocs' last stand, a Klamath River ranch family's invitation gave Muir a reason to go. Over rails and rutted stagecoach tracks, he jostled nearly five hundred miles into a region most newspaper readers would never visit.

The first five essays appearing in the *Bulletin* described places popularized by the recent Indian uprising but generally unknown. Muir opened the series with a piece about a salmon hatchery on the McCloud River in a valley south of Mount Shasta: "Long may McCloud salmon swim!" Recent construction of California's first rural hatchery was meant to mitigate the extensive stream damage incurred by a quarter century of unchecked mining and logging, so the facility was a symbol of the state's new commitment to environmental stewardship. Led by a Wintu youth whom the writer judged a "bright, inquisitive fellow," Muir explored the valley for a few days—his longest association yet with an indigenous person. Ensuing dispatches described a snowy ascent of Mount Shasta, local wildlife, bees, and the "dark, mysterious lava-plain" where Captain Jack and his men made a prolonged and bloody stand.[34]

Through a land visited by perhaps two dozen tourists in 1874, Muir tramped and scribbled observations in black notebooks. As he wandered across a landscape "calculated to inspire terror," inspecting fantastic lava sculptures vomited from the earth's core, Muir's mood darkened. In a rare departure for the apolitical naturalist, "Modoc Memories" inserted popular social opinion into his usual scientific/experiential exposition. In a passionate voice that presaged his environmental rhetoric years later, Muir framed the Modoc War in moral terms. As he completed his tour of the tortured landscape, Muir marveled at the Modocs' adaptation to the "most complete natural Gibraltar I ever beheld," followed by an audacious rebuke:

> Modocs, like most other Indians, are about as unknightly as possible. The quantity of the moral sentiment developed in them seems infinitely small, and though in battle they appear incapable of feeling any distinction between men and beasts, even their savageness lacks fullness and cordiality. The few that have come under my own observation had something repellant in their aspects, even when their features were in sunshine and settled in the calm of peace; when therefore, they were crawling stealthily in these gloomy caves, in and out on all fours, unkempt and begrimed, and with the glare of war in their eyes, they must have looked very devilish.[35]

Lacking the "cordiality" of true savages, the Modocs of Muir's imagination were assigned to the same hell he would reserve for the "wealthy wicked" a few decades later. A Bay Area readership demanded retributive language to feed the heroic narrative of General Canby, thirty-five soldiers, and over three hundred settlers slain by "wild savages," a passion Muir shared. Fifteen years later, the naturalist perpetuated the characterization by rewriting the article as a chapter in *Picturesque California* with Modocs cast as "demons of the volcanic pit."[36]

Except as place names, nowhere else in his *Daily Evening Bulletin* series did Muir mention Indians. Wars still raged in the Black Hills, Red River Valley, Bitterroot Mountains, and Arizona borderlands, but the Modoc defeat signaled available land for the white conquerors. News of Captain Jack's hanging diverted whole wagon trains southward from the Oregon Trail to the Applegate Trail and into Klamath country. Rivers and tule marshes were soon drained for ranch and farm families, whose roads and fences crisscrossed the fault scarp ridges of the eastern Sierra. Crossroads grew into Klamath Falls and Alturas, towns that signaled normalcy for many of Muir's urban readers, who yearned for the language of trees and temples. Some even aspired to explore this newly wild land.

For the next three years, "wild John" alternated summers in the Sierras with the off-season in San Francisco, where he lodged in the home of Mary and John Swett, friends of the McChesneys and Carrs. John Swett served as the first California superintendent of public instruction and was a school principal when he met Muir. The two Johns immediately connected, forming a friendship that led to an offer of free room and board. When his new comrade insisted on paying, Swett conceded that Muir work off rent as a hiking companion in Yosemite, an arrangement that held. Mounting demands on Muir's time, however, kept him closer to town than either preferred. More than ever, the naturalist required solitude for his growing writing responsibilities, which, as usual, tormented him. Despite the long hours and constant revision, Muir was so unhappy with his drafts that Mary Swett judged, "He had a poor opinion of his own powers."

As much as he agonized at the slow, solitary work, Muir delighted in a live audience. Escape from his desk meant strolls in the neighborhoods, then games and stories with one or more of the eight Swett children, perhaps closing the day by dispensing long-winded lectures in the parlor. "He was very interesting as a talker," Mary reminisced. "We used to sit long evenings and talk, that is he did the talking."[37]

In a Scotch brogue that thickened as needed, Muir effused "w' th crackie" of his forebears. Like people in most societies, his core communication style arose from culture and family behavior: storytelling grandfather, sermonizing dad, taciturn mother, seven sibling co-laborers. Until the "lang-tongued chiel" left home at twenty-two, most of his experience with unregulated society came Sunday afternoons when he and his brothers played freely. The remainder of every week was defined by "long, sweaty dog days," recalled the eldest son who bore his labors with unblinking stoicism. Literally raised as an indentured farmworker, Muir found release in the Scottish tradition of protest, becoming the "contumacious quibbler" who so irked his father at bedtime.

Debating at the University of Wisconsin channeled and refined his oratory. The Muir who descended Sierra Nevada slopes to the city was embraced by educator-friends such as the Carrs and Swetts who encouraged his oratorical tendencies. His transcendental and geological beliefs deepened into default narratives often launched at the slightest provocation. He condemned the dominant belief that the earth was God's gift to man. That such an "enormous conceit is allowed to go unchallenged," he said, ignores the greater truth that humans stand beside every "animal, plant and crystal" not as consumers but "stewards."[38]

"No one who did not know Muir in those days," an old friend told a biographer, "can have any idea of Muir's brilliance as a conversational antagonist in an argument."[39]

Whoever questioned or contradicted the wilderness prophet invited a tireless opponent. At the Swetts's dinner parties Muir was a centerpiece among luminaries such as *Overland Monthly* editors Ina Coolbrith and Charles Stoddard. Because he "had a habit of soliloquizing," some withered in his verbal wake, but most were enchanted by his Old World dialect and razor-edged mind. A few kindred souls like John Swett and Scottish American painter William Keith rejoiced. "Muir is Scotch, I'm Scotch, so we quarrel all the time," said Keith. Swett sparred for hours with Muir, unwilling to relent. Education was a frequent topic: Swett believed in free public schooling; Muir held families responsible.[40]

"They would argue and argue and argue," Mary Swett wrote. "For someone who didn't realize these were two strong minds, one honing his mind on the other, it was quite a sight."[41]

As more articles appeared in print, so grew readers' fascination with the Range of Light and its zealous promoter. With interest having outgrown the Swetts's dinner table, John and Mary thought it time for Muir to speak in public.

Muir vigorously declined. He had never given a formal lecture and preferred never to give one.

Despite his ease among children, friends, and family, Muir instinctively withdrew from strangers and crowds. Without formal training or modeling beyond his father's harangues, he harbored no concept of himself as a public speaker. Even in smaller groups he might be personable and interested, but his limited small talk skills sometimes led to awkward reticence. He abhorred politics, war, and fashion, so added little to popular discourse. That is, of course, until challenged to explain the relevance of glaciers or birdsong.[42]

"Like most men who have spent much of their lives in the mountains," wrote zoologist and close friend C. Hart Merriam, Muir was an "independent thinker" capable of delivering "well-digested opinions on a surprisingly large number of topics." Extended stints of wilderness solitude compelled Muir to contain and refine his thoughts until he eventually wrote them down for publication or spilled them onto the dinner table. Even before the meal was served, Muir was releasing a torrent of "reminiscence, description, exposition, all relieved with quiet humor, seasoned with pungent satire, starred and rainbowed with poetic fancy." Instead of trying to stem his verbal monopoly, listeners were mostly enthralled. One dinner acquaintance thought Muir an absent-minded scholar until asked about mountains, at which instant the "bashful man became an orator and the awkward pedant the most charming poet."[43]

Increasing offers for public appearances pushed Muir and Swett into new grounds for debate. John's refusal finally crumbled when an invitation arrived from the Literary Institute of Sacramento, a lecture series that attracted prominent leaders—politicians, professors, preachers—to hear the best thinkers in the state. Not only would the appearance promote Muir's theories to an esteemed assembly, it paid well. Far too often, Muir admitted, "the Scotch in me" drew him to money, even for work he despised.[44] His lecture followed two weeks after a well-received presentation by the Reverend A. L. Stone of San Francisco, who proposed a "law of compensation" that contrasted human society with nature to "prove" the inevitability of positive reciprocation. The academic or learned person, Stone posited, compensates for physical deficiencies by developing intellect while the weaker mind compensates with a strong body. "For every cloud there is a rosy lining," Stone concluded, "and for every adverse circumstance some compensation."[45]

On January 25, 1876, the glacier expert boarded a carriage for an event he had dreaded since he decided to go. Muir carried a large painting loaned to him by "Willie" Keith, who assured him that the oil rendering of "Headwaters of the Merced" would soothe his nerves. "Just look at the painting, Johnnie. You'll think you're back in the mountains. You'll relax and be fine."

Five hours later, a deluge pummeled the hack as it halted in front of the Congregational Church, a soaring Gothic structure in Sacramento with seating for a thousand. Instead of the modest numbers promised by friends, a "large and very superior" gathering awaited. Muir quelled his jitters with a stroll on the muddy sidewalks around the block, then climbed the stone steps into the cavernous narthex. With slow, leaden steps he advanced to the dais. He glanced at Keith's painting displayed in plain view, then turned to his audience.[46]

The task filled him with great trepidation, Muir confessed, because he had never lectured, lacked training, and "was not certain that he should not utterly fail." The self-negating introduction "fell dismally" upon the throng but was forgotten as the speaker's vast knowledge became apparent. For nearly two hours, listeners hung on depictions of an ancient ice sheet draped over the Sierras, the molding effects of its movement, and Muir's excursions into its heart. Except for a few rapturous moments, his voice

John Muir Portrait, ca. 1875. Photograph, MSS048.f23-1249.tif, John Muir Photographs, Digital Collections, Holt-Atherton Special Collections, University of the Pacific Library, Stockton, California.

rarely breached dinner-table volume, words streaming like spring freshets. Geomorphological details filled two blackboards. Immersed in his favorite subjects, the reluctant Scotsman became "so easy and so social, his style so severely plain and so homely his language and logic as often to provoke a smile . . . Mr. Muir was at once the most unartistic and refreshing, the most unconventional and positive lecturer we have yet had in Sacramento. He was profoundly entertaining."

At the close, Muir's newest admirers pressed forward to shake hands and "thank him heartily" for the uplifting talk. The next day's newspaper extolled the remarkable man who had "found beauty, grandeur, [and] God in all nature, and was at once a student, a thinker, and a practical searcher in the archives of the rocks."[47]

Even at frontier's doorstep, growing numbers of urbane Californians wearied of their cities on the hill, yearning instead for the luminous heights of William Keith and others of the Rocky Mountain school of landscape painting. Alongside the iconic images, Muir supplied a narrative that invited his audience to transcend their daily routines by encountering the Eden next door. Motivated by the rhetoric of redemption, tourists became pilgrims on a spiritual quest. "However frivolous and inappreciative" some travelers might seem, Muir wrote in an earlier *Bulletin* dispatch, wilderness tourism was a "hopeful and significant sign of the times, indicating at least the beginning of our return to nature, for going to the mountains is going home."[48] Yosemite offered visitors a home with a divine view in every room and, like homes in Sacramento or Oakland, provided refuge from real or imagined threats—bears, wolves, and "wild" Indians.

As gadflies swooned in Sacramento, Muir launched one of his earliest direct advocacy efforts. Two weeks after the speech at First Congregational, the Sacramento *Record-Union* ran the article, "God's First Temples—How Shall We Preserve Our Forests?" underscoring the value of forest conservation to protect climate, soil, and watersheds. Although Muir acknowledged wasteful timber-industry practices, he argued that fires set by "sheep-men" were far worse. Citizens would never ignore the burning of a cathedral, but God's own King Sequoia might vanish for lack of interest. He dismissed the regulatory resolve of the "loose-jointed government," suggesting a comprehensive survey of all forest resources.[49] Two more decades of Muir's heated campaign would supply enough steam to create the National Forest Commission of 1896, of which Muir was member.

For the first few engagements, John Swett paid hall rental and other costs, but revenues soon outpaced expectations, at once satisfying Muir's need for economic security by sacrificing his precious solitude. He feared the lecture circuit would impede an already-glacial writing pace but nevertheless hefted speech-making onto his "toil-doomed shoulders."[50] A month after Sacramento, Muir lectured at the San Jose Normal School, following with a flurry of speeches in the Bay Area. The season for mountain scrambling couldn't come soon enough.

Until that spring, field study and exploration typically occupied Muir's summers, including the previous season's six-hundred-mile hegira accompanied only by a mule. Success, however, meant sacrifice. For the next few seasons, a rising tide of professional and social obligations restricted his rambles. Contacted by a crew of prominent geologists, Muir worked with the U.S. Coast and Geodetic Survey (still under George Davidson) as a guide in Utah and Nevada. Time limitations required focus on specific studies in the central Sierra. Ever conscious of a widening circle of influential friends, the naturally reclusive Muir tried to extend himself, including a journey to Los Angeles in late summer to visit lifelong mentor Jeanne Carr and her husband, Ezra.

Thanks to Jeanne Carr's matchmaking, Muir also took up a vigorous correspondence with John and Louisiana Strentzel of Martinez, and their daughter, Louisa Wanda. From his forays in the West, Muir sent botanical samples to the Strentzels along with descriptive commentary and travelogue. Indians, as usual, wafted on the periphery of his reports: they were "harmless as sagebushes, though perhaps about as bitter at heart."[51] His reference to surly Indians in the December letter likely reflected national news that even Muir could not evade. A soldier's murder of Crazy Horse in September was seen by whites as bitter retribution for Custer's death the year before. That story was eclipsed in October newspapers by the surrender of Chief Joseph to Maj. Gen. O. O. Howard in the Bearpaw Mountains of Montana. Given Muir's disdain for Natives, such events only reinforced old expectations.

There was no time to dwell on it. He had work to do. Muir paid for his mountain forays with long, miasmic winters in town, days at a desk assembling the details of his triumphal landscapes. Though he might complain of the drudgery of the "scribble room," he far preferred it to the grueling anticipation he endured before each lecture.

Three years after his first address to the Sacramento Literary Institute, the "Thoreau of the Sierras" returned to the First Congregational before a robust audience, this time speaking of Utah and the Great Basin. As before, he captivated the crowd with the geologic secrets of deserts and mountains once considered wasteland. Most "amusing" for listeners were Muir's glimpses into the lives of "the human beings of the Great Basin," by which he meant Mormons. Never had he "met a people so wrong-headed on religion, and so right-headed on practical, especially agricultural, affairs." Through industry and efficiency, he warned, the collective force of Brigham Young's beehive was expanding into Arizona and Idaho. They were building a vibrant society in passed-over lands.[52]

In April 1879, Muir turned up the heat on his nuanced romance with Louie by writing the first letter he ever addressed exclusively to her. "I failed to see you Tuesday night," he began, "the absurd old black horse having for once been on time." The box of flowers she left for him jostled the writer from his usual restraints. "Boo!—aren't they lovely! . . . an orchard in a bandbox. Who wad ha thocht it?" Six days later, he wrote a follow-up note bemoaning the tragedy of wilted flowers.[53]

When Muir accepted a hundred-dollar offer to speak twice in early June at the National Assembly of Sunday Schools, he probably had already made plans to spend some part of summer in Martinez with Louie and her parents. The Yosemite venue, however, required an appearance. Though public address evoked fear and dread in Muir, prospects of speaking to a church full of religious leaders presented ideal conditions for mass conversion to his glacier gospel.

Before Sheldon Jackson's June 8 speech in Yosemite Chapel, the naturalist knew little of the Presbyterian campaigner and likely regarded him with the same suspicion he reserved for most missionaries. As the sawed-off reverend extolled the scenic details of Alaska's raw beauty, however, Muir softened. Conversely, his anxiety climbed as he anticipated following Jackson's talk, but, of course, his presentation "electrified" the assembly. Later offstage, the two speakers briefly shared their common interests in glacier country, and Jackson suggested that Muir join his party of ministers to inspect their newest mission in Alaska. The steamer *Dakota* sailed in twelve days.

Muir fairly leapt at the chance. He posted his next letter to Louie and her parents from Fort Wrangell in July.

7 :: Unbecoming Indians

Imagine this scene: Seated on the first riser from the central firepit of his great house in Yandeist'akyé, Daanawáak studies the flickering reflections in his council's eyes. Opposite the sháade háni is his principal shaman, Skandoo'o, and brother Yen-da-yonk. Adjacent the shaman is Daanawáak's nephew and second-in-command, Lunaat, from Dyea. Nearer to the headman sit subchiefs Ahkaha and Kakee. Old Karskarz, wizened shaman-chief of Chilkoot village, shares a plank with the headman. The leaders confer into the night as they have for years, somber faces illuminated by a stack of blazing hemlock logs. Hunting stories and clan politics aside, the discussion eventually circles back to Boston men.

They bring new opportunities for Tlingit wealth, argues Daanawáak. Firelight glints off the wire-rimmed spectacles from which he derives his name, Silver Dollar Eyes, worn to show the gravitas of the occasion. White men arrived two days ago with official papers from Fort Wrangell. Daniel McKenzie, white prospector, carried an affidavit signed by manager John Vanderbilt of the Northwest Trading Company post and R. D. Crittenden certifying that the Natives would safely guide the white men to a gold prospecting site. A red wax seal in the corner identifies the customs collector for the District of Alaska, highest federal official in the territory.

The sháade háni proposes to offer his services and ventures a justification.

Long gone are the seasonal trading ships from the Hudson's Bay or Russian-American Companies. They were the best kind of business partners, lingering only for a day or two before they sailed away. Boston men want more—they seek our gold. Tlingits grew rich from the furs we acquired from Athabaskan partners and sold to sailing ships. Silver fox and wolf pelts from the Interior brought us money; salmon, seal, and eulachon at our doorstep make us rich. We had so much that we never thought about gold on our land. But Boston men keep asking, and if they find gold here, they say they will pay us and leave.[1]

The council responds with silence, partly in deference to Daanawáak's words, partly because they have heard it all before. A hemlock knot flares and fades. Across from the sháade háni, Skandoo'o slowly shakes his head, body-length dreadlocks bending side to side. His eyes narrow.

Money is not the problem. They might remember to pay us. But if miners find gold, more will follow. Many ships with God's Men and soldiers—watch—it will be our undoing.

Catlike and cautious, Skandoo'o nudges up a riser into half-shadow where he gazes into his hands and softly mews in Ravenspeak. The shaman's otherworldly voice blends with the murmuring flames.

Eventually, Lunaat speaks. The young Dyea leader recalls the voyage two years earlier when his paddlers conveyed Sheldon Jackson from Stikine to Fort Simpson.

You watch—God's Men bring wealth. Jackson built a new house for his Tsimpsian headman and a school for the village. He told me he would send a God's Man to us with all the benefits gained by other Indians. One came to Stikine last year. Sitka has many. Kake, Auk, Yakutat, Taku, Hoonah, even one of the Hutsnuwu villages has a God's Man. They are all learning the white man's tongue and getting jobs while we are left behind. I have seen it myself—God's Men want to save Indians' souls, they don't want our land.[2]

A low hiss from Skandoo'o's corner.

Faces stare into the firepit, each remembering the promises of white men.

Only five summers earlier in 1874, George Holt of Sitka paid Chilkoot Jack and two slaves to escort him over the Chilkoot Pass, the first white man to traverse either trade route owned by the northern Tlingit. Upon his return to the coast, Holt announced a gold strike and produced nuggets as proof. Several parties set sail immediately, but when they returned months later with empty pokes, the mood soured. Gold rushers heard nothing about a discovery up north but learned that Interior Natives had sold nuggets to a

   DLEIT AANḴÁAWU

white man. The Native men claimed they found the gold in a Yukon River tributary called Tr'ondek, which white men pronounced Klondike. The word roused dozens of schemers in Sitka driven by their impatience and debt, but again they stalled. Before anyone got a straight story from Holt, he was murdered by men thought to be Tlingit. Conspiracy theories sprouted in the fertile clan relationships between Sitka and Klukwan, in effect hindering would-be prospectors from heading to Chilkat Country. Best to wait for a military escort.[3]

Cracking the Chilkat-Chilkoot stronghold came closer to reality the following summer when Maj. Gen. O. O. Howard sailed into Sitka.[4] Public interest in Alaska was aroused by a new Alaska map from John Wesley Powell published by the U.S. Geological Survey, and Howard needed to assess the security issues of this huge, unknown territory. The decorated Union hero, known as "the Christian general" for his piety, viewed military service as God's work fortified by the rousing sermons and bibles bestowed on former hostiles. With the zeal of Isaiah, Howard had wielded his "terrible, swift sword" against the enemy, first of whom were remnant Seminole bands hidden in the watery expanses of Lake Okeechobee in Florida. From his victories in the swamps, Howard went to West Point where he taught mathematics until the outbreak of the Civil War broke, in which he commanded troops under Major Generals McClellan, Grant, and Sherman. As Howard commanded Union troops at the Battles of Antietam and Fredericksburg in September and November, the Santee Sioux in Minnesota rose in rebellion, killing nearly seven hundred men, women, and children. To avenge these deaths, Minnesota volunteers and militia under Col. Henry Hastings Sibley counterattacked, violently crushing the uprising with infantry, artillery, and fire. Sioux warriors surrendered to Sibley's forces or fled far north and west. A military tribunal tried the prisoners and sentenced 303 insurgents to hang. President Lincoln pardoned all but 38.

After the brutal conclusion to the War of Brothers, General Howard joined Bvt. Maj. Gen. George Crook's troops in Arizona to subdue the Western Apaches. A year later he was transferred to Oregon to relieve General Davis who had just ended the Modoc War. Once a personal guest of Koh'klux, General Davis likely briefed Howard about the "warlike" Chilkats before the new commander of the Department of the Columbia in the Pacific Northwest Division steamed north in summer 1875 to assess the Tlingit threat.

Daanawáak and his kinsmen knew none of this, but retained vivid memories of the general's visit to the Chilkat Valley. From the shore at Yandeist'akyé they had spied the steamer *California* anchored in Chilkat

Inlet and paddled out to it. With full beard and medal-laden uniform, Howard's appearance suggested the stature of a Tyee as great as previous visiting dignitaries such as William Seward and George Davidson.

A large American flag flapped from the stern-pole of the first canoe that drew alongside the ship. Steeled against the worse, General Howard (not to be confused with Captain Howard eight years earlier) relaxed when a big Tlingit man boarded in a "grand style" befitting the diplomatic occasion. The Tlingit "prince" was Kaltseixs, known as Sitka Jack, Kaagwaantaan leader of Sheet'ká ḵwáan and brother-in-law of Koh'klux, ally to Chilkats and Chilkoots. While in Sitka, Howard had sought the notorious headman without success, so was pleased to meet Sitka Jack in Chilkat. Deep ties with Sitka and Chilkat country made Jack's friendship a strategic necessity.

After each exchanged formal credentials and assurances, the general told Jack that he had orders from the Great Father to resolve an existing conflict. Months earlier, a northern subchief (probably Chilkoot) was sentenced to time in the Sitka guardhouse. Utterly despondent, he committed suicide. As payment for the man's death, Tlingit law of reciprocity required the life of a white man—any white man. General Howard now offered reparations: ten new HBC blankets. He accepted Sitka Jack's invitation to meet Native leaders in Yandeist'aḵyé, and as the ship's rowboat crawled two miles up the eastern channel of the Chilkat River to the village, Howard listened to the Sitka leader call pilot instructions from the bow.[5]

Whatever apprehension either party felt prior to the meeting dissipated as General Howard shook the hand of each solemn leader. Aside from the blanket exchange and the usual rituals of a state visit, the only other aspect of Yandeist'aḵyé that particularly interested the general was an "enormous meteorolite" that he tried to purchase for the Smithsonian Institution in Washington, D.C. Daanawáaḵ refused his offer, for the rock was promised to a white prospector who was upriver in Klukwan at the time.

Given Howard's penchant for preaching the Gospel "on street corners, [on] steamboats," in barracks—just about anywhere—he likely seized a moment or two to spread the Word. As he had with other tribes, he probably attempted to distribute English bibles to his heathen hosts and indicated the presence of a God who could grant eternal salvation and other rewards of Christian salvation. Of course, the recipients could not read, so the books became symbolic, their printed words evincing almost magical power.[6]

Satisfied that the Chilkat-Chilkoot threat was quelled for the moment, General Howard sailed out the great fjord and along along a thousand miles of crenulated coast before turning east to steam up the Columbia River to

Fort Vancouver. The next summer, 268 U.S. cavalry fatalities at the Little Big Horn River emboldened Natives throughout the West, prompting a heightened military response to round up every last Indian.

In June 1877 Howard served a thirty-day notice to an isolated Nez Perce band that refused to move to the reservation that surrounds Lapwai, Idaho. Instead of relocating to the detention center a week's journey south, Chief Joseph turned his 500 men, women, and children north toward Canada. For more than thirteen hundred miles, U.S. troops under Generals Howard and Nelson Miles pursued the runaway Indians, each side sustaining over a hundred casualties. After seventy-five days on the run, Chief Joseph was thirty miles from the border when he surrendered. A "forlorn procession" of 418 survivors tramped out of the Bearpaw Mountains into the army encampment. Howard assured Joseph that they would be sent back to the Nez Perce reservation but was overruled by Miles. Washington ordered them transported to Indian Territory in Oklahoma.[7]

While U.S. Indian policy dispossessed the last insurgent bands of Nez Perce, Cheyenne, and Apache of their homelands, the federal military presence in Alaska all but evaporated. The power vacuum tempted some Tlingit leaders in Sitka and elsewhere to threaten a return to traditional authority. When Special Agent William Gouverneur Morris (son of the Revolutionary war hero) demanded in 1877 that Sitka Jack free his slaves, the Kaagwaantaan headman held a large ku.éex' at his new "white man's" house. Not only did Jack refuse the emancipation order, but he threatened Morris with a thousand clan warriors poised to "seize all . . . valuable properties" in Sitka. Because of the increasingly porous nature of the plank-and-post fence separating white Sitkans from the Ranche, Morris believed Jack's threat. The special agent was appalled that Natives sometimes attended "white" events, where they "obtruded themselves . . . in a haughty, insolent, and overbearing manner," but he felt powerless to make demands. In a report to Washington, Morris described Sitka residents "slumbering upon a volcano" that one day would "belch forth and engulf them." In October, the San Francisco *Chronicle* reported Tlingits to be "entirely masters of the situation" in Sitka, held in check only by the "abject poverty" of white residents.[8]

If the Americans' poverty was disincentive for attack, the ancient warship USS *Jamestown* evoked slightly more fear. Manned by a few members of the U.S. Marine Corps and Revenue Service (later U.S. Coast Guard), the ship anchored just offshore was the sole symbol of American strength in Alaska. The occasional round of inspections in nearby villages passed for law enforcement, with far fewer tours into the inner sanctum of the northern

Tlingit. The tiny federal detachment faced enough problems in villages closer to Sitka, where they blamed alcohol on rising Native unrest.

Absence of U.S. presence energized some traditional leaders and fired up regional hooch production. Since distilling came to the Hutsnuwu on Admiralty Island in the 1860s, the foul beverage had spilled into every corner of Southeast Alaska. Usually distilled from a fruit mash of apples or prunes, hooch required molasses to transform twenty-proof sludge into hundred-plus-proof white lightning. The short supply of copper tubing and glass beakers in Alaska forced innovative Tlingit distillers to substitute bull kelp. Found in floating beds along the North Pacific coast, the hollow seaweed whip grows over a hundred feet in length from a bulbous base and, when dried, proved an ideal alternative. Sitka bootleggers ordered huge stores of perfectly legal molasses distributed by the keg to outlying villages. Arguments over a barrel sometimes exploded into violence between clans, evinced by the multiple conflicts in Chilkat that came to be known as the "Hooch Wars." Unable to regulate the flow of molasses, white enforcers looked away.[9]

Hooch hit Klukwan hard. The upper-valley location of the Mother Village provided a natural quarantine that delayed the ravages of civilization, but like smallpox two generations before, once alcohol found its way up the Chilkat Valley, it stayed, wiping out entire house groups. Village grief was further complicated by hooch-related violence that set into motion the traditional process of reciprocation. Not only did one death demand another, but lesser violations, such as facial wounds, might also justify fatal revenge. Dark days clung like ice fog to the village, perpetuated by cycles of mortal conflict between houses and clans.[10]

By the way he tenderly holds it, the paper in Daanawáak's hands projects an authority worthy of his deepest respect.[11]

In the morning after the council of elders, the sháade háni—shrunken, bespectacled, wearing a Union cap and Chilkat blanket—signs his "X" and passes the document to the other clan leader, Ahkaha, who signs his. The prospector, Daniel McKenzie, adds his signature and extends his hand to each man who responds with a long, solemn handshake. According to the paper, if McKenzie found gold in "paying quantities," the headmen received "equal interest in the claims." In case of a bust—no compensation.[12]

The sháade háni's canoe whisks the party to the back of Lutak Inlet for the mile-long walk up Chilkoot River to its head at Chilkoot Lake. From there McKenzie's men paddle a smaller canoe across the lake to the mouth of the upper river. The white men set up base camp on the broad lake beach and admire the sweeping vertical walls that hem either side of the valley.

After days of scanning sediment samples for a glint of gold, McKenzie gives up. The white men paddle back across the lake and share the disappointing news with their prospective Native partners before finding passage back to Fort Wrangell.

No gold rush ever penetrated the Chilkoot Valley. While prospectors streamed into other watersheds nearby, the Chilkoot was forgotten almost as it is today—the realm of brown bear, wolf, and sockeye salmon.

But Tlingit residents did not forget their agreement. The same document that designated safe passage and percentages in 1879 still hung on a wall in Daanawáak's clan house in 2016.

:: "THAT WILD JOHN"

Twelve days after Sheldon Jackson invited John Muir to join a Presbyterian tour of Alaska missions, the forty-one-year-old naturalist ascended the gangplank onto the steamer *Dakota* in San Francisco. Accompanying Muir was J. Thomas Magee, a San Francisco realtor whose newsletter carried the red-bearded Scot's calls to end grazing and logging in the Sierras. The ship sailed up the coast to Victoria, British Columbia, then headed south into Puget Sound and along the forest-fringed Pacific Northwest Coast. While his fellow passengers sought shelter from the rolling seas, Muir stood at the rail, transfixed by the presence of great, unbroken wildness. The tree-minded gawker marveled at the contrast between the bristling evergreen jungle here and the golden slopes that rose from California's shore. From the crests of sea swells, Muir watched the Olympic Range tumble to the coastline and snow-crested Cascade volcanoes pierce the sky. The majestic scenery sorely tempted the avid mountaineer but not so much that he would delay his Alaska destiny.[13]

When their ship docked in Portland, Magee caught the *Oregon* back to California, and Muir boarded the *California* for Alaska. Accompanying Reverend Sheldon Jackson were the Reverend Aaron Lindsley, pastor of the First Presbyterian Church of Portland, and Dr. Henry Kendall, secretary of the Presbyterian Home Missions Board. Kendall was the revered eminence of the group and called "Great Chief" by thousands of Native Americans touched by his network of finishing schools for girls.[14]

Although he eagerly chatted about the landforms and forests observed from the deck, Muir tucked his religious views in a vest pocket. The parochial parenting style of his Campbellite father engendered in John a lifelong suspicion of religious zealots. Joining in rituals such as mealtime prayers affiliated Muir with mainstream Protestantism, but disdain leaked into his private writings in repeated references to the seers and their pious wives as "divines." Dismissed by the Presbyterians as "that wild John," Muir was stand-offish during the voyage, preferring to lean with the roll of the ship as he gazed at the fractured continental edge looming just out of reach.[15]

Securing Presbyterian hegemony in Alaska was a principle theme for the esteemed clergy, whose conversations often turned to saving souls. Jackson theorized that most Alaska Native people were poised for a great conversion. Eighty-five years under the czar led the Alutiiq and Yupik to affiliate gradually with the Russian Orthodox creed, but the U.S. Purchase produced a spiritual vacuum. Most Native communities desired the Good Word, but beyond vestigial Russian priests, no denomination had yet established a firm base. Recent construction of missions in Sitka and Wrangell positioned Presbyterians ahead of the scattered Methodists, Moravians, and Catholics also starting schools in the territory. After planting over a hundred churches throughout the American West in little more than a decade, Jackson set his sights on a legacy in Alaska.

In all the North, he told his fellow passengers, only one tribe had openly resisted the advances of missionaries. Remote location and a reputation for "warlike" behavior kept most whites away from the Chilkat Tlingits (common collective reference to Chilkat-Chilkoot peoples). Even in civilized Sitka, Chilkats were known as power brokers who sometimes threatened the safety of the meager white population. Adding to their notoriety was Skandoo'o, the Yandeist'aḵyé íx̲t' who condemned the church and railed against vaccinations while evading capture. That such a man still ruled in Chilkat was an affront to Christianity. His defeat would be a victory for the Cross.

Jackson gazed into his listeners' eyes. These were days of miracles. Two years prior to their voyage, he was carried for days in a canoe by a Chilkat chief, his shaman, and a dozen savages. They spoke no English, but hosted him with the utmost care. When they arrived at Fort Simpson, the leader, Lunaat, located a translator and approached Jackson. His people were ready for a God's Man. They would become children again, he said, ready to learn about Eternal Life. Jackson's prayers were answered. He promised to send a God's Man to Chilkat. That day was near.

The clerics should pool their funds to hire a steamer to Chilkat, the evangelist promoter suggested, and together convert the last, wild heathens. Only a week's canoe voyage from Fort Wrangell, Chilkat was two days by steamboat. How appropriate that such high-ranking clergy should close that dark chapter of American history. Jackson's companions agreed to finance the pivotal occasion.

North from Vancouver Island the ship's side-wheels churned seawater between headlands and islands palisaded by primeval woods and stone-toothed beaches. Landforms grew steeper, more foreboding. Whenever the ship ventured into outer waters, Muir thought of a dolphin diving in and out of massive rollers flung by the force of a muscular ocean. Built thirty-one years earlier to carry mail and supplies between New York and San Francisco, the 203-foot SS *California* held over two hundred passengers, a thousand tons of freight, and 520 tons of coal. In the heyday of the California gold rush, the three-masted ship delivered over four thousand dreamers willing to endure the long voyage 'round the Horn for a shot at the mother lode. In the years leading up to Muir's voyage, gold strikes in Stikine country financed the aging steamer's forays with freight and prospectors to Fort Wrangell, a dilapidated reminder of Russia's dubious tenure.[16]

Two weeks of drifting past landscapes swaddled in gauzy overcast brought the *California* to a strait inside Zarembo Island, then around Woronkofski Point for John Muir's first view of Fort Wrangell. Through "a dismal blurring rain," he spied the shambling fort from which scores of houses dribbled along the sinuous coastline. Within the spruce-log palisades was a stockade, customs house, barracks, and officers' quarters—now used by missionaries and others since the army withdrew two years earlier. Outside the fort walls, Muir thought the settlement "a moist dragglement of unpretentious wooden huts and houses that go wrangling and angling along the boggy, curving shore." Distended cloud bellies engulfed the crowns of immense spruce on the hill behind the waterfront. On the tips of sagging tree branches outsized ravens appeared as notes blotted on a musical score.[17]

Late in the afternoon, Muir and the Presbyterians sailed for Sitka to inspect their first Alaska mission and the grounds that would later become Sheldon Jackson College. For a few sodden days, Muir explored the forests and muskegs on the outskirts of the old Russian capital, a "rusty, decaying" town built around the "imposing" architecture of Saint Michael's Cathedral. This was more like the frontier towns he knew, ramshackle, with "dirty Indians loafing about."[18]

By the time they returned to Fort Wrangell on the southbound *California,* the rain had stopped and the clouds were thinning. A rowboat lightered passengers to shore, where they disembarked in low-tide muck and slogged to shelter. Presbyterians followed Jackson to their quarters; Muir accompanied trading-post manager John Vanderbilt to his home for supper and conversation. Close proximity to living glaciers fueled the garrulous naturalist, but he also listened intently as the thirty-one-year-old trader offered details from his year at the outpost. Like the churchmen, Vanderbilt eagerly anticipated a conversion of the Chilkats, but for a different reason. Once the northern tribe embraced Christianity, he said, the Northwest Trading Company could move in. Missionary influence compensated for the lack of law enforcement in the territory. A religious coup in Chilkat guaranteed an end to the threat of armed conflict, he reasoned, and would open the market to silver fox and other premium furs hauled from the Interior by trains of Tlingit packers. Vanderbilt aimed to capture that market. The two men traded ambitions and stories into the night until, exhausted and excited, the glacier-chaser collapsed on a fragrant pile of shavings in the carpenter's shop.

Ensuing days in the muddy gash of a village produced a rare melancholy in Muir, who admitted feeling "strangely alone." Wrangell was worse than any boomtown he had seen in California or Nevada, and Muir deplored its absence of "the slightest subordination to the points of the compass." Massive, mossy stumps blocked the two main avenues, diverting heavy foot traffic—livestock and human—onto a maze of boggy paths "too thin to walk in, too thick to swim in." But rising from the soupy terrain, Muir noted, were Indian houses as "solidly built of logs and planks as those of the whites." Likewise, the original inhabitants seemed to function as actual community members fully engaged in subsistence activities: fishing, hunting, berry-picking, food preparation. Moreover, the Tlingits whom Muir met on the swampy ruts displayed genuine "family pride," parents and children interacting freely and clan members supporting kin.

Many clan members, in fact, wore white-man clothes and had been practicing versions of Christianity since the Russians erected Fort Dionysus there two generations earlier. Months after the U.S. Purchase, General Davis had ordered the redoubt rebuilt and christened Fort Wrangell after a former manager of the Russian-American Company. The Fort was flanked on its south side by the Stikine village of five hundred; to the north, "Foreign Town" held hundreds of prospectors and non-Stikine Natives. From that context, Muir called the fifty white people within the fort "golden nuggets of civilization which shine all the more brightly in their somber surroundings." Foremost in his glowing assessment were resident missionaries, Hall Young and Amanda McFarland, whose deeds seemed to reflect a genuine commitment to their Native charges. A vigorous advocate for young women, stout Mrs. McFarland's build and disposition proved effective when extracting students from the arms of white prospectors.[19]

From the moment they shook hands, Muir felt a close connection with Reverend Young.[20] Adventurous, energetic, and righteous to a fault, the two idealists shared faith that the Lord would deliver them from threats

Rev. S. Hall Young. Illustration from Sheldon Jackson, *Alaska, and Missions on the North Pacific Coast* (New York: Dodd, Mead and Company, 1880).

they encountered in His garden. From Young's heartfelt stories of smashing stills and confronting shamans, Muir recognized in the minister a true believer, a man on an unswerving quest. Even better, when the geologist waxed ecstatically about the divinity of glaciers, Young seemed to share his enthusiasm. Generally wary of evangelicals, Muir relaxed in the company of his new friend but remained aloof among the divines. Even in a dispatch to the San Francisco *Daily Evening Bulletin*, he found space to cluck that some missionaries were "devoting themselves to the Indians, while others seem to be devoting themselves to themselves."[21]

Rarely did Muir reveal his scorn for established religion, but sarcasm dripped from his next *Bulletin* letter, an account of the expedition to convert the "warlike and conservative Chilkat Indians." Besides himself, the dozen passengers aboard the small Stikine River sternwheeler included Reverend Young, the "Doctors of Divinity" and their wives, and John Vanderbilt, all headed north to answer a call. "Like the Macedonians," the skeptical scientist wrote, "these savages so warlike and inflexible in their opposition to the entrance of miners into their mountains, called for the missionaries and invited them to establish a church and school in their midst." For three hundred dollars, the esteemed clergy launched a five-day round-trip voyage to Chilkat, eager to save souls and take in a little scenery.

For the naturalist, the outing was all about the view. Souls aside, Muir's greatest desire on the excursion was to study the best-known tidewater glacier in America—the Davidson. Since George Davidson announced its existence to the world, American newspaper readers had grown familiar with stock lithographs of the three-mile-wide glacial fan. Muir clipped a copy for his own files, where it remains today. Part of the hundred-foot-high glacier snout was submerged at high tide when Davidson saw it in 1867; by the summer of 1879 it had retreated above the high-tide line. Muir yearned for just a little time on the sandy promenade at the beachfront phalanx of ice towers. So many questions for the elders before they melted!

The day shone like a mid-summer jewel. The ship's prow sliced through seas that mirrored an unruffled blue sky. Spirits soared as passengers marveled at the pastoral scenes sliding by but slipped when the *Cassiar*'s "economical engineer" announced a reduction in coal due to faulty boilers. For more than two hours, the sternwheeler crawled around the broad outer Stikine River delta, threading between sand bars, around floating logs, and through surging currents before turning northeast into a sheer-sided fjord for their first stop, Le Conte Glacier. Named for the Berkeley geology professor with whom Muir climbed in the high Sierras, the Le Conte tumbles from a high ice cap between black-rock canyon walls until it crashes into the sea. The ship lingered among house-sized icebergs long enough for Muir to sketch and gawk before resuming the slog north.

In midafternoon the *Cassiar* rounded into Thomas Bay, where Muir witnessed a "noble group of glaciers (all) flowing from a highly complicated chain of crater-like fountains." As the glaciers' most-avid student attempted to absorb the scene, he became aware of a changed mood aboard the ship. Exasperated with the plodding speed, the ship's captain, Nat Lane (son of Oregon senator Joseph Lane), repeatedly urged the engineer to burn more coal but was refused each time. For the sake of ice and souls respectively, Muir and Young preferred to press on, but the divines became alarmed over the rising price tag of conversion when they realized "that the cost of the efforts to reach and save the souls of the Chilkats would be from five to ten dollars too much for each person comprising the party. Therefore, after considerable expenditure of fruitless negotiation with the purser, the majority ruled that we return the next day to Wrangell, unsaved Indians, beautiful islands, sunny waters reflecting God, the grand glacial revelations and all, seeming . . . to have suddenly become mere dust in the balance."[22]

As the *Cassiar* neared its home port, Captain Lane announced that the truncated voyage allowed time to visit an abandoned Stikine village fourteen miles south of Fort Wrangell. When a passenger attempted to cheer

Muir with the news, the disconsolate glacier-chaser shrugged it off: "It's all Chilcat to me. It seemed something grim [that] so ponderous a mission of divines to the most warlike and most alive of all Alaska tribes should end thus lightly in an official picnic curiosity trip to the dead Stickeens." When viewed from the deck, however, Muir changed his tone. Towering old-growth spruce trees, a rushing stream, and the protected beach of the old community made for "a perfectly delightful place to spend a life." Though deserted sixty or seventy years earlier, the yellow cedar house timbers still held, "beautifully carved" pillars supported massive ridgepoles, and in front of each house stood a totem pole fifteen to forty feet high. In the enduring works of old-style Tlingit culture, Muir recognized a perfection "of a wild and positive kind, like that which guides the woodpecker in drilling round holes, and the bee in making its cells." The fine woodwork was ample evidence of an indigenous culture in tune with its environment. He had never known people on such intimate terms with nature.

Small groups of gawkers wandered amidst the "noble ruins" to admire historic treasures and perhaps take them. Among the most prolific takers was Sheldon Jackson, whose sharp eyes scanned the grounds for the "curios" he considered a missionary's rightful spoils. Forty years of avid pursuit built large collections housed today at Princeton University and the Sheldon Jackson Museum in Sitka, Alaska.[23]

As Muir sketched art and architecture, a chopping rhythm intruded from the beach, followed by a heavy thud. Excited voices drew Muir to the hearth of another house where an "archeologist doctor" had hired a few men to remove a prominent cedar statue of a woman over three feet wide at the shoulders. Angry talk flared up among the Tlingit crew, but only the owning clan had a right to confront the white man directly. The protests hushed when a young leader stepped forward. Headman of the clan that owned the purloined woman, Kadachan was also a leader in the Wrangell First Presbyterian Church. For several moments, his dark gaze locked with the eyes of the "reverend doctor," then he said, "How would you like to have an Indian go to a graveyard and break down and carry away a monument belonging to your family?"

Profuse apologies and a few "trifling presents" smoothed stormy waters faster than Muir expected. The monument was not returned. As the ship carried it back to Wrangell, Muir feared that such ruin and desecration foreshadowed "too surely the fate of the Stickene tribe," placing much blame on the Presbyterian power brokers.[24]

For the rest of their month in Wrangell, the divines and Muir endured their prickly relations through avoidance, but the tension hardly dissipated. What the naturalist perceived as hubris in the sanctimonious triumvirate was the very reason for their success. Reverends Jackson, Kendall, and Lindsley were devotees of a message they felt could change the world, draped in piety that Muir interpreted as egotism. Though he agreed with their spiritual premise, overexposure to his father's hellfire homilies soured Muir toward Christian promoters. His later published work revealed a profound spirituality, but Muir never proselytized others, a behavior he considered in bad taste. Converting Chilkats was a political move, Muir reckoned, to serve the purposes of Jackson and his cohorts while guaranteeing the downfall of Indians, "who gain a hymnbook without the means of living [then] mope and doze and die . . . like tamed eagles in barnyard corners."[25]

In the close quarters of the *Cassiar,* "wild John" tried to hold his tongue but still annoyed the Presbyterian apostles by what they saw as reckless behavior. On the next excursion, the sternwheeler muscled against a 150 miles of Stikine River current to arrive in midafternoon at Glenora, British Columbia, gateway to the Cassiar gold-fields. Muir announced his intention to hike a twenty-mile round trip to the crest of a prominent mountain range, promising to return before the steamer departed in the morning. When Young volunteered to accompany the mountaineer, Muir vigorously opposed him on grounds that the younger man would lag behind. As the friends had planned in advance, Young insisted over the disapproval of Muir and divines, whose protests sputtered against the minister's rock-solid decision. Elders and wives shook their heads and muttered as the two men disappeared into the wilderness rising from the banks of the Stikine River across a broad alpine shoulder to the base of a mountain with a seven-thousand-foot vertical gain to its summit.

Keeping apace with Muir pleased the missionary. Since arriving in Wrangell, the freshly minted seminarian had worked continually with Mrs. McFarland to exercise Christian influence over the rough-and-tumble population. Compounding his time at church, a pregnant wife kept Young even closer to home. He relished a chance to test himself against the land with the remarkable Muir, who seemed as wild as the country through which they traversed but whose pronouncements were no less reverent than those of a Christian prophet. As the master translated sacred landforms, Young felt like a "student sitting at his feet" to hear a fresh interpretation of "God and His way of making the world." Instead of sitting, however, Young chased Muir on a spongy carpet of moss, heather, and dwarf blueberry as the naturalist reiterated that they "must see the sunset from the top." The hikers hurried even on the sheer basalt of the summit, where the novice attempted to duplicate every step and handhold of the seasoned mountaineer.[26]

About forty feet from the top, they faced a steep gash in the cliff route over which the bearded goat leapt, then raced along a narrow ledge, pressing his companion onward. In his "haste to overtake Muir," the minister hopped to a stone he hoped would hold. Gravel that embedded it into the gully gave way. Instantly, Young turned face in, arms up, hugging loose gravel in a chute that opened below to a thousand vertical feet of air and, at the bottom, the blue-crevassed mantle of a glacier. His cry brought Muir back to the gash, where he exclaimed, "My God!" Shouting assurances and whistling Scottish airs, he examined the rock face for a foothold strong enough for two. Eternities passed in the moments before Muir's arms appeared over the edge to grab the missionary by the belt. Then his "wonderful friend" pulled Young close enough to bite his collar, lock jaws, and inch backwards fifteen feet up the gully to the ledge.

Ugly scrapes and a dislocated arm were the least of Young's concerns as he tumbled down the mountain after Muir. The adventurers shambled up to the *Cassiar* a few minutes past its scheduled departure time. Mixed with cries of relief were shouted orders to prepare the ship for sailing. Some rushed immediately to the battered climbers, others gathered closer to watch, but one man glared from the rail. Face frozen in profound displeasure, Dr. Kendall finally pronounced his discontent. "You have a family and a church," he boomed, "and it is very wrong for you to jeopardize your life in foolhardy scrambling."

Steamed and impatient, Captain Lane shoved an elbow into the indignant man: "Oh, hell! This is no time for preaching. Don't you see the man's hurt?"

The holy harangue continued until Kendall's wife thrust a spoon in his face and ordered her husband to "shut up and leave." He obeyed.[27]

:: "HURRY! WE ARE DAILY LOSING THE MOST
IMPORTANT NEWS OF ALL THE WORLD"

By the end of the month's inspection, tourists and locals alike were ready to move on. A few nights before the Presbyterian luminaries boarded the *California,* To'watte and the church-going clans hosted a "grand dinner," at which Muir was also an honored guest. He noted the absence of Native foods, which were replaced by "imported canned stuff served Boston fashion." A performance of Tlingit dancing followed the meal: plodding rhythms hammered on waist-high box drums, resonance reinforced by the heels of dozens of dancers on thick spruce planks. On the periphery, elders jabbed the floor with heavy staffs. And over the thudding syncopation, a brown bear chorale chanted throaty anthems.

Whatever the vibrational effects inside the box-drum house, equally captivating was the visual display. Each dancer wore regalia brought out only for highest ceremonies. These clan treasures, at.óow, define Tlingit identity and provide a link to the clan and to their ancestors. Clan affiliations bind wearers and watchers to animal hides and Chilkat blankets, beaded vests and leggings, and masks: Raven, Bear, Killer Whale. Intricate, ornate designs with multiple images filled every space of a robe, hairpiece, or house post, each acknowledging the person(s), animal(s), and incident(s) that inspired the artistic statement. A roomful of animated at.óow—bouncing, leaping, gyrating—moved participants toward a sort of synesthetic ecstasy. Taken as an amusing vestige of the Old Ways, even the lace-collared Victorian ladies were entertained. Muir's highlight was a dancer clad in full bear-skin whose movement and manner perfectly imitated the animal's behavior.

When the thunder of the last drum-beat faded, a Tlingit leader stood and spoke through Young's interpreter, Sarah Dickinson: "Dear Brothers and Sisters, this is the way we used to dance. We liked it long ago when we were blind, we always danced this way, but now we are not blind. The Good Lord has taken pity upon us and sent his son Jesus Christ, to tell us what to do. We have danced today only to show you how blind we were to like to dance in this foolish way. We will not dance any more."[28]

One after another, Tlingit speakers declared allegiance to their newfound faith while the scribbling Muir looked up occasionally from his black journal to drink in the rich ambience of a tribal house filled with beautiful objects. Each orator denounced traditional Tlingit culture and reasserted vows to end Native dancing, food, clothing, and beliefs. Kadachan confessed his initial reluctance to the New Way but now pledged himself and family to the church: "When I first got Mr. Young, I hear the truth. I fight against it. Temptation hold me back. But I couldn't stand it any longer. I must go back and talk with Mr. Young. I fight the truth no more. Now I love the truth."[29]

Giving the last speech, Old Chief Shakes conceded "We have been long, long in the dark. You have led us into a strong, guiding light and taught us the right way to live and the right way to die. I thank you for myself and all my people, and I give you my heart."

As proof of their commitment, a headman announced that Tlingits would surrender all dance regalia to their guests. Dancers gave Jackson and his associates furs and shaman paraphernalia. Muir accepted a medicine man's "fantastic head-dress," probably a shakee.át. "Altogether," he recalled, "it was a wonderful show."[30]

Muir likely evaded the crowd that gathered on the beach to watch the Presbyterians board their southbound ship. Originally, the naturalist intended to return on the same run, but he simply needed more time with ice. The extended visit meant further investigation up the Stikine River network, often for days at a time, to study earthworks of the Master Artist. Reverend Young sometimes accompanied Muir into a glacier-sculpted backcountry penetrated by few humans white or Native. In one drainage they met prospectors who had briefly ventured into northern Lynn Canal and described it as a region of ice, rock, and unfriendly heathens—a seductive combination for the two. The reverend returned to Fort Wrangell in mid-September, just in time for the arrival of their firstborn child, Abby Lindsley Young.

Autumn rains that drowned muddy streets and flooded local streams also confined the explorers under the pastor's roof—Young tending his new family and Muir crouched over his *Bulletin* dispatches. Each was fully engaged with his responsibilities, but when the naturalist supped with the Youngs or palavered late with the pastor, he rarely failed to mention a journey north. The window of acceptable weather was nearly shut, elevating the urgency in Muir's sales pitch.

"We are going to write some history, my boy," Muir counseled his friend, wholly mindful of the historical footnote Young might earn from civilizing the fearsome Chilkats. "Think of the honor! We have been chosen to put some interesting people and some of Nature's grandest scenes on the page of human record and on the map. Hurry! We are daily losing the most important news of all the world!"[31]

His wild-hearted friend deserved holy time with glaciers, the missionary concurred. And where his sanctimonious superiors had failed in their quest to tame the last heathen Indians, Young planned to succeed.

8 :: To'watte's Canoe

U.S. Navy captain Lester Anthony Beardslee understood the complexity of his mission when he was assigned as commanding officer for Alaska in spring 1879. Reasserting federal authority in the territory after a two-year military absence was as onerous and delicate a mission as any task on the American frontier. Bootlegging had soared, and with free-flowing hooch had come neglect, abuse, and violence. Each village suffered the ravages of alcohol, and in the Chilkat-Chilkoot aaní, where three thousand Natives maintained the Old Ways and forbade white settlement, stills were unchecked by the church or law enforcement. In the inner recesses of Lynn Canal, so-called "hooch wars" raged behind a curtain of isolation and complicity.[1]

Alcohol was just one of the problems that made Alaska a nuisance to the new president of the United States. Elected by a hair's breadth in 1877, Rutherford B. Hayes was a moderate Republican teetotaler who promised to revive a national budget gored by a decade of Reconstruction in the South following the Civil War. In his single presidential term, the former Ohio governor faced not only depleted resources but a polarized nation, a massive railroad strike, and the ongoing Indian Wars. To roust and confront Chief Joseph's Nez Perce bands in Idaho and Montana demanded a full federal response, so during his first weeks in office, Hayes withdrew all federal troops stationed in the former Confederacy, likewise abandoning Alaska to its own chaos and tumult. Hayes considered the huge territory a fiscal black hole. To keep the peace on about forty-seven thousand miles of coastline, he retained a tiny detachment of U.S. Treasury agents on two revenue cutters. Thus did the only president to ban booze from the White House precipitate a howling hooch crisis in Southeast Alaska.[2]

Enter Captain Beardslee with his officer's cap, cinnamon mutton chops, and keen sense of human behavior, guided by an Executive Order to "restore harmonious relations between the whites and Indians."[3] Barely middle-aged and already twenty-nine years into a naval career, the new Alaska commander was known as a solid administrator, reliable, firm, and fair. Signed at fourteen as a midshipman, Beardslee accompanied Com. Matthew C. Perry to open U.S. trade with Japan three years later. At twenty, he graduated from the U.S. Naval Academy. He was on the ironclad ship *Nantucket* when it attacked Charleston, South Carolina, in the Civil War, served on the *Wachusett* off Brazil, and flew the first American colors through the Suez Canal. He learned about Alaska from the decks of the USS *Saginaw* when he participated in the bombardment of Kake in 1869. Few naval officers were as well suited to the task of taming America's last wild fringe.

Once installed on the USS *Jamestown,* Beardslee quickly assessed that the source of civil unrest in Sitka had less to do with Natives than with the brazen behavior of white "outlaws and fugitives."[4] Much of their power derived from the sale of molasses to Natives, whose distillatory talents yielded a lethal spirit. Fear of provoking war kept previous military governors from dedicating their few troops to destroying stills in private homes. In Beardslee's view, however, prohibition was essential to establishing law and order. After prohibiting all molasses sales, Beardslee appointed Native police officers, a common practice on the "Indian frontier" but a first among the Tlingit. The four clan leaders—Sitka Jack (Anaaxoots), Shukhoff, Katlian (K'alyáan), and Dick—had openly criticized past U.S. authorities, but as authorized policemen, they honored the new boss by eradicating all Native stills in Sitka within a month.[5]

No sooner had local enforcers cleaned up the Ranche than they heard news about a brutal clash between Chilkat and Chilkoot tribes. A dispute over a molasses keg had turned deadly, igniting a fight that may have killed up to nine on each side, but more alarming to Kaagwaantaan kinsmen were rumors that Koh'klux was seriously wounded. The Chilkat sháade háni's brother-in-law, Sitka Jack, immediately prepared canoes for the weeklong voyage to resolve the conflict in Klukwan.

     DLEIT AAN<u>K</u>ÁAWU

Despite the ongoing fracas, Captain Beardslee was unable to mount a military response. His only vessel was the *Jamestown*, expensive, cumbersome, and still under repair from damage in a winter storm. Experience with bombings in Charleston and Kake proved the man capable of deadly force, but without a warship he was forced to rely on surrogates. Beardslee inserted into the peace delegation two policemen and their lieutenants. The word of an Indian officer was like his own, he told Sitka Jack, the official "orator," so the Chilkats and Chilkoots were wise to listen. The orator should tell "Klotz-Kutch" that the time had come for the great chief to open his country to the white miners and traders and that Commander Beardslee would help him prevent further violence among Natives and whites. Besides, he added, if they allowed prospectors into the reputed goldfields beyond Chilkat and Chilkoot passes, Tlingit gatekeepers would be "enriched" in their traditional trade and even more so as packers and guides. In return for Sitka Jack's promise to relay "the value of white friendship and the danger of the opposite," Beardslee rewarded the delegation with provisions and gifts.[6]

The peacekeepers launched on the flood tide of October 3. They headed northeast through Sergius Narrows, a tidal rapids squeezed between two of the largest islands in the United States—Baranof and Chichigof—and then sailed east through Peril Strait until its confluence with ten-mile-wide Chatham Strait. From that point, the three canoes turned left and maintained a northerly course into the troubled Chilkat citadel 150 miles away.

The northern Tlingits welcomed into their homes the Sitka delegates, who repaid the cordiality of their hosts with Beardslee's offerings.[7] Among the most-desirable gifts were American flags, some stored in Klukwan homes today along with older flags distributed by William Seward and General O. O. Howard and now elevated to a status similar to the handcrafted at.óow of Tlingit ancestors.

In a few weeks, the Sitka diplomats would stand beside their hosts as a canoe arrived bearing four Tlingit guests, a God's Man and a long-bearded one whose glacial fixation earned him the honorific, Dleit Aankáawu, which he heard as Glate Ankow and interpreted as Ice Chief. Of local Tlingits today who still protect at.óow in clan houses, chests, and closets, each carries stories of beloved forbears as well as that of a white man who forever transformed their lives.

As sodden September slurried into October, Reverend Young prayed that winter held off until they completed the upcoming sea voyage. Heads bowed, Fannie Young and her husband asked that he might be the first to preach to the feared Chilkat. Never mind rumors of hooch wars or that the "season of constant rains" was upon them. Only weeks old, their firstborn thrived as her mother recuperated. Faith led the Youngs to Alaska; faith forged their commitment to God; faith assured the reverend's success and safe passage.[8]

Faith also fueled the passions of their ice-struck guest, who surely added his own prayers whenever the topic arose. Although John Muir found worthy subjects in nearby Stikine glaciers, he yearned to venture north to the land of living ice. The naturalist knew by heart the charts sketched by Captain Vancouver on his 1793–1794 voyage of the *Chatham* as it skirted the mouth of the berg-choked bay. Four or five miles inside the oceanic indentation rose a glittering wall over a hundred feet high behind which "a compact sheet of ice" gradually ascended until it filled the entire northern horizon. Anchored safely beyond the pale, Vancouver and crew observed the glacial spectacle for a week while a patrol led by Lt. Joseph Whidbey investigated the grand fjord named after King's Lynn, the captain's birthplace. Upon his return, Whidbey reported a close brush with well-armed, hostile Natives. Attired in "brilliant" garb, two hundred Tlingits in four war canoes had repelled the lieutenant's three modest craft. Discouraged by the superior force, Vancouver turned south, never actually sailing into Lynn Canal (see chap. 2).[9]

Eighty-five years hence, Muir speculated, retreat of the frozen plain would reveal a scene never described to the Western world—a literal unveiling of new land. No wilderness was more pure. "Wild John" ached for his life's prize, from which he was separated by watery miles and a means of transport.

Despite his urgency to leave, the glacier-chaser had warmed to Wrangell. Short excursions up the Stikine by steamer and canoe gave him access to the higher ice fields, which he often traversed alone, sometimes with the truant minister. Their friendship deepened with each outing. Though not the "usual" sort of Christian by his "outward display," Muir impressed Young as one of the most "intensely religious" men he knew, an ecstatic witness to the divine scheme in every flower, rock, and mountain. Whenever moved by spectacular landscapes or natural phenomena, Young heard Muir exclaim,

"Praise God from whom all blessings flow," yet never knew him to attend a church service.[10]

Apostle for purity, Muir disparaged contamination. Until he witnessed Tlingit people at home, Muir's disdain for Indians reflected a lifetime of watching them fall from grace. Wilderness is perfection, he held; civilization the inverse. He held fast to the Transcendentalist principle that Nature was a manifestation of God's love, that His Word was writ large in each marsh marigold, water ouzel, and river boulder. By degrees, "Lord Man's" touch debased Eden. As a young man in his sickbed, Muir refused garden flowers from young admirers, sending them instead to gather "God's posies." In 1875, he argued for the quality of wild wool over domestic in an article that concluded with "a little pure wildness is the one great present want, both of men and sheep." The naturalist blamed the fall of American Indians on missionaries, who, "in the attempt to Christianize savages" wielded hymnbooks that dulled "wild instincts (until) they become very nearly nothing." Whenever possible, Muir avoided shepherd and flock.[11]

But Alaska was different. Muir's feelings about missionaries changed when he made friends with one. In Alaska, it appeared that "Christian teachers stood between Natives and the degrading vices of civilization." During his ten weeks among the Stikine tribe, Glate Ankow came to know his Native guides and interpreters as members of families, clans, and communities. Besides their "Mongol looks," Muir judged the primary difference between Tlingits and other Indians was their willingness to work. "They are industrious when free from the contamination of bad whites," who, he observed, lured their targets into drunkenness and debauchery. Missionaries Young and McFarland assailed Muir with tales of wresting enslaved Native girls from white miners, smashing hooch stills, and quelling witch hunts. The three agreed that Tlingits were better for these intrusions. Muir grew to know the Natives who were closest to the mission and occasionally took him hunting or fishing. The canoe outings afforded Muir time to appreciate the humor and wisdom of his hosts, whom he confounded and amused.[12]

"A good deal of sport was made of my pity for the animals," Muir wrote, because he rocked the canoe whenever the men tried to shoot ducks or seals. When a group of white miners chided To'watte for overhunting waterfowl, the old sháade háni responded that it was impossible to kill too many because "the duck's friend would not let him." In a later incident, Muir scolded a Tlingit companion for killing a seagull without reason, to which the man responded that "he had learned from the whites to be careless about taking life."[13]

The naturalist could not deny the blame. He mourned the death of wildness in each innocent being—human or seagull—sacrificed to the impulses of Euro-American conquerors. Among the Tlingits, he recognized the wisdom of lives interwoven with nature. If "civilization" vanished, these Natives would hardly notice. Tlingits were the most self-sustaining people Muir had ever known; thus he deemed them ready for Americanization. "They are industrious, willing to give good and fair work for fair wages, and to adopt all the benefits of civilization within reach. They would compare favorably with the very best of the uneducated of any people under the sun," Muir journaled after two weeks among them. "Unprincipled whiskey-laden traders are their bane; common-sense Christian teachers their greatest blessing."[14]

Of the attributes he admired in Tlingit culture—family, work ethic, traditional ecological knowledge—one lingering tradition deeply disturbed Muir, a practice he felt distinguished "wild" people from civilized: heathen superstition. He could hardly toss off Reverend Hall's terrifying confrontations with shamans nor forget that the íxt' still held sway in outlying communities, where Young claimed they whipped up witch hunts that led to torture, even death. The plight of the Chilkats justified his new friend's urgent undertaking. Though the flinty fundamentalism of his youth repelled Muir from Christian proselytizing, he was prepared to support his new friend's mission, even to preach, if necessary.[15] He'd do anything to enter the kingdom of ice.

For his character models, Muir looked no farther than the "church Indians," particularly To'watte, the "nobleman" whose meeting with Sheldon Jackson only two years earlier opened the Stikine kwáan to Presbyterians. To'watte lived with his family in the first of a line of frame houses between the fort and the old village, followed by Kadachan, Shakes, and Johnson, each a member of Young's congregation. When their pastor decided in the first week of October 1879 that a northbound expedition should proceed, he directed the clan leader, over eighty years old, to roust a crew for the voyage. To'watte weighed the prospects. The timing was horrible. Autumn in southeast Alaska is a short, sodden slide from summer's end in September to the blizzards of November. Low-pressure troughs sometimes pummeled the archipelago for weeks in the season of dying light, when smart residents remained indoors. It was time to carve, tell stories, mend nets, stay put.

God's work is never convenient, Young reminded To'watte, but the rewards are eternal.

Blustery weather was not the worst of To'watte's fears. He believed that God could guide their passage through rough waters, as his preacher promised, but the elder wondered about His capacity to restrain the Chilkats, old enemies with long memories. As a people yet to know the Gospel, they still adhered to the traditional law that dictated retribution for To'watte's youthful participation in raids against them. They would surely seek to balance the score. With God on his side, Reverend Young was unmoved.

Despite misgivings, To'watte pledged his canoe and leadership. As church patron and Young's primary sponsor, the headman had already cast his lot. Two generations of impoverished Russian Orthodoxy had done little for the well-being of Stikine people, even less after the Americans moved in. Two years before he encountered Jackson, To'watte noticed a dramatic shift in the behavior of Haidas, southern neighbors whom he once considered "the worst Indians on this coast" but now were generous and peaceful. In addition to a doctrine of salvation, their God's Man also brought free education, good housing, and increased trade. With the help of a soldier, To'watte and others dictated a letter requesting a missionary and mailed it to General Howard in Vancouver, Washington. The "Christian General" contacted Sheldon Jackson, tireless promoter of the Presbyterian West.

Jackson found in To'watte the respected elder he needed to open doors among the Tlingit. Sometime after their meeting, Jackson sent his newest convert to a religious convention in Port Townsend, Washington Territory, where the Stikine elder spoke to a large audience of whites and Indians. "We are content," he said, about the change from Russian to American hands. When the Great Chief in Washington purchased Alaska, "he purchased us" and so must act responsibly toward his new property. To'watte explained, "All we ask is justice. We ask that we be civilized, Christianized, and educated. Give us a chance and we will show the world that we can become peaceable citizens."[16]

For his second-in-command To'watte chose next-door-neighbor Kadachan, who, in his late twenties, was already a family leader, clan provider, and church pillar. Deeply pockmarked and stern in appearance, Kadachan was also the strongest orator of the Stikine, "a born after-dinner speaker and a master of metaphors, oily phrases, and compliment." A classically-trained Tlingit orator with passable English, Kadachan enjoyed a regional reputation as culture bearer and peacemaker. As if pulled by strings, listeners drew near his strong, moving voice at memorials and celebrations.[17]

Seasoned paddler and speaker, Kadachan was a natural choice for the voyage, but for To'watte, the young Stikine diplomat was perhaps most valued as the son of notorious Chilkat sháade háni Koh'klux. Not long after the total eclipse of 1869, one of the headman's two wives had admitted to an infidelity, for which she was banned from Klukwan. The disgraced woman returned home with her teenaged son to live among the Stikine. She and Kadachan eventually allied with Mrs. McFarland and Reverend Young. Nearly a decade had passed since Kadachan last shared a meal with his northern relatives, an absence tied to the unresolved dispute between Chilkats and Stikines. Rather than their presence fueling a conflict, To'watte wagered that the return of the Chilkat heir would inspire harmony.[18]

Rounding out the crew were two younger men, each of whom possessed qualities vital to a successful voyage. Like Kadachan, part of Sitka Charley's value was strategic—his Hoonah-Sitka lineage was a calling card in their realms. As a child of two k̲wáans, the twenty-nine-year-old knew the best canoe routes and camping sites throughout the archipelago; as son of Sitka Jack, he held the Chilkat card. Raised in part by fort officers, Stickeen Johnny possessed the strongest English and domestic skills, so he would serve as translator and cook. Each young man was an accomplished hunter and fisher, always honored to fill the dinner plates of their families and missionary staff.[19]

To'watte directed his men to collect provisions, which he placed inside wooden boxes to be cinched tight and stored under a waterproof tarpaulin stretched across the inner canoe. His midlength vessel was best for such a trip, and To'watte was a legendary navigator. On the morning of October 14, the Tlingit crew carried the thirty-six-foot yellow cedar dugout to a beach where they made final preparations. Along with countless fishing and hunting expeditions, generations of travelers had paddled to gatherings around Southeast Alaska. The community depended on the canoe—and its captain—to stay whole.

A knot of frowning women materialized nearby. Kadachan's mother, a "woman of great natural dignity and force of character," marched down the steps to the beach and across the tidal mud to the canoe. She fixed her "dark, bodeful eyes" on Reverend Young with an intensity that presaged a red-hot upbraiding. With "great solemnity and gesture," the woman accused Young of using undue influence to persuade her son into believing that such a foolhardy excursion was God's will. Did Young truly believe that God would save them from horrible weather and hostile rivals? "Like an ancient sibyl," Kadachan's mother detailed an array of dangers awaiting the party, predicting disaster at every turn. At the conclusion of her speech, she paused, locked a fatal gaze on Young, and swore her oath: "If my son comes not back, on you will be his blood, and you shall pay."

Young raised a hand as if to catch or bless her threat. He was on a mission for the Lord. She should remember that they traveled in the protective light of an all-knowing God who gave His only son for her. The Reverend pledged himself to care for Kadachan as if he were his own son, and "and if need be die in his defense."

"We shall see whether or not you die," she snapped.[20]

Kadachan responded neither to Young nor his mother but kept his head down with the other men as they hurried toward the launch. Muir noticed To'watte's usual solemn expression creased into a mask of doomed resignation and asked the captain about his gloomy appearance. With words like heavy stones dropped into water, the elder mixed Tlingit and English, but his face told every detail. Domestic unrest plagued him as well. When To'watte said goodbye to his wife, Julia, she wailed bitter tears and predicted that if he did not perish in the strange, icy bay, their mortal enemies, the Chilkats, would finish him off.

Her husband was steadfast. "I'm going to take my missionary to these Indians to tell them of the Man from Above who came to earth to die for us. Maybe these Indians kill me—all right. I go quick to Heaven."

The comment drew louder protests. As To'watte prepared to leave, he paused at the door to shake her hand, but Julia refused, repeating "the Chilkats will kill him; they will kill him!"[21]

:: "NOT SO MUCH AS THE ANGLO SAXON"

After forcing the 1877 surrender of Chief Joseph and the Nez Perce in the Army's last major Indian war, Maj. Gen. O. O. Howard led his troops down the Columbia River back to Fort Vancouver. From the Nez Perce and Custer debacles, Howard learned to attack with unexpected speed and deadly force, a strategy he employed for his remaining four years as regional army commander. Whether troops deployed by the "Christian General" were ordered to defend churches and businesses or dispossess Native communities for new ones, his efforts to roust out troublesome "raiders and freebooters" proved effective. Once God's Men exorcised the "wild" from their flocks, Howard envisioned a long parade of settlers bringing light to heathen realms, Christian families bent to the Lord's work of making the land pay. Placer miners dredged mountain streams; farmers plowed rich valley loam; stockmen grazed herds in lush meadows. Divinely seated, the general pledged his righteousness to the Lord's work.

The next summer Howard received an urgent message from Sarah Winnemucca, a Paiute "Agency Indian" who escaped an encampment of warriors. Hidden high in the remote Steens Mountains of southeastern Oregon, over a thousand Bannock, Umatilla, Klamath, and Paiute warriors had converged with plans to rub out white ranchers and farmers across the high inland plateau. After re-entering the war camp and successfully freeing dozens of tribal members, Winnemucca guided the general and hundreds of troops across the harsh geography of the John Day region. Armed with carbines, howitzers, and Gatling guns, Howard's troops pursued a thousand Native combatants over impossibly rugged terrain: "jagged rocks, precipitous slopes, knife-edged divides [and] deep canyons with sides steep and difficult." Outnumbered and outgunned, the warriors faded into the landscape. Howard responded with a systematic search over hundreds of square miles, imprisoning any able-bodied man found and herding families to distant reservations.

While John Muir sauntered over Stikine glaciers in August of 1879, General Howard's troops were again tracking Native renegades, including remnants of warrior bands involved in the John Day battles and now aligned with disaffected bands of Northern Shoshone called "Sheepeaters" by white settlers. This time, U.S. soldiers chased their enemies in the backcountry between Hell's Canyon and the Seven Devils, volcanic postpiles rising above the Middle Fork of the Salmon River. Both sides endured fierce conditions and deadly surprise attacks until U.S. troops overcame the warriors, killing many and forcing a mass surrender. It would be the last "Indian War" waged against Pacific Northwest tribes.

For sixty-two days overlapping with Muir's voyage of discovery, the soldiers marched their captives "through fearful snows over rugged mountains" to the Columbia River, then transported them downriver for long-term confinement at Fort Vancouver. After one of the enemy combatants turned out to be a former army spy or informer in his employ, a colleague asked General Howard if he found Natives generally treacherous. "Not so much as the Anglo Saxon," Howard replied. As a rule, Native promises were ironclad, unlike those of whites. Beyond the heat of battle, Howard was unaware of any Indian devising "a deliberate plan to deceive and injure me and mine, as many an educated white man has done."[22]

As they glowered at the wake spreading behind To'watte's rudder, the women on the beach mulled over the preacher's promises. God or no God, four able-bodied men were gone for a month or more, tricked by the missionary and his strange friend. What if they died? Icy bay, bad weather, dangerous water, hostile Chilkats—all were dangerous, even lethal, and could take their men. More than personal tragedy, their deaths leave empty plates at home and a huge gap in tribal leadership.

The men felt happier with each paddle stroke. From his seat in the raised stern To'watte squinted into the western sun, knotted hands gripping the oversized steering paddle he used for course corrections. Kneeling forward of his captain, Kadachan rolled powerful shoulders into each stroke of his ornately carved paddle. Sitka Charley and Stickeen Johnny toiled amidships with the well-oiled rhythm of familiars. On the bow-thwart behind the foremast, white men sat side by side in mackinaws and wool caps, one wearing mutton-chops and the other sporting a long, reddish-brown beard straggling across his chest. Both wielded a paddle but were often distracted in the manner of "children" entering a "wonderful playhouse full of unknown toys."

The upturned bow of the thirty-six-foot cedar canoe sliced into the table-topped surface of a perfect day. The azure dome overhead seemed imperturbable; surely it was a sign of easy travel ahead. A mile or two from shore, the men raised twin square sails to catch a Stikine wind westward into Sumner Strait, a great ocean passage that flows east-west between islands the size of some states. From there, a week of calm water and light breezes would transport the missionary to his prime objective, the sandy shoals of the Chilkat River. Muir would see his ice at Davidson Glacier and, if the weather held, in Vancouver's icy bay.

Little more than an hour out, the travelers set ashore for lunch. The white men were impressed by how quickly Stickeen Johnny lit a fire for coffee and grub, but withheld from sharing their pot of reheated beans with him and the others. Reverend Young was advised to let Natives pack their own food or risk being "cleaned out," so the crew kept their hard biscuits, venison, dried salmon, and seal grease while the non-Natives ate flour, sugar, rice, milk, beans, and potatoes. Of "Boston food," Tlingits most coveted butter, which, like eulachon or seal oil, satisfied their considerable craving for lipids. Invited once to dine with the white men, To'watte serenely sliced off a third of a butterball, which when popped into his mouth, produced an unctuous grin across the normally stoic face.[23]

Two days of paddling along the southern shores of Kupreanof Island paralleled a consummate Northwest Coast tide-line of fluorescent seaweeds ramping into a fringe of red alder that lapped against an abrupt wall of spruce, hemlock, and occasional cypress (yellow cedar). Gravel and sand beaches were rare; a sighting often presaged a lunch stop or campsite. Less than an hour's paddle from the southwestern point of Kupreanof, To'watte elected to land at such a beach, which, with its large creek, was a favorite stopover. After supper, Young paid a visit to a Kake family camped nearby and, through John and Kadachan, explained their mission, introduced Muir, and asked whether their village wanted a school and teachers.

"We have not much to say to you fellows," the patriarch replied. "We always do as we have done to you, give a little of whatever we have, treat everybody well and have no quarrel with anyone. That is all I have to say." Further conversation was futile, so Young and the others soon parted, enduring the Tlingits' laughter and chatter as they strolled away.[24]

Steady drizzle fell the next morning, "wind ah-ing in the noble swaying trees." Just as the tents were dismantled, air currents shifted from south to north and the rain got colder. To'watte and Kadachan insisted they stay put. As eager as the white men were to proceed, no one balked. The Natives rambled down the beach on a hunt while Muir nosed in the intertidal zone, where he observed the signatures of glaciers on rocks polished by the weight of ice. His journal entry reveled at the discovery, unable to resist scoffing at the "ex cathedra tones" of lectures by scientist and author William Dall, who argued that such rock was rare in Alaska.[25]

The breeze laid back the next day, so the canoeists paddled to Point Barrie, where To'watte steered the vessel into Keku Strait and north ninety degrees with Kupreanof Island on starboard and Kuiu Island on port. Sumner Strait seemed like an inland sea compared to Keku, which squeezed into a six-mile passage between the two large islands. At its most tapered, Rocky Pass separates the two islands by a few hundred feet of water known by mariners for its extreme hazard. North and south entrances to Keku Strait open to huge water bodies from which high-volume flood tides are drawn, creating sea-rivers that rush from opposite directions into the pinched channel. The two rivers collide at Rocky Pass, a place of whirlpools and boiling brine around dozens of rock teeth that gnash the water's surface.

Slack high tide is the only time vessels may attempt Rocky Pass without peril. Twice a day, ocean inflow reaches a maximum height when it achieves stasis for up to a half-hour before it begins the race to low tide. To'watte timed their passage well, for Muir noted nothing of the water, just "very fine" scenery as they paddled between the islands' volcanic edges. He devoted much more journal space to his Native companions' efforts to retrieve a dead duck, a group portrait of perseverance and humor.

As the canoe approached the Kake villages the next afternoon, Muir noticed potato patches, brown from recent frost, in seaweed mounds just above the high-tide mark. Upshore from the landing rose eight totem poles, each representing a clan living in the sprawl of timber-framed houses. Escorts led them through the village, where Young observed many new structures but also several buildings in ruins, splintered and charred monuments to the "forest diplomacy" of U.S. Navy cannons a decade earlier. As he strolled past the potato beds, Muir saw human bones unearthed in the freshly cultivated beds, reminders of a battle with Sitka marauders, whose dead were tilled into the soil where they fell. When Young discovered that half the population was out for a late king-salmon run, he prepared to travel across the strait to another Kake village. Those people were also gone, replied the headman, who declared he had waited all year for a visit from Young. Muir stood by as the Kake leader "coaxed and flattered" the God's Man until he promised to stay an extra day.[26]

As they often did before bedding down, that evening the travelers sat around a campfire and talked. Muir especially enjoyed the Natives' accounts of life before white men when elders knew the animals better and were more engaged with teaching subsistence methods. In the midst of the discussion, a wolf began howling from an island a half-mile from shore. As the plaintive howl continued, Kadachan turned to his pastor and asked if wolves had souls. The question mystified Young—why should wolves be among God's chosen ones? They show great wisdom as hunters, the Tlingit man answered. When wolves swam after seals, they hid their heads behind mouthfuls of grass. Wolf packs demonstrated complex communication skills on deer hunts. Wolves' combination of speed, strength, intelligence, and cooperation, consistently brought down prey. Then why don't they kill off the deer population? Muir inquired. Too smart. Wolves know better than to wipe out a food supply.

Glate Ankow recognized the ecological and spiritual basis of Kadachan's answers and interpreted the comments as further proof of Tlingit intimacy with the wild.[27]

Perhaps two hundred listeners assembled inside the big clan house the next morning to hear Reverend Young preach. Gifts of rice and tobacco were distributed as the missionary opened a "floodgate of talk" by telling the "Great New Story" translated by Stickeen Johnny. God offered eternal life; the Great Father in Washington offered civilization. The Tlingits could remain as children lost in the dark or follow the Presbyterian light. The Stikine had chosen the "righteous path," as had their former enemies, Tsimshian and Haida. All had dropped old grudges in favor of schools, medical care, and immortality. Throughout the sermon, babies cried and listeners shouted to those people listening beyond the wall planks. To'watte and Kadachan considered them "mannerless barbarians."[28]

Following Young's invocation, Muir stood, reluctance scrawled around gray eyes that usually glittered with contention and intelligence. He shunned the podium, a lifelong aversion, but circumstances compelled his contribution. In a "few struggling syllable sentences," Muir advised the audience to expect "two kinds of Boston men—one selfishly seeking gold, and the other trying to do good," and to seek only the company of the latter. Race, he said, was not a factor in the good or bad in people because humanity is united in the "Fatherhood of God." As humans, Muir thought Kake people "shrewd, industrious and rather good-looking;" as Indians, they affirmed his high regard for the Tlingits.

The Russians had inculcated basic Christian concepts in this and many other Tlingit villages but had never stationed a priest in Kake. Most residents maintained a version of the Old Ways touched by elements of Western religion, like burial rather than cremation. Still, shamans served as intermediaries with the spirit world.[29] Multiple families lived in clan houses where men often kept two or three wives. "Eye for an eye" served as justice. But the arrival of missionaries in Stikine and Sitka piqued interest in outlying villages like Kake because Boston men brought schools and increased trade. Two headmen spoke. The younger, "Yana-taowk," said that he was glad to ally with Boston men who knew about agriculture and other things unknown to Tlingits. As a warrior who had slain many men, including two whites, Yana-taowk did not care to be a child lost in darkness. He sought the light. To Muir, the second headman exuded "benevolence and strength" by virtue of his advanced age, huge head, Roman nose, and bushy eyebrows. "This is just what I want," declared the elder. "I am ready to welcome him [Young] at any time."[30]

The warm reception was intoxicating for the novice clergyman and his Stikine congregants, but their mood plummeted at news of war in Klukwan. Rumors flew that a keg of molasses had ignited a fight resulting in ten deaths and many wounded. Even more alarming, Kadachan's father, Koh'klux, was said to be mortally wounded and might already be dead. The death of the Chilkat sháade háni might provoke an all-out clan war—one of To'watte's

 DLEIT AAN<u>K</u>ÁAWU

greatest worries and certainly his wife's nightmare. In the morning, however, the aged captain confronted a more imminent danger.

On Monday, October 20, the white men roused their crew at 2:30 a.m. for a 5:00 launch. The Tlingits were always reluctant risers, but their recalcitrance this time stemmed from more than the early hour. From the voyage's beginning, To'watte and his men had openly shared their dread of crossing twenty miles of exposed water in Frederick Sound. The route was risky in fine weather and suicidal in bad. As the paddlers pulled away from the safety of Kake Harbor they picked up a brisk southeast breeze at the stern and raised the sails. Point Gardener glowered like a dark cloud on the northwest horizon.

"I am surprised that you are not frightened to cross here," a crewman said to Muir, renewing a flurry of fretting among his comrades. To'watte confessed that he laid awake nights worrying about those dangers Muir could never anticipate. "You will be scared to death before you get across," he predicted. Eyes blazing with adventure, Muir returned the challenge: "All right, some of you Indians will show it first."

A six-foot swell rolled in from the ocean entrance of Chatham Strait southwest of the sailing canoe. Green water poured into the craft when the high prow dipped into the waves, but a heavy tarpaulin and an alert bailer kept things dry. Through hours of palpable tension, no one betrayed an emotion until the canoe rounded Point Gardener at the southern tip of Admiralty Island. Protected from ocean turbulence, the Native crew burst out laughing and joking like "schoolboys on a vacation frolic."[31]

A robust breeze fattened the sails for another twenty miles. Seven hours after leaving Kake, the men pulled To'watte's canoe onto the beach at Neltushkin, the first of three "Hootsenoo" (Hutsnuwu) communities on the west coast of Admiralty Island. Over two hundred villagers emptied onto the beach and followed Muir and Young around "as if they had never seen a white man." A "remarkably good-looking and intelligent" young man guided the party up to his large, new house and apologized for the traditional food: raw turnips, "slobbery" potato soup, and venison chunks in seal oil. Stickeen Johnny explained that the white men had yet to learn how to eat Indian foods but appreciated the sentiment.[32]

Dishes were cleared away while other headmen filed inside to hear the white men speak. Young delivered his usual lecture about God, Jesus, and heaven followed by Muir's comments about temperance, treatment of animals, and "the brotherhood of man of all nations." Clan leaders responded as they had in Kake; they were eager to shed the darkness in their lives for a guiding bright light. The headman's emotional plea for the village children showed Muir that "he truly loved them," demonstrating the "right intelligent insight" necessary to lead his tribe through the transition ahead.[33]

Buoyed by their warm welcome at the first Hutsnuwu village, the men sustained high hopes Tuesday morning as they paddled north to the main community. For Muir, the promontories and islets scrolling by on starboard were sculptures in limestone and marble. And he marveled at the wilderness looming above the shore! At 1,684 square miles Admiralty Island is the seventh largest island in the United States and home today to the densest coastal brown-bear population on earth. Ursine dominance was also apparent to Tlingit settlers in the first millennia; they called their home Hutsnuwu, Stronghold of the Bears. The two largest villages, Killisnoo and Angoon, guarded adjacent bays where brown bears stood in nearby stream mouths to scoop wriggling salmon into their Pleistocene jaws.

Young considered his options as the canoe rounded Point Samuel and glided into the islet-studded bay fronting Angoon. As in Kake, Hutsnuwu people were touched by Russian Orthodoxy, but absence of institutional support left only a veneer of understanding and practice. Unlike their neighbors on Keku Strait, Angoon residents remained in the thrall of a fierce shaman, Klee-a-keet, who months earlier had clashed with Reverend Young in Stikine and was driven out by the church Indians. Moreover, alcohol was pervasive in a community infamous as the birthplace of hooch, the incendiary beverage of the last frontier. Since a white soldier had initiated Angoon home distilling fifteen years earlier, the practice had spread into every corner of the region, disrupting millennia of social evolution through chronic inebriation, neglect, and violence. As a result, at least one clan or family group in each village had sent for a minister. So it was in Angoon where the preacher prayed that he might speak with them—plant a seed from which faith might grow.

As enforcers of the absolute ban of shamans and alcohol by their God's Man, To'watte and Kadachan studied the determined faces of Young and Muir, each resolute in his mission, and prayed that God was on their side.

A blood-curdling answer pierced the stillness of the early afternoon as they approached the imposing timber frame houses of Angoon, followed by a chorus of shrieks and screams the Stikines called "whiskey howls." The pebbly scrape on the hull of the canoe ended a moment of hesitation when Muir hoped Young might recant rather than preach while the "poor sufferers were afire." The crew's rising reluctance shifted into despair as they stepped onto the exposed beach. In the shadowed entry of a prominent beachfront house appeared several "demoniac faces," which promptly

    DLEIT AAN<u>K</u>ÁAWU

withdrew. Moments passed before two "old crouching black men" wobbled out, stared, then shouted into the dark entrance. A howling erupted from inside; the noise "sounded like hell" to Muir, who stood with Young on the village frontage a few paces ahead of the crew. Many Hutsnuwus crawled out of the big house to see the strangers before scuttling back, but shortly, a committee of three women and four men staggered forward, "smelling villainously," and invited them inside the big house. Reverend Young withdrew, his relieved comrades trailing close behind.

The white men strolled to the north end of the village to gaze across the mouth of Mitchell Bay. Back at the first house, To'watte encountered a man who nursed an old grievance and was drunk enough to wreak havoc. For a half hour, To'watte endured a barrage of screams and taunts from his tormentor and allies while he silently gazed "like a lion at bay." The travelers watched from the canoe as their captain weathered the harangue until it finally subsided and he rejoined them for a quick exit.[34]

Every stroke added distance between paddlers and the fading howls. A steady breeze pushed the canoe fifteen miles up the coast to the night's camp under the branches of a huge spruce. The south wind grew overnight, a detail ignored by the paddlers until the next morning when a gust smacked the sails as they nosed beyond the protected cove. The craft took a near-fatal dive, an ominous reminder of the terrible power of Inside Passage waters.

A south gale roared up Chatham Strait, forcing the crew to stow the sails and dig their paddles deeper in the froth to stay atop the following seas. Amidships, Johnny and Charley wielded long oars to minimize rocking. To avoid smashing into reefs and rocks, To'watte steered the craft as close to the coastline as possible on starboard. Portside, eight miles of squall separated them from Chichigof Island.

As they ducked into a sheltered notch, Kadachan declared the storm too dangerous for Indians, but he said their good luck would hold because God loved the white men. In the best scenario, the strong winds might blow them straight up to Chilkat in three days, but doubts plagued Kadachan's peers. Extreme maritime conditions were common for the season, but not all Tlingits were seasoned mariners. During the stormiest half of the year, most stayed close to their warm, dry households; only the direst circumstances justified the enormous risk of an open crossing. For a people who traditionally practiced cremation to send off the deceased, death by drowning was a horrifying prospect.

To'watte noticed a canoe beached in a grassy harbor and steered toward shore with hopes of hearing news about events in Chilkat. A Hoonah shaman sat under an ancient spruce with three women, waiting out the storm before crossing the strait. Their canoe was loaded with walnut-sized "Russian" potatoes in large sacks of woven spruce root. Yes, the shaman replied, his wife's sister had recently returned from a northern visit with confirmation of rumors in Klukwan. Ko'klux's death could set off a terrible war. In preparation for armed conflict, he had heard, residents were gathering in barricaded clan houses. To'watte and Kadachan advised the white men to delay a Chilkat meeting and let tempers cool. "Knowing the character of the Cats," Young and Muir opted for their "scalps' sake" to divert to Hoonah and the icy bay.

The delay was a reprieve for the crew and a delight for Muir. He ached to explore the "ice mountains" that Sitka Charley described from his travels, eager to unveil geological secrets that could transform his abstract theory into living proof or indisputable fact, in only a matter of days. The travelers overnighted farther up the coast of Admiralty Island where Chatham Strait narrows to about four miles. Muir closed the day's entry: "Had a wet camp—took 2 hrs. to make a fire. Not a very flattering testimony to the woodcraft of our Indians."[35]

:: "LIKELY TO MEET DEATH AND NOTHING ELSE"

The water laid down the next morning. A fair breeze carried the canoe across Chatham to the north end of Chichigof Island where paddlers rounded Point Sophia to find a large village tucked along the shores of a strategic harbor. The community sustained about eight hundred Hoonah Tlingits, whose territory extended west to the open coast and north across berg-littered Icy Strait into the bay of glaciers. Influential clans among the Hoonah originally lived in villages in the north bay (Klem'sha'shakeen, Chookanheeni, and others) but migrated centuries ago when advancing ice destroyed their homes. In recent generations, retreating glaciers allowed villagers to resume harvesting seals and sea gull eggs in the bay, though they feared the sea ice and treacherous currents. Muir hoped to find someone willing to guide their party into the farthest reaches of the bay of glaciers.

A Union Jack ran up a pole in front of the largest house along the beach. To'watte responded with an American flag on his stern pole. "Barefooted and bareheaded," sháade háni Kashoto looked every bit a leader as he strode from his house to meet the canoe. He greeted the party with apologies for his poverty and traditional food. A broad smile replaced the headman's grave demeanor when Young indicated through Stickeen Johnny that they would accept his hospitality.[36]

After the white "chiefs" ate enough Indian food to call it a meal, a large group of men and women assembled in the big house accompanied by packs of "wondering children." Young delivered his routine program of prayer, sermon, and song, then Kashoto requested a speech from Muir. "The brotherhood of all races" was again Muir's theme, bolstered with evidence of God's love and the interest of good "white brethren" in the welfare of Indians. Muir praised the hospitality of his listeners, saying he "seemed to be among old friends ere I had been half an hour in the house." By their "nods, ughs, and smiles," Muir thought the audience especially interested in his story about Natives who ate missionaries, though he felt confident that Tlingits would "put them in their hearts instead of their stomachs."[37]

In a heartfelt response, Kashoto affirmed his people's distress at being "little children in the dark" and desired a missionary to guide them. He agreed with Muir that similarities among humans proved they were children of the same God, and thanked them for traveling to Hoonah to preach. He warned them, however, that their venture into the icy bay was fraught with danger and that they were "likely to meet death and nothing else." In one inlet lay the kooshdaaḵáa, an otter demon waiting to drag the canoe to an underwater purgatory; in another lived a killer whale that could swallow them whole. Kashoto also "strongly advised" against traveling north because of the "war raging" among Chilkats.[38]

The headman's thoughtful, dignified manner impressed Muir as characteristic of the culture, different from Native Americans he had known or imagined. Equally notable among the Tlingits, he observed, was their "willingness to abandon" any substandard aspect of traditional lifestyle for the improvements brought by white men. "They are not savages in the ordinary sense of the term," Muir scribbled in the entry for October 23, 1879.

"I have never seen Americans or Europeans of the poorer classes," he explained, "who would compare favorably to them in good breeding, intelligence, and skill in accomplishing whatever they try to do with tools . . . or in their conceptions of a spiritual kind, moral sense, and government, political, judicial, or domestic. I have never seen a child ill-used even to the extent of an angry word. Scolding, so common a curse of the degraded of Christian countries, is not known here at all. But on the contrary, the young are fondled and indulged without being spoiled."[39]

The dire warnings from their Hoonah hosts only sharpened the white men's hunger to "explore the wonders beyond," so the travelers moved out in early morning. The canoe cut north across Icy Strait to Pleasant Island, where the paddlers paused for coffee and wood. Knowing only forest and muskeg, the Tlingits fell silent as the ice-scoured plains and peaks rose into view. They assuaged their mounting dread by collecting driftwood for later cooking fires. Another hour of sailing propelled the canoe over the bold line demarcating the nudge of blue-green seawater against the bay's milky turquoise, its surface textured with floating ice sculptures. The travelers set up camp on a sheltered beach in Bartlett Cove.

Smoke rising from an island shore the next day diverted the canoeists from their course. As they neared the seal hunters' camp, "an infernally black-faced Hoona" emerged from a bark hut, fired a warning shot, and demanded identification. "Missionary from Wrangell," Johnny replied. Fifteen people of varying ages poured out onto the beach, including a man with a rifle who drew Kadachan's sharp rebuke. No weapons! Didn't he know how to behave around a God's Man?

"Though the place would seem too small for two," everyone filed into the low structure—twenty-one total. Despite the cramped chamber, Muir saw ample stores of salmon and seal meat, and a variety of skins. The Hoonahs had heard of the missionary, but it seemed strange that he should come where no humans lived. It soon became apparent that the white men knew nothing about the locale, and the Stikines, little more. Charley was disoriented; the bay had changed since he had last visited. After some discussion, the clan headman proffered his services as a guide. When Young accepted, the man's wife silently assembled a duffel with a "tired blanket, a bit of matting, and some dried salmon and seal sausage made by plaiting strips of lean meat around a center strip of fat." As the white men prepared to leave, she smiled and said: "It is my husband that you are taking away. See that you bring him back." As he had on the beach at Fort Wrangell, Young promised her man's return.[40]

The ensuing week was dedicated to Muir's investigations. Gone hours before dawn, he did not return until after nightfall. He explored ice cathedrals, traversed ice cataracts, and spanned ice bridges. He noted abrasions on bare rock surfaces, movement of boulders in the valleys, patterns of glacial retreat. He studied the succession of plants that spread like a delicate carpet from the toes of glaciers: mosses, lichens, cottongrass, fireweed, ferns, sedges, willow, alder, spruce. He sketched mountain vistas, sunsets over berg water, and frozen rivers cascading to the sea. He marveled at the daily panorama of landscape so recently released from the throes of an ice plain thousands of feet thick and sung hosannas to the Creator, who allowed him to walk upon this fresh-born earth.

So consumed was Muir by the new country that any obstacle or delay evoked passionate debate. "Sternly stormy" weather was no excuse for

West Arm of Glacier Bay. Photograph by Kim Heacox. Reproduced by permission.

shying from these "terrestrial manifestations of God." When the Hoonah guide called for a midday camp only hours away from the Grand Pacific glacier, the naturalist complained bitterly about "how easily the missionary had been fooled," but Young prudently stood with guide and crew. Muir yearned to paddle ever closer to the blue walls of tidewater glaciers, but the crew held back. Their reasoning was confirmed by each explosive collapse and calving of ice cliffs and the shock waves that caused icebergs to tumble and collide. The canoe could be crushed in an instant.[41]

Transcendent as the week was for Muir, it was hell on the Tlingits.

To'watte's forbearance broke on the Sabbath, his day of rest, when a frustrated Muir rose long before "graylight" to hike into the bare, boulder-strewn mountains, and did not return after dark (see prologue). The headman was worried sick; as captain of the expedition, he felt personally responsible for the safety of each member; as a Tlingit, he feared retribution if Muir should die. No balanced person wanders off in a bleak country like this, To'watte believed, especially in a numbing downpour. To'watte and Kadachan carried pitchwood torches to the top of a nearby hill. There was no sign of the white man. Hours passed. Around midnight, someone heard footsteps in the dark; Muir's grizzled visage appeared in the firelight.

Only a witch seeks wisdom in storms and ice, To'watte declared. He abhorred the barren land, his stomach ached with fear, and he thought of the place as an ice prison. Kadachan agreed. If Muir died, he explained, they were culpable.

The mountaineer calmed them with his boundless faith and hearty assurances that good luck would prevail. For ten years, he told them, he had hiked the Sierra Nevada with nary a scratch. God watched over His people. To'watte wanted with all his heart to believe that, but he also believed Muir's penchant for risk endangered the entire group. The young man was impulsive and self-absorbed. It was not the last time To'watte would scold Glate Ankow for reckless behavior.[42]

9 :: Brotherhood

The soggy south blow that nagged at the voyagers for most of the journey died on their final evening in "Icy Bay." Air calmed, seas flattened, cloudcover dissipated. Golden beams shot through rents in the gauzy ceiling to cast a "spiritual purity upon innumerable peaks," all igniting John Muir's transcendental longing. Then came a ceiling of stars, pinpricks in the smothering black. Temperatures plunged.[1]

The Tlingits were disturbed. In normal conditions they hunted while the white men traipsed into the mountains, but they were prisoners in this lifeless landscape, compelled to stoke the fire and worry over Glate Ankow. He might not notice or even care when winter's full force bellowed from the skies. Good luck or not, To'watte knew their mission to Chilkat required many more days in an uncertain realm where the weather could be harsh and tribes hostile. If harm came to Young, To'watte declared to Muir, his blood was on Glate Ankow's hands. "It does not matter whether I live or die, but you shall not sacrifice the life of my minister." Against Muir's fervid protest, Reverend Young affirmed his captain's resolve.[2]

After reuniting the Hoonah guide with his clan, the men sailed southeast, back across the demarcation of glacial milk water into the dull, dark turquoise of Icy Strait. Instead of crossing to Hoonah, To'watte steered due east. The old headman was glad to see the dreary place recede in the wake as he tracked Icy Strait's northern coastline to its intersection with Chatham Strait. In the maze of islands that comprise Alexander Archipelago, Chatham is a broad, diagonal slash starting low from its ocean mouth off the south tip of Baranof Island and cutting nearly two hundred miles northwest to its junction with Icy Strait before shooting north another hundred miles as Lynn Canal. At its head, the great sea canyon splits into three inlets, each fed by a glacial river sizzling with salmon, each claimed and guarded by fierce defenders of the Chilkat stronghold.

Near the place where strait meets canal, To'watte landed the cedar canoe on a beach in the jigsaw islands behind Point Couverden. Men appeared out of the woods and, following a short palaver, hoisted the canoes and supplies beyond the tide's reach. Like most other remote Tlingits, these people seemed honored by the esteemed party. The Chilkats were at peace, they reassured their visitors, and safe to approach. Along the path to the headman's house, Muir noted a storage hut packed to the rafters with salmon, fish oil, and mountain-goat mutton—insurance against the hard winter ahead.

As they entered the large timber-framed dwelling, the travelers discovered the clan leader's family engaged in hooch production. Clearly embarrassed, they dismantled the still while the headman offered profuse apologies for the conditions, including, as usual, a lack of "Boston food." He told the white men that their presence gave him hope that "the light of a better day" might shine on them," and he would "gladly do whatever the white teachers told him to do and have no will of his own."[3] Reverend Young led a brief service with gifts of tobacco and rice; Muir added his usual thoughts on "the brotherhood of peoples of whatever color" and credited the headman for seeking better conditions for his tribe. Muir noted the tidy upkeep and well-behaved children, who "gazed like curious animals, but with intelligence." Their host repeatedly thanked them and promised to pray daily. His only request was that that the missionary might replace the "luck board" nailed over his door. It read: "The Lord will bless those who do his will. When you rise in the morning and when you retire at night, give him thanks. Heccla Hockla Popla." The headman explained that if they gave him a new one, he would present the old board to a rival tribe that once tried to steal it, now a gift of spite. He invited them to stay the night in his house, but the white men feared "wee beasties" that might run about, so refused the offer.[4]

Later in the evening, Kadachan and To'watte approached Muir and Young at their tent in the beach grass. They were offended by the white men's response to their hosts' hospitable gestures. The right thing to do was share a meal and sleep under the same roof. "If this is the way you are to do up at Chilkat, we will be ashamed of you." Properly chastised, missionary and naturalist promised to "behave like good Chilkats" and to eat whatever was served.

A steady north headwind the next day meant constant, strenuous paddling up Lynn Canal. From Point Couverden, the portside view was filled with the Chilkat Range rising gradually into a procession of cirques and sharp-carved ridges flanked by year-round snowfields. As the ocean corridor narrowed—Chilkats on the western flank, Coast Range on the east—mountain slopes plummeted from six or seven thousand feet to sea level, confining the tides to rock-walled passages.

At times the canoe barely seemed to make progress, but the crew was undaunted. Even the white men, often awash in expostulation, were hushed by the hard work. Young gazed past the spray to the highest mountains ahead, designing sermons for heathen Chilkats. On his mental palette, Muir sketched the grand entrance into Lynn Canal on a day so clear that all glacial evidence is laid bare. Previously permitted only cloud-hole glimpses of Glacier Bay, Muir was exhilarated by his views into the massive fjord.

For days, the paddlers labored head-on against turbulence. To'watte kept the canoe two or three hundred feet offshore away from breakers that flung foamy knots of kelp and bladder wrack on granite boulder beaches. From his lurching vantage, Muir observed wind-sculpted hemlocks gripping rocks and cliffs hammered by a churning sea. He gazed back into U-shaped valleys where glaciers still devoured mountains. During periodic landings, Muir followed the vegetation succession up from the carpet-strips of autumn-rust cinquefoil and goose-tongue in the high tide seaweed mounds. A few feet farther, desiccated beach-grass shuddered under a skeletal alder hedge. Ten paces inland was a wall of green. An interlocking phalanx of spruce and hemlock marched into lower glacial valleys and up sharp slopes until it succumbed to alpine tundra at around two thousand feet in elevation. Muir noted how "remarkably well-developed" the biggest trees were in the lower stands.

About three hours out of Point Couverden the tide turned, forcing the canoeists to seek the shelter of a pocket cove. While the crew set up camp, Muir wandered into the forest, where he found a large patch of yellow cedar, a species prevalent in the southern reaches of Southeast Alaska but rare in the north. Prized for its durability and range of use, yellow cedar was the preferred carving wood among Northwest Coast artisans and canoe builders (and still is the wood of choice today). These wispy eighty-foot specimens, however, hardly matched the prodigious cedars of Prince of Wales Island in Alaska and of Haida Gwaii in British Columbia, at least ten days' journey south by canoe. Lynn Canal soil is thin, and the winters are bitter. As for this grove, Muir noted that nearly every tree showed the scars from limbs hacked by Tlingit travelers for use as paddles and fiber.

Back at tidewater, passing Native canoeists noticed Muir perched on a sea cliff. The father held a child in his arms as he steered the canoe close to shore. He reported bad news: Sitka Jack and his relatives were in Klukwan for a big potlatch where hooch was "flowing like water." The Hoonah man predicted renewed interclan hostilities. The news was "depressing" to the preacher Young, who feared for his crew, especially To'watte, who had killed Chilkats in battles a half-century earlier. Tlingit law demanded no less than his death. Compared to this situation, the drunken reception in Angoon felt benign.[5]

Despite To'watte's counsel against night travel, the white men insisted on proceeding when the tide turned after dark. For hours, paddlers muscled their craft into a black headwind until the sheltered waters of Saint James Bay opened on port. The canoe glided up to a beach encampment just as snow began to fall. The three bark shelters belonged to Chilkat families in their last mountain goat camp of the season. Booming voices demanded to know the strangers' business. Kadachan's equally powerful voice announced their divine mission. Both parties took to the huts for a 3:00 a.m. parley while Johnny and Charley set up the tents. As the weary travelers prepared to bed down, To'watte approached his preacher and "read him a lecture at the first opportunity." If the white men were in a hurry, he said, they should start in early morning. But to "travel in the night like thieves" was untenable. Muir and Young vowed that they would approach Chilkat territory in daylight, buoyed by faith and good luck.[6]

The "hard, dull work" of paddling the next day pushed the party about twelve miles to a protected "rocky nook" behind which To'watte ducked his canoe. They camped with a Hoonah family that offered the strangers salmon, walnut-sized potatoes, and a "big tin pail full of berries and grease," which the crew wolfed down at an "extravagant rate of speed."[7]

The wind changed by morning, oily cloud-sheets whipping up from the south. A full day's sail would drive the canoe to its destination, but Young forbade work on Sundays, a dictum Muir considered "weak and craven out here in the wilds where God himself works on Sunday."[8] Headwinds and breaking swells on Monday compelled Johnny and Charley to pull long oars as much to prevent backsliding as to crawl forward. Five more southbound canoes sailed past, likely returning from the party in Klukwan, but conditions prohibited any exchange. Muir pressed for Davidson Glacier, a goal To'watte thought unwise; about an hour's sail from the glacier, the skipper

DLEIT AAN<u>K</u>ÁAWU

pulled into a cove on Sullivan Island. Muir swallowed his disappointment by looking for a flat spot to sleep on and found a human skeleton embedded in the moss. The Native crew was hardly impressed. The remains belonged to a slave, they explained, whose body was discarded by the owner. Rather than bury their dead as Christian-influenced Indians did, Chilkats still cremated their loved ones; slaves' bodies were tossed in the woods. Muir completed the "pitiful work" of burying the remains.[9]

A favorable breeze the next morning sent the travelers to a beach at the toe of Davidson Glacier, "a broad flood reaching out two or three miles into the canal with wonderful effect." Like readers from coast to coast, Muir knew of the "grandly descending" ice fan from George Davidson's sketches reproduced in newspapers.[10] Professor Davidson saw the glacier first in 1867, then two years later when he returned to observe the total solar eclipse in Klukwan. Recording the astronomical event was simply Davidson's job, but for the northern Tlingits, such a visit by the "great tyees" signaled personal access to a powerful nation. A decade later, Muir offered a compelling vision of fraternity that the Tlingits believed guaranteed access to improved living conditions.

The canoe landed at Glacier Point on the exposed pebble beach that bordered the fanlike periphery of ice. A few paces above the high-tide mark, a dense forested margin up to two hundred feet wide stretched three miles across the glacier's face. The final approach to the glacier was marked by boulders and silt ponds. Along portions of the frozen snout, one might easily hop onto ice for a traverse of the glittering mass to its origins in the high "mountain fountains." Other sections rose in pale blue cliffs a hundred feet high or more and split into coxcombs and promontories which, no matter how huge and solid, eventually crumpled and fell into the muck. Muir yearned to explore all of it but complained that he was "fenced off" by the interlocking forest hedge. He hardly had time to sketch, much less to investigate.[11]

A bare whisper of breeze at their backs aided the canoeists' progress into Chilkat Inlet. About an hour out of Yandeist'a<u>k</u>yé, To'watte landed his craft on a beach where Muir's companions proceeded to groom "beyond recognition." The Tlingits washed, perfumed, and oiled themselves, cut one another's hair, and made "a complete change in their clothing, even to white shirts, new boots, new hats, and bright neckties." The preacher donned a "Sunday sermon suit from a satchel and washed and combed and looking-glassed to a rather ridiculous extent." Owning "nothing dressy," Muir adorned his cap with an eagle feather. The white men ran an American flag up the stern pole and hoisted the sails. Supine, the canoe glided into a realm of hostiles and heroes.[12]

John Muir's Sketch of the Davidson Glacier. Illustration, item 1.3.1.1.04, Shone Collection, Holt-Atherton Special Collections, University of the Pacific, Stockton, California.

Contemporary Chilkat elders chuckle at Muir's implications of his colleagues' excessive vanity. Given the rumors of war, they say, those men weren't just dressing up—they were "fixin'" to die.[13]

:: "I HAVE NEVER UNTIL NOW HEARD A WHITE MAN SPEAK"

As they drew closer to the inlet's head, the canoeists saw smoke lines dangling over the north corner of the river mouth indicating Yandeist'a<u>k</u>yé, gateway to the valley, where "everything from afar drifts ashore." On starboard passed the shoreline of Chilkat Peninsula featuring bonsai hemlock on rock tuffets, protected coves, and wild-rose meadows. Portside, two miles of lakelike ocean surface stretched to the opposite shore, where steep mountains slashed the western horizon. A tight, green weave of alder and devil's club covered the lower slopes before surrendering to alpine meadows that soon gave way to scree fields, knife ridges, and black, granite towers that loomed more than a mile over the canoe. The geology was just like Yosemite, Muir thought, except for the glaciers everywhere and the seawater standing a hundred miles from open ocean and diluted by the cement-hued blood of ancient ice.

   DLEIT AAN<u>K</u>ÁAWU

"We were in sight long before we landed," Muir deduced from a man they saw standing on a beach a few miles from the village. "Who are you? What are your names? What do you want?" he asked in "a heavy, far-reaching voice." Stickeen Johnny responded with equal volume: "A great preacher-chief and a great ice-chief have come to bring you a good message." The man shouted the message to another man waiting a quarter-mile down the beach who relayed it to a "living telephone" line that stretched all the way to the headman's house.[14]

Mountains crowd the banks where the milewide Chilkat River empties into the sea. Dozens of channels jigsaw a sandy delta drowned twice daily by high tides. To'watte nosed his boat into the large starboard channel and called for all hands to paddle hard into the upstream current. A quarter mile from the village, another man ran to the water's edge.

"*Gusuwah-eh?*" he asked. Who are you?[15] Moments after Johnny's answer echoed down the line, thirty or forty men fired a volley of musket shot, some zinging dangerously near the canoe. The startled white men stopped paddling.

"*Ut-ha!*" barked To'watte. "*Ut-ha!*"[16] Young and Muir didn't have to understand Tlingit to interpret the urgency of their captain's tone. Gunshots were a good sign, Kadachan explained. To stop paddling might be mistaken as intent to return fire, transforming the celebratory gesture into a tragedy. Stray shots whizzed by as the paddlers drew near the front landing. To'watte spoke in low, mournful English: "My wife said my old enemies would kill me. Never mind." He put his hand on his heart. "I hope they shoot me here."[17]

From a lawn chair at her ancestral fish camp on the Chilkat River in 2013, Klukwan elder Sally Burratin ("Grandma Sally") recalled the incident as told to her by her uncle, Austin Hammond. One of the welcome party saw a rifle in the canoe and shouted, "What are you trying to do? Where are you going? What you doing with that gun?'"

"We're here to do Christian stuff!" Johnny said.

"What you got that gun in the boat for if it's Christian stuff?"

"Oh—just for bears!"

"Protection! Oh, come ashore then."[18]

The crowd of warriors shouted at the approaching visitors, then disappeared behind houses. At least twelve timber-framed structures stood above the beach, each one home to two or more extended families, including the large house in the middle owned by Chilkoot sháade háni Daanawáak. As the canoe prow touched sand, the men dashed back down to the river chanting: "Hoo-hoo! Hoo-hoo!" The welcome party surrounded the canoe, lifted it into the air, and trotted craft and occupants up the beach to the headman's

Sally Burratin. Photograph by author.

doorstep. Muir marveled at nearby children who ran races and swam in the frigid river, seemingly uninterested in the strangers.[19]

Burratin waved an arm expansively from the river to her camp. "So they came ashore. Bunch a guys come out. Ordered them to stay in the boat. They lifted it on their shoulders and carried everything to Daanawáak's doorstep. Can you imagine that? You think they're gonna play pussyfoot with these guys? They *better* start preachin'."

The grandma's ruddy cheeks rose into a victor's grin: "Ha!"[20]

Muir and his men filed into the imposing fifty-by-fifty-foot post-and-plank house. They strode onto the upper tier encircling the interior wall, stepped down to the middle platform, and were led to a figure sitting alone on the first-level floor.

In calico shirt and Chilkat blanket, the headman faced the central house pit, staring into the fire even as he shook hands with the white men. Family members scurried about their routines for several minutes, completely ignoring the visitors. For at least three decades, Daanawáak had greeted white travelers to his village—Russians, HBC men, U.S. generals—but he had never met a God's Man. He knew one was coming because two years earlier, his nephew and lieutenant, Lunaat, requested a missionary when he escorted Sheldon Jackson to Port Simpson. Now as Stickeen Johnny introduced the party and their intent, Daanawáak felt unprepared.

The sháade háni's weathered face turned to his guests, then back to the fire. Flames glinted in the oversized spectacles from which his name was derived. His trademark Union cap was slung low, and his slender frame, bent to the flickering light. After a long silence, the Chilkoot leader spoke: "I am troubled. It is customary when strangers visit us to offer them food in case they might be hungry, and I was about to do so when I remembered that the food of you honorable white chiefs is so much better than mine that I am ashamed to offer it." Hearing John's translation, Reverend Young assured the headman they would be honored to dine with him. Daanawáak straightened and stood, visibly relieved. He called out for a meal. A young man acting as steward repeated the commands, setting the household into motion.[21]

The hospitality question resolved, the hosts wanted to talk. Other "chiefs" joined the circle, including an outspoken middle-aged man who was probably Lunaat. He stood while Daanawáak sat on the floor, speaking so much like "a polished diplomat that all polish motive was hidden." At first, their appearance surprised the villagers, Daanawáak said. All previous white men appeared in summer, and then "only to trade and gain what they could." But these visitors were different. Anyone who braved the "cold and dangerous" season in a canoe must have great courage and noble intentions. The northern tribes were ignorant of white ways, the speaker confessed. Worse, he was too old to learn but was comforted to know that a teacher was coming for the children's sake. The missionary's arrival was also timely as Daanawáak sought a favor. Because a Chilkoot woman had died from alcohol provided by Hutsnuwu people, he was about to lead a group to Angoon to exact retribution in blankets or blood money. If the God's Man gave them permission, the operation might proceed peaceably. He "begged" the whites to pray that no one be killed.[22]

In neither journal nor memoir does Muir record Young's response. Neither does the naturalist recount with much enthusiasm the next event, a supper Young declared a "never-to-be-forgotten banquet." Served in huge, blue HBC washbasins, "the feast of fat things" commenced with dried salmon in an oil dressing derived from the annual run of local smelt called eulachon. High in lipids, the oil was, ounce for ounce, the most valuable trade item in the North. The headman was serving his best. In a diplomatic ploy to deflect the rancid paste, Muir and Young asked for grease in separate bowls. Basins were removed, cleaned, and returned with large hunks of deer back fat floating in eulachon oil. The third bowl brimmed with small potatoes in more eulachon oil (Muir called it "pelican oil"). Leftovers were contained and taken out to the travelers' canoe, where boys guarded the food against dogs and bears. Dessert bowls of red-orange rosehips drizzled in seal grease inspired Muir to elbow Young. "Mon, mon," he said in his thickest Scottish brogue. "I'm fashed we'll be floppin' aboot i' the sea, whiles, wi' flippers an' forked tails."[23]

Among those serving the group was a "good-looking" young woman whose attentions were placed solely on Daanawáa_k. Only she cooked his food or lit his pipe. Muir discovered she was a slave, a custom still practiced "among the richest of the headmen," and from what he saw, her "servitude seemed by no means galling." Muir and Young agreed that she was treated like a family member, a status affirmed by Daanawáa_k's promise to "dress her well" and enroll her in school when the church sent a teacher. "Formerly," Muir added, slaves were sacrificed on "great occasions" such as completion of a totem pole or house, but now they were apparently beloved. Civil War or not, each Northerner was sufficiently moved to share his perceptions of this apparently kinder, gentler form of slavery in his memoirs.[24]

When the dishes were cleared, someone announced the imminent arrival of the Chilkat sháade háni Koh'klux and his Klukwan entourage. Three or four hours passed as the house became "crowded to suffocation," but no Koh'klux. In his welcoming speech, Daanawáa_k reiterated the tribe's needs by using the same metaphor and speech structure Young had heard from other Tlingit leaders: "A dark night, a canoe, a trip in the storm without a paddle or sail, men lost, starving and in danger; then a light, a sheltered harbor; food and comfort; the usual round of compliments."[25]

Young responded with the first of many sermons he delivered over the next four days, rehearsed since seminary, tailored to save wild souls: We are all sinners. As sinners we are doomed to burn in hell, but there is one way out: God's way. He loved us so much that he sent his only Son to tell us the way. Sinners killed the Son, but He still loved them to the end, then rose into heaven to be with His Father. If you follow His way, you can go there, too. Pray and live according to the Way, and eternal life is yours. "As always," Young wrote, his Tlingit audience became "motionless and avid" when he described the Resurrection.

Likely, too, Young issued his usual strong warning against the Old Ways of shamanism, slavery, and potlatching. He promised severe penalties for manufacture of hooch. First articulated in Wrangell a year earlier, Young's well-traveled speech posed a fatal dichotomy for all forbidden acts: "Are you going to have the friendship of the captains of the war vessels and of the government of the United States, or are you going to be enemies of these great men?"[26] Come away from darkness, brothers, into the light.

"Gunalchéesh ho ho," said Daanawáa_k as Young concluded. Thank you

very much. Applause rumbled under many feet tapping floorboards but faded quickly as To'watte stood and said, "Amen."

Surrounded by enemies with unresolved issues, the elder Stikine felt the sting of angry glares from those offended by his presence. Some gestured at To'watte and uttered short, sharp threats. He bowed his head and prayed in a voice seasoned by a lifetime of oratory. The long pause after his "Amen" allowed To'watte to gaze into the crowd before he launched into a speech that, noted Young, was a "model of kindliness and diplomacy."

"We are not different tribes," he began. "We are all one family. God is our father; Mr. Young and Mr. Muir are our brothers. No one is better than the other. All are equal.

All remembrance of former hurts and anger and war is wiped out by this new Word. Let us be at peace. If I have offended any Chilkat, I ask his pardon."[27]

Whether To'watte borrowed from Muir or Muir from To'watte, each recognized the rhetorical power of brotherhood as an ethical standard proven by one's capacity to forgive.

Johnny and Kadachan followed with several hymns while Charley, To'watte, and Young distributed tobacco and small gifts.

After an acceptable silence, Daanawáak turned to Glate Ankow and asked him to speak. Cook-fire shadows flickered in Muir's shaggy face. He shook his head and muttered a few self-deprecations. Daanawáak repeated his message to Stickeen Johnny, who conveyed to Muir the gravity of the headman's request. The naturalist's reluctance was fed by a packed audience starved for news of the Man-God he had once revered but now rejected. Muir's God was manifest in mountains, ice, and forests—works as divine as Reverend Young's Bible. Muir's message was incongruent with the revival, Muir admitted to Johnny, because he thought the region's natural wonders at least "as interesting as the gospel."

The Chilkoot elder insisted. He wondered about the eclipse that drew George Davidson to the Chilkat Valley, and how the moon controlled the rise and fall of tides. And what of Glate Ankow's icy mission? What secrets did he expect to reveal by exploring the very places Tlingits usually avoided?

"Daanawáak called him out," said Sally Burratin. Koh'klux was nowhere to be seen, and the audience was unimpressed with the program thus far. Though most thought Reverend Young preachy and boring, the old headman patiently endured his sermons, glad to hear about eternal life. But like most audience members, Daanawáak brimmed with curiosity about Glate Ankow. Like Davidson, the glacier walker possessed knowledge about the natural world that had long mystified Tlingits.

"Grandma Sally" heard the story many times in her youth, but she insisted that elders "never said one word, not one word" about the Reverend S. Hall Young.[28]

The Ice Chief stood. From his central position at the hearth, Muir scanned the room. A large and intricate totemic design framed the low doorway in the front wall. Massive timbers comprised the post-and-beam frame sheathed by ten-foot adzed spruce planks. Fire threw light on a sea of faces and fine regalia. Ornate patterns leapt from the robes and blankets wrapped around the hundreds of "eager intelligent listeners" crammed into the room. Even the smallest child was hushed and alert. Then the "cracking, tearing" sound of wall planks wrested from the building to accommodate onlookers. Men hung from log beams, attuned to every word.[29]

Why was he here?

Ice.

But ice is an impediment, a destroyer.

Quite the opposite, Muir countered. From ice, all good things emerge. In moderate voice and personable affect, he delivered the "glacier gospel" with the sincerity of a white man mindful of his ice-tempered audience. Ice is the mother of mountains, rivers, forests, animals. Humans, too, are nurtured by glaciers. That's what brings me to your wonderful land. I must know more about ice to discover how it moves mountains to bring us life. In the blue catacombs of a glacier I have seen a great, crystal heart beating to the eternal rhythm of a living planet. The blood flowing from that glacial heart pursues an ocean-bound destiny, taking with it a pulverized mountain. The greatest miracle comes from the life it brings—trees, plants, salmon, eagles, bears, whales . . . and you. I am honored to be a guest of such powerful hosts. Your generosity will be rewarded in Heaven when you heed the preacher's advice to follow a higher calling.

Then I spoke of the brotherhood of man—how we were all children of one father; sketched the characteristics of the different races of mankind, showing that no matter how far apart their countries were, how they differed in color, size, language, etc. and no matter how different and how various the ways in which they got a living, that the white man and all the people of the world were essentially alike, that we all had ten fingers and toes and our bodies were the same, whether white, brown, black or different colors, and speak different languages. If one family of Tlingit boys and girls were scattered far abroad and raised in different places, they would forget their own language, their habits, and their looks would be colored by climate. If they all happened to meet again, they would seem strange to one another.[30]

In a rare emotional admission, Muir confessed that his hosts "seemed my own people and though I had been with them but a day I seemed to know them always and that I felt like leaving the whites and living with them to teach them and do them good." Muir watched a rare smile spread across To'watte's stoic face. Glate Ankow's speech affirmed his own brotherhood message. Despite being surrounded by old enemies, the Stikine headman began to believe he might survive.[31]

More waiting. Speakers were drained, travelers were bone weary, but no one left the room. Some chuckled and pointed to a boy hanging from the rafters, fast asleep. Before dinner, runners had been dispatched twenty miles upriver to Klukwan, so a time lag was calculated. Reverend Young considered the delay a political maneuver, certain that Koh'klux was trying "to impress us with his dignity as supreme chief."[32]

Close to midnight someone announced the arrival of the Chilkat sháade háni.

When the entryway was cleared, the man Young called the "worst old savage of Alaska" strutted into the room, elegantly attired with chinchilla robe hanging from his broad shoulders. A Chilkat entourage followed in the proud headman's wake as he advanced toward the firepit. The audience adjusted to the packed conditions without complaint.

With a six-foot frame draped in fine regalia and a face ravaged by gunshot, Koh'klux demanded respect. He extended a hand to Daanawáak, who accepted with a solemn expression, then to Muir, Young, and his long-absent son, Kadachan. He passed To'watte without a glance. Before he sat on his designated bale of HBC blankets, Koh'klux turned and flared his robe to display an inscription stitched in bold letters: "To Chief Shathitch, from his friend William H. Seward." Young and Muir shared surprised glances, but in subsequent writings only the preacher mentioned the robe or even the Chilkat leader's appearance. In a few words, Koh'klux honored his hosts, thanked the white men for their visit, invited the party to preach in Klukwan, and abruptly exited.[33]

For three more days, Reverend Young preached "from early morning until midnight, relieved periodically by Muir and the responsive speeches of the natives." House and clan leaders offered speeches of gratitude and remembrance. In a room bristling with orators, Muir was subdued.

An infant's unrestrained howls through most of one evening's services prompted Muir's inquiry. Stickeen Johnny spoke with a woman who said the mother had died and no one was available to nurse an extra child. The translator spoke in a matter of fact tone: "Maybe one, two more day it cry, then it die." A distressed Muir ordered Johnny to fetch all the condensed milk in the canoe; he returned with eight cans. Muir bathed and fed the baby and carried him around the interior of the great house until sleep came. In the morning Muir gave the remaining milk to the headman. Touched by the gesture, Daanawáak offered him the child, but Glate Ankow gently refused. The boy should grow up as a Tlingit. A woman awaited him in California, he explained, soon to be his wife. Her family expected him to run the farm. Though they hoped for children someday, he could not return to San Francisco with one in his arms.

Tlingit protocol dictated a different level of obligation. Seven years later, a woman approached Reverend Young in Wrangell and presented him with the boy. Since Muir would not take him, Daanawáak decreed that if the boy survived, he belonged to the preacher. The woman pushed the youngster toward the man. "He is not ours any longer. He is yours." Young accepted his new charge, whom he christened John after the man who saved his life. The boy attended several grades in Wrangell and completed his training at the Presbyterian school in Sitka.[34]

On the fourth day in Yandeist'akyé, Daanawáak asked Muir to be their missionary, promising him as many wives as he desired and enough boys to remove all stones from his path. Again the explorer demurred. Though he might lose himself forever in this ice-sculpted land, social obligations led him elsewhere.

In the afternoon, Daanawáak and other Chilkoot leaders escorted their guests to Deishú, the narrow isthmus joining the Chilkat Peninsula with the mainland, for the purpose of selecting a mission site. Among them was Skandoo'o, the copper-haired shaman who had long opposed missionaries. He said nothing to the preacher but sided with Daanawáak on the ideal site for the Presbyterians—an area of soggy meadows dotted by old spruce. Sandwiched between two great inlets, the site that eventually became the community of Haines seemed fine to Young. It had fresh water, open land, seawater access, and a spectacular view.

"Perfect for a white-man town," chuckled elder Ed Warren at a Klukwan History Day event in 2011. "They like scenery. But you notice no Tlingit living there. Why is that?" A smile spread across the octogenarian's face. "We got the good spots, the strategic locations. Klukwan, Chilkoot, Dyea, even Yandeist'akyé are more sheltered than Deishú (Haines townsite), all with southern exposure and close to salmon. In Deishú, snow's deep and winds pound you from any direction. But you don't argue with free land."[35]

Muir declined the tour, opting to climb G̲eisán, the steep mountain that towers over the village. He judged the thirty-seven-hundred-foot summit of what is now called Mount Ripinsky to be fifty-five-hundred feet, an easy mistake when the tree line is about two thousand feet. In the foreground of one sketch, Davidson Glacier pours between towering gargoyle peaks, then spreads in a great fan within a few hundred feet of tidewater. Another gives a view of the Chilkat Valley with five glaciers squeezing out between bordering peaks to surrender their meltwater to the gray, churning river. From the same viewpoint today, Chilkat Valley glaciers are gone and the Davidson is an icy staircase tucked into a canyon six miles from the sea.

The same rhetorical routine closed religious services each night: Daanawáak̲ or Lunaat requested that Muir speak, but he resisted. Only when they prodded him with natural history questions did Glate Ankow rise to respond.

On the final evening the audience was especially interested to hear Muir talk about the contrasting intentions of white men. They must be judged on their merits, he said, just as Native brothers who built reputations on the quality of their behavior. One's humanity was evident in his "kindness and good manners," Muir declared, a statement that drew a chorus of affirmations from his earnest listeners.[36]

At the close, the eldest shaman rose to his feet for the first time all week. This was Karskarz, sháade háni and principle íx̲t' of Chilkoot village. The close relative of Skandoo'o was a benevolent and wise man who led a village that never quite recovered from smallpox a century earlier. "With a high wrinkled forehead, large, strong Roman nose and light-colored skin," Karskarz appeared highly dignified to the white men.

> I am an old man but I am glad to listen to those strange things you tell, and they may well be true, for what is more wonderful than the flight of birds in the air? I remember the first white man I ever saw. Since that long, long-ago time I have seen many, but never until now have I ever truly known and felt a white man's heart. All the white men I have heretofore met wanted to get something from us. They wanted furs and they wished to pay for them as small a price as possible. They all seemed to be seeking their own good—not our good. I might say all my life I have never until now heard a white man speak. It has always seemed to me that while trying to talk to traders and those seeking gold-mines that it

Sailboats Fishing for Hooligan at 4-mile. Photograph, A3 no. 61, Haines Sheldon Museum, Alaska.

was like speaking to a person across a broad stream that was running fast over stones and making so loud a noise that scarce a single word could be heard. But now, for the first time, the Indian and the white man are on the same side of the river, eye to eye, heart to heart.[37]

In his short speech, the íxt' certified Glate Ankow's capacity for a collaborative relationship. After a century of defending the aaní from white incursions, during that November week the Chilkoot-Chilkat leadership changed its attitude. Muir's vision of brotherhood, a promise to uphold the group first, fit with tribal ways.

"He was the first white man who didn't want something from us," said Kim Strong, former Klukwan village council chair, in 2007. Muir showed humility and kindness, speaking in a collegial tone as he praised their "foodful" country and offered new insights into ice, tides, and white men.[38]

From her fish camp in the Chilkat River, Sally Burratin recalled how elders said that Muir projected "more of God's power" than "what's his face." Although she often heard the story from Uncle Austin Hammond and other elders, none mentioned his companion. In an audience of master orators, she suspected, some interpreted Young's evangelical inflection as unnatural and disingenuous. They had never heard a stranger speak to them at such length in a style so peculiar. One thing historians never mention, Burratin stage-whispered, eyes wide, is that for the entire week, Muir and the Natives "didn't know they were speaking English and Tlingit." The

     DLEIT AAN<u>K</u>ÁAWU

round-faced woman leaned in, gaze locked into mine: "They understood each other. Never forget it."[39]

An incidental boost for Muir may have been his brevity. Often characterized as rapturous and long-winded, the eco-prophet gave shorter speeches in Yandeist'a<u>k</u>yé. According to Joe Hotch, Muir's restraint may have further contributed to his perception by and standing among the Tlingits. Although Tlingit public speaking is famous for length, in Chilkat tradition "you make your talk as short as you can." Some speeches are longer than others, as appropriate to the topic or circumstance. Still, Hotch maintains, "If you talk too long it's like words piling up. If you talk too long, it costs us money. Recognize everybody, thank them, honor them, talk for a little bit, then move on."[40]

At the close of the final night, translator Stickeen Johnny told Glate Ankow that the audience felt warm toward him, that he "knows how to talk and beats the preacher far." Brotherhood bound Muir to his listeners. Linking one's destiny with an audience, wrote rhetorician Kenneth Burke, builds common cause, the "consubstantiality" necessary to move a group to action. Just as Muir would use his rhetorical powers to convert citizens to environmental causes, nature's evangelist inspired the conservative Chilkats to welcome their American brothers.[41]

Glate Ankow repeatedly turned down his new friends' proffered gifts, but by week's end selected an item. A hundred-pound rock near the headman's house caught his eye—a grotesque beast's head, surface burnished to brightness and pocked by "nut-shaped hollows." It was the same weird boulder General Howard had wanted two years earlier, a bid Daanawáa<u>k</u> had rejected. Judging it to be an aerolite (meteorite), Muir asked the headman if he might take a fragment for testing. If it was, in fact, extraterrestrial, Glate Ankow might wish to buy it.

The meteorite was a thing of great value to the tribe, Daanawáa<u>k</u> explained. Over a century ago, the father of one of the oldest living villagers watched it fall from the sky, so he mounted an expedition to Chilkat Pass, about fifty miles distant. Five generations since the man hauled the space-sculpture back to Yandeist'a<u>k</u>yé it was less a cosmic reminder to locals than a symbol of the fortitude and wisdom of Old Ones. Parting with the item was not possible without ample time and cautious deliberation. From the nickel-plated mass, Muir chipped a sliver that he wrapped in cloth for transport to the California Mining Bureau. Daanawáa<u>k</u> promised to refrain from selling the specimen to anyone until he heard from Muir.[42]

Koh'klux's invitation to hold services in Klukwan hung in the air unanswered. Acceptance would extend their late season journey at least four days. To'watte worried that bad blood marred his relationship with Chilkats and that locals held a grudge against him for a careless insult uttered years earlier. Rumors of hooch-induced violence added traction to To'watte's growing fears. Runners from Klukwan eventually confirmed To'watte's suspicions. The Chilkat sháade háni welcomed all but the Stikine headman. Further, the liquor was flowing. Koh'klux's brother-in-law, Sitka Jack, remained in the village with a keg and was prone to reciprocating To'watte's slur with blood.

After considerable discussion with the crew, the white men reluctantly came to terms with the possibility of trouble upriver. Once the decision was made, Muir advocated sailing out that day. Ice sheets drifting on the river confirmed the creeping chill. The fair breeze would scoot the canoe southward and out of Lynn Canal in half the time it took to come up. The crew, "who loved dearly to doze and eat in those big square houses," favored a three-day delay. The men settled on a ten o'clock departure the next morning.[43]

The canoe left on an outgoing tide, sail stretched taut by a steady north breeze. Reverend Young carried a note from Dannawáak verifying that the white men had met with him and departed alive, insurance that if they perished, he was blameless. In his journal that day, Muir reflected on the traits of his "warlike and hospitable friends," whose lifeways seemed so much more authentic and humane than those of civilized folk. To his Chilkat-Chilkoot hosts Muir attributed the same sort of superior qualities that made all wild things more desirable than domestic ones. Children were never scolded or punished, yet seemed quiet and obedient. Multiple-family households encouraged cooperation in contrast to the "civilized selfishness" Muir disdained in modern humanity. More satisfied, confident, and *natural* than any American—Native or otherwise—he had ever known, the Tlingits met a standard for Native Americans (and Scotsmen) that he had set in boyhood.

"It is a common saying that savages respect only power," he opined. "These seem literally to kiss the rod and love it, and therefore need it seldom."[44]

:: "WHAT RAVEN CAN SAVE ME?"

Winter flung the cedar canoe from the immense sea canyon. Though pitched by frothing rollers, To'watte's steady hand kept the craft on course for the eastern shore, into Berner's Bay and to inside channels farther south. In the protected waters near present-day Juneau, the travelers encountered several small groups of Tlingits—mostly Auk and Taku—many in the process of making, transporting, or consuming hooch. The crew openly despised the Auk, whom To'watte called "dogs." Months earlier, a rogue Auk force had been repelled from Stikine by club warfare, exacerbating long-held tensions. Against To'watte's recommendation, the white men paid a visit to the Auk headman, who apologized for the drunken behavior of his people and requested a service. Young obliged, but the Stikine elder refused to participate.[45]

Beyond another short prayer meeting with a few Taku at another camp, Young's missionary impulses were dampened by the flagrant use of alcohol. In the evening of the third day, the canoeists heaved ashore to find the first white person they had seen in a month: a jolly, drunken Irish prospector who lied about everything. The travelers moved on.

Two days out of Fort Wrangell, To'watte located a comfortable campsite on the north side of Point Vanderpeut, a long, narrow point protruding into Frederick Sound. Two hours before dawn, the paddlers set out to round the narrow peninsula. They began in flat water, but by the time the canoe reached the point, a south gale "lashed the Sound into white-cap waves." Passage was complicated further by a shallow reef that extended a mile beyond the point, now a frothing seawall.

What happens next depends on which white man you trust to tell the tale.

"We cannot round the reef in this gale," Young remembered To'watte saying. "We must turn back and camp."

Glate Ankow heard differently. "Though cautious," he journaled, the Stikine headman "determined to break through the ring of foam." Amidst pitching seas, To'watte guided the canoe parallel to the reef until he located a narrow notch between two boulders and, with expert timing and grace, caught a large roller and surfed between rocky obstacles into the calmer lee. Later that night around the campfire, according to Muir, To'watte told stories about similar close calls in his youth.

A dozen years after Muir's death, Young relayed details perhaps more consistent with the men's typical behaviors.

"As usual," To'watte's discretion drew protests from Muir. No need to delay so close to home, the Scotsman argued. "Go on and make a further effort to get around the reef." Admitting that he, too, was eager for home, Young urged his captain ahead to "see if we cannot make it." "Inch by inch," the canoe crawled the length of the reef, sharp eyes searching for a gap. When south headwinds blew hard enough to stop their progress entirely, Muir shouted, "Keep on going! Cross the reef and get along."

Stickeen Johnny interpreted To'watte's sharp response. "He say it's dangerous; the canoe will be wrecked."

"Ah, you are all cowards," Muir cried. "Go across, go across."

Upon hearing the translation, To'watte replied instantly. "Very well, if we die you die, too," and steered the canoe's bow toward the reef. When the white men ceased paddling as the canoe scraped past roaring rocks, the wizened captain yelled orders made plain in any language: "Paddle you fools, paddle!"

At precisely the right moment, according to Young, a large wave heaved them over the gnashing rock teeth and into calm water. Old To'watte steered the canoe into a protected cove, stepped onto the wet sand, and called to Muir. "You know many things," he declared through the translator, "I do not." Towatte bluntly explained:

> You can tell us about the sun and stars and the great world outside; you have traveled on the steam horse to many lands, but you *do not* know Alaska and her waters. Many times you acted like a silly child. If we had listened to you we would not be alive now. You forced us to cross that reef when we were taking our lives in our hands. Perhaps you, Charley, John, and Kadachan might have swum to shore if our canoe had been smashed, but Mr. Young and I are not strong, and I am old, and we would have been drowned. Would you be happy now on the shore with us lying among the breakers? Hereafter, let me manage this canoe. Don't act like a fool anymore.

Despite a characteristic blindness to his own faults, Muir was abashed. "Meek as a child," the naturalist silently endured the headman's scolding and, at the conclusion, acknowledged his foolish behavior.[46]

The remaining two days' travel passed without Glate Ankow's usual harangue.

Landing at Wrangell on November 20 brought a brief outpouring of relief from worried wives and families before the voyagers faced overdue obligations. Keenly aware of the dark, sloppy months ahead, the Tlingit men attended to house repairs, firewood, and food stocks. When not consumed by his ill wife and baby, Young sought to rebuild the faltering membership of his little church. Satisfied that the mountains were "locked for the winter," Muir organized his notes and composed *Bulletin* articles as cold rain on the roof became slush, ice, and finally deep, white drifts.[47]

For a man who chided miners for their ignorance of the natural world, Muir's cautious boosterism in his essay "Alaska Gold Fields," seems antithetical. Composed in the restrained language of science, the piece nonetheless prodded would-be gold rushers to head north: "The gold of Alaska is still in the ground," Muir opened. "Probably not one vein of placer in a thousand has yet been touched by the prospector's pick . . . all its mineral wealth about as darkly hidden as when it was covered by the ice-mantle of the glacial period. But light sooner or later is sure to come." Muir predicted that having emptied the Nevada and California mountains of riches, "thousands of sturdy miners" would soon push northward to "make the land tell its worth."

Systematically, the naturalist reviewed past and ongoing mining efforts in Southeast Alaska, his account replete with tantalizing tales of lodes and goose-egg nuggets. Along with descriptions of successful extraction operations, Muir announced that the Chilkats, widely known as "hostile to miners entering their country," had laid down their arms and were eager to guide white men over once-forbidden trails to Interior gold-fields.

In the days before mass media, an article such as Muir's was discussed at supper tables and ballyhooed from barstools before being clipped and sent to friends and relatives. In this manner, dozens of readers across the country might pore over the same clipping, perhaps even contribute cash to grubstakes or themselves set off for the newest Eldorado. The feared northern Tlingits were mollified, Muir assured the desperate and desirous, and their fresh mood assured public access to a "virgin wilderness" studded with gold.

A month after completing the canoe voyage, Muir boarded the steamer *California* for Sitka, from which he wired his dispatches to San Francisco. While most Alaskans hunkered down for the long stretch of frigid darkness, Muir anticipated rambles in search of "plant gold" in the oak savannahs and coastal marshes of the Bay Area. He imagined emerging from his scribble room in the spring to marry Louie just before resuming his studies in Alaska. How, he wondered, should he best seek her blessing for a second expedition?[48]

To'watte faced the winter with pain in his heart. For once, his wife was not the source. Her anxieties were soothed by the voyagers' return and a larder replenished by younger clan members. Village tensions, however, were high.

Bullets flew between the houses of two Stikine families in an ongoing "state of warfare." Rumors of an impending raid by Hutsnuwu supporters of the shaman Klee-a-keet set everyone on edge. A sober resolve sustained Reverend Young's "church Indians" during his six-week absence, but since most were members of To'watte's clan, they had little influence on the affairs of other clans.[49]

Community issues plagued To'watte, but he was equally occupied by a crisis of faith. Rather than ease his fears about white men, prolonged contact had provoked serious doubts about his spiritual and cultural choices. He harbored no doubt about Aankáawu—Great Spirit or God. But some Americans seemed impulsive, even dangerous. To'watte had initially called for a God's Man on the assumption that a minister would give his people strength against disease, alcohol, prostitution, and other symptoms of cultural transition. And now? He had witnessed too much change. It wearied him.

Two years earlier To'watte's heart had been full of hope when he steamed to the Presbyterian convention in Port Townsend and delivered, at the behest of Sheldon Jackson, a speech to the assembly. He spoke of the "barbarous" ways of old-style Indians who lacked technology and engaged in perpetual wars. But a change was underway. Christian influence had forged peace among former enemies by refocusing their attentions from hooch to God. "I have changed for the better," To'watte told the audience of Natives and whites. "I am in my old age becoming civilized." He urged Christians to make the Stikines "a happy people" by guiding them whenever they were "led astray from the right path."[50]

Now To'watte prayed for the strength of his grandchildren to withstand the onslaught.

According to Kaagwaantaan elder Rachel "Dixie" Johnson, not long after coming home, "Muir's skipper" was called to Sitka to oversee the repair of his uncle's clan house. As nephew and clan leader, he was compelled to go. Once in Sitka, however, a Presbyterian missionary (probably John Brady) forbade the elder from participating in the "heathen" custom of "potlatching" and communal living. Clan members openly mocked To'watte for his Christian restrictions, setting off a "battle inside of him" that culminated in a song to show his feelings.

"My grandfather's land is turned upside-down with me," he sang slowly and mournfully. "What Raven can save me?" As song leader for the Gei Saan Dancers of Haines in the last quarter of the twentieth century, Dixie Johnson kept To'watte's song alive as a reminder of the anguish and confusion that arose from cultural upheaval, a burden passed to future generations.[51]

"Trouble was in the air," Young wrote of the New Year. Bedridden since the expedition, the pastor suffered from a debilitating headache and fever. To'watte was back from Sitka when a Hutsnuwu war canoe landed in the Foreign Town section of Stikine. A Baptist preacher for that sector confirmed Young's foreboding when his small congregation was completely absent for a regular service. Upon finding most of his flock thoroughly intoxicated, the preacher ran to the fort where he rousted two of To'watte's clan, Matthew and Aaron. They returned to the "drunken mob" intent on breaking up a

The Meeting, 1879. Illustration by Pete Andriesen. Reproduced by permission of artist.

hooch still that was "going full blast." A melee erupted during which Aaron's face was deeply gashed. In Tlingit tradition, facial wounds were a source of deep shame usually resolved by payment of blankets. Absent blankets, the victim responded with violence.

The fight evaporated. Aaron returned the next morning flanked by ten clan members wielding pick handles. The stone-sober Stikines inflicted black eyes and bloody noses on many hung-over Hutsnuwu before retreating to the fort.

"I think my time has come," To'watte said to Reverend Young at his bedside. "My family have not God in their hearts. I will do all in my power to make peace, but they will not listen to reason." The headman offered to make a large blanket payment to quell the dispute, but none would have it.

The pastor was roused in the early morning of January 10 by a breathless delegation of church Indians. The community was in an uproar; rifles in hand, men shouted defiant speeches from opposite shores. Drums throbbed as gangs of war-dancers poured onto the front street and beach. Reverend Young urged his people to hide in their homes. To'watte sent a message requesting a meeting with the Hutsnuwu leader, who, although willing, was unable to subdue his party. Reeling from fever, Young arose, donned his heavy woolens, and ran outside to muster a posse of whites. Despite his pleas, the men were reluctant to intervene. One well-known bootlegger shrugged off Young's demands: "Let them alone and let's see the fun."

The Stikines' retreat further enraged the Hutsnuwu. Interpreting the behavior as abject cowardice, they broke into a well-to-do church Indian's house and smashed his expensive furniture. Young lurched forward as waves of combatants collided but was blocked by several men until being dragged away by a screaming woman. Guns were drawn by the time the pastor regained the periphery. Aggressors aimed from behind boulders or houses, but To'watte stood on the beach with a few others, among them his brother, Kitch-gow-ish, and Stickeen Johnny, Muir's translator. As a sign of authority, the headman held a heavy spear of tropical wood into which alien designs had been carved by an unknown hand. Young dashed up to To'watte, whose usual impassive face appeared almost serene.

"Don't you see the Hoochenoo are massing in front of you?" Young asked. "They are many and you are few. Go back!" He placed a hand on To'watte's shoulder. "Come back with me to your house."

As the headman locked eyes with the God's Man, a broad smile creased his face.

"*Yak'éi*" (good), he replied, and commanded the Stikines to put down their arms.

Less than ten feet away from To'watte, a Hutsnuwu fired. The bullet entered the center of the headman's forehead and he crumpled to the beach. Kitch-gow-ish and two other church Indians were killed, and a dozen others, wounded.

"It seemed as if the world had come crashing about me," Young recalled.[52]

10 :: Wilder Than

:: **"REASON ENOUGH FOR YOU TO FIND OUT"**

Chilkat and Chilkoot tribes opened their homeland to settlers; Old Ways succumbed to the American Way; Muir advanced his glacial gospel to the world.

So what?

Besides profound irony, do these threads of historical narrative lead to any enduring insights? Did Muir's meeting with the northern Tlingits alter his subsequent views of Native Americans? What effect, if any, did the encounter have on his campaign for wilderness preservation? And what of Muir's impact on his model citizens? Was Tlingit culture affected in any measurable way by the man they called Dleit Aankáawu? What does their meeting tell us about non-Native relations with indigenous people at the time? Today?

The man to whom I first addressed these questions in 1983 was unsure about how to respond. While I studied the rhetoric of Muir in graduate school, serendipity led me to Holway R. Jones, author of *John Muir and the Sierra Club*, published in 1965, and national Sierra Club chair for wilderness. Jones also happened to be the head reference librarian at the University of Oregon library, where I inhabited a tiny study carrel. Our chance meeting led to an interview.

"Muir came out when the frontier was disappearing," Jones said. "His passions were stirred by tremendous changes in American culture at the time." Prior to Muir, most arguments for nature preservation stressed human aesthetics and recreation. Likewise, Muir linked wilderness with mental and physical health, but further advocated "pure nature" for its own sake. Flowers, birds, and mountains were citizens of equal standing in a global community. "Muir's shift from anthropomorphic to biocentric was a keystone," said Jones, who studied and emulated his hero's rhetorical strategies for the dozens of preservationist campaigns he led in Alaska and the Pacific West.[1]

As we ended our chat, I asked what he thought about the incident at Yandeist'akyé.

Several seconds passed as Jones searched my face for sarcasm or sincerity, then shrugged: "I don't know." He freed a monosyllabic chuckle. "Which, I suppose, is reason enough for you to find out."

Jones's offhanded challenge lingered the next month as I boarded an Alaska-bound ferry and in late summer when I lobbed the same questions to Austin Hammond, traditional leader of the Chilkoot Tlingits. We sat on benches around the firepit of his culture camp on the western shore of Chilkoot River, where a village once thrived. A circle of elders—Richard King, Eva Davis, Archie Klaney, Nathan Jackson, Dixie and Pete Johnson, and Matilda and George Lewis—waited for Hammond's response. In name and tribal status, their leader was direct heir to the same Daanawáak in whose longhouse Muir delivered a speech that forever transformed his people. The seventy-four year-old Hammond paused as he considered my questions. Like his historic namesake, the headman gazed at me through silver-rimmed spectacles, perhaps assessing my capacity to listen and understand.

"Talk tomorrow."

As I approached the fire circle the next morning, Daanawáak rose to his feet. From broad shoulders hung the Sockeye Robe, a large Chilkat blanket considered the legal deed to traditional Chilkoot lands. In at least one instance, a local magistrate allowed the robe as evidence of property ownership. I asked about Hammond's origins. He was born at fish camp in Taiyasanki Harbor on Alaska Day in 1910. "So I'm an Alaskan man," he chuckled. What about his earliest memories? Hammond grinned and glanced around the circle at his comrades. "I used to be crazy." Some chortled or smiled; others nodded or shook their heads and muttered in Tlingit. The sháade háni refocused his eyes somewhere just above my head and spoke his mother tongue with a strong, husky tenor, starting with the Flood.

　　　　　　　　　　　　　　　　　DLEIT AANḴÁAWU

Dixie Johnson injected translation into each of Daanawáak's frequent pauses.

Two hours later, Hammond collapsed into a lawn chair. I quickly tossed out a John Muir question. A deeply whorled hand lifted his ball cap while the other mopped his forehead. His eyes caught mine: "I'm out of questions for now."[2]

A dozen solemn elders broke up laughing.

A generation passed before an answer landed.

:: "I HOPE YOU ARE GOOD AT HAIR-SPLITTING ARGUMENT"

Head filled with Alaska, John Muir sailed home to a nation at war.

After a generation of raids on settlers and soldiers to regain homeland lost in the Treaty of Guadalupe Hidalgo, Mimbreño Apache leader Victorio conducted several strikes in late 1879, inflicting more than twenty military and civilian causalities. Settlers fled sustained Apache raids. A half-year later, the *Sacramento Daily Union* reported nearly eighty white fatalities from Apache incursions in May alone and that homesteaders in threatened areas had all but abandoned their ranches.[3] As with most reports of Indian attacks in the press, hyperbole from newspapers and politicians inflamed the perception of "war," justifying a violent response. U.S. troops pursued Apache bands into the rugged mountains of Chihuahua, where Mexican soldiers pushed Victorio's warriors into a box canyon. The ensuing battle killed dozens of Apaches, including Victorio, who died in the sights of a Tarahumara marksman.

Muir knew little of the war when his southbound steamer tied onto the Portland wharf in January 1880. After months of exploring the vast solitudes of Alaska, Muir was suddenly "pounced upon & kuffed into the lecture business" by well-heeled Oregon progressives eager to share the esteemed scientist with their public. In addition to various civic talks, Muir agreed to deliver three paid lectures: "Glaciers of Alaska and California," "Earth Sculpture: The Formation of Scenery," and "Resources and Gold Fields of Alaska."[4]

"Not remarkable" was General O. O. Howard's initial impression of the shy man in rough, rural clothes standing before the packed hall of the first lecture. But the general's judgment shifted abruptly, he confessed in the *Morning Oregonian,* when Muir's "face lighted up as he talked about the history of the world."[5]

As commanding officer of federal troops based at Fort Vancouver, the reviewer was better known as a Christian humanitarian who superintended the Freedmen's Bureau and strove to reform America's "heathen" wards following the Civil War. Months after the conflict, the one-armed general founded all-black Howard University to prepare former slaves for the ministry. In 1872 Howard brokered a treaty with Chiricahua Apache leader Cochise, who declared that "the Indians and the white man shall eat bread together," then died two years later on an Apache reservation in southeastern Arizona. Five years later, Howard forced the sixteen-hundred-mile retreat of Nez Perce leader Chief Joseph, who submitted to the General with a "sad and sick heart." Between surrenders, Howard toured Southeast Alaska with a stopover in Yandeist'akyé for a parley with Daanawáak and Sitka Jack. Villagers may have heard their first Christian pitch when "Old Prayer-Book" likely launched into his routine sermon to "heathens" on how the death of God's Son meant eternal life for his followers.[6]

Upon hearing Muir's lecture, however, the general became a convert to the glacial gospel. For two hours, the "young man of great modesty" transported Howard to a state he usually achieved only at church, infusing him with passion he could not "sleep off."[7]

Enthusiastic crowds embraced each of Muir's lectures, but their interest crested in the third talk when the topic shifted from glaciers to gold. Listeners leaned forward as Muir gestured toward several blackboards on which he had earlier sketched detailed illustrations. The bearded scientist "clearly showed" the great gold and silver formations of the West Coast veering north, the *Oregonian* reported, proof that a "mineral belt doubtless extend[ed] to Alaska." A sudden hush engulfed the hall. For example, Muir continued, a gold strike near Sitka, Alaska, was located on the "same great lead [vein] as those in Nevada."[8]

Elbows nudged neighbors. Murmurs rippled through the hall. Gold? Sitka, Alaska? How far was it? How did a man get there?

Whatever jolt Muir's bold assertion may have given Oregon listeners had already resonated among a widening audience in Sitka where Captain Beardslee spread the news of Koh'klux's invitation to prospectors. Beyond his official naval reports and unofficial magazine writings, the commander selected a team of soldiers and prospectors suited to breech the Chilkat Curtain.[9] The "Bean expedition" steamed to Dyea shores in May 1880, where they were met by a group of Chilkoot men who quickly secured employment as guides and packers for the twenty-two-mile tramp from sea level to thirty-five-hundred-foot Chilkoot Pass. After months of probing the Yukon watershed, the white men returned with little gold but enough stories to fuel rampant speculation. Word ran like sluice down a flume, attracting more people each successive year until 1898, when hundreds of Native packers escorted twenty thousand Klondike stampeders over the fabled notch.

Beyond the iconic image of humanity tramping single file over the icy pass, five generations of miners in the Klondike so fouled water, land, wildlife, and human health that modern historians concur on the massive environment damage resulting from "the giant swindle known as the Klondike."[10]

Muir would return to Jilḵáat aaní to observe the stampede, but on the heels of his first Alaska voyage, he thought of little but glaciers and landforms and, on occasion, Louie. Though he attempted to sequester himself in the home of a San Francisco bookseller, Muir often slipped away to Martinez to visit Louie and her parents. Whenever John took a breath between telling Alaska stories, discussion likely touched on their lives ahead, beginning with a modest April wedding. Ten days before the April 14 ceremony, Muir dropped the "bombshell" in the Russian Hill parlor of his old friends, Mary and John Swett.

"John and I are jubilant over the match," Mary wrote to Louie, but the bride needed to understand Muir's penchant for debate:

> I hope you are good at hair-splitting argument. You will need to hold your own with him. Five times to-day he has vanquished me. Not that I admitted it to him—no, never! He not only excels in argument, but always takes the highest ground—is always on the right side. He told Colonel Boyce the other night that his position was that of champion of a mean, brutal policy. It was with regard to Indian extermination, and that he (Boyce) would be ashamed to carry it with one Indian in personal conflict. I thought the Colonel would be mad, but they walked off arm in arm. Further, he is so truthful that he not only will never embellish . . . but retains every unsightly feature lest his picture should not be true.[11]

By necessity of nuptial advice from an older woman to the younger, Mary Swett distilled Muir's prickly side into some of the same personality traits examined in this book: argumentative, persistent, fraternal, unvarnished. For each harrowing disagreement that Louie would confront in the "contumacious quibbler," Swett asserted an inherent value.[12] Though her groom's dogged opinions might infuriate some women, at thirty-four Louie, a reserved homebody, could do worse than marry this paragon of scientific truth.

His "Indian extermination" comments reveal a remarkable shift in Muir's view of Native Americans. Motivated by profound humanism, he would never have argued for the bloodthirsty policy before his first Alaska trip; still, living among Tlingits had fundamentally changed the man. Direct experience among Natives engendered real empathy. Over several months Muir navigated day-to-day relationships with indigenous people whose lives convinced him of the viability of sustainable cultures and communities. For the Ice Chief, Tlingits were living proof that ecologically whole Native American communities still remained.[13] With the proper education, he believed, they could be ideal citizens: "A few good missionaries, a few good cannon with men behind them, and fair play, protection from whiskey is all the Alaska Indians require. Uncle Sam has no better subjects, white, black, or brown, or any more deserving his considerate care."[14]

A week after the wedding on April 14, 1880, in Martinez, Muir received a letter from trading-post manager John Vanderbilt offering to "take good care of you" if he returned to Fort Wrangell for the season.[15] Still haunted by glaciers overlooked on his first voyage, Muir made clear to Louie his desire to continue the unfinished investigations.

Louie knew his heart and—as she did for the rest of her life—urged John away into the wild. Though Muir's Alaska friends hoped to meet his new wife, she stayed home. Travel to Alaska was inconceivable to a woman who rarely ventured more than a day or two away from Martinez.[16] If the newly-weds made any trade-offs or promises before Muir sailed on July 30, Louie had hers. Muir's first expedition had stretched five months. He vowed this trip would be half as long.

:: "AS IF THROUGH A WINDOW"

In a letter from Victoria, Muir told Louie that while strolling the streets "something like a missionary spirit came over me" as he thought about the Tlingit people he had met the previous year. Why the sudden outpouring of emotion from a man of science? Perhaps he was stirred by shop displays of Chilkat blankets or heard Tlingit language spoken on the sidewalks.[17] Perhaps his eyes met the open gaze of a Native child. In the next letter to Louie written the following day, Muir described a single-sail canoe gliding into the Victoria harbor. The sight triggered memories of paddling with his companions among icebergs in Glacier Bay. Whatever Muir's inspiration, he allowed a fondness for Tlingit people that he rarely expressed for any specific culture.

"Poor fellows," he lamented, "I wish I could serve them."[18]

Muir spied familiar Tlingit faces five days later as he strolled down the gangplank onto the muddy Wrangell beach, but upon seeing Reverend

Young, he called out, "When can you be ready?" Caught offguard by his unexpected visitor, Young sputtered about time and responsibilities until Muir interrupted. "Man, have you forgotten? Don't you know we lost a glacier last fall? Do you think I could sleep soundly in my bed this winter with that hanging on my conscience? . . . Get your canoe and crew and let us be off."[19]

Timing was good for Young, whose progressive campaign had killed local hooch production and relieved the village of certain "trouble-makers." Although To'watte's death was a painful loss, the church stayed strong when surviving Tlingit members stepped forward into leadership roles.[20] Young's problem was finding transportation. Without To'watte at the rudder, the old paddling crew had dispersed. Sitka Charley was out of town, probably back in Sitka where his father, Sitka Jack, was a clan leader. Stickeen Johnny was working the Cassiar mines far up the Stikine River. Káadashaan, the first Stikine church elder, was "getting drunk in the old style," Young told Muir, and likely to lose his membership in the church.[21]

While Young assembled the crew, Muir continued on to Sitka where he met Commander Beardslee with news of progress in outlying villages. Accompanied by Maj. Governeur Morris, the Commander was preparing to sail the *Favorite* north to "look after Government interests among the different tribes." In a letter to Louie, Muir noted that Beardslee's Bean expedition, which had yet to return, was "the first party of whites that the war-like Chilcats have allowed to pass through their country." Closure of the Cassiar mines made Fort Wrangell "very dull," he reported, but Sitka residents were buzzing with speculation about the Chilkat lode.[22]

The southbound *California* docked in Fort Wrangell on August 14 and again Muir walked off the gangplank to meet Young who announced that the expedition sailed in two days. Canoe owner and captain was Lot Tyeen, middle-aged successor to Shustaak, a respected Stikine leader aligned with To'watte's family. His paddlers were Hunter Joe, "a stout, intelligent Stikine," and Billy Dickinson, whom Muir called "Smart Billy" for his quick mind and multilinguistic talents. The lanky, teenaged son of Sarah and George Dickinson assumed Kadachan's role as orator and go-between.

The crew kept a northbound route with side investigations of glaciers in Sum Dum Bay and Taku Inlet. Muir recalled his Chilkat friends as the canoe glided on the milky seam where Taku River meets the sea. Like the Chilkat River, he wrote, the "Tahkou" swept down from the land beyond the Coast Range, and like the northern tribes, the Tlingits held "possession of the river and (compelled) the Indians of the interior to accept their services as middle-men" for all business with merchant ships.[23] Muir refrained from further judgment, willing to accept the Tlingit cartel as a necessary part of an economic model.

The scientist failed to hold his tongue, however, when Hunter Joe casually shot a passing gull. After ignoring Muir's repeated commands to halt, Joe earned "a severe reprimand for his severe cruelty" to which he replied that he "had learned to be careless about taking life from the whites." Older and more traditional, Lot Tyeen upbraided Joe for his casual attitude. Tlingits should not be swayed by wanton acts of white men—no one should kill animals needlessly as it was "likely to bring bad luck." Joe bore the responsibility.[24] Memory of the incident stayed with Muir and eventually would appear in his final book, *Travels in Alaska,* as an example of his evolving conception of animal rights. The gull's death evoked Muir's alignment with Tlingit beliefs that "animals have souls, and that it was wrong and unlucky to even speak disrespectfully" of them.[25]

The travelers camped near a Tlingit family in view of the Taku Glacier. As Muir was feeling pressed for time, Reverend Young postponed services among Taku and Auk tribes. Tyeen steered the canoe westward for the last forty miles to Glacier Bay.

Young heralded their passage into Muir Inlet as "the greatest scenic trip in the world," an impression enlarged by the Ice Chief's ensuing lectures and writings.[26] Notes and drawings from the expedition filled a sketchbook and most of a 4 in. x 7 in. black-leather trip journal. The expedition camped for a week near the "radiant ice-flood," which Reverend Young would christen Muir Glacier. The explorer rose at two or three each morning and returned late, guided into camp by a huge signal fire fed by the crew. In nearby Taylor Bay, Muir narrowly survived one of his best-known adventures with a small, furry stowaway named Stickeen. With the "wildest gentle dog I ever saw" scampering at his heels, Muir raced the darkness across the Brady Icefield, sometimes inching along ice slivers over bottomless crevasses.

Though earlier in the voyage Muir had thought the dog cold and inscrutable, their common struggle helped him see Stickeen with "clearer sympathy" than he had felt for any animal. Similarly, the perilous conditions he shared with Tlingit companions engendered an abiding respect for their lifeways and "joyous adaptability to harsh surroundings."[27] For a man otherwise preoccupied with his passions, shared adventures facilitated a fresh way to see "as if through a window" people or dogs in an intimate relationship with the wild.[28]

After ten days on ice, the canoeists paddled to Sitka where Muir and Young huddled with Captain Beardslee and officers to sketch charts of their travels. The crew paddled back to Fort Wrangell and continued on their separate ways. Young steamed north to help Sheldon Jackson build Haines Mission, and Muir caught the southbound *California.*

When Muir next entered Jilḵáat aaní almost two decades later, personal and public perceptions of him had shifted from being a curiosity ("poetico-trampo-geologist-bot[anist] and ornith[ologist]-natural, etc etc. etc.") to honoring "the eminent scientist" known for vivid travelogues, daring exploration, and fervent wilderness advocacy.[29] With much of the intensity he had reserved for natural history, Muir refocused his energies on managing the Strenzel ranch, a path that led to wealth, stability, and a range of relationships including the birth of two daughters, Wanda and Helen. Other than occasional outings, nature's most ardent botanist cultivated the skills of a master horticulturalist and blossomed into a successful businessman.

Yet the Ice Chief still dreamed of wilderness: mountains locked in perpetual ice, sheer granite walls, flower-flooded meadows, glaciers sweeping up to the sky.

An opportunity to "come home" to his beloved mountains arose in 1887 when Muir became editor of an expansive literary project called *Picturesque California,* a thirty-part subscription (and later book) with dozens of essays and over eight hundred illustrations. The project was a grand excuse to slip away to a redwood grove or High Sierra lake, for which Muir paid with hundreds of hours confined to his "Scribble Den" in Martinez. More than the editor's many essays, contributions from Joaquin Miller, Jeanne Carr, Frederick Remington, William Keith, and others built an impressive document designed to attract potential tourists to the Pacific West. It supplied a vision of the new, improved frontier, a wonderland of recreational and aesthetic possibilities interpreted by America's premier nature guide. Gone were the days of starvation, bears, and wild savages, Muir assured readers. The warrior chiefs were dead, with surviving tribal members "civilized into comparative innocence, industry, or harmless laziness." Tourists had more to fear from ants than hostile Indians.[30]

Natives encountered on Muir's third and fourth Alaska voyages respectively in 1881 and in 1890 further validated his perception of them as apart from other Native Americans. He observed Alaska Natives utilizing resources from defined territories to sustain traditional ways of life. Because they lived where white men seldom ventured, northern peoples stayed closer to nature. At times they seemed "the wildest animals of all," like the Athabaskan families Muir watched on the banks of the Yukon River.[31] Others he entrusted as guides, such as the Tlingit seal hunters who approached Muir in the icy backwaters of Glacier Bay. Long-term relationships with Reverend Young and his followers softened Muir's toxic view of missionaries. Religious training (about which he maintained reservations) aside, Glate Ankow supported English education, hygiene, and temperance as necessary standards for U.S. citizenship. Like his "old friends" Lot Tyeen and Shakes in Fort Wrangell, Muir admired people—Native or not—whose wild affinities were tempered by a dollop of domesticity.[32]

Beyond two Alaska voyages and a few Sierra camping trips, Muir occupied the ensuing decade close to farm and family. A premonition in 1885, however, led him halfway across the country. A few weeks after he received word that his father was ill, a vision of the old man's impending death prompted an immediate trip to Kansas City, where Daniel Muir lived with a daughter. For years, John had yearned for reconciliation—he sensed a last opportunity. Before arriving at his father's bedside, Muir called at the homes of five siblings and convinced them to accompany him for the first such reunion in more than twenty years. Writing at the dying man's bedside, Muir informed Louie that his father failed to recognize him, but once took his hand and asked, "Is this my dear John?" before falling back on a pillow. Sister Joanna assuaged John's aching loss when she conveyed their father's recent admission of remorse over the abuse he had inflicted on his eldest son.[33]

Muir wrote slowly, publishing nothing in the 1880s. The dry spell ended when "The Treasures of the Yosemite" appeared in *The Century Magazine* in August 1890, followed by two successive essays advocating national park status for Yosemite. To that end, editor Robert Underwood Johnson introduced Muir to a well-heeled readership ready to be guided through landscapes recalling the luminous works of William Keith and Alfred Bierstadt: "awful in stern, immovable majesty, how softly these mountain rocks are adorned and how fine and reassuring the company they keep."[34] Given the nation's frontier legacy, most nineteenth-century Americans considered rocks indifferent, probably inconvenient, maybe even life-threatening. In his Yosemite writings, however, Muir offered scenery of Old Testament proportions cushioned by New Testament intimations of a relationship with the ineffable. "Christianity and mountainanity are streams from the same fountain," he once declared in a letter to J. B. McChesney.[35] In the Sierras, he maintained, resided the essence of God.

Conversely, Satan dwelt in the unconscionable acts of timber and grazing interests at the proposed park's periphery. Whole groves of ancient sequoias were "doomed to feed the large mills" with tragic results, yet their destruction was relatively minor compared to the "whole belts" of forests burned by stockmen to create pasturage for their growing swarms of "hoofed locusts."[36]

In the quirky, semireclusive writer, the New York editor recognized the ethos of a prophet, a movement leader with the rhetorical power and compelling personality that could shape public opinion. From his first Yosemite article in the New York *Tribune* in 1871 until Pres. Benjamin Harrison signed the park into law in October 1890, Muir wrote and published dozens of articles and other materials detailing the natural character of the Central Sierra, but not until his *Century Magazine* work did he turn to goal-driven advocacy. Nearly two decades had passed since Yellowstone became the first national park in the world. As another grand example of Western landscape exceptionalism, argued Johnson and Muir, Yosemite should be next.[37]

Celebration of their success was brief. Though the U.S. Army claimed a Yosemite Valley base in May 1891 to protect the new federal possession, Johnson knew the park's status was subject to political whim, so he helped orchestrate the Yosemite Defense Association, soon called the Sierra Club. Powered by Muir's writings, the Club sustained political pressure in the East while luring liberal urbanites in the West to the newest national park. Johnson pressed Muir to lead the Sierra Club, and although the scientist admitted misgivings about heading a political group, he accepted the office of president, a position he held until his death.[38]

As chief spokesperson for the Sierra Club, John Muir evolved his public language beyond the luminous exposition of a poet-naturalist to the unyielding absolutism of a standard-bearer. In language reminiscent of his father, Muir conveyed evangelical certainty in a battle that was "part of the eternal conflict between right and wrong," but instead of heaven at the feet of God after death, he offered a heaven on earth, untrammeled wilderness, in life.[39] Through his involvement with the Club, Muir's knowledge of threats to American landscapes armed the righteous defense of key values—beauty, spirit, refuge—against the destroyers' creed of profit, utility, growth. Beyond his writing and publishing, Club leadership forced the lifelong reluctant orator to speak as part of his official duty to protect God's handiwork from "every action that the unweariable thieves and robbers present."[40]

From 172 charter members in 1892 , the tiny outdoor club has grown to nearly a million U.S. members in 2017, evolving into the flagship of the American environmental movement. The piercing gaze and long beard of the reluctant icon soon came to symbolize a profligate nation's desire to preserve pieces of its pre-industrial past. Millions of people were drawn to the light of Muir's vision, but in the nineteenth century (and some argue, today) the brilliance of wilderness preservation was vastly outshone by the gleam of gold.

The lure of golden nuggets energized bands of pioneers ready to pursue their dreams in the western frontier. They were risk-takers, wrote historian Frederick Jackson Turner, exiles, immigrants, and dreamers whose subjugation of wild lands and "savage lords" contributed directly to the natural "buoyancy and exuberance which comes with freedom." The raw, remote environs of the pioneers, Turner suggested, forged a unique "American intellect" defined by "dominant individualism" characterized by a "restless, nervous energy," perhaps "lacking in the artistic but powerful to effect great ends." The 1849 California gold rush reflected the ideas and rhetoric of Turner's theory, echoed by successive rushes in Colorado, Wyoming, South Dakota, Montana, Idaho, and, at the close of the century, Alaska.[41]

In 1897 John Muir ventured into the "wild, discouraging mess" of the Klondike gold rush as a well-paid correspondent for the San Francisco *Examiner,* his first outing into the Tlingit stronghold since his visit to Yandeist'akyé.[42] In the seventeen years since Daanawáak and Koh'klux lifted the ban on white people, business had skyrocketed for Chilkoot and Chilkat packers. Hundreds, then thousands of stampeders spilled from steamers onto wharves at Skagway and Dyea eager to hustle tons of gear over the pass and down the Yukon River four hundred miles to Dawson and the Klondike gold-fields. Between 1896 and 1900 as many as forty thousand people crossed the Chilkoot Pass, often assisted by Tlingit packers, who usually carried packs weighing a hundred pounds each. At twelve to fifteen dollars per hundred-pound load (up to a dollar a pound at the peak), many Tlingit packer families earned more money than their non-Native clientele in the rush.[43] When they returned to Chilkat Valley homes at season's end, some packers exercised conspicuous consumption with fancy clothes, carriages (later, the first automobiles in the region), "white-man houses," and, of course, sumptuous potlatches.[44]

Most of Muir's first newspaper installment laid out the geologic odds of striking a lode, which he insisted were no better than average. "Nobody has a right to expect to get rich in Alaska or any other goldfield on the globe," he wrote, "without giving the better part of his life to the business." Nonetheless, he conceded, the Yukon Basin was mostly comprised of "auriferous gravel" with rich pay dirt potential.[45]

Oddly, the writer lied about his hiking prowess. "I shall walk over Chilcoot Pass," he wrote. "I have been there before. I have no pack to carry. I know how to protect my feet and nose, and to men who are accustomed to this kind of travel the trip is not arduous. I have crossed in November."[46]

 DLEIT AANḴÁAWU

As seen in this book, journal entries from November 1879 offer a detailed account of Muir's five-day stay with Daanawáak, including sketches from the mountain he climbed behind Yandeist'akyé, but the length of that visit simply does not accommodate the minimum four extra days needed to paddle to Dyea, speed-walk the forty-four-mile roundtrip to and from Chilkoot Pass, and paddle back. Neither does the episode appear in his companions' recollections.

If any affection for the northern Tlingits remained, none showed in the *Examiner* articles. Despite hundreds of Tlingit men, women, and children engaged in the free-flowing economy of the Klondike gold rush, they were invisible to Muir, who reported seeing "three to four thousand gold-seekers" at the head of the Chilkoot Trail along with two thousand ragged, under-nourished stock animals "struggling like salmon in a bowldery pool at the foot of a fall."[47] While miners thrashed and wallowed in the mud for footing, Tlingit packers plodded up the trail miles ahead.

Thirty miles west, Muir ceded, the longer, more-gradual ascent to Chilkat Pass was "best for cattle and horses" but historically subject to "the extortionate charges and tantalizing delays of the Indian packers" of Klukwan. After centuries of preventing competitors from traveling their trails, the Chilkat attitudes shifted when they heard "how greatly the Stickeens had profited" from open trade, so "they changed their minds and encouraged prospectors to go their way."[48] A few gold-hunters traveled over Jack Dalton's primitive "road" along Chilkat River and over the Pass, but most stayed aboard the steamship for Dyea or Skagway, an hour or so to the north.

The Chilkoot Trail was shorter and faster, but most stampeders chose it because they thought the trail was the *only* route. In the years between Muir's 1880 "Alaska Mines" and his 1897 *Examiner* series (and *Century* feature), enough writers had contributed literature about the "Golden Staircase" to elevate it to myth. Few wrote about the Chilkat side. A coherent map of the "Grease Trail" from tide line (near the Haines Mission) four hundred miles north to the confluence of the Pelly and Yukon Rivers was unavailable until 1901 when a brief article appeared in *Mazama,* a small Oregon climbing journal. Titled "Explanation of an Indian Map," the unassuming report by University of California professor George Davidson introduced the map drawn for him by Koh'klux and his wives thirty-two years earlier.[49]

The map was given to reciprocate Davidson's assumed orchestration of the 1869 total eclipse in Klukwan. Although the astronomer carefully explained the relationship between the earth and its moon, Koh'klux still suspected his guest of somehow influencing the event (see chap. 3). Koh'klux offered the details of his people's trade route as a gesture proportionate to the scientist's celestial wisdom. "Unusually sensitive to American Indians," wrote historian John Cloud, Davidson likely delayed publishing the map to avoid a gold rush with the inevitable "devastation that would follow the whiteman."[50] Such was the condition of the Chilkoot side, which reminded John Muir of a "nest of ants taken into a strange country and stirred up by a stick."[51]

As Muir sought a journalistic story in the pandemonium, his old friend Hall Young serendipitously boarded the same Alaska-bound steamer intent on saving souls. Each wrote later about his experiences with memories that often diverged. Surveying the crowded decks of the *Queen,* however, both men agreed they had never witnessed such an unruly mass. Standing beside the reverend, Muir clucked and shook his head at the "horde of fools" crowding onto the gangplank. "I don't envy your job of proclaiming the gospel to such a mob," Muir said. "Why, it's like preaching to a pack of wolves!"

"I look upon them as my parish," Young replied. "Immortal souls, all of them."[52]

The turbulent throng was, in fact, at the heart of his mission.

Until resigning from his post in 1888, Young remained active in the region by building churches in Juneau, Haines, Hoonah, Howkan, Kasaan, and Klukwan while sustaining his congregation in Wrangell. His wife, Fannie, poured her effervescent energies into the Industrial Training School for Girls. Young was especially proud of being the first missionary in Alaska to require English language in church services. Despite a Presbyterian policy that encouraged clergy to write Native language dictionaries and translate hymnbooks, Young refused on grounds that it was "a useless and even harmful task" to extend Native traditions instead of letting them "die."[53] However, after a decade of struggling to apply the standard in his own church, Young found congregants understood little unless he used Native language in "nine-tenths" of his services. Consequently, the reverend sensed he was "deteriorating mentally and spiritually," so he relocated his family to southern California. He assumed pastoral duties in a half-dozen churches in four states while remaining an ardent campaigner for missionary work in Alaska. Just as he was inspired by Sheldon Jackson two decades earlier, Young aimed to carry on the crusade to convert the frontier.

A nine-year absence did not erase Alaska from Young's thoughts or speech. His "constant lecturing" around the country forged a personal link—at least among some Presbyterians—with America's northern possession. More than travelogues, his lurid depictions of shaman confrontations and abductions of teenage girls roused righteous audiences and raised funds wherever he spoke. As had Jackson, Young collected the artwork (including at.óow) discarded by his "church Indians," much of which is held today in the Princeton University Museum. Young's work even caught the attention of Pres. William McKinley, who briefly considered appointing him governor of Alaska territory.[54]

When tales of horror and depravity in the Klondike began to filter out into the general public, Young seized the opportunity to lobby for his missionary reprise. A battery of letters and speeches persuaded the Presbyterian Home Mission to send Young and two medical missionaries to what the media had rapidly transformed into the bull's-eye for sin in America: Skagway, Alaska. The bonus of Muir's company was a divine sign. After a week together, Young bade adieu to his "dearest friend" on the southbound steamer and set out on the long, harrowing journey to Dawson—a community of "seven thousand crazy people!"—where he would build a church.[55]

In the ensuing years, the two men pursued their passions. Young established religious order throughout Alaska; Muir promoted wildness wherever he trod. Young wrote books about his northern adventures, including two memoirs, a collection of poems, and a novel about the Klondike gold rush. Much of Muir's work as Sierra Club president consigned him to the "Scribble Room," where he produced articles and books extolling the splendors of rivers, redwood groves, and mountain "temples," powered by a moral imperative to preserve them.

Rarely was Muir relieved of his desk, but in 1899 he reserved the summer for studying Alaska with the "Floating University" assembled for the Harriman Expedition. Fascinated by America's northern frontier but appalled at the dearth of knowledge, railroad magnate and Muir's close friend, Edward Harriman, assembled a cadre of scientists and artists on the steamship *George Elder* with the purpose of publishing several volumes as evidence of vast natural wealth in the nation's massive, unknown territory. It was to be the sixth and final Alaska voyage for Glate Ankow.

For nearly two months, the thirty esteemed members observed and recorded as much as was possible of the northern coastline from the deck of a posh steamer until making a final Alaska stop at Cape Fox on July 26. Located a few miles south of present-day Ketchikan, the Tlingit village had been abandoned for a few years but still contained at.oow, carved treasures including nineteen totem poles that stood beside fifteen empty houses.

Some expeditionaries, like Muir and fellow naturalist John Burroughs, strolled the grounds, pausing to admire the dramatic works, perhaps to sketch or scribble notes. Conversation among others centered on the poles, which most assumed would rot away. "Why not, therefore, secure some of these totem poles for the museums of the various colleges represented by members of the expedition?" Burroughs asked in a later essay. The ring of axes and rattle of rigging continued into the evening of the second day when the men hauled back "five or six of the most striking poles."[56] Though Burroughs's camp endorsed the extraction, Muir "watched the taking in disgust," articulating sentiments that had not fully formed on his first Alaska voyage, when totem theft by Presbyterian officials prompted Kadachan to ask how they would react if a Native desecrated their family cemetery.[57] Twenty years later, Muir now knew where he stood.

Absorbed by their causes, Muir and Young exchanged little correspondence until 1910 when Young sent Muir the manuscript of a nearly finished memoir, *Hall Young of Alaska: "The Mushing Parson."*

Because Young's personal papers were destroyed four years earlier when the steamboat *Leah* sank in the Yukon River, Muir's reply is the only known surviving letter to his friend. In light of Young's vast store of Alaska experiences, Muir wrote, it was his time to write a book. "I have always said that I would not bother writing books until I was too old to climb mountains, but I have been at work lately," Muir related, listing as evidence *The Mountains of California, Our National Parks,* and *Stickeen.* He also hoped to write a book about Alaska but conceded that his notebooks and studies from their travels had "hardly been touched."[58]

About Young's manuscript, Muir offered no general opinion, but he did note two specific criticisms, the first relating to details from the rescue on Glenora Peak. "After you fell on that mountain, you evidently lost track of your way," Muir chided as he refuted Young's claim to have climbed across glaciers, "but such mistakes do not interfere with the main truthful effect of the adventure."

The second and larger problem was the title. "I am pretty sure you should change the name of the book," Muir advised. "'Mushing' is slang, even in Alaska, and parsons should be better described no matter how they travel. I'm sure that it would be a very bad title."

Chafed by the opprobrium, Young responded in his next letter that "literary Alaskan friends," among others, were "quite taken with the title. . . . In fact, there is no other word used up here to express the same idea."

Despite his reputation as a dogged debater, Muir fell silent. The relationship stalled. But for a Chinese manservant, he persevered alone in Martinez. Louie had "gone to the better land," and their daughters were married.[59] Advocacy, writing, and travel occupied his days until December 1914 in Los Angles when a downpour caught him without a raincoat and pneumonia compelled him to a sickbed. For two weeks Muir coughed incessantly as

Last House Standing in Yandeist'akyé. Photograph by author.

fluid gradually filled his lungs. Most days propped up in bed, he sat before his papers, at last editing and rewriting notes from the Alaska explorations.

Muir died on Christmas Day. Strewn across his bedclothes were pages from the unfinished manuscript, among which was his longest, warmest essay about Native Americans, "The Country of the Chilkats."[60]

The particulars of Muir's Tlingit encounters appeared the following year when his *Travels in Alaska* was published by Houghton Mifflin. In the same year, Presbyterian-owned New York publisher Fleming Revell produced S. Hall Young's *Alaska Days with John Muir,* which launched the author into an extensive tour to peddle his book, to memorialize his friend, and sometimes to offer an alternative view of events. On February 16, 1916, Young celebrated Muir before a thousand rapt listeners at a missionary conference in San Francisco. Even though the man of science betrayed no sign of outward religiosity, Young had witnessed him deliver to the "heathen of Alaska . . . some of the most intensely religious sermons that I have ever listened to, and some of the most effective."[61]

Case in point was the Chilkats, a tribe known widely as "insolent, proud, war-like, cruel, and heathen." For five days, Young recalled preaching "from morning to night" to a crowd so tightly packed into Daanawáak's house that some crawled on the roof and peered into the smokehole. Whenever he paused from exhaustion, eager audience members refused to allow him rest, crying out "Tell us more!" When Young finally collapsed late each night, the audience stayed in place, demanding Muir.

"As a result of that first visit with John Muir," Young concluded, "today three-fourths of that tribe are humble followers of Christ—a transformed people."

The remainder of the address was devoted to breathtaking details from his rescue on Glenora Peak, including the moment that Muir chomped onto his collar and dragged him uphill to safety.

"He risked his life a thousand times for me," the reverend concluded.[62]

Young persisted in his Alaska crusade for another decade, founding new parishes in Fairbanks, Nome, Cordova, and Skagway. The Presbyterian General Assembly called for Young's illustrated lectures at national meetings in order to "keep Alaska before the Presbyterian public."[63] He even managed to steal occasional moments to edit and rewrite his full memoir.

In May 1927, seventy-year-old Young spoke again before the General Assembly about missionary work in Alaska. "Never had he seemed more vigorous in body and buoyant in spirit than he did then," observed John Marquis, national secretary for Presbyterian missions. He conferred with Young about arrangements for publication of the manuscript and agreed to meet in September to apply final adjustments.[64]

En route to the meeting, Young's driver stopped to fix a flat tire. The reverend stepped outside to stretch his legs and walked directly into a passing trolley car. He was killed instantly.

Hall Young of Alaska, "The Mushing Parson" was published three months later.

11 :: Trampling the Shaman

Across the vast, unpopulated spaces between communities of Southeast Alaska in 1880, news of To'watte's death spread like a red tide. With relationships already frayed, Angoon-Stikine attitudes were murderous. From Sitka, Captain Beardslee dispatched a gunboat to Wrangell. Up in Jilḵáat aaní, the murder of To'watte settled old scores for some, including Koh'klux, who was forced to reconcile his newfound Christian faith with traditional Tlingit law.

"Indian policemen" continued to facilitate the cultural transition. Deputized by Beardslee, Sitka Jack and his comrades led well-attended meetings in clan houses where they explained American laws and expectations. They joined their northern kin in communal activities such as subsistence and memorial ḵu.éex', nurturing relationships to prepare their audience for a new moral code that promised eternal life. Indian policemen likely stood in Daanawáak's house to hear Muir, To'watte, and Young. Upon their return to Sitka in February 1880, they presented to the commander a document signed by Koh'klux, who promised peace and granted miners entry into Chilkat country. Though northern Tlingits knew little English, Beardslee wagered that a "superstitious respect for written words" would cement their vows. In a post-Custer frontier (with a shrunken military budgets), Beardslee preferred to send policemen with papers rather than soldiers in gunboats.[1]

News of Koh'klux's "invitation" sparked fevered preparations in Sitka: boats were built; crews, mustered, supplies, ordered and received. The title of Beardslee's official published report to the Department of the Navy in Washington, D.C., spread the frenzy outward: "OPENING OF THE CHILKAT AND CHILKOOT COUNTRY TO THE WORLD."[2] In spring, Beardslee directed E.P McClellan to speed to Chilkat "under sail and oar" with thirteen soldiers and two-dozen miners. Upon landing, McClellan would arrange an "interview with the chiefs" in full military dress. The lieutenant would remind leaders that in the previous Chilkat-Chilkoot conflict, the Navy chose to send Native policemen rather than troops. Naval patrols plied the Lynn Canal because Chilkats desired peace with the Americans; consequently, he expected Koh'klux and his headmen to treat whites as guests, so they might "live peaceably and friendly with the Indians." Even further, Beardslee stressed, Koh'klux must allow whites to trade with Interior tribes once restricted by the "Chilkat monopoly." Failure to do so, Beardslee added, would result in the ban of all Chilkat persons from landing in Sitka "for trade or other purposes." Further, all Chilkats residing in Sitka would be subject to a hiring freeze.[3] Not only would the sanctions sever vital economic ties between communities, but for Koh'klux, a Kaagwaantaan clan leader, breaking away from kinsmen was unthinkable.

Unlocked by his "X" on paper, the Tlingit Curtain opened.

On June 5, 1880, the Navy launch returned to Sitka, bearing news that "Chilkhat country was now fairly open to the whites." Within days, Commander Beardslee posted a letter to Pres. James A. Garfield, and, from the USS *Jamestown*, a letter to Koh'klux, lauding the "good conduct" of Chilkats. Keeping their promise, Beardslee vowed, enabled the tribes "to make money by selling all of their furs, oil and other things."[4]

Beardslee told Koh'klux how pleased the Great Father would be to know the chief's decision to allow miners free passage in Chilkat country. Village leaders were "wise" for seeing the economic value of relationships with white men. If the great chief guaranteed safe passage for prospectors, their discoveries would "enrich the Indians also." Above wealth, however, Beardslee underscored his faith in Koh'klux: "I am glad you kept your promises, and I felt sure you that you would. Brave men of all colors are alike; they will not lie."

As a symbolic gesture, the commander broke his own rule against giving gifts by sending Koh'klux a fine American pipe and some tobacco. "Keep the pipe as long as you live, then give it to the next chief, to be used always as a pipe of peace."[5]

A threat, a promise, and a gift made for the sort of diplomacy Koh'klux expected from the Americans. They would be powerful partners.

The first non-Native to settle in Jilkáat aaní arrived six months later when the Northwest Trading Company built a store at Portage Cove. The landing party included one of Amanda McFarland's star students, Sarah Dickinson, her Anglo husband George, and their two children, Billy (Muir's 1880 translator) and Sarah. The trading post carried a civilizing inventory of "cloths, buttons, shoes, hats, beads, blankets, combs" as well as "bogus meerschaums and cheap medicines," which George traded for the rich furs packed by Chilkats from the Interior and for the oils they rendered from "whales, porpoises, and seals." As directed by Reverend Young, Sarah taught English and Bible studies.[6]

Mrs. McFarland's school had groomed Sarah Dickinson to be a model Christian teacher. The Tongass Tlingit woman possessed linguistic and cultural understandings that brought the Good Word close to her audience. As Young's interpreter in Wrangell, she faced down a powerful shaman, stood between combatants, and coaxed reluctant parents to surrender their daughters to boarding school. Now in her early thirties, Sarah brought to Haines a righteous fervor tempered by uncommon compassion. Young credited her with reforming the common Native practice of "entering complaints against and berating one another in prayer-meetings and confessions." Access to English, religion, and Boston goods in one place attracted Native families, many of whom relocated near the school and trading post at Deishú.[7]

The steamer *Favorite* paid several visits to the Dickinsons that year, each time disgorging a rough mix of soldiers, prospectors, traders, and occasionally company manager John Vanderbilt. On one trip, he bore a letter from John Muir authorizing the State of California to purchase the "Chilkat meteorite" from Daanawáak. Though other white men had made competitive offers, the headman honored his pledge to Glate Ankow. The trading company shipped the "pre-terrestrial plastic deformation" to San Francisco, where it was on display for decades at the California Museum of Natural History.[8]

Less than two months after the Dickinsons arrived, hostilities again broke out between Chilkats and Chilkoots. A white miner named Steele was discovered to be circumventing Tlingit middlemen by dealing directly with their traditional trading partners, the "Stick Indians" of southern Yukon.[9] Discontent turned dark, fueled by a hooch river that flowed through "nearly every house" toward a sea of trouble. Tensions soared in August over a barrel of molasses sold by trader Pierre Erassard. A nephew of Koh'klux declared a "blood feud" with Erassard as payback for being stabbed by a white man in Wrangell the year before. Mindful of his agreement to Commander Beardslee, the old headman protected the French trader. The nephew nonetheless settled his score by shooting and killing a Chilkoot man who had bitten off his ear in a past brawl. Honor-bound, tribal partisans descended into a deadly civil war.[10]

The Dickinsons's prayers were answered when the *Favorite* steamed into Portage Bay on August 24, carrying troops led by Commander Beardslee and Maj. William Governeur Morris. A Union officer in the Civil War, Morris had recently been appointed collector of customs in Sitka. He and Beardslee listened at length to a distraught George Dickinson, who related the details of his family's frightening ordeal. Months later, Beardslee's military report recounted the events in the crisp, functional language of the bureaucrat; but using the pseudonym "Piseco," Beardslee penned a jaunty dispatch that appeared in the November 25, 1880, edition of *Forest and Stream* magazine. From both narratives an unusual account of frontier diplomacy emerges.

The drunken grudge match, Beardslee wrote, arose from white encroachment on Interior trading partners, the main reason northern tribes had "always been opposed" to opening their homeland to outsiders. Steele, the culprit in this case, had slipped away, so rival groups vented their frustrations on each other. Beardslee sent messengers to invite key headmen to a meeting aboard the *Favorite* the next day to resolve the dispute in a "civilized" manner.

Sailors requested shore leave to hunt and fish, but the commander ordered them to their stations, where they awaited the Tlingits' response in the "the monotony of expectancy." Early the next morning, however, flocks of ducks landing in a Deishú marsh tempted Beardslee and Morris to slip ashore. After a few minutes on a trail, they met Pierre Erassard walking with five Natives. Among them was Koh'klux, "a tall, well-built, dignified old fellow from whose good looks, however, a wad of cotton, stuffed into a hole in his left cheek, somewhat detracted." He was accompanied by "Kak na tay," another headman whom Beardslee estimated to be older, probably in his seventies. Erassard, a powerfully built voyageur "arrayed in red," displayed to the commander a "most profound obeisance" expressed with a "true shrewdness and French politeness" that verged on fawning.

As Beardslee struck up a conversation with Koh'klux, his concern about his own civilian attire faded when, "stripped of all external show of power," the two men sat under a large tree to talk over the problem. In addition to pressures on Interior trading partners, Koh'klux complained to the commander that "white men demoralized the Indians by selling them liquor and debauching their women." These grievances, the journalist-officer

          DLEIT AAN<u>K</u>ÁAWU

concurred, were "only too true." When Beardslee's cigars were smoked down, Koh'klux brought out the pipe he had received from the officer in June. As they talked and smoked, the men paused from time to time to shoot a bird with Beardslee's breechloader. "If the true history of wars and diplomacy could be written," opined Piseco, "how many times have such little matters had more weight than elaborate speeches, convincing only their utterer?"

Free of his attendants, Koh'klux "unbosomed" himself to Beardslee, admitting that his family was to blame and he was eager to make peace. The murdered man was "not worth a hundred blankets," the sháade háni claimed, but "he would pay two hundred if not less would heal the breach." The greater crime, Koh'klux maintained, was disrespect from transient whites, whose attitudes about alcohol, women, and money produced deadly tensions. Since fear of reprisal kept most Tlingits from striking white men, Natives fought each other. Traditional law based on reciprocity tended to amplify and prolong interclan conflicts. Koh'klux would keep his promise to protect whites, but Beardslee must protect his tribe.

Later that morning, Commander Beardslee and Major Morris met at the trading post with the aggrieved parties. U.S. officers now dressed in glittering full uniform; Tlingits wore regalia that "vied with our splendor." Flanked by their kinsmen, Chilkat leaders Koh'klux and Colchika gathered on one side of the building; Daanawáak, Karskarz, and the Chilkoots assembled on the opposite. Signaled by a gunshot, they together boarded a dory rowed by soldiers to the *Favorite*.[11]

Once aboard the steamer, Beardslee read from a prepared speech that framed a history of U.S.-Tlingit relations driven by old threats and promises. Back in 1869, the "great Tyhee" William Henry Seward had been "greatly pleased" with the abundant resources of Chilkat lands and his friendly treatment by "brave and intelligent tribes." Beardslee reminded listeners that in ensuing years, his naval patrols were called to settle troubles stirred by Indians and whites alike. In most cases, the United States had relied on the threat of a trade embargo to secure the cooperation of Native leadership. Beardslee was "very grieved and mortified" over the latest clash. "Like a little fire," it "can easily be put out by a cool breath," but if allowed to burn, the flames will spread and "destroy the country." To prevent the Navy from squelching the blaze with unilateral action, Beardslee asked Native leadership to "help me blow it out."

A headman spoke. If each party told its version of the war, would the commander arbitrate?

Beardslee refused, emphasizing that he came as a friend, not a judge: "We know that you Indians have laws, and that by them this dispute can be settled better by your chiefs in cool, deliberate council than by young men, crazy with hoo-che-noo, killing each other."

Koh'klux agreed that the dispute was best resolved by traditional means. He would speak with the family of the deceased to determine the number of blankets owed and make the payment himself. The old sháade háni's pledge enlivened Daanawáak and Karskarz, who broke their silence to engage in "friendly consultation." After Beardslee received assurances that the leaders would pursue peace, Major Morris spoke at length about the liquor trade. If the Tlingit leaders cooperated, he said, the navy promised to build a schoolhouse around which a new village would be constructed with Chilkoots residing east of the store and Chilkats, to the west. And should the Tlingits halt their use of "trouble-brewing molasses," Morris added, the *Favorite* would bring them "good, wholesome beer" from the Sitka brewery. Headmen chuckled and nodded as Major Morris patted his ample belly to show how beer drinkers became "fat and healthy." Beardslee reported that they were "very willing to have the experiment tried."[12]

Before the Tlingit leaders disembarked, sailors demonstrated the force of their weaponry. In testimony twenty years later, Skandoo'o's brother, Yen-da-yonk, recalled hearing "shots over the hill" during the howitzer demonstration. Rounds from a Gatling gun were especially impressive to the men aboard the gunship, for the repeating weapon showed "what one man could do to a fleet of canoes coming from all directions."[13] Back ashore, the headmen met to determine Koh'klux's payment, then returned to the ship to sign the peace treaty.

"So Haines was founded," ethnographer George Thornton Emmons pronounced in his seminal account, *The Tlingit Indians*.[14] Although the actual town was a quarter-century from incorporation, the new place name displaced the previous Native appellation with a secure, uncomplicated Anglo-Saxon reference. A ten-thousand-dollar donation from New Jersey benefactor Mrs. Francis E. Haines, who never visited her Alaska namesake, produced a mission school from lumber delivered on a steamer by Sheldon Jackson himself.

The arrival of missionaries Eugene and Carrie Willard in summer 1881 marked the official installation of eastern gentility in Jilkáat aaní. Like Hall Young, the Willards came from solid Pennsylvania Presbyterian stock, armed with fervor for Christian social reform. Carrie was born in New Castle, twenty-eight miles from Butler, the Wrangell preacher's hometown. Three years after coming to Haines, she would publish the first book from a woman residing in Alaska, *Life in Alaska,* then again in 1891 with a quasi-fictional account of Chilkat culture before and after Christianity in

Kin-Da-Shon's Wife (see chap. 4). The Willards' installment coincided with renewed hostilities in the ongoing "hooch wars," some of which was highly dramatized in her second book.

Alarmed by reports of internecine Chilkat violence resulting in several deaths, Sec. of the Navy William H. Hunt ordered men to Klukwan to investigate and "take any action possible." Respected regionwide as a marine surveyor (updated versions of his charts of Sitka are still used today), Navy Master Gustavus C. Hanus sailed from Sitka with Capt. Edward P. Lull, two Tlingit interpreters, "a party of Marines," and a photographer.[15]

On June 25, 1881, the steamer *Favorite* anchored in Portage Cove, where the officers rowed ashore to meet the Dickinsons. George, described by Hanus as "a man easily scared," had seen nothing firsthand but was so unnerved by events that his interviewers found it "impossible to get a precise statement" about the conflict. Fright nearly paralyzed Sarah, who could hardly speak. Hearing only "foolish and vague rumors" around the trading post, Hanus determined to lead the detachment upriver. Before they left the Dickinsons, however, Hanus ordered all molasses kegs transferred from the store to the *Favorite*.[16]

Early the next day, Koh'klux arrived with his entourage. The Chilkat sháade háni explained that he had "done all he could to promote peace" between combatants, but eight deaths—including two high-caste Ravens—had kinsmen clamoring for many more lives in payment. As an opposite clansman, Koh'klux's hands were tied. Confronted by his "greatest tribal difficulty," the Chilkat leader asked for help. Hanus read Secretary Hunt's orders, which, upon translation, Koh'klux followed with an invitation.[17]

In two small canoes, members of the Sitka party paddled up the Chilkat River against the summer flood of melting glaciers until a full day's work brought them to Klukwan. Koh'klux lodged his guests in the Cinnamon Bear treasure house, where Seward and Davidson had slept a dozen years earlier. A few hours in the village convinced Hanus that "nearly all the trouble is caused by hoochinoo."

The next morning Hanus met with Koh'klux and about a hundred Ravens (he called them "Crows") on their side of town. The Tlingits patiently listened to the officer's "long speech" urging them to end fighting, quietly conferred, then announced they would "make peace if the Whales would pay a thousand blankets." Hanus walked the offer a half-mile to the other end of the village where he delivered the deal in a similar speech to clan members barricaded inside houses, which functioned as forts with "portholes cut at intervals." Multiple bullet holes perforated many walls. Hanus walked the path across the village several more times until disputants settled on a hundred blankets, Lull reported, "and in my presence they shook hands and promised to live peaceably."[18]

Classes at Haines Mission began on August 8, 1881.

Despite the reconciliation in Klukwan, deep divisions lingered, but change was in the air. Upon hearing the news from Hanus and Lull, Reverend Willard sent word upriver to Koh'klux for permission to conduct a missionary meeting. The response came quickly: welcome. The headman was ready to seal interclan promises of peace with Christian conversion.

Eugene and Carrie Willard set out September 1 with interpreter Sarah Dickinson and others on the first Christian mission to Klukwan. Following a scenic tour of the Chilkat River described in *Kin-da-shon's Wife,* Carrie reconstructed the grand meeting between missionaries and the "rich old chief," Koh'klux. Since the headman was "in nowise involved in the war," Willard was vexed that he maintained "a position so neutral that he could confer with either side while attempting to control neither."[19] The sháade háni proved himself a generous host, lodging his visitors in the Cinnamon Bear house "with its hundreds of carved vessels and boxes of blankets and oil and every Indian treasure." Lavish adornment, however, did not distract the missionaries from the "pall" hanging over what was once a "busy, thriving town."

The roots of the conflict were saturated with hooch, Willard wrote, reaping a dark harvest for her novel's "emissary of evil," Yealh-neddy. Her shaman retained his power by using alcohol to keep villagers "in a state of abject slavery," while Koh'klux remained concerned but disengaged. It seems a set-up for a last heart-pounding denouement, but instead, Willard's villain simply slunk into the dark wilderness away from the "light of Christ," never to return.[20]

Hundreds of Ravens and "servants" jammed into the sháade háni's big house. In a manner approved by Reverends Hall Young and Aaron Lindsley, Eugene Willard bore to them the "suffering, struggling world" from which, with faith, a "message of peace and love" could emerge. Their "shame" was paid for by the Son of God, who died so that they could live forever. For such a reward, however, God required His true sons and daughters to follow a divine code: "To be *received* His love must be *obeyed.*"[21]

The long hush in the wake of her husband's sermon sounded to Carrie Willard like the breath of transformation. "Hard faces softened, dull faces kindled. Their hearts had been touched. The Chilkat war was at an end." Brimming with new faith, villagers assured the missionaries that this promise is not like the one they made to the navy, which was "a quick and easy way of getting them out of the country." Real peace is different. "When the taste of blood is out of our mouths, we see that we are brothers," a speaker said. To demonstrate the weight of their commitment, Whale and Raven headmen would live as honored guests in former enemies' houses for a week as a way of "proving thus their own sincerity" and following traditional protocol.

Carrie Willard described the scene in a letter to Sheldon Jackson. Koh'klux adopted her the day after Reverend Willard's sermon; she was the first white woman to be given a Chilkat name. When the sháade háni told her the name's meaning (which she never revealed in print), she claimed an "even more precious meaning:" that Chilkats were "priceless bits of copper" once separated by "bitterness," now bound by love, cast by "the great Chief above," who melded the fragments into one. As copper-bearer for a new covenant, Mrs. Willard assured Jackson that while Tlingit culture was complex and colorful, the Old Ways must perish.[22]

"Oh, what a pitiful thing," moaned Klukwan elder (and Assembly of God minister) Sally Burratin in 2013 regarding Willard's influence. Rather than a beneficiary of the early mission, Burratin considers herself a survivor. "The Presbyterians promised to teach our people how to read, write, sing." Her volume swelled. "Instead they built this big home like a prison, then starved our children down on the beach while the preacher's wife just laughed at 'em!" Long pause while Sally's eyes flashed at me, tears glistening as she repeats, whispering, "just laughed at them." The elder's narrowed eyes gripped mine, a smile rearranged her generous face. A rye chuckle escaped.

"They were trying to civilize us poor savages."[23]

In spring 1881, Koh'klux invited Reverend Willard and ethnographer Aurel Kraus to witness a shaman's initiation in Klukwan. The white men joined a large crowd in the headman's house, where hundreds of soles pounded a booming rhythm. In the midst of the thunderous dancing, Koh'klux spoke to interpreter Billy Dickinson who translated to the white men: "This initiation is the last of its kind. His people want to live the new way."[24]

Encouraged by the headman's actions, Sheldon Jackson later proposed to Koh'klux that he honor their first God's Man by changing Klukwan's name to Willard. The leader took the proposition to his council.

"Always been a village" kept its name.[25]

In the deep-fried prose one expects from the back of a 1950s café menu ("The Best Food in Alaska"), Haines businessman I. B. Howser offered his story of Skandoo'o for hungry customers awaiting their "Real He-Man/ She-Woman Breakfast Plates." Aside from concocting cures, "the last of the great Medicine Men" could predict the future and "show off his mystic powers." Crowned with dangling red locks sprouting from double cowlicks, "Scundooo" cut a fearsome figure.[26]

His power, however, was eroding. Elements of the New Way—disease, liquor, Boston food, science, medicine, and theology—cut into his ethos. When the people stopped believing in their íx̲t' business suffered. The shaman increased his forays to other villages, demanding blankets in payment for relief from nonexistent maladies. U.S. Navy gunboats sought him, but the "copper-haired" Scundooo "didn't do that back seat stuff;" his "bombastic methods" continued.

"In the midst of all this upheaval," the menu explained, "an official of the vicinity took sick," so Scundooo came for the cure. Despite a display of "mystic powers befitting such an important man," the patient died. The medicine man was tried for murder and sentenced to forty years at McNeill Island Federal Prison in Washington.

By this time, I. B.'s wife, Merle, glides back into the steamy diner with refills ("Coffee goes with a meal—No limit to number of cups") and conversation with customers. Most are locals—loggers and fishermen—with a few stragglers from the weekly steamship. An occasional vehicle rolls off with folks asking about conditions on the new Haines Road, 150 miles of potholes to a junction with the newly built Alaska Highway. Merle can count on those outsiders to crack a comment or query. What about this Skundooo? Was he for real? Where's he buried? She chuckles, offers the action end of her coffee pot, taps the menu. Read on.

Not long after settling into a cell at McNeill, the shaman had a vision. A large cash theft in the Chilkat Valley gave rise to Skandoo'o's offer to identify the culprits in exchange for a pardon. After a year in prison, the shaman returned to Haines to finger the four Natives "guilty of this dastardly deed of stealing the white man's money." Exonerated, Skandoo'o became known as "Judge Scundoo" until his death at eighty-three. His body was wrapped tightly in skins and placed atop a cliff overlooking Yandeist'ak̲yé and the Chilkat River delta. In the ensuing years, "lowly thieving men" pilfered bones and valuables from the gravesite, leaving only "a couple of short ribs, a vest, and some pieces of wooden boxes."

Skan-Do Grave (ca 1910). Photograph, 266 A8 no. 14, Haines Sheldon Museum, Alaska.

Breakfast clatters onto the speckled Formica table-top. Merle cocks her head and beams a trademark smile. Whad'ja think? Distracted by rising vapor from a He-Man platter (ham, bacon or sausage links with "spuds, oleo, jelly, and coffee"), speculation becomes a chore. Using a forefinger emboldened by caffeine, the patron slides his coffee cup forward. Where'd you say that rascal was buried?

Decades of coffee shop chatter constructed a mythic sense of Skandoo'o, "the last medicine man." As the most accessible shaman biography in town, locals knew the story by heart. When Howser's Café closed in the 1980s, the big black-and-white menus nearly disappeared, but someone thought to pass on a stack to the local museum.

Boil the six-hundred-word blurb down to the truth and this much is clear: Skandoo'o ("one who is enraged at him") was a red-headed shaman called Dr. Scundoo before he was sentenced to San Quentin (not McNeill) and returned three years later as "Judge Scundoo." He did not have a mystic vision in prison. Grave robbers stole his treasures.

Beyond hearsay and menus, local knowledge about Skandoo'o is scanty. Historical records reveal a bit more. Though not the last Tlingit to practice shamanism, Skandoo'o—Reverend Young's nemesis—was notoriously resistant to its demise. After Sitka Jack disbanded his raiders and allied with

Boston men in the late 1870s, the Shangukeidí íx̲t' drifted among Chilkoot relatives who shielded him. For over a decade, the slippery shaman evàded all efforts at capture.[27]

Skandoo'o's submergence coincided with the rise of a non-Native population around the trading post and mission, and, by 1882, the operation of two salmon canneries. "That's when our culture started to break apart," said Chilkat headman Joe Hotch in 2014, "when our people left their homes to live near the mission and the money."[28]

The íx̲t' persisted on the periphery, still deeply tied with his community. According to U.S. census records, Skandoo'o was married and fathered a daughter, likely born in the mid-1880s.[29] In the traditional Tlingit way, the infant girl—called Kaatkwaax̲snei—was betrothed to a toddler boy, Stoowukaa, grandson of Koh'klux. After their marriage in 1902, Florence and Louis Shotridge became known nationally as artists and ethnographers who introduced mainstream America to Tlingit culture.[30] As a curator for the University of Pennsylvania Museum, Louis brokered the acquisition of hundreds of clan treasures ranging from Chilkat blankets to a sixty-foot cedar canoe.

Their remarkable lives—and attendant tragedies—stir strong emotions even today among anthropologists and Native kinsmen and supply the grist for this book's companion volume.

Not until Sheldon Jackson published an account of Skandoo'o's alleged atrocities in an 1888 newsletter did the force of public opinion arouse a military reaction from Sitka. Jackson charged that persistent, high-charged witch hunts led by "Doctor Scundoo" terrorized Native and non-Native residents. The medicine man was most active, reported Jackson, in the coldest months, when "storms are raging their highest" and cloistered villagers were susceptible to rumor and fear. Dramatic accounts of Native savagery stimulated donations to the missions, so the infamous "Skundoo" became an antagonist suitable for the cause. Kadachan played the victim for Jackson's newsletters to wealthy East Coast Presbyterians.[31]

According to Jackson, the shaman's first victim that winter was Emma, "higher caste" wife of Lunaat's tribal successor, John. Through loud, relentless badgering, Skandoo'o inflicted such "shame upon her as a witch, [that] she procured a rope and deliberately hanged herself to a rafter of her home." A few months later, Skandoo'o accused eighteen-year-old Minnie of bewitching her aunt, but she insisted the real witch was Kadachan, orator in John Muir's crew, who had recently relocated from Wrangell to serve at the Haines mission. Fearful for his life, he sought protection by sailing to Sitka, so Skandoo'o bound Minnie with ropes and her own hair until Kadachan returned weeks later. The Presbyterian elder was immediately hogtied along with Minnie and subjected to the shaman's fury until Kadachan offered to resolve the affair with a "generous potlatch." Descendants today remember Kadachan as a bridge-builder, "our peacemaker," recalled a relative.[32]

Weeks later, the *Favorite* brought troops up Lynn Canal to apprehend Skandoo'o and, in a public ceremony, attempted to break perceptions of his power by shearing his dreadlocks. He continued to practice until March 1894, at the close of another long winter, when Chilkat Valley Tlingits sent for the U.S. marshal after witnessing the torture and death of another alleged witch, a fourteen-year-old girl named Ches'aax. Skandoo'o had bound the girl with heavy rope in a small room for days, according to the marshal, with the intent to "starve, kill, and murder." Daanawáak immediately sent a deposition to Sitka alleging Skandoo'o's crime and his possible hideout in Dyea. A week later, an unlit cutter landed in darkness on the Taiya River mud flats. Led by a Dyea headman, more than a dozen armed men rousted the íxt' from a clan house then escorted him back to Juneau. A manslaughter conviction in U.S. District Court in Alaska landed Skandoo'o in San Quentin in California for three years.[33]

Through the 1980s and 1990s, I listened to Tlingit elder Dixie Johnson lead the Gei Saan Dancers in the "San Quentin Song" written by Skandoo'o during his prison stint. As the twenty or so Chilkoot elders performed, their mournful tone and movement conveyed the emotional meaning of Tlingit words to any audience. "He's crying for his land," Dixie told me. "He won't feel whole until he comes back home."[34]

At the end of his hitch, Skandoo'o returned to Lynn Canal a changed man. He morphed his infamous outlaw persona into Judge Scundoo, a Main Street eccentric with a tin star on his breast and a drum for the Salvation Army. For pay, he performed. In 1906 photographers Winter and Pond commissioned Skandoo'o to recreate shamanic rituals in sessions at their Juneau studio for a series of images still seen today as part of Alaska popular culture. The next year, an unnamed photographer took a portrait of Skandoo'o flanked by his brothers, Karskarz ("Monkey Man") and Yen-da-yonk (sometimes Schwatki). Schwatki ("child of Schwatka") acquired his name as lead guide for Lt. Frederick Schwatka, an army explorer, who was, among other things, the United States' choice to seek the lost Franklin expedition. Under the lieutenant, Schwatki guided U.S. troops on several missions into the Yukon Interior, including a traverse over Chilkoot Pass, which was soon known as gateway to Klondike gold-fields.

Among local Native names heard by stampeders on the muddy streets of Skagway and Dyea, that of the notorious íxt' stuck—a seed from which storytellers could cultivate myth. When twenty-one-year-old Jack London heard the stories, he recast the actual Skandoo'o as the noble, all-seeing "Scundoo, shaman of shamans" in *Children of the Frost* published in 1902.[35] A year later, London became a household name with the advent of *Call of the Wild,* a book that has never gone out of print.

Brothers Skandoo'o and Yen-da-yonk died in 1908, each laid to rest in his appropriate space. The íx̱t' perches alone on a high cliff top; guide lies in the Christian cemetery. The grave of Yen-da-yonk is marked today by a marble monument: "In-da-yonk/100 Years." Skandoo'o's remains were interned in a small death house on which was painted a Killer Whale, his clan crest. Alongside the bier, a twenty-foot cottonwood canoe held precious personal items: Chilkat robes, furs, bear-claw necklaces, headpieces, carvings, yéik amulets. All were intended to accompany the íx̱t' to the next world.

Christian or not, Tlingit belief is very firm that one should never touch the belongings of an íx̱t', so Natives avoided Skandoo'o's grave. But the Howsers' Café menu was right about one thing: the deeds of "lowly thieving men." Old-timers say soldiers from Fort Seward raided the site and sold everything. Soldiers apparently pressed I. B. Howser to buy the shaman's skull, but he refused. Following a rash of unexpected appearances around town, the grisly artifact (which may have been painted gold) was reputedly sold out of state.[36]

After exhausting public records and café hearsay, on a drizzly day in September 2009 I knocked on eighty-five-year-old Charlie Brouillette's door at three-mile Haines Highway. His is one of the few houses near Yandeist'aḵyé, which is now deserted. Charlie and his wife, Harriett, were in their final hour of preparation before leaving Haines to be near a hospital in Seattle. Wife and daughter finished last-minute packing and cleaning while Charlie and I talked at the kitchen table.

Charlie's mother, Mary, was Skandoo'o's great-niece, which in Tlingit matrilineal tradition, he reminded me, made him the medicine man's closest living relative. Elders spoke little of Skandoo'o while Charlie was growing up. He wasn't aware of any child of the íx̱t', whose sister was his great-grandmother, Tsu'si. Yes, Charlie said, it's possible that Florence was Skandoo'o's daughter, but his Tlingit mother never talked about Native ancestors when he was a kid. He suspected she preferred silence to battling with his father, Charles Brouillette Sr., a French-German teamster who hated Skandoo'o. Anything he said about the old shaman "wasn't very nice," Charlie chuckled. Once when Charles Sr. was driving a load through Klukwan, Skandoo'o accosted him for a ride back to Haines in the horse and wagon, but the elder Charles was headed farther up the valley to Porcupine. He loudly refused.

    DLEIT AAN<u>K</u>ÁAWU

Charlie and Harriett Brouillette. Photograph by author.

Between hideous exclamations, the shaman scooped dust from the road and blew it at Brouillette, who drove away shouting his own epithets. Charlie recalls another story his father told about pitching in a baseball game in front of a local crowd that included the medicine man. "He thought Skandoo'o was trying to put a jinx on him somehow or another so he threw a wild pitch and hit him accidentally on purpose." Charlie laughed. The íx̱t' slunk away.[37]

What of Skandoo'o's opposition to missionaries? The details don't come easily, but since he was a boy, Charlie heard "nothing but bad attitude" in the Presbyterian Church, of which he is a lifelong member. "We Tlingits called him a shrewd businessman, but they (non-Natives) called him stingy, sharp. A funny way, a different way."

Charlie described the mainstream opinion of Skandoo'o as somewhere between hapless relic and evil holdover, but as a Tlingit, he said it was hard to dismiss obvious connections between the medicine man and the spirit world. He recalled a story about a Yandeist'a<u>k</u>yé í<u>x</u>t' who foresaw enemy canoes headed up the fjord, so villagers had time to hide high up <u>G</u>eisán (Mount Ripinsky). Another í<u>x</u>t' was well-known for his ability to fly between Yandeist'a<u>k</u>yé and Klukwan, even to Taku, a hundred miles away. Besides his witch hunts, Skandoo'o was known for exuberant performances and supernatural demonstrations. Charlie recalled old Ed Shotridge telling him that he became convinced of Skandoo'o's powers when he watched the old shaman cast eagle down on a swift river and the feathers floated upstream, against the current.

Of the old beliefs, Charlie shrugged. His eyes met mine. "They took what they saw and what they had."

When witches are part of those beliefs, what of the crime that sent his great-uncle to prison? Charlie held up his arms, palms up, fingers out-stretched. "He thought he was doing what was right," the former high school teacher declared. "Whoops, she died you know."

In Charlie's eyes shone the same sepia-toned gleam of his infamous ancestor arrayed in amulets and furs, crouched, an ornate rattle in each hand, ready to spring.

Epilogue: *The Wild Line*

Three months and five hundred miles after Maj. Gen. O. O. Howard declared war on the Nez Perce, Chief Joseph (Hinmatóowyalahtq'it) found a haven. In the midst of an eleven-hundred-mile retreat known as the Nez Perce War, the leader guided several hundred children, women, and men into the Yellowstone Basin for thirteen days of rest and repair.

As a tourist visiting the newly established park, General in Chief William Tecumseh Sherman was furious when he learned that Chief Joseph's group had passed within shouting distance of his ostentatious campsite. After Sherman departed, his scouts guaranteed the safety of nine frightened vacationers but vanished when the tourists later confronted a Nez Perce scouting party. Gunshots echoed across the meadows. The horsemen faded into the forest, leaving one white man dead and another gravely wounded. Troops mustered around the tourists in wait for raids. A day or two later, Chief Joseph sent a subchief and horsemen to disavow the violence and care for the white survivors. Gunfire foiled their approach, so the refugees resumed their northward exodus.

Firebrand of Grant's Indian Wars, Sherman parleyed his close encounter into military strategy with a wire flashed to Col. Nelson A. Miles at Fort Keogh, three hundred miles north. Joseph's tribe would pass nearby—an easy interception. Just two days from the Canadian border, Miles's forces confronted the Nez Perce in the Bear Paw Mountains of Montana. Exhausted

Davidson Glacier and Lake, June 2004. Photograph by author.

and outnumbered, Chief Joseph surrendered: "From where the sun now stands, I will fight no more forever."[1]

Sherman forced his captives to march four hundred miles to Leavenworth, Kansas, then relocate years later to the Colville Reservation in central Washington. Joseph never returned to his homeland in Oregon's Wallowa country, much of which is designated wilderness today.

By seeking cover in Yellowstone, Chief Joseph led his people into a region long considered a sanctuary by intermountain tribes, a place apart from white settlers where the First Ones withdrew to hunt, fish, and gather. The creators of Yellowstone National Park in 1872 codified a line around the land to keep wildness in and keep former residents out. As with later designations in Yosemite and Glacier National Parks, U.S. troops were stationed to enforce the line. But for token Natives at trading posts and "Wild West" shows, early tourists—privileged white Americans—sought wilderness in its purest form: without humans.

Chief Joseph crossed the line and paid the price.

All for the semblance of Eden, a national Native dispossession movement precipitated the wilderness preservation movement.

"Wilderness is a made-up word," a Tlingit leader told me one spring morning in 2013, as we sat around a table in the Kettleson Library in Sitka.

Preferring to remain anonymous, the man held a steady gaze and solemn expression that underscored the weight of his claim. Native Americans stewarded the continent for millennia before Muir, he said, "yet white people act like he was the first to think of it." Much of the United States, whose beauty Muir extolled, had been ethnically cleansed not long before he saw it: Winnebagos in Wisconsin, Cherokees in southern Appalachia, Seminoles in Florida, Ahwahneechees in Yosemite, Modocs at Mount Shasta, and many, many more tribes.

The way the man saw it, Muir founded "a religion called conservation" in which his disciples believe fervently. For Native Alaskans, like many indigenous people, the so-called "wild" line makes little sense. Wilderness designation aims to nullify an ancient relationship with place and snuffs out a way of life. Your family fished this stream for a thousand years? Too bad. It belongs to nature now.

Some people place their faith in lines to protect landscapes. Some lines protect habitat for egrets and bears and fish. Some keep out those who know the wilderness best and love it most. Some lines are defended, some are ignored. Some wounds heal, some ache for generations.

I recall the tingle that shot through my nine-year-old body when I first saw the line. For three summers my family camped at a favorite fishing hole on the South Fork of the Payette River in central Idaho. On days when midday heat numbed trout and small children, a grownup might lure us onto a trail with promises of Vienna sausages and candy bars. A few hundred yards up what is now called the Idaho Centennial Trail, we routinely paused to admire a wooden sign marking our entrance into the Sawtooth Primitive Area. Here was a place where animals ran free, my folks said, where humans only visited.

The line became more real when I encountered a new sign in July 1965: Entering Sawtooth Wilderness Area.

"This is all that's left of the great American frontier," Dad explained. He and Mom had recently joined the Wilderness Society and were reading the organization's magazine. In the simplest, most romantic way he could muster, Dad explained how the Wilderness Act became law the previous fall as a last-ditch effort to save the natural treasures of a great nation. Lover of history and close calls, Dad regaled us with nail-biters about John Muir, the "grandfather" of wilderness, who survived by grit and blind faith.

"Muir was a wild guy," Dad said, "but he was lucky. The Paiute (whom Dad taught on the rez) thrived for centuries out here not because of luck, but because it was home. Now you tell me—who's wilder?"

My father's question lingered as I tried to discern the division of an otherwise innocuous lodge-pole pine meadow. As the others turned for camp, I hopped back and forth over the line between spine-tingling wilderness and just plain-old forest. I swore it felt different on the wild side.

The incident propelled me through a half-century of inquiry into the wild line. As a student of "frontier rhetoric," I explored Native and non-Native relationships with the natural world, an investigation that, over time, confirmed my father's allusion to the racist implications of the word "wild." Tecumseh and Thoreau notwithstanding, tracing the roots of American conservation advocacy invariably led to the man whose name I first heard while standing on the line with Dad.

In his crusade to preserve his beloved Sierra Nevada and America's forests, John Muir sharpened a rhetorical tack dodged by Emerson and Thoreau. While American philosophers and poets waxed romantic over the beauty and restorative powers of wild places, Muir was among the first to argue for their necessity. Like few Euro-American contemporaries, Muir's sheer personal vigor and scientific acuity deepened his relationship with nature beyond utility or taxonomy. Product of an evangelical upbringing, the conservationist projected images of wild nature safe and wholesome enough for a Christian nation.

Read *evangelical* as righteous passion. Like all true believers, Muir drew a line in the duff between good and evil, arguing specifically for the superiority of wild over domestic. But lines are funny things. Even when inviolate, they can move, pivoting on an axis, as it were. A line looks different depending on your perspective, depending on which side of the line you stand. For Native people, the wild line all too often meant exclusion, and the inevitable collapse of the Old Ways.

This reality became especially clear to me when I moved to Alaska a century after Muir's first visit and felt the environmental icon's presence in vast landscapes seemingly untouched by humans. How, I wondered, did Alaska Natives respond to "preserved" lands? Does wilderness status kill culture by removing and locking Natives from their traditional lands, or does it protect the Old Ways by managing lands and resources for future generations?

When Muir ventured into Alaska in 1879, he brought along the mainstream belief that postconquest Native Americans were pitiable has-beens with "no place in the landscape." Aboard the SS *California,* Muir's missionary companions spoke of the northern Tlingit people as the last of the "wild tribes"—untreatied, warlike, animistic—in a geographic and cultural stronghold nearly untouched by Euro-American influence. Though the naturalist disdained the hubris he attached to the "Divines," he nonetheless confirmed their overall mission to domesticate heathens by his work with

Reverend Young. After all, Muir's "discovery" of Glacier Bay was financed by the Presbyterian Church. His life-long friendship with Young was bound not only by shared adventures but by shared responsibility for the mass conversion in Yandeist'akyé.

Few tribal members today recall details about Muir's ordained companion; most will tell you that, for better or worse, it was Dleit Aankáawu who persuaded them to redraw the line. In their writings, Young and Muir acknowledged Stickeen Johnny as the translator, yet collective memory seven generations later holds that Muir and his listeners understood each other *without* translation. As the first white man to offer Chilkat-Chilkoot people brotherhood and scientific inquiry—no strings attached—Muir set a new standard as a white man whose ethos was stronger than words.

For a century and a half, northern Tlingits defended a bold line against any white settlement in the region. Koh'klux's signed invitation of 1880 opened a freshet of white miners to render gold and rumor sufficient for a calamitous gold rush eighteen years later. Though one may claim the economic success of Tlingit packers as just compensation, there are no words to frame the cultural impacts to an ancient people when outsiders supplant and dislocate them. After disease wiped out two-thirds of the population, survivors were left to reconstruct an elaborate past or get a job. Their legacy lagged.

In a rare act of contrition, in 1971 Congress passed the Alaska Native Claims Settlement Act as an attempt to compensate Natives for a century of cultural upheaval with a billion dollars and the return of forty-four million acres to Native ownership. Some Native lands were logged, mined, and drilled, and some preserved as habitat. Like their white brothers and sisters, indigenous adversaries learned how to sue each other over land use.

A crowning achievement for Muir's disciples was the Alaska National Interest Lands Conservation Act of 1980, which granted special status (parks, monuments, preserves) to 157 million acres, including 56 million turned into wilderness. In the Last Frontier, wilderness set-asides are subject to an "Alaska exception" that authorizes, among other things, motorized access to pursue traditional subsistence foods for Natives and rural residents. Most Alaska wilderness lands protect vital habitat for key subsistence species, which are often stewarded by those people who have the most to lose. For the first time, tending the wild line became a common concern for those living on both sides of the boundary.

Gradually, some Alaska Natives came to embrace the wild line as a firewall against encroaching development, a tool used in defense of traditional ways. Arrival at this conclusion is difficult. Living with the line is often a lengthy, painful process as indigenous residents re-experience the loss of access to or control of ancestral lands with ensuing degradation of memory and culture.

These issues weighed on the Klukwan Tribal Council in 1982 when it voted to oppose creation of the Alaska Chilkat Bald Eagle Preserve, a state bill to set special protections in the forty-four thousand acres of rich habitat surrounding the village. Council members voted against the preserve not because they disliked eagles but because all the way back to Russian days, Tlingits had drawn and redrawn the lines of Jilḵáat aaní, ceding a little more control with each land or resource cession. Those times, leadership decided, were over. Despite village opposition, Republican governor Jay Hammond sought special status for the Chilkat Council Grounds, the delta expanse in front of Klukwan where each fall up to four thousand bald eagles congregate for salmon. He hailed the law as "a crown jewel in the annals of cooperative resource management."

Disputants still wince at that line.

But none deny that the wild line to protect eagles also conserves the salmon runs that have sustained Klukwan for at least a thousand years, providing up to 75 percent of villagers' annual protein. In the milky runoff of glaciers throughout the fourteen-hundred-square-mile watershed wriggle all five species of Pacific salmon plus healthy runs of steelhead, Dolly Varden, and eulachon. The subsistence nets that stretch into the Chilkat River along the Klukwan riverfront are prime indicators of community wellness. Full nets mean healthy diets, economic resilience, and community purpose. Empty nets lead to additional twenty-mile drives to town for processed foods and health care.

In an age when glaciers melt faster than at any time in human memory, Chilkat people are more protective of their river than ever. In 2014 the Klukwan village council acknowledged the latest threat to pristine Chilkat headwaters—rich deposits of copper, zinc, gold, and silver ore may signal massive development in the near future. Years of exploration have led Constantine Metal Resources to the brink of full-scale production. "Tremendous expansion potential" claims the Canadian firm's website about the mine it calls the "Palmer Volcanogenic Massive Sulphide Project." In the next decade Constantine envisions a "world-class" source of minerals with "ready access to Asian concentrate markets." As required by law, the multinational giant promises to monitor salmon-spawning streams and fund "stream mitigation" but offers few details about the long-term effects of heavy metals from impoundment reservoirs leaching into salmon-producing streams. In an area prone to earthquakes and flash floods, the company's pledge to contain toxic leach-fields for centuries seems disingenuous to downstream populations who fear the prospects of a poisoned legacy for their grandchildren.[2]

"When it comes to fish, we draw the line," says Klukwan village manager Brian Willard of the community's stance. Brown-bear-sized Willard endured four years of my high school English classes and more in college. He's now forty-three with a village on his broad shoulders. If anything, he has learned the value of a clear, uncluttered message. "It's not that we're against all mining," says Willard. "But without salmon we're gone. Poof."[3]

By teaming up with local and international conservation groups, Klukwan is leveraging the wild line for subsistence rights, and once again its people are asserting themselves as protectors of Jilḵáat aaní. In fall of 2014 the village council passed a resolution to compel the State of Alaska to authorize an Environmental Protection Agency designation of "Outstanding National Resource Water," in effect holding the Canadian mine to the highest possible watermark. Beyond its role as a source of protein and cultural identity for Tlingit people, the council argued, the Chilkat River nourishes a rich ecosystem that sustains both wildlife and human populations. In 2012 the watershed supplied salmon enough to net $12.5 million for local commercial fishers.

It turns out that foremost among EPA standards for an "outstanding" designation is that the nominee flows across a line marking protected habitat, such as wilderness, national park, or wildlife preserve such as the Bald Eagle Preserve.

The Eagle Preserve fits.

"They're gonna harm our fish since the water's going into the river," Joe Hotch told me in 2014. The traditional leader's hands gestured like water. "So we need to make them aware that our fish are harmed enough already." A finger slashed a line in the air. "Instead of fighting more."[4]

Refracted through a modern lens, John Muir's wild lines may seem simplistic, naïve, or even racist. In a nation of postage stamp wildernesses surrounded by vast lands open to sacrifice, the cynicism of Native America is predictable and inevitable. But when residents align with stakeholders to preserve the sanctity of a few special places, miracles happen. For tribes in Alaska and elsewhere, advocates for future generations are discovering that cultural survival depends on protecting habitat. Meaningful alliances are being forged between non-Native groups and Native tribes—Tlingit, Nez Perce, Gwich'in, Umatilla, Hupa, to name a few—for the sake of wildlife and wild lands.

Over definitions of "wild" and "wilderness," we might debate into the

Dancing Costumes of Chilkat Indians, ca. 1900. Photograph by J. M. Blankenberg, 1975.304.0001, Haines Sheldon Museum, Alaska.

night. Were the Chilkat-Chilkoot people any more "wild" before they met John Muir than after? Is Jilḵáat aaní a wilderness or a neighborhood? Do wild salmon require wild waters to be wild? Did Muir reserve a place for humans inside his wild line?

After witnessing the ways of his Tlingit hosts, something shifted in Muir, a wound was healed, new faith bloomed.

"I never saw a child or servant scolded or punished, or any resentment about taking the best place at the fire, or the best bits of food," Muir scribbled in his journal on his final night in Yandeist'akyé. "Many a good lesson might be learned from these wild children. They should send missionaries to the Christians."[5]

Selected Chronology

1741   Russians "discover" Southeast Alaska.

1774   Spanish ships sail into Lynn Canal.

1794   British lieutenant Joseph Whidbey and crew are escorted out of Lynn Canal by two hundred Chilkats in five war canoes.

1795   Aleksandr Baranov sails into "Chilkat Bay," where he places markers at prominent points to identify Russian territory.

1800–1830 Reign of Xet-su-wu as headman of Klukwan. He commissions Kadjisdu.axt and family to carve the legendary Whale House totems.

1802   Kiks.ádi Tlingits defeat Russian aggressors.

1803   Russians estimate two thousand adult males in the Chilkat and Chilkoot villages.

1804   Russians defeat Sitka-area Tlingits in a battle for control of the region.

1805–6 Chilkats chide Kiks.ádi tribe for losing Sitka to Russians, then lead tribal groups in a threat against Russian occupiers.

1807   Seventy Chilkats die when they attempt to board and loot a Boston brig in Lynn Canal.

1819   Koh'klux (Kaalaxch') is born in Klukwan, Alaska.

1838   Smallpox epidemic hits Klukwan.

       John Muir is born April 21 in Dunbar, Scotland.

1839 Hudson's Bay Company census of Chilkat records 498 residents

1840 Russia leases "Labouchere" (Pyramid Harbor) to the British for trade with the Chilkats.

1847 S. Hall Young is born in Butler, Pennsylvania.

1849 John Muir leaves Scotland with his family for a homesteading life on the central Wisconsin frontier.

1850 George Davidson begins surveying the West Coast north from Cabo San Lucas in Baja California, Mexico.

Russian crews are forced to abandon ships near Yandeist'akyé. Chilkats salvage four cannons.

1852 A Chilkat war party including Koh'klux and Skandoo'o travels four hundred miles to destroy Fort Selkirk, a Hudson's Bay Company trading post.

1860 John Muir's early-rising machine, clocks, and other inventions win him acclaim at the State Agricultural Fair and a partial scholarship to University of Wisconsin.

1864 The valley of the Yosemite is reserved as a state park.

1867 The U.S. flag is raised in Sitka and Yandeist'akyé.

Gen. Jefferson C. Davis is appointed military commander for the District of Alaska.

After nearly blinding himself, John Muir sets off on a thousand-mile walk from Indiana to Florida.

George Davidson surveys the southern coast of Alaska and plants U.S. Coastal Survey Marker Number 1 on God's Island (later Pyramid Island).

1868 John Muir arrives in San Francisco on March 28.

Gen. Jefferson C. Davis labels the Chilkats the "most formidable and hostile" of all Alaska Natives and proposes a military post in their midst.

1869 George Davidson joins William H. Seward in Klukwan to observe a total eclipse.

1871 John Muir meets Ralph Waldo Emerson in Yosemite.

1872 Yellowstone National Park is established.

1874 John Muir publishes his first essay, "The Wild Sheep of California," in the *Overland Monthly.*

George Holt is the first white man to cross the Chilkoot Pass.

1874–76 John Muir writes a series of articles for the San Francisco *Daily Evening Bulletin* and criticizes the "unknightly" Modoc tribe.

1875   Maj. Gen. O. O. Howard arrives in Chilkat and meets Sitka Jack for a tour of Yandeist'a_kyé.

1876   John Muir delivers his first public lecture at the Congregational Church in Sacramento, California.

1877   Amanda McFarland opens a school for Native girls in Wrangell.

1878   S. Hall Young arrives in Wrangell.

1879   U.S. naval officer Lester A. Beardslee is appointed commander of the USS *Jamestown* in Sitka and becomes federal administrator of Alaska.

John Muir meets Sheldon Jackson at the Presbyterian conference in Yosemite Valley on June 8.

John Muir departs San Francisco aboard the *Dakota* on June 20. Muir arrives in Wrangell, Alaska on July 14.

Muir steams aboard the *Cassiar* with "the divines" from July 21–23.

Muir departs Wrangell in a canoe with S. Hall Young and four Tlingit men: Tow'atte, Kadachan, Sitka Charley, and Stickeen Johnny on October 14.

Muir arrives in Killisnoo on October 21.

Muir in Hoonah on October 23 .

Muir departs Hoonah for Glacier Bay on October 24.

Muir's party paddles from Glacier Bay to Yandeist'a_kyé from October 31–November 4.

Muir delivers his "brotherhood of man" speech to hundreds of Tlingit listeners each night from November 4–8.

Muir climbs Mount Ripinsky to sketch Lynn Canal and Chilkat Valley on November 7.

Oldest Chilkoot shaman declares that Muir and the Tlingits are on the "same side of the river, eye to eye, heart to heart" on November 7

Tow'atte scolds Muir for recklessness that nearly capsizes the canoe on November 19.

Muir's crew returns to Wrangell on November 21.

Muir writes dispatches from Sitka on December 23 and 27.

1880   John Muir arrives in Portland around January 6.

Tow'atte is killed in Wrangell while mediating between warring groups on January 10.

John Muir marries Louie Wanda Strentzl on April 14.

George Dickinson establishes a Northwest Trading Company post at Deishu in spring, and his wife, Sarah, is the first teacher.

Beardslee sends the Bean expedition (miners and military) across the Chilkoot Pass in May 1880.

Muir departs San Francisco for Alaska on July 30.

"Hooch War" brings Beardslee to Klukwan, he conducts a peace ceremony, and Koh'klux signs a letter declaring the area open to whites, in August.

S.Hall Young returns to Deishu with John Vanderbilt to plant a trading post and mission school in August.

1881   John Muir cruises on the *Corwin* into the high Arctic in search of the lost *Jeanette* expedition.

The Reverend Eugene Willard and Caroline Willard arrive at Haines Mission in July and begin teaching classes in August

Klukwan community conducts the last shamanic ceremony before converting to Christianity in summer

1882   John Muir becomes the manager of the orchards of the Strentzl Ranch east of San Francisco and mostly stays home for the next decade.

1889   John Muir meets *Century* editor Robert Underwood Johnson, who convinces him to promote his ideas on a national stage.

1890   John Muir explores Glacier Bay for third time.

1891   After John Muir wages a national campaign to protect the Yosemite, Congress establishes Yosemite National Park.

1892   John Muir founds the Sierra Club and serves as its president until his death.

1894   Skandoo'o apprehended. A military court finds him guilty of manslaughter and sends him to San Quentin in California.

1897   On assignment from the San Francisco *Examiner,* John Muir goes to Skagway, Alaska, to report on the Klondike gold rush.

Skandoo'o returns to Alaska.

1899   John Muir tours with the Harriman Alaska expedition.

1900   Pres. William McKinley is assassinated. Theodore Roosevelt becomes president.

1902   American Alpine Club founded by Frederick Cook, George Davidson, Thomas Hill, Joseph LeConte, John Muir, Robert Peary, and others.

1903   John Muir camps for three days in the Yosemite Valley with Theodore Roosevelt.

1905   Theodore Roosevelt advocates for and receives an expansion of Yosemite National Park.

1906   The Antiquities Act gives the president the power to designate as
       national monuments areas of federal land with scientific or historical
       value.

       An earthquake shakes San Francisco and fires erupt on April 18.

1908   Skandoo'o and his brother Yen-da-yonk die in Haines, Alaska.

       John Muir advocates for protection of the Grand Canyon of the
       Colorado River, which President Roosevelt designates a National
       Monument.

       Muir begins publishing national articles condemning San Francisco's
       plans to dam the Hetch Hetchy Valley in Yosemite National Park.

       Theodore Roosevelt hosts a conference of governors at the White
       House on the subject of conservation.

1909   John Muir publishes *Stickeen*.

1913   U.S. Congress votes to dam the Hetch Hetchy River to supply water to
       San Francisco.

1914   John Muir dies with *Travels in Alaska* manuscript at his bedside on
       December 24.

1915   S. Hall Young publishes *Alaska Days with John Muir* and gives a speech
       about the conversion of Natives at Chilkat during his visit with John
       Muir.

1927   S. Hall Young dies. *Hall Young of Alaska* is published.

Glossary of Tlingit

AANÍ	traditional territory of a Tlingit tribal group
AANḴÁAWU	Great Spirit, "Lord above," high diplomat
AT.ÓOW	artwork elevated to clan ownership; treasured objects
CH'ÁAK	eagle
DLEIT	white or ice
GUWAKAAN	deer; ceremonial "peace hostage"
GUNALCHÉESH	thank you
GUNANAA	outsiders; different people
HÉENI	river or creek
HIT, HITSAATI	house, clan house keeper
ÍX̱T'	shaman; medicine man
ḴWÁAN	community
KOOSHDAAḴÁA	Land Otter Man; dangerous spirit
ḴU.ÉEX'	memorial event; "potlatch"
SHÁADE HÁNI	headman, community leader
SHAKEE.ÁT	ceremonial headdress sworn by shaman, used in dancing
XAQ'NAAKEIN	Chilkat robe
YEIL'	raven
YÉIK	shaman's spirit helpers
YÁAY HÍT	Whale House
YAK'ÉI	good

Notes

INTRODUCTION

1. Muir, 21 July 1879, *John of the Mountains: The Unpublished Journals of John Muir*, ed. Linnie Marsh Wolfe, 2d ed. (Madison: University of Wisconsin Press, 1979), 262.

2. Muir, 23 December 1879, *Letters from Alaska*, ed. Robert Engberg and Bruce Merrell (Madison: University of Wisconsin Press, 1993), 56.

3. Austin Hammond, quoted in Daniel Henry, "Chilkoot Heritage: Living on Stories," *Chilkat Valley News*, 16 August 1985, p. 5 (with author notes). The author has also drawn on notes taken during his interview of Hammond and coverage of the event for the *Chilkat Valley (Haines, Alaska) News*. These notes are in his possession.

February 2007, Klukwan, Alaska.

5. Marsha Hotch, *Tlingit Time*, KHNS-FM, 5 March 2006, Haines, Alaska. Hotch's program still airs in 2017. Victoria Barber, "An Expert Opinion on Whether John Muir Was Really an 'Honorary Chief,'" *Anchorage Alaska Dispatch News*, 30 December 2016.

6. Henry, "Chilkoot Heritage," 4.

7. Nora Dauenhauer and Richard Dauenhauer, *Haa Kusteeyi, Our Culture: Tlingit Life Stories* (Seattle: University of Washington; Juneau: Sealaska Heritage Foundation, 1994), 207-8.

8. Henry, "Chilkoot Heritage," 5.

PROLOGUE

1. *Gunuk* is likely The Reverend S. Hall Young's rendering of Tlingit *gunanaa*, which translates in English to outsider or stranger. Quotations in this scene are drawn from *Hall Young of Alaska*; Samuel Hall Young, *Alaska Days with John Muir* (1915; reprint, introduction by Richard Fleck, Salt Lake City, Utah: Peregrine Smith Books, 1991),

199–200; and John Muir, *Travels in Alaska* (1915; reprint, New York: Houghton Mifflin, 1979), 145–48.

2. John Muir, 4 November 1879, journal, JMP.

CHAPTER 1

1. *Hall Young of Alaska, "The Mushing Parson": The Autobiography of S. Hall Young* (New York: Fleming Revell, 1927), 101–2; George Thornton Emmons, *The Tlingit Indians*, ed. Frederica de Laguna with Jean Low (Seattle: University of Washington Press; New York: American Museum of Natural History, 1991), 51.

2. Emmons, *The Tlingit Indians*, 351–55; Joseph Kawaky, *Haa Shagoon* (Haines, Alaska: The Association, 1983), filmstrip.

3. Austin Hammond Sr., oral history with author, Chilkoot Culture Camp, Haines, Alaska, 10 August 1985, Haines Sheldon Museum and Culture Center, Alaska.

4. The Chilkoot River was called the Lḵoot by Natives in the precontact era. Louis Shotridge, "A Visit to the Tsimshian Indians," [part 1] "The Nass River" and [part 2] "The Skeena River," *The Museum Journal* 10, nos. 1-2 (March/June 1919): 49-67; no. 3 (September 1919): 117–48. Thomas F. Thornton, *Klondike Gold Rush National Historical Park Ethnographic Overview and Assessment* (Skagway, Alaska: National Park Service, Alaska Regional Office, 2004), 15–16; Wallace M. Olson, *The Tlingit: An Introduction to Their Culture and History*, 3d ed. (Juneau, Alaska: Heritage Research, 1997), 12–15.

5. Ronald L. Olson, *Social Structure and Social Life of the Tlingit in Alaska*, University of California publications, Anthropological Records, vol. 26 ([Berkeley]: [University of California Press], [1967]), 69–80.

6. Austin Hammond Sr., oral history with author, 10 August 1985.

7. Paul Phillips quoted in Rita A. Miraglia, "Yindastuki and Chilkoot Village: The Fates of Two Chilkat Tlingit Villages Claimed under ANCSA 14 (h) (1)," *Chasing the Dark: Perspectives on Place, History and Alaska Native Land Claims*, ed. Kenneth L. Pratt, Shadowlands series, vol. 1 (Anchorage, Alaska: United States Department of the Interior, Bureau of Indian Affairs, Alaska Region, Division of Environmental and Cultural Resources Management, ANCSA Office, 2009), 124. Jenny Tlunaut said that Chilkat meant "big fish," and according the Klukwan locals, Chilkoot, "many fish."

8. Kristin Bigsby, "Ancient Fish Trap Discovered," *Juneau (Alaska) Empire*, 10 September 10 2003, http://juneauempire.com/stories/091003/loc_fishtrap.shtml.

9. Aristotle, *The Rhetoric of Aristotle,* trans. and intro. Lane Cooper (1932; reprint, Englewood Cliffs, N.J.: Prentice-Hall, 1960), 6–7.

10. Cooper, ibid., xx.

11. The "Chilkat reputation" was based on a perception that the northern Tlingits were "warlike," a view reinforced by dozens of nineteenth-century documents. Capt. Lester A. Beardslee of the U.S. Navy built a lengthy case in his "Report," *Case of the United States before the Tribunal Convened at London . . .* , in *Proceedings of the Alaska Boundary Tribunal: Convened at London, under the Treaty between the United States of America and Great Britain . . .* (Washington, D.C.: Government Printing Office, 1903), 365–68 (hereafter *Case of the United States, ABT*).

12. Thornton, *Klondike Gold Rush National Historical Park Ethnographic Overview and Assessment*, 16; Peter Nabokov, *A Forest of Time: American Indian Ways of History* (New York: Cambridge University Press, 2002), 81.

13. Austin Hammond Sr., oral history with author, 10 August 1985; Joe Hotch Sr., interview with author, 2014, Haines Sheldon Museum and Culture Center, Alaska; Sally Burratin, interview with author, Klukwan, Alaska, 2013; Richard King, interview with author, 1991, Haines Sheldon Museum and Cultural Center, Alaska.

14. Russell Sackett, *The Chilkat Tlingit: A General Overview* (Fairbanks: Anthropology and Historic Preservation, University of Alaska Cooperative Park Studies Unit, 1979), 14–16; Thornton, *Klondike Gold Rush National Historical Park Ethnographic Overview and Assessment*, 15.

15. Cathy Connor et al., "The Neoglacial Landscape and Human History of Glacier Bay, Glacier Bay National Park and Preserve, Southeast Alaska, USA," *The Holocene* 19, no. 3 (May 2009): 381–93; Ellen A. Cowan et al., "Fjords as Temporary Sediment Traps: History of Glacial Erosion and Deposition in Muir Inlet, Glacier Bay National Park, Southeastern Alaska," *Geological Society of America Bulletin* 122, nos. 7–8 (July 2010): 1068–69; Rick S. Kurtz, *Glacier Bay National Park and Preserve Historical Resources Study*, (Anchorage: National Park Service, Alaska System Support Office, 1995), 3; Susie James, "Glacier Bay," Nora M. and Richard Dauenhauer, *Haa Shuká, Our Ancestors: Tlingit Oral Narratives* (Seattle: University of Washington Press; Juneau: Sealaska Heritage Foundation, 1987), 249; Ronald Limbaugh, *John Muir's "Stickeen" and the Lessons of Nature* (Fairbanks: University of Alaska Press, 1996), 110.

16. Frederica de Laguna, "Tlingit," *Northwest Coast*, ed. Wayne P. Suttles, vol. 7 of *Handbook of North American Indians*, ed. William Sturtevant (Washington, D.C.: Smithsonian Institution, 1990), 206.

17. Joe Hotch Sr., speech to English class at Haines High School, Alaska, 4 February 2000; Emmons, *The Tlingit Indians*, 24; Joe Hotch Sr., in *Our Language, Our Stories, Our Life* (Juneau, Alaska: Joel Bennett Productions, 2008), filmstrip.

18. Sally Burratin, interview with author, Chilkat River fish camp, 9 August 2013; Joe Hotch Sr., interview with author, Haines, Alaska, 11 August 2014.

19. Louis Shotridge, "Ghost of Courageous Adventurer," reprinted in Nora Marks Dauenhauer and Richard Dauenhauer, eds., "Louis Shotridge and Indigenous Tlingit Ethnography: Then and Now," *Constructing Cultures Then and Now: Celebrating Franz Boas and the Jesup North Pacific Expedition*, ed. Lauren Kendall and Igor Krupnik, Contributions to Circumpolar Anthropology, no. 4 (Washington, D.C.: Arctic Studies Center, National Museum of Natural History, Smithsonian Institution, 2003), 165–84.

20. Emmons, *The Tlingit Indians*, 351–55; Testimony of Rosita Worl, 25 January 1993, p. 404, trial transcriptions, Whale House Artifacts Trial, Sheldon Haines Museum and Cultural Center, Haines, Alaska.

21. Joe Hotch Sr., History Day talk, Klukwan, Alaska, April 2009. A video of Hotch's talk is held by the Chilkat Indian Village Archive, Klukwan, Alaska.

22. Richard King, interview with author, March 1991.

23. Shotridge, "Ghost of Courageous Adventurer," 174.

24. Andrei Val'Terovich Grinev, *The Tlingit Indians in Russian America, 1741–1867*, trans. Richard L. Bland and Katerina G. Solovjova (Lincoln: University of Nebraska. Press, 2005), 216; Thornton, *Klondike Gold Rush National Park Historical Park Ethnographic Overview and Assessment*, 89–94.

25. Lee Heinmiller, interview with author, Haines, Alaska, 2010; Annie Ned, "Old-Style Words Are Just Like School," in Julie Cruikshank, *Life Lived Like a Story: Life Stories of Three Yukon Native Elders* (Lincoln: University of Nebraska, 1990), 271.

26. Joe Hotch, interview with author, 2014.

27. Steve Williams, "Frozen Man Strengthens Native Ties," *Chilkat Valley (Haines, Alaska) News,* 7 October 1999, p. 1; Micah True, "DNA testing seeks family links to icebound hunter," ibid., 28 June 2007, p. 1.

28. Al Morgan, public comments, Haines Sheldon Museum and Cultural Center, 2010.

CHAPTER 2

1. The opening scene is recreated from the author's conversations with George Lewis and Jim Brouillette, Haines, Alaska, 1988–1990. The underwater shaman in discussed in Aurel Krause, *The Tlingit Indians: Results of a Trip to the Northwest Coast of America and the Bering Straits* (1885; reprint, trans. and ed. by Erna Gunther, Seattle: University of Washington Press, 1979), 196–97.

2. Wallace Olson, *Through Spanish Eyes: Spanish Voyages to Alaska, 1774–1792* (Auke Bay: Heritage Research, 2002). Olson cites numerous accounts recorded in original ships' logs.

3. Robert Boyd, *The Coming of the Spirit of Pestilence: Introduced Infectious Diseases and Pestilence among Northwest Coast Indians, 1774–1884* (Seattle: University of Washington Press, 1999), 22–27, 36.

4. Judson Brown, interview, 16 June 1983, Archives, Sealaska Heritage Institute, Juneau, Alaska.

5. Gerasim Gigor'ivich Izmailov and Dimitrii Ivanovich Bocharov, journals, June 1788, trans. Lydia Black, in Nora Marks Dauenhauer, Richard Dauenhauer, and Lydia T. Black, eds., *Anóoshi Lingít Aaní Ká / Russians in Tlingit America: The Battles of Sitka, 1802 and 1804* (Seattle: University of Washington Press, 2008), 44–46.

6. N. P. Rezanov, "Estimated Enumeration of the Tlingit nation in the vicinity of Port Novo-Arkhangel'sk residing along the waterways beginning with Yakutat, with the names of their settlements known to Russians," 1805 or 1806, ibid., 112.

7. Miraglia, "Yindastuki and Chilkoot Village," 111.

8. Tommy Jimmie Jr., interview with author, Haines, Alaska, 23 July 2008.

9. Paddy Goenett, speech at 1929 Alaska Native Brotherhood Meeting, Haines, Alaska, cited by Lee Heinmiller, interview with author, 2010; Sackett, *The Chilkat Tlingit,* 33.

10. Muir, *Travels in Alaska,* 168.

11. *The Alaska Travel Journal of Archibald Menzies,* ed. and annot. Wallace M. Olson (Fairbanks: University of Alaska Press, 1993), 168–78.

12. Ray Dennis and Joe Hotch, trade routes panel discussion, Haines Public Library, 29 January 2010.

13. Joe Hotch Sr., History Day talk, Klukwan, Alaska, 20 April 2009.

14. George Vancouver quoted in Emmons, *The Tlingit Indians,* 349.

15. *The Alaska Travel Journal of Archibald Menzies,* 173–76.

16. Lani Hotch, "Yanwaa Sháa" (unpublished essay, March 2011, copy in Chilkat Indian Village Archives, Alaska), 3.

17. Andrea Verplank McClellan, "The Evolution of Tlingit Daggers," *Sharing Our Knowledge: The Tlingit and Their Coastal Neighbors,* Ed. Sergei Kan with Steve Henrikson (Lincoln: University of Nebraska Press, 2015).

18. Author notes on Agnes Bellinger, Elders meetings, Klukwan, Alaska, 8 November 2004. Sailor hats are sometimes worn by women at memorials in the Chilkat Valley.

19. Sergei Kan, *Memory Eternal: Tlingit Culture and Russian Orthodox Christianity through Two Centuries* (Seattle: University of Washington, 1999), 172.

20. Richard King, oral history with author, March 1991.

21. Krause, *The Tlingit Indians*, 30.

22. Robert De Armond, *Early Visitors to Southeastern Alaska* (Anchorage: Alaska Northwest Publishing, 1978), 78–79

23. Baranov, "Ceremony and Procession, Sitka, October 1799," in Marks Dauenhauer, Dauenhauer, and Black, eds., *Anóoshi Lingít Aaní Ká / Russians in Tlingit America*, 127–28.

24. Baranov, "Letter to Unknown Recipient, April 7, 1800," ibid., 133.

25. Kan, *Symbolic Immortality,* 225; A. P. Johnson, "First Encounter with the Russians, Dry Bay Area," in Marks Dauenhauer, Dauenhauer, and Black, eds., *Anooshi Lingit Aaní Ká / Russians in Tlingit America*, 115–21.

26. Ted C. Hinckley, *The Canoe Rocks: Alaska's Tlingit and the Euramerican Frontier, 1800–1912* (Lanham, Pa.: University Press of America, 1996), 27.

27. Lt. Col. Robert N. Scott, "Report on Indians," *Proceedings of the Alaska Boundary Tribunal*, 353.

28. George Thornton Emmons, "The Whale House of Chilkat," *Raven's Bones*, ed. Andrew Hope III (Sitka, Alaska: Sitka Community Association, 1982), 68–90.

29. Louis Shotridge, "The Founder of the Whale House," manuscript, Shotridge Ethnographic Field Notes, Louis Shotridge Collection, University of Pennsylvania Museum of Archaeology and Anthropology, Philadelphia; Steven B. Brown, "A Tale of Two Carvers," *American Indian Art*, autumn 2005, pp. 49–59.

30. Brown, "A Tale of Two Carvers," 49-59.

31. Barry Herem. "The Curse of the Tlingit Treasures: The Struggle for Possession of the Secret Masterworks of North American Art," *Connoisseur*, March 1991, p. 86.

32. Emmons, *The Tlingit Indians*, 61.

33. Grinev, *The Tlingit Indians in Russian America*, 167.

34. Yeil.xaax, "Testimony of Yel-hak," *Proceedings of the Alaska Boundary Tribunal*, 548.

35. Edward Glave, "Pioneer Packhorses in Alaska: The Advance," *The Century Magazine* September 1892, 671–82.

36. Ned, "Old-Style Words Are Just Like School," 280.

37. Boyd, *The Coming of the Spirit of Pestilence*, 121.

38. Emmons, The Tlingit Indians, 83; Boyd, *The Coming of the Spirit of Pestilence*, 122.

39. Emmons, The Tlingit Indians, 56.

40. Author notes on Agnes Bellinger, elders meeting, Klukwan, Alaska, 8 November 2004.

41. Clifford Wilson, *Campbell of the Yukon* (Toronto: Macmillan of Canada, 1970), 121–28.

42. Joe Hotch, History Day talk, 20 April 2009.

43. Campell quoted in Wilson, *Campbell of the Yukon*, 121–28.

CHAPTER 3

1. *New York Times*, 14 March 1909.

2. Kenneth Burke, *A Rhetoric of Motives* (Berkeley: University of California Press, 1969), 42.

3. Hinckley, *The Canoe Rocks*, 110; James Douglas to George Davidson, in Davidson, *The Alaska Boundary* (San Francisco: Alaska Packers Association, 1903), 234; William H. Seward, *Alaska: Speech Delivered at Sitka, 12 August 1869* (Washington, D.C.: Philip and Solomons, 1869).

4. Doris Kearns Goodwin, *Team of Rivals: The Political Genius of Abraham Lincoln* (New York: Simon and Schuster, 2005), 443.

5. Oscar Lewis, *George Davidson: Pioneer West Coast Scientist* (Berkeley: University of California Press, 1954), 1–40 passim.

6. John Cloud, "George Davidson and the Point of the Beginning: 'Once Seen, It Will Never Be Forgotten,'" *California Coast and Ocean* 23, no. 2 (2007): 2.

7. Charles G. Yale, "Brief Sketch of the Public Services of George Davidson," *Mining and Scientific Press*, August 1885, http://www.history.noaa.gov/

8. George Davidson, *Pacific Coast: Coast Pilot of Alaska, First Part, from Southern Boundary to Cook's Inlet* (Washington, D.C.: Government Printing Office, 1869), 3.

9. Norman L. Smith Sr., "To the Mouth of the Chilkaht," (paper presented at the Alaska Historical Society, Haines, 4 October 2006), 4.

10. George Davidson, *Coast Pilot of Alaska*, 35.

11. Smith Sr., "To the Mouth of the Chilkaht," 1, 2; George Davidson, "Coast Survey Report for 1867," *The Case of the United States*, ABT, 342.

12. "The Late Eclipse of the Sun," *Albany (N.Y.) Evening Post*, 1869, clipping, scrapbook (newspaper items relating to work on Western Coast), carton 27, George Davidson Papers, 1845-1911, Bancroft Library, University of California, Berkeley.

13. W. A. Howard to Sec. of the Treasury Hugh McCullough, 30 November 1867, "Papers Relating to Cession and Transfer of Alaska to United States," in *The Case of the United States*, , ABT, 341-44.

14. Andrew Higgs, "Encounters with Kohklux: Historical Images of the Charismatic Chilkat Chief Shotridge" (paper presented at the annual meeting of the Alaska Historical Society, Haines, Alaska, 23 September 2003), 4.

15. Eliza Ruhamah Scidmore, *Alaska: Its Southern Coast and the Sitkan Archipelago* (Boston: D. Lathrop, 1885), 115–16.

16. George Davidson. 17 October 1867, Davidson Papers, Bancroft Library. Item was forwarded in Steve Langdon, email to author.

17. W. A. Howard, testimony, in U.S. House, *Papers Relating to Cession of Alaska to United States*, 40th Cong., 2d sess., 1868–1869, H. Ex. Doc. No. 177, p. 195. 339; Harold Hopper, "The First Alaska Day Celebration," speech delivered in Haines on Alaska Day, 18 October 1991 (paper archived in Haines Sheldon Museum and Cultural Center, Alaska); McIntyre quoted in Hinckley, *The Canoe Rocks,* 75.

18. Bvt. Maj. Gen. Jefferson C. Davis to Bvt. Maj. Gen. J. B. Fry, 27 May 1868, *Papers Relating to Cession of Alaska to United States,* 354.

19. Ezra J. Warner, "Jefferson Columbus Davis," *Generals in Blue: Lives of the Union Commanders* (Baton Rouge: Louisiana State University Press, 1964), 115-16; Ralph P. Thian, comp., *Notes Illustrating the Military Geography of the United States, 1813–1880,*

ed. John M. Carroll (1881; reprint, with a foreword by Robert M. Utley, Austin: University of Texas Press, 1979), 52; "General vs. General and a Horrible Betrayal of Slave Refugees," http://open.salon.com/blog/laura_wilkerson.

20. Bvt. Maj. Gen. Jefferson C. Davis, to Bvt. Maj. Gen. J. B. Fry, 27 May 1868, *The Case of the United States, ABT*, 19.

21. Capt. W. A. Howard to Sec. of Treasury Hugh McCullough, 4 June 1867, ibid., 342.

22. Gen. Jefferson C. Davis to Bvt. Maj. Gen. J. B. Fry, 3 August 1868, ibid., 355.

23. Bvt. Maj. Gen. Jefferson C. Davis, to Bvt. Maj. Gen. J. B. Fry, 5 January 1869, ibid., 356.

24. "An Instance of His Daring Courage . . . ," *St. Louis Globe,* Jefferson Columbus Davis Papers, 1867-1878, The Newberry, Chicago, Illinois, cited in Hinckley, *The Canoe Rocks,* 99–100.

25. Hinckley, *The Canoe Rocks,* 102.

26. Ibid., 91.

27. George H. William to Sec. of War W. W. Belknap, 13 November 1873, AFSA, Roll 2. *Sitka Alaska Times,* 21 May 1869.

28. Morgan B. Sherwood, "A Pioneer Scientist in the Far North: George Davidson and the Development of Alaska," *The Pacific Northwest Quarterly* 53 (April 1962): 77.

29. *San Francisco Daily Alta,* 13 June 1869, scrapbook, carton 27, Davidson Papers, Bancroft Library.

30. George Davidson, "Explanation of an Indian Map of the Rivers, Lakes, Trails, and Mountains from the Chilkaht to the Yukon Drawn by the Chilkaht Chief, Koh'klux, in 1869," *Mazama,* April 1901, p. 76, reprinted in Koh'klux (Chilkat Chief), *The Koh'klux Map* (Whitehorse: Yukon Historical and Museums Association, 1995), 16.

31. Sherwood, "A Pioneer Scientist in the Far North," 77.

32. John Muir, 5 September 1879, in *Letters from Alaska,* 22.

33. Davidson, "Explanation of an Indian Map," 16.

34. *San Francisco Daily Alta,* 10 August 1869, scrapbook, carton 27, Davidson Papers, Bancroft Library.

35. S. D. C. Hastings, Abijah Fitch, and William Smith, 27 August 1869, Victoria, British Columbia, "The Cruise of the Active—Interesting Report," *The British Colonist,* Davidson Papers, Bancroft Library.

36. Frederick W. Seward, *Seward at Washington as Senator and Secretary of State, 1861–1872* (New York: Derby and Miller, 1891), 415.

37. Ibid., 418, 425–26.

38. The story of Klukwan villagers fleeing from the sun appears in a number of internet sources such as *history.com, wikipedia.org, endnotes.com.* Print sources include Sherwood, "A Pioneer Scientist in the Far North"; Linda Johnson, "The Day the Sun Was Sick," *Yukon Indian News,* summer 1984; and *The Koh'klux Map,* 7.

39. Seward, *Seward at Washington as Senator and Secretary of State,* 426–28. This section was reprinted as Frederick W. Seward, "Eclipse at Chilkat," *The Alaska Journal* 2 (winter 1972): 18–20.

40. Davidson, "Explanation of an Indian Map," 78–82.

41. John Cloud, "Benjamin Peirce and the 'Science of Necessary Conclusions,'" http://www.lib.noaa.gov/noaainfo/heritage/coastandgeodeticsurvey/Peircechapter.pdf. Koh'Klux, Map of the Chilkhat: [Alaska and Yukon], 1852, Bancroft Library, University of California, Berkeley.

42. *Alaska Speech of William H. Seward, August 12, 1869* (Washington, D.C.: Philip and Solomons, 1869),1–16.

43. "Mr. Seward's Speech in Salem, Oregon," in ibid., 21–31.

44. *The Sitka Alaska Times* in Thornton, *Klondike Gold Rush National Historical Park Ethnographic Overview and Assessment*, 117.

45. Hall, *Alaska Days with John Muir*, 90.

46. E. C. Merriman, "Report," 29 May 1883, *The Case of the United States, ABT*, 429.

CHAPTER 4

1. Mrs. Eugene S. Willard [Caroline], *Kin-da-shon's Wife*, 3d ed. (New York: Fleming H. Revell, 1892). Mrs. Eugene S. Willard [Caroline McCoy White Willard] created fictional names loosely based on Tlingit originals.

2. Mrs. Willard, *Kin-da-shon's Wife*, 36–44.

3. Many versions of this story are told on the Northwest Coast. The core of this comes from Aurel Krause, *The Tlingit Indians*, 174–75.

4. Emmons, *The Tlingit Indians*, 368–75; Ronald Olson, *Social Structure and Social Life of the Tlingit in Alaska*, 111–16.

5. Austin Hammond Sr., oral history with author, Haines, Alaska, 10 August 1985.

6. Charlie Jimmie Sr., interview with author, Haines, Alaska, 22 September 2009.

7. Address by Austin Hammond Sr., Native American Spirituality workshop, Alaska Environmental Assembly conference, Juneau, Alaska, 13 February 1988. From author's notes.

8. As early as 1840, Father Veniaminov identified Chilkat as one of the last strongholds of the shaman. Emmons, *The Tlingit Indians*, 375.

9. Hinckley, *The Canoe Rocks*, 129–30. My great-grandfather's earliest memory was being shoved on a buckboard upon hearing of Custer's defeat as his family hurriedly vacated their home in Ogallala, South Dakota.

10. William Henderson, letter, *Sitka Alaska Times*, September 1869.

11. Thornton, *Klondike Gold Rush National Historical Park Ethnographic Overview and Assessment*, 117.

12. Alexander M. Pennock to Sec. of the Navy George M. Robeson, 31 August 1873, *The Case of the United States, ABT*, 363.

13. Thornton *Klondike Gold Rush National Historical Park Ethnographic Overview and Assessment*, 119; called "money trail" by Agnes Bellinger, George Lewis (dlh); Berton, Pierre, *The Klondike Fever: The Life and Death of the Last Great Gold Rush* (1958; reprint, New York: Carroll and Graf, 1985), 9.

14. Lt. Alexander McCrackin to Lt. Com. John S. Newell, 11 June 1887, *The Case of the United States, ABT*, 392–94.

15. Emmons, *The Tlingit Indians*, 54.

16. Rev. Sheldon Jackson, *Alaska, and Missions on the North Pacific Coast* (New York: Dodd, Mead, 1880 [1884?]), 255–60.

17. Hinckley, *The Canoe Rocks*, 129–35; "The American Occupation—The Administration of the Military Authorities," *The Case of the United States, ABT*, 90.

18. *Sitka Alaska Times*, 21 May 1869.

19. Hinckley, *The Canoe Rocks*, 1.

20. Mrs. Eugene S. Willard [Caroline], *Life in Alaska: Letters of Mrs. Eugene S. Willard*, ed. Mrs. Eva McClintock (Philadelphia: Presbyterian Board of Publication, 1884), 14.

21. Mrs. Willard, *Kin-da-shon's Wife*, 217.

22. *Hall Young of Alaska*, 96.

23. Jackson, *Alaska, and Missions of the North Pacific Coast*, 132–39; Jackson, *Missions*, 194; *Hall Young of Alaska*, 77; Hinckley, *The Canoe Rocks*, 132; Pauline V. Burkher, "Amanda McFarland: Mother of Protestant Missions in Alaska," http://www.yukonpresbytery.com/history/Interviews/amanda.htm.

24. Hinckley, *The Canoe Rocks*, 137.

25. Mrs. Willard, *Kin-da-shon's Wife*, 275; J. Arthur Lazell, *Alaskan Apostle: The Life Story of Sheldon Jackson* (New York: Harper and Brothers, 1960), 61; Lee Heinmiller, interview with author, 26 July 2012, Haines, Alaska, Haines Sheldon Museum and Cultural Center, Alaska.

26. Jackson, *Alaska, and Missions of the North Pacific Coast*, 259; Mrs. Willard, *Life in Alaska*, 30.

27. "United States v. Scum Doo, whose real name is unknown," U.S. District Court for the District of Alaska, *Case of the United States, ABT*, 439.

28. *Hall Young of Alaska*, 213.

29. Charlie Brouillette, interview with author, Haines, Alaska, 22 September 2009, Haines Sheldon Museum and Cultural Center, Alaska.

30. Emmons, *The Tlingit Indians*, 372.

31. Ibid., 411; Biography of Phoebe Warne Samsen, Presbyterian Home Mission archive, 1970.003.0002, copy in Haines Sheldon Museum and Cultural Center, Alaska. Koh'klux was born around 1819 according to Higgs, "Encounters with Koh'klux"; Charles Brouillette, interview with author, 22 September 2009. Brouillette claimed to be the last living relative of Skandoo'o and, in the final months of his life, identified the three brothers. Emmons writes that Karskarz, principal headman and shaman of Chilkoot village, was Daanawáa̱k's younger brother. See Emmons, *The Tlingit Indians*, 372. Thornton, *Klondike Gold Rush National Historical Park Ethnographic Overview and Assessment*, 184–86.

32. Grinev, *The Tlingit Indians in Russian America*, 254; Emmons, *The Tlingit Indians*, 404.

33. Eliza Ruhamah Scidmore, "The First District from Prince William Sound to Yakutat Bay," United States, Census Office, *Report on Population and Resources of Alaska at the Eleventh Census, 1890* (Washington, D.C.: U.S. Bureau of the Census, 1893), 46–47.

34. Frank Oscar, oral history, Wrangell-St. Elias National Park, Project Jukebox, Oral History Program, University of Alaska, Fairbanks, *http://jukebox.uaf.edu/WRST/71301.html*.

35. *Hall Young of Alaska*, 156; Jack London, *The Children of the Frost* (New York: Regency Press, 1902), 91.

36. Hinckley, *The Canoe Rocks*, 95.

37. Sitka Jack, genealogy, http://wc.rootsweb.ancestry.com/cgi-bin/igm.cgi?op=GET&db=klea&id=I35871

38. C. E. S. Wood, *The Century Magazine*, July 1882, p. 3, in Hinckley, *The Canoe Rocks*.

39. Hinckley, *The Canoe Rocks*, 129.

40. Jackson, *Alaska, and Missions of the North Pacific Coast*, 240, 98–101.

41. *Hall Young of Alaska*, 62–65.

42. Ibid. 22.

43. Ibid., 49.

44. Ibid., 63.

45. Ibid., 64–69.

46. Ibid., 73–74. All italicized language in Young's quotation are original to his text. Lazell, *Alaskan Apostle*, 56–57.

47. *Hall Young of Alaska*, 88, 93, 259.

48. May Lee Davis, *We Are Alaskans*, ill. Olaus Johan Murie (Boston: W. A. Wilde, 1931), 246; *Hall Young of Alaska*, 92.

49. *Hall Young of Alaska*, 90–93.

50. Ibid., 156.

51. Ibid., 112–16, 121–25

52. Ibid., 126.

53. Ibid., 129, 147, 149–56, 164–66.

54. A[aron] L. Lindsley, *Sketches of an Excursion to Southern Alaska* (Portland, Ore.: First Presbyterian Church, 1881), 16; *Hall Young of Alaska*, 157.

CHAPTER 5

1. Boyd, *The Coming of the Spirit of Pestilence*, 121, 134–35, 130, 310–13, 324–27.

2. Bernard Grun, *The Timetables of History,* 3d ed. (New York: Simon and Schuster, 1991), 389; *Oxford Encyclopedic Dictionary*, s.v. "People's Charter."

3. Paula Mitchell Marks, *In a Barren Land: American Indian Dispossession and Survival* (New York: Quill/William Morrow, 1998), 90–94.

4. Geoffrey Parrinder, ed., *World Religions: From Ancient History to the Present* (New York: Facts on File, 1971), 451.

5. Donald Worster, *A Passion for Nature: The Life of John Muir* (New York: Oxford University Press, 2008), 37–38, 40.

6. Turner quoted in Linnie Marsh Wolfe, *Son of the Wilderness*, 36.

7. John Muir, *The Story of My Boyhood and Youth* (1913; San Francisco: Sierra Club, 1988), 19, 49.

8. Daryl Morrison, "John Muir and the Bains," *John Muir: Family, Friends, and Adventures*, ed. Sally M. Miller and Daryl Morrison (Albuquerque: University of New Mexico Press, 2005), 37.

9. Ralph Waldo Emerson, *Nature* (Cambridge, Mass.: James Munroe and Company, 1836), 12.

10. Muir, *The Story of My Boyhood and Youth,* 46; Worster, *A Passion for Nature*, 49–50.

11. Patricia Nelson Limerick, *The Legacy of Conquest: The Unbroken Past of the American West* (New York: Norton, 1987), 188–91.

12. Chief Seattle quoted in Albert Furtwangler, *Answering Chief Seattle* (Seattle: University of Washington Press, 1997), 12–13.

13. Richard F. Fleck, *Henry Thoreau and John Muir among the Indians* (Hamden, Conn.: Archon, 1985), 25, 37.

14. Muir, *The Story of My Boyhood and Youth*, 134–141, 151.

15. John Muir to Galloways, fall 1861, quoted in Worster, *A Passion for Nature*.

16. Goodwin, *Team of Rivals*, 300–301, 352.

17. Wolfe, *Son of the Wilderness*, 88–89.

18. Ibid., 94–97; Worster, *A Passion for Nature*, 96–100.

19. Dee Brown, *Bury My Heart at Wounded Knee: An Indian History of the American West* (New York: Holt, Rinehart and Winston, 1970), 122–32; Charles A. Eastman, *Indian Heroes and Great Chieftains* (Boston: Little, Brown, 1918), 14–15, 121.

20. Merrill Moores, "Recollections of John Muir as a Young Man," 1938, William Frederic Badé Papers, John Muir Collections, Holt-Atherton Special Collections, University Library, University of the Pacific, Stockton.

21. Frederick Turner, *Rediscovering America: John Muir in His Time and Ours* (San Francisco: Sierra Club Books, 1985), 129.

22. Muir quoted in Wolfe, *Son of the Wilderness*, 105.

23. Moores, "Recollections of John Muir as a Young Man,"; Wolfe, *Son of the Wilderness*, 107.

24. A selection from *A Thousand-Mile Walk to the Gulf* by John Muir, in *The Wilderness World of John Muir*, ed. Edwin Way Teale (New York: Houghton Mifflin, 1954), 76; Worster, *A Passion for Nature*, 125.

25. Worster, *A Passion for Nature*, 138.

26. Paula Mitchell Marks, *In a Barren Land*, 89-125; S. C. Gwynne, *Empire of the Summer Moon: Quanah Parker and the Rise and Fall of the Comanches, the Most Powerful Indian Tribe in American History* (New York: Scribner, 2010), 211, 238; Robert M. Utley, *The Indian Frontier of the American West, 1846-1890* (Albuquerque: University of New Mexico Press, 1984),100-105.

CHAPTER 6

1. John T. Faris, *The Alaskan Pathfinder* (New York: Fleming Revell, 1913), 31, 121; "The Pacific Excursion," *Sunday School Journal for Teachers and Young People,* September 1879.

2. Karl Marx, *Chicago Tribune,* 5 January 1879, Marx-Engels Internet Archive, http://www.marxists.org/ archive/marx/bio/ media/marx/79_01_05.htm; Richard L. Lehman, "The 1879 National Sunday School Assembly Convention in Yosemite Valley," *Yosemite Nature Notes,* January 1957, p. 9; Wolfe, *Son of the Wilderness*, 202.

3. "The Pacific Excursion," *Sunday School Journal for Teachers and Young People,* September 1879, p. 6.

4. Lehman, "The 1879 National Sunday School Assembly Convention in Yosemite Valley," 8–10.

5. Whitney quoted in Frank Buske, "John Muir's Alaska Experience," *John Muir: Life and Legacy,* ed. Sally M. Miller (Stockton, Calif.: University of the Pacific for the Holt-Atherton Pacific Center for Western Studies, 1985) in *The Pacific Historian* 29, nos. 2–3 (summer–fall, 1985): 114.

6. "The Pacific Excursion," *Sunday School Journal for Teachers and Young People,* September 1879, p. 6; *San Francisco Daily Evening Bulletin,* 27 September 1879, p. 1, and 29 October 1879, p. 1; "Mountain Sculpture," *Sunday School Journal for Teachers and Young People,* September 1879, p. 1.

7. *Sacramento (Calif.) Daily Union,* 14 June 1879, Alaska file, William and Maymie Kimes Collection, John Muir Papers, John Muir Collections, Holt-Atherton Special Collections, University Library, University of the Pacific, Stockton, California.

8. Wolfe, *Son of the Wilderness*, 203.

9. John Muir, *The Yosemite*, Natural History Library (1912; reprint, New York: Doubleday, 1962), 4-9.

10. John Muir, *The Yosemite* 4, 9; Muir, *John of the Mountains*, 43, 60, 86.

11. Mark David Spence, *Dispossessing the Wilderness: Indian Removal and the Making of the National Parks* (New York: Oxford University Press, 1999), 101–5.

12. "Yosemite Valley," http://www.nps.gov/yose/historyculture/archeology-yosemite-valley.htm; David A. Smith, "California and the Indian Wars: The Mariposa War," http://www.militarymuseum.org /Mariposa1.html; http://thehive.modbee.com/?q=node/180

13. Muir, *The Yosemite*, 173–76.

14. John Muir to Jeanne Carr, "September or October, 1871," The *Life and Letters of John Muir*, ed. William Frederic Badè, vol. 1 (Boston: Houghton Mifflin, 1924), 299.

15. Fleck, *Henry Thoreau and John Muir among the Native Americans*, 37–39; Spence, *Dispossessing the Wilderness*, 109.

16. Muir quoted in Mark Dowie, *Conservation Refugees: The Hundred-Year Conflict between Global Conservation and Native Peoples* (Cambridge, Mass.: MIT Press, 2009), 6; Spence, *Dispossessing the Wilderness*, 109.

17. Therese Yelverton, *Zanita: A Tale of the Yo-Semite* (1872; reprint, with an introduction by Margaret Sanborn, Berkeley, Calif.: Ten Speed Press, 1991), xxxiv, 5.

18. Moores, "Recollections of John Muir as a Young Man," pp. 11-15, Badè Papers, Muir Collections.

19. Fleck, *Henry Thoreau and John Muir among the Native Americans*, 37–39; Spence, *Dispossessing the Wilderness*, 109.

20. Gary Scharnhorst, *Bret Harte: Opening the American Literary West*, The Oklahoma Western Biographies (Norman: University of Oklahoma Press, 2000), 50; Daniel A. Wells, "Mark Twain in the 'Overland Monthly' (1868–1900): An Annotated List of Citations," *American Literary Realism, 1870–1910* 20, no. 2 (winter 1988): 85.

21. Benjamin P. Avery, "Summering in the Sierra, No. 1," *Overland Monthly*, January 1874, p. 82.

22. George Davidson, "Abrasions of the North-Western Coast," *Overland Monthly*, January 1874, pp. 35–40.

23. Worster, *A Passion for Nature*, 194.

24. Daniel Muir, to John Muir, 19 March 1874, Correspondence and Related Documents, John Muir Papers, John Muir Collections, Holt-Atherton Special Collections, University of the Pacific, Stockton, California.

25. Frederick Turner, *John Muir*, 213-215; Ralph Waldo Emerson, "The Oversoul," *First Texts* (1841), http://www.emersoncentral.com/oversoul.htm; Henry David Thoreau, "Hymn to the August Morn," in *The American Transcendentalists,* ed. Perry Miller (New York: Doubleday, 1957), 70.

26. Richard Cartwright Austin, *Baptized into Wilderness: A Christian Perspective on John Muir* (Atlanta: John Knox Press, 1987), 12–13.

27. "The Religion of John Muir," clipping, John Eastman Shone Collection, John Muir Collections, Holt-Atherton Special Collections, University of the Pacific, Stockton, California. This item was delivered as a lecture in a Stockton church by William Frederic Badè, president of the Pacific School of Religion in Berkeley, California, and Muir's literary executor. Henry Fairfield Osborne, draft review of Badè's *Life and Letters of John*

Muir, ibid.; Hall Young, address to Laymen's Missionary Conference, San Francisco, California, 23 February 1916, Badè Papers, Muir Collections.

28. John Muir, "By-Ways of Yosemite Travel," *Overland Monthly,* September 1874, pp. 272–74.

29. John Muir to Catherine Merrill, 12 July 1871, *The Life and Letters of John Muir,* ed. Badé, vol. 1, p. 288.

30. John Muir to Sarah Muir Galloway, 17 April 1876, Correspondence, Muir Papers.

31. Brown, *Bury My Heart at Wounded Knee,* 225–40. A book-length account of this conflict is Jefferson C. Davis Riddle, *The Indian History of the Modoc War* (1914; reprint, with an introduction by Peter Cozzens, Mechanicsburg, Pa.: Stackpole Books, 2004).

32. Delano quoted in "The Modoc War," *New York Times,* 14 April 1873.

33. Brown, *Bury My Heart at Wounded Knee,* 240.

34. Muir, "Shasta in Winter," *John Muir Summering in the Sierra,* ed. Robert Engberg (Madison: University of Wisconsin Press, 1984), 30–37; Muir, "A Perilous Night on Shasta's Summit," ibid., 19; Muir, *Steep Trails* (New York: Houghton Mifflin, 1918), 57–81.

35. Muir, "Shasta in Winter," 55–58.

36. Wolfe, *Son of the Wilderness,* 314; Asst. Chief Ranger Don C. Fisher and John E. Doerr Jr., "Outline of Events in the History of the Modoc War," *Park Naturalist Nature Notes from Crater Lake* 10, no. 1 (June 1937), http://www.craterlakeinstitute.com/online-library/nature-notes/vo110no1-modoc-war.htm

37. Jackson, *Alaska, and Missions of the North Pacific Coast,* 228–29. Mary Swett is quoted in Ruth E. Sutter, "John Muir and the John Swett Family," *John Muir,* 15–29.

38. Wolfe, *Son of the Wilderness,* 49; Muir, *The Story of My Boyhood and Youth,* 124; "Wild Wool," *Overland Monthly,* April 1875, pp. 364-65.

39. Badè, *The Life and Letters of John Muir,* 9.

40. Margaret Sanborn, introduction to Yelverton, *Zanita,* xxvii; Ronald Limbaugh, "California's Kindred Spirits: John Muir and William Keith," in Miller, *John Muir,* 69; John Swett, in *Kindred and Related Spirits: The Letters of John Muir and Jeanne C. Carr,* ed. Bonnie Giesel (Salt Lake City: University of Utah Press, 2001), 9.

41. Mary Swett quoted in Sutter, "John Muir and the John Swett Family," 23.

42. Sutter, "John Muir and the John Swett Family," 18; Engberg, ed., *Summering in the Sierra,* 10.

43. C. Hart Merriam, "To the Memory of John Muir," unpublished manuscript, Badè Papers, Muir Collection; Melville B. Anderson, "The Conversation of John Muir," *American Museum Journal* 15 (March 1915): 116–121; "An Evening with Muir," fragment, [n.d.], Muir Papers.

44. Muir quoted in Sutter, "John Muir and the John Swett Family," 19.

45. E. L. Stone, "Literary Institute, Lecture by Dr. A.L. Stone," *Sacramento (Calif.) Daily Union,* 12 January 1876.

46. Steve Pauly, "The Importance of John Muir's First Public Lecture, Sacramento, 1876," *John Muir Newsletter,* winter 1998–1999, pp. 1–4.

47. "The Glaciers of California—Interesting Lecture by John Muir," *Sacramento (Calif.) Daily Union,* 26 January 1876, Kimes Collection, Muir Papers.

48. Muir, "Summering in the Sierra," *San Francisco Daily Evening Bulletin,* 24 August 1876, clipping, Muir Papers.

49. Badé, *The Life and Letters of John Muir,* vol. 2, 58–59.

50. John Muir to Sarah Muir Galloway, 17 April 1876, Correspondence, Muir Papers.

51. Muir quoted in Badè, *The Life and Letters of John Muir,* vol. 2, 102.

52. "The Great Basin—Some Interesting Facts About It—Lecture by John Muir." *Sacramento (Calif.) Record-Union,* 14 January 1879, clipping, Muir Papers.

53. John Muie to Louie Strenzel, 18 April 1878, Correspondence, Muir Papers.

CHAPTER 7

1. Non-Native pressure for access to Chilkoot lands was likely a topic of many discussions led by Daanawáak among the Chilkoot subchiefs. Evidence of Chilkoot-Anglo cooperation is found in four letters cited in N. and R. Dauenhauer, *Haa Kusteeyi, Our Culture,* 750–53.

2. *Hall Young of Alaska,* 190–93.

3. Thornton, *Klondike Gold Rush National Historical Park Ethnographic Overview and Assessment,* 119.

4. O. O. Howard, *My Life and Experiences among Our Hostile Indians: A Record of Personal Observations, Adventures, and Campaigns among the Indians of the Great West . . . .* (Hartford, Conn.: A. D. Worthington, 1907), 96–99, 151–62.

5. Howard, *My Life and Experiences among Our Hostile Indians,* 307–13.

6. Hinckley, *The Canoe Rocks,* 119-20.

7. Howard, *My Life and Experiences among Our Hostile Indians,* 278–300.

8. *San Francisco Chronicle,* 31 October 1877, and 1 January 1878.

9. Hinckley, *The Canoe Rocks,* 91–93.

10. Judson Brown, interview, Sealaska Heritage Institute.

11. Steven J. Langdon, "Unreciprocated 'Reverence': 'Papers,' Political Recognition, and Tlingit Engagement with US Governmentality in the late 19th Century," *Ethnohistory* 60, no. 3 (July 2013): 505-36.

12. N. and R. Dauenhauer, *Haa Kusteeyi, Our Culture,* 750–54; The original agreements, which hung on the wall of Austin Hammond's home for decades, are currently held in the Haines Sheldon Museum and Cultural Center, Alaska.

13. John Muir to Strentzel family, 9 July 1879, Muir Papers, http://www.pacific.edu/Library/Find/Holt-Atherton-Special-Collections/Digital-Collections/John-Muir-Correspondence.html; Muir, *Travels in Alaska,* 8–11.

14. Jackson, *Alaska, and Missions of the North Pacific Coast,* 229.

15. Wolfe, *Son of the Wilderness,* 203.

16. "SS *California,*" http:// en.wikipedia.org/wiki/SS_California_(1848).

17. John Muir, 8 August 1879, *Letters from Alaska,* 11–17.

18. Muir, journal entry, *John of the Mountains,* 259.

19. John Muir, 8 August 1879, *Letters from Alaska,* 11–17.

20. Hall, *Alaska Days with John Muir,* 12.

21. John Muir, 8 August 1879, *Letters from Alaska,* 18.

22. John Muir, "Alaska Glaciers: An Ounalaska Yosemite: Glacial Theology and Sermons in Ice: The Rocks, Plants, and Trees of Alaska," *San Francisco Daily Evening Bulletin,* 23 September 1879, clipping, Muir Papers. A newsprint image of the Davidson is in the Muir archives.

23. Rosemary Carlton, *Sheldon Jackson, the Collector* (Juneau: Alaska State Museums, 1999), 31.

24. John Muir, "Wanderings in Alaska: A Lovely Sail—Majestic Mountain View," *San Francisco Daily Evening Bulletin*, 1 November 1879, p. 1, clipping, Muir Papers.

25. Muir, journal entry, *John of the Mountains*, 275.

26. S. Hall Young, "Alaska Days with John Muir," speech to Layman's Missionary Conference, San Francisco, California, 23 February 1916, Badè Papers, Muir Collections.

27. Wolfe, *Son of the Wilderness*, 207.

28. Muir, *Travels in Alaska*, 35.

29. Jackson, *Alaska, and Missions of the North Pacific Coast*, 235.

30. Muir, *Travels in Alaska*, 36.

31. Young, *Alaska Days with John Muir*, 67.

CHAPTER 8

1. Hinckley, *The Canoe Rocks*, 149–52.

2. "Withdrawal of the Federal Bayonets from Alaska," *New York Tribune*, reprinted in *Harper's Weekly*, 21 April 1877, p. 309.

3. Hayes's order is reproduced in *The Case of the United States, ABT*, 365.

4. Hinckley, *The Canoe Rocks*, 149–50.

5. Ibid., 150; Utley, *The Indian Frontier of the American West*, 219–20.

6. *The Case of the United States, ABT*, 365–66.

7. Jackson, *Alaska, and Missions of the North Pacific Coast*, 257.

8. Young, *Alaska Days with John Muir*, 60; *Hall Young of Alaska*, 182.

9. Rick S. Kurtz, *Glacier Bay National Park and Preserve: Historic Resources Study* Anchorage: National Park Service, Alaska System Support Office, 1995), 7; *The Alaska Travel Journal of Archibald Menzies*, 177–78; Emmons, *The Tlingit Indians*, 131; Krause, *The Tlingit Indians*, 25.

10. Young, Speech, 23 February 1916; Young, *Alaska Days with John Muir*, 99.

11. Dennis C. Williams, *God's Wilds: John Muir's Vision of Nature* (College Station: Texas A&M University Press, 2002), 200–201; Austin, *Baptized into Wilderness*, 24–28; Entry in late July 1879, John Muir journals, Muir Papers; Muir, journal entry, *John of the Mountains*, 275; Moores, "Recollections of John Muir as a Young Man," Badè Papers, Muir Collections; John Muir, "Wild Wool," *Overland Monthly*, April 1875, clipping, Muir Papers.

12. John Muir, "Wanderings in Alaska: A Lovely Sail—Majestic Mountain View," *San Francisco Daily Evening Bulletin*, 1 November 1879, p. 1, clipping, Muir Papers.

13. Entry in late July 1879, John Muir journals, Muir Papers; Muir, *Travels in Alaska*, 186.

14. Entry in late July 1879, John Muir journals, Muir Papers.

15. *Hall Young of Alaska*, 82–83; Kan, *Memory Eternal*, 202.

16. To'watte's speech was quoted in *the Port Townsend (Wash. Terr.) Weekly Argus*, cited in Jackson, *Alaska, and Missions of the North Pacific Coast*, 169–71.

17. Carol Feller Brady, conversation with author, 8 November 2013, Juneau, Alaska. Brady is Kadachan's granddaughter. *Hall Young of Alaska*, 185–86.

18. Lee Heinmiller, interview with author, 17 October 2008.

19. "Sitka Charlie," Tlingit, Haida, and Tsimshian Genealogy of Alaska, http://wc.rootsweb.ancestry.com/cgi-bin/igm.cgi. He is buried at the "Cottage Cemetery" in Sitka, Alaska.

20. Muir, *Travels in Alaska*, 115; Muir, *Journals*, 14 October 1879; *Hall Young of Alaska*, 185; Young, *Alaska Days with John Muir*, 70.

21. *Hall Young of Alaska*, 185–86.

22. Howard, *My Life and Experiences among Our Hostile Indians*, 398–420, 433.

23. *Hall Young of Alaska*, 187; Young, *Alaska Days with John Muir*, 72.

24. Entries for October–December 1879, John Muir journals, image 4, Digital Collections, Muir Papers.

25. Ibid., image 5, Digital Collections, Muir Papers..

26. Ibid., images 6, 8, Digital Collections, Muir Papers.

27. Ibid., image 8 Digital Collections, Muir Papers; Muir, *Travels in Alaska*, 124; Fleck, *Henry Thoreau and John Muir among the Indians*, 52.

28. Ibid., image 9, Digital Collections, Muir Papers; Young, *Alaska Days with John Muir*, 74.

29. Kan, *Memory Eternal*, 158, 209.

30. Entries for October–December 1879, John Muir journals, image 9, Digital Collections, Muir Papers.

31. Ibid.

32. Ibid., image 10, Digital Archives, Muir Papers; Frederica de Laguna, *The Story of a Tlingit Community: A Problem in the Relationship between Archeological, Ethnological, and Historic Methods* (Washington, D.C.: U.S. Government Printing Office, 1960), 55.

33. Entries for October–December 1879, John Muir journals, images 10–12, Digital Archives, Muir Papers.

34. Ibid., image 13, Digital Archives, Muir Papers.

35. Ibid., image 14, Digital Archives, Muir Papers.

36. Ibid.

37. Ibid., image 15, Digital Archives, Muir Papers.

38. Ibid.; Young, *Alaska Days with John Muir*, 101–2

39. Entries for October–December 1879, John Muir journals, image 15, Digital Archives, Muir Papers.

40. Muir, October, *Letters from Alaska*, 48; Entries for October–December 1879, John Muir journals, image 16, Digital Archives, Muir Papers; Muir, *Travels in Alaska*, 142–43.

41. Entries for October–December 1879, John Muir journals, image 17, Digital Archives, Muir Papers; Muir, *Travels in Alaska*, 153.

42. Entries for October–December 1879, John Muir journals, image 18, Digital Archives, Muir Papers.

CHAPTER 9

1. Entries for October–December 1879, John Muir journals, images 22–23, Digital Archives, Muir Papers. Muir was referring to the back of the West Arm between Johns Hopkins and Grand Pacific Glaciers.

2. Young, *Alaska Days with John Muir*, 120.

3. Muir, *Travels in Alaska*, 162.

4. Entries for October–December 1879, John Muir journals, image 27, Digital Archives, Muir Papers.

5. Muir, *Travels in Alaska*, 164; Entries for October–December 1879, John Muir journals, image 29, Digital Archives, Muir Papers.

6. Entries for October–December 1879, John Muir journals, image 29, Digital Archives, Muir Papers. Muir reported that the camp was after "wild sheep," but they were probably hunting mountain goats.

7. Ibid.

8. Ibid.

9. Muir, *Travels in Alaska*, 167.

10. Muir, 5 September 1879, *Letters from Alaska*, 22. John Muir, sketch of Davidson Glacier, November 1879, Drawings, Muir Papers.

11. Entries for October–December 1879, John Muir journals, image 31, Digital Archives, Muir papers.

12. Ibid., image 29, Digital Archive, Muir Papers; Muir, *Travels in Alaska*, 167.

13. Tlingits have suggested this interpretation to me a few times. Most recent is Al Morgan at a meeting, May 2011, Sheldon Museum and Culture Center, Haines, Alaska.

14. Entries for October–December 1879, John Muir journals, image 31, Digital Archives, Muir Papers; Muir, *Travels in Alaska*, 168; Young, *Alaska Days with John Muir*, 84–85. Muir and Young disagree about the details of their approach to Yandeist'akyé. I attempted to resolve contradictory stories and selected versions common among Chilkat and Chilkoot people today.

15. The Tlingit phrase "Goosú wa.é?" actually translates as "Where are you?" Keri Edwards, correspondence with author, 6 June 2016. Edwards is an ethno-linguist. See her *Dictionary of Tlingit* (Juneau, Alaska: Sealaska Heritage Institute, 2009).

16. Probably "Axaa," the command to paddle. Keri Edwards, correspondence with author, 6 June 2016.

17. Young, *Alaska Days with John Muir*, 84–85; Entries for October–December 1879, John Muir journals, image 34, Digital Archives, Muir Papers.

18. Sally Burratin, interview with author, family fish camp on Chilkat River, Haines, Alaska, 9 August 2013.

19. Entries for October–December 1879, John Muir journals, image 32, Digital Archives, Muir Papers; Young, *Alaska Days with John Muir*, 86.

20. Burratin, interview with author, 9 August 2013.

21. Muir, *Travels in Alaska*, 170.

22. Entries for October-December 1879, John Muir journals, image 32, Digital Archives, Muir Papers.

23. Young, *Alaska Days with John Muir*, 89. Muir referred to "pelican oil" in entries for October-December 1879, John Muir journals, image 33, Digital Archives, Muir Papers.

24. Entries for October–December 1879, John Muir journals, image 33, Digital Archives, Muir Papers. *Hall Young of Alaska*, 211.

25. *Hall Young of Alaska*, 208, 209. Each offers his own order of speeches. Muir and Young often disagree about the sequence of events that week.

26. Ibid. The sketch of Young's sermon is a distillation lacking the etymology of standard Presbyterian sermon and meant to balance his summation of the Natives' speeches.

27. Ibid., 208; Muir, *Travels in Alaska*, 171.

28. Burratin, interview with author, 9 August 2013.

29. Entries for October–December 1879, John Muir's journals, image 33, Digital Archives, Muir Papers; *Hall Young of Alaska*, 208.

30. Muir quoted in Fleck, *Henry Thoreau and John Muir among the Indians*, 89–90.

31. Entries for October–December 1879, John Muir's journals, image 32, Digital Archives, Muir Papers.

32. Young, *Alaska Days with John Muir*, 89.

33. *Hall Young of Alaska*, 208–9.

34. Ibid., 212.

35. Edward Warren Sr., Klukwan History Day, 19 April 2011.

36. Entries for October–December 1879, John Muir's journals, image 32, Digital Archives, Muir Papers.

37. Muir, *Travels in Alaska*, 172. Chilkoot headman Karskarz (or Kar'schartzt) was the name of Skandoo'o's brother and may have also been the name of their father. The elder delivered the speech.

38. Kim Strong to author, Klukwan, Alaska, 30 January 2007.

39. Burratin, interview with author, 9 August 2013.

40. Joe Hotch Jr., speech to Haines High School class, Alaska, 14 February 2000.

41. Burke, *A Rhetoric of Motives*, 54; Muir, *Travels in Alaska*, 173. The importance of oratory among the Tlingits is discussed extensively in the works of Nora and Richard Dauenhauer, especially in *Haa Tuwunaagu Yis, for Healing Our Spirit: Tlingit Oratory* (Seattle: University of Washington, 1990), of Julie Cruikshank, *Do Glaciers Listen? Local Knowledge, Colonial Encounters, and Social Imagination* (Vancouver: UBC Press; Seattle: University of Washington Press, 2005), 165.

42. "A Fine Meteorite from Alaska," *New York Times*, 5 July 1881; Henry G. Hanks, California State Mining Bureau, *Fourth Annual Report of the State Mineralogist for the Year Ending May 15, 1884* (Sacramento: California Division of Mines and Geology, 1884: 264–65; Earle G. Linsley, "A Description of Meteorites Available for Public Inspection in the San Francisco Bay Region," Notes from the Society for Research on Meteorites, *Popular Astronomy* 42 (1934): 474–75.

43. Entries for October–December 1879, John Muir journals, image 34, Digital Archives, Muir Papers.

44. Entries for late July 1879, John Muir journals, image 20, Digital Archives, Muir Papers.

45. Entries for October–December 1879, John Muir journals, image 37, Digital Archives, Muir Papers; Muir, *Travels in Alaska*, 180.

46. Towatte quoted in *Hall Young of Alaska*, 217; Entries for October–December 1879, John Muir's journals, image 38, Digital Archives, Muir Papers.

47. Muir, *Letters from Alaska*, 52.

48. Ibid., 52–57.

49. *Hall Young in Alaska*, 220.

50. Jackson, *Alaska, and Missions of the North Pacific Coast*, 169–71.

51. Rachel "Dixie" Johnson, Talk, Haines Sheldon Museum and Cultural Center, Alaska, 7 November 1991.

52. *Hall Young in Alaska*, 221–25.

CHAPTER 10

1. Holway R. Jones, interview with author, Eugene, Oregon, 15 March 1983.

2. Hammond, oral history with author, 10 August 1985, trans. Dixie Johnson, Haines

Sheldon Museum and Cultural Center Archives, Alaska. See also, Keri Edwards Eggleston and Helen Sarabia, "Transcription and Translation of [a] Narrative Told by Austin Hammond Regarding Lukaax̱.ádi," 1985 (manuscript, Sealaska Heritage Institute Archives, Juneau, Alaska). See also William L. Paul Sr., in Narratives and Conversations in Tlingit Recordings Collection, 1972-2012, Archives, Sealaska Heritage Institute, Juneau, Alaska.

3. "The Apache Indian War," *Sacramento (Calif.) Daily Union*, 29 May 1880.

4. John Muir to Louie Strentzel, 6 January 1880, Correspondence, Muir Papers.

5. O. O. Howard, "Glaciers in Alaska," *Morning (Portland) Oregonian*, 24 January 1880, p. 1.

6. Utley, *The Indian Frontier of the American West*, 140; Howard, *My Life and Experiences among Our Hostile Indians*, 552; Chief Joseph, speech, *Great Speeches by Native Americans*, ed. Bob Blaisdell (Mineola, N.Y.: Dover Publications, 2000), 148; Arthur Hart, "Idaho History," *Boise Idaho Statesman*, 26 October 2014.

7. Howard, "Glaciers in Alaska," p. 1.

8. "Alaska: Its Mines and Other Resources," *Morning (Portland) Oregonian*, 24 January 1880, p. 3.

9. L[ester] A. Beardslee, "Report," 28 April 1881, *Case of the United States, ABT*, 365–68. Beardslee published an article under the pseudonym "Piseco" in *Forest and Stream*. See chapt. 11.

10. M. J. Kirchoff, *Dyea, Alaska: Rise and Fall of a Klondike Gold Rush Town* (Juneau: Alaska Cedar Press, 2012), 86.

11. Mary Swett to Louie Strentzel, 8 April 1880, in Badè, *The Life and Letters of John Muir*, vol. 2, 132.

12. Muir, *The Story of My Boyhood and Youth*, 135–36.

13. Fleck, *Henry Thoreau and John Muir among the Indians*, 58.

14. Muir, journal entry for late July 1879, *John of the Mountains*, 274.

15. John Vanderbilt to John Muir, 20 April 1880, Muir correspondence, Digital Archives, Muir Papers.

16. Badè, *The Life and Letters of John Muir*, vol. 2, 137.

17. Boyd, *The Coming of the Spirit of Pestilence*, 76.

18. John Muir to Louie Muir, 3 August 1880, in Badè, *The Life and Letters of John Muir*, vol. 2, 143, 146.

19. Young, *Alaska Days with John Muir*, 126.

20. *Hall Young of Alaska*, 249.

21. John Muir to Louie, 14 August 1880, in Badè, *The Life and Letters of John Muir*, vol. 2, 156.

22. John Muir to Louie Muir, *Letters from Alaska*, 64.

23. Muir, *Travels in Alaska*, 241.

24. Muir, *Letters from Alaska*, 95.

25. Muir, *Travels in Alaska*, 171.

26. *Hall Young of Alaska*, 251.

27. Muir quote in Limbaugh, *John Muir's "Stickeen" and the Lessons of Nature*, 126.

28. Fleck, *Henry Thoreau and John Muir among the Indians*, 35.

29. John Muir to Robert Underwood Johnson, 13 September 1889, quoted in Muir, "The Creation of Yosemite National Park," *Sierra Club Bulletin* 29 (October 1944): 50.

30. John Muir, "Washington and Puget Sound," *Picturesque California and the Region West of the Rocky Mountains, from Alaska to Mexico*, 2 vols. (New York: J. Dewing Publishing Company, 1888–1890), 447.

31. John Muir, *The Cruise of the Corwin,* ed. and intro. William Frederic Badè (1917; reprint, with a foreword by Roderick Nash, San Francisco: Sierra Club Books, 1993), 65.

32. Muir, *Travels in Alaska,* 276.

33. John Muir to Louie Muir, in Badè, *The Life and Letters of John Muir,* vol. 2, 204–9.

34. John Muir, "The Treasures of the Yosemite," *The Century Magazine*, August 1890, copy in Manuscripts and Published Works, Muir Papers.

35. John Muir to J. B. McChesney, in Badè, *The Life and Letters of John Muir,* vol. 1, 378.

36. John Muir to Robert Underwood Johnson, in Badè, *The Life and Letters of John Muir,* vol. 2, 244.

37. Muir, "The Treasures of the Yosemite," copy in Muir Papers.

38. Holway R. Jones, *John Muir and the Sierra Club; the Battle for Yosemite* (San Francisco: Sierra Club Books, 1965), 8.

39. John Muir, Sierra Club speech, 1895, in Robert Engberg, "On John Muir: Letters from Alaska," *John Muir Newsletter*, winter 1992, p. 1.

40. John Muir to William Colby, 31 March 1911, quoted in Jones, *John Muir and the Sierra Club.*

41. Frederick Jackson Turner, *The Frontier in American History* (1920; reprint, Tucson: University of Arizona 1994), 37, 144.

42. Bruce Merrell, "A Wild, Discouraging Mess: John Muir Reports on the Klondike Gold Rush," *Alaska History* 7 (fall 1992): 30.

43. Thornton, *Klondike Gold Rush National Historical Park Ethnographic Overview and Assessment*, 177.

44. Historical details are forthcoming in this book's companion volume.

45. John Muir, "Trails of the Gold Hunters on Northern Seas and in Mountain Passes," *San Francisco Examiner*, 11 October 1897, p. 1, clipping, Muir Papers.

46. Merrell, "A Wild, Discouraging Mess," 32.

47. Muir, "Trails of the Gold Hunters on Northern Seas and in Mountain Passes," 1, clipping, Muir Papers.

48. John Muir, "Pathless Treasure Fields of the Frozen Northlands," *San Francisco Examiner*, 23 August 1897, p. 1, clipping, Muir Papers.

49. George Davidson, "Explanation of an Indian Map of the Rivers, Lakes, Trails, and Mountains from the Chilkaht to the Yukon Drawn by the Chilkaht Chief, Koh'klux, in 1869," *Mazama*, April 1901, p. 75.

50. John Cloud, "George Davidson and Native Peoples," *California Coast & Ocean* 23, no. 2 (2007): 25; Linda Johnson, "The Day the Sun Was Sick," 15.

51. Muir, "Pathless Treasure Fields of the Frozen Northlands," 1.

52. Ibid.; *Hall Young of Alaska*, 320.

53. *Hall Young of Alaska*, 259.

54. Ibid., 312, 314.

55. Ibid., 320, 341.

56. John Burroughs, *The Art of Seeing Things: Essays,* ed. Charlotte Zoe Walker (Syracuse, N.Y.: Syracuse University Press, 2001), 112.

57. Rosita Worl, "Standing with Spirits, Waiting," *The Harriman Alaska Expedition*

Retraced: A Century of Change, 1899–2001, ed. Thomas S. Litwin (New Brunswick, N.J.: Rutgers University Press, 2005), 32–33.

58. Muir quoted in Bruce Merrell, "A Muir Letter," *John Muir Newsletter*, spring 1991, pp. 5–6.

59. Ibid., 6.

60. John Muir scholar Ronald Limbaugh told this to me during a 1991 visit to the Muir Archives at the Holt-Atherton Special Collections, University Library, University of the Pacific, Stockton, California. See also Worster, *A Passion for Nature*; Wolfe, ed., *John of the Mountains*; Teal, ed., *The Wilderness World of John Muir*.

61. S. Hall Young, address to Layman's Missionary Conference, San Francisco, California, 23 February 1916, pp. 1–4, Badé Papers, Muir Collections.

62. Ibid., 4.

63. Italics in original. *Hall Young of Alaska*, 429.

64. John Marquis, introduction to *Hall Young of Alaska*, 8.

CHAPTER 11

1. Piseco [Lester A. Beardslee], "Chilcat and Chilcoot [*sic*]," a dispatch from Chilkoot Inlet, Chatham Straits, Alaska, 24 August 1880, in The Sportsman Tourist, *Forest and Stream*, 25 November 1880, p. 325. The power of paper is fully discussed in Langdon, "Unreciprocated 'Reverence.'"

2. Beardslee, "Report," *Case of the United States, ABT*, 365–66.

3. Lester A. Beardslee to E. P. McClellan, 20 May 1880, and Lester A. Beardslee to the Chiefs of the Chilkhats, Klotz-Kutch, and Elquesah [*sic*], 20 May 1880, published in ibid., 366–68.

4. Lester A. Beardslee to Klotz-Kutch, 10 June 1880, published in ibid., 369.

5. Ibid.

6. Piseco, "Chilcat and Chilcoot [*sic*]," 325.

7. Victoria Wyatt, "Female Native Teachers in Southeast Alaska: Sarah Dickinson, Tillie Paul, and Frances Willard," in *Between Indian and White Worlds: The Cultural Broker*, ed. Margaret Connell Szasz (Norman: University of Oklahoma Press, 1994), 183; *Hall Young in Alaska*, 92, 150, 165.

8. Hanks, *Fourth Annual Report of the State Mineralogist for the Year Ending May 15, 1884*, 264-65; Linsley, "A Description of Meteorites Available for Public Inspection in the San Francisco Bay Region," 474-75.

9. Lester A. Beardslee to Sec. of Navy R. W. Thompson, 1 September 1880, *Case of the United States, ABT*, 370-71.

10. Krause, *The Tlingit Indians*, 108.

11. Piseco, "Chilcat and Chilcoot [*sic*]," 325.

12. Interview of Lester A. Beardslee and Gouverneur Morris with Native leaders, 25 August 1880, *Case of the United States, ABT*, 372–73.

13. In-da-Yonk (Yen-da-yonk), Deposition, 26 March 1903, Ibid., 441.

14. Emmons, *The Tlingit Indians*, 332.

15. Carrie Willard's books are *Life in Alaska* and *Kin-da-shon's Wife*. Henry Glass to Sec. of the Navy William H. Hunt, 9 July 1881, *Case of the United States, ABT*, 379.

16. Gustavus C. Hanus, "Report," 1 July 1881, *Cases of the United States, ABT*, 381–82.

17. Ibid., 381. In his account, Crows are the equivalent of today's Eagles; Whales represent the Raven moiety.

18. Edward P. Lull, to Sec. of the Navy William H. Hunt, 8 September 1881, ibid., 382.

19. Willard, *Kin-da-shon's Wife*, 257–58.

20. Ibid., 258.

21. Italics in original. Ibid., 259.

22. Ibid., 260. Willard, *Life in Alaska*, 85–86.

23. Sally Burratin, interview with author, 6 July 2013.

24. Thornton, *Klondike Gold Rush National Historical Park Ethnographic Overview and Assessment*, 144.

25. George Thornton Emmons, "Report," 13 May 1887, *Case of the United States, ABT*, 406.

26. I. B. Howser, Howser's Café menu, c. 1950, Haines, Alaska, author's collection.

27. *Hall Young of Alaska*, 213.

28. Hotch, Joe, interview with author, 11 August 2014, Haines, Alaska.

29. Scundoo, Chilkat, 1900, p. 41, Southern District, Alaska, Federal Population Census Schedules, Twelfth Census of the United States, 1900, reel 1831 (1900), micofilm, T623, National Archives Microfilm Publications, Records of the Bureau of the Census, Record Group 29, National Archives Records Administration, Washington, D.C.

30. Louis and Florence Shotridge marriage certificate, 25 December 1902, Haines, Alaska. The Shotridge wedding certificate hangs in his former home, now owned by Dwight and Nancy Nash of Haines.

31. Sheldon Jackson, "Witchcraft among the Chilkats," *The Sitka (Alaska) North Star*, August 1888, p. 34, clipping, Archives, Haines Sheldon Museum and Cultural Center, Alaska.

32. Carol Feller Brady, interview with author, 10 November 2013, Juneau, Alaska.

33. Charges filed by U.S. Attorney Lytton Taylor against "Scum Doo," U.S. District Court, District of Alaska, 1894, *Case of the United States, ABT*, 439–40.

34. Rachel "Dixie" Johnson, oral history with author, Haines, Alaska, 1990, Archives, Haines Sheldon Museum and Cultural Center, Alaska.

35. Jack London, *Children of the Frost* (New York: Regent Press, 1902), 91.

36. Jenny Lynn Smith, discussion with author, Haines Sheldon Museum and Culture Center, Alaska, 20 July 2009.

37. Charlie Brouillette, interview with author, 22 September 2009.

EPILOGUE

1. Helen Addison Howard, *Saga of Chief Joseph* (Caldwell, Idaho: Caxton Printers, 1965), 330.

2. Palmer Volcanogenic Massive Sulphide (VMS) Project, Constantine Metals. http://www.constantinemetals.com/projects/palmer/.

3. Brian Willard quoted in Daniel Lee Henry, "Wild Line," *Community College Moment*, vol. 16 (Eugene, Ore.: Lane Community College, Spring 2016), 75.

4. Joe Hotch Jr., interview with author, 11 August 2014.

5. Entries for October–December 1879, Muir journals, image 34, Digital Archives, Muir Papers.

Bibliography

PRIMARY SOURCES

Archival Manuscripts

Alaska State History Library, Juneau (ASHL)

Bancroft Library, University of California, Berkeley (BL)

    Davidson, George. Papers, 1845-1911.

    Koh'Klux. Map of the Chilkhat: [Alaska and Yukon], 1852.

Chilkoot Indian Association (CIA)

Haines Sheldon Museum and Cultural Center, Alaska (HSM)

    Whale House Artifacts. Trial Notes.

Biography of Phoebe Warne Samsen. Presbyterian Home Mission Archive.

    1970.003.0002. Copy.

Muir Collections, Holt-Atherton Special Collections, University Library, University of

    the Pacific, Stockton (JMP)

    Muir, John. Papers. Correspondence and Related Documents.

    Badé, William Frederic. Papers.

        Merriam, C. Hart. "To the Memory of John Muir." Manuscript.

        Moores, Merrill. "Recollections of John Muir as a Young Man," 1938.

        Young, S. Hall. Young, S. Hall. "Alaska Days with John Muir." Address to Layman's

        Missionary Conference, San Francisco, California, 23 February 1916.

    Kimes Collection. Alaska File.

    Shone Collection. Clippings.

University of Pennsylvania Museum of Archeology and Anthropology, Philadelphia.

    (UP)

    Louis Shotridge Collection.

Interviews, Speeches, and Conversations

Bellinger, Agnes. Elders Meetings. Klukwan, Alaska, 8 November 2004.

Brady, Carol Feller.

———. Conversation with author. Juneau, Alaska, 8 November 2013.

Brouillette, Charlie. Interview with author. Haines, Alaska, 22 September 2009. Haines Sheldon Museum and Cultural Center, Alaska.

Burratin, Sally. Interviews with author. Klukwan, Alaska, 6 July 2013; and Haines, Alaska, 9 August 2013.

Brown, Judson. Interview. 16 June 1983. Archives. Sealaska Heritage Institute, Juneau, Alaska.

Edwards, Keri. Correspondence with author. 6 June 2016.

Hammond Sr., Austin. Address to Native American Spirituality workshop. Alaska. Environmental Assembly conference, Juneau, Alaska, 13 February 1988. From author's notes.

———. Oral History with author. Chilkoot Culture Camp, Haines, Alaska, 10 August 1985. Trans. Rachel "Dixie" Johnson. Haines Sheldon Museum and Culture Center, Alaska.

———. "Transcription and Translation of [a] Narrative Told by Austin Hammond Regarding Lukaax̱.ádi." Trans. and Ed. Keri Edwards Eggleston and Helen Sarabia. 1985. Manuscript. Sealaska Heritage Institute Archives, Juneau, Alaska.

Heinmiller, Lee. Interviews with author. Haines, Alaska, 2008, 2010.

Hotch Sr., Joe. Interview with author. Haines, Alaska, 11 August 2014. Haines Sheldon Museum and Culture Center, Alaska.

———. History Day Talk. Klukwan, Alaska, 20 April 2009.

———. Speech. Haines High School, Alaska, 14 February 2000.

Hotch, Lani. Interview with author. Klukwan, Alaska, 30 January 2009.

Jimmie Sr., Charlie. Interview with author, Haines, Alaska, 22 September 2009.

Jimmie Jr., Tommie. Interviews with author. Haines, Alaska, 23 July 2008; and 5 May 2009.

Johnson, Rachel "Dixie." Oral history with author. Haines, Alaska, 1990. Haines Sheldon Museum and Cultural Center Archives, Alaska.

———. Talk. Haines Sheldon Museum and Cultural Center, Alaska, 7 November 1991.

Jones, Holway R. Interview with author. Eugene, Oregon, 15 March 1983.

King, Richard. Interview with author. March 1991. Haines Sheldon Museum and Cultural Center, Alaska.

Lewis, George. Conversations with author, Haines, Alaska, 1988-1990.

Morgan, Al. Interview with author. May 2011. Haines Sheldon Museum and Culture Center, Alaska.

———. Public Comments. Haines Sheldon Museum and Cultural Center, Alaska, 2010.

Oscar, Frank. Oral History. Wrangell–St. Elias National Park. Project Jukebox. Oral History Program. University of Alaska, Fairbanks. http://jukebox.uaf.edu/WRST/71301.html.

Goenett, Paddy. Speech at 1929 Alaska Native Brotherhood Meeting, Haines, Alaska. Cited by Lee Heinmiller. Interview with author. Haines, Alaska 2010.

Dennis, Ray, and Joe Hotch Jr. Trade Routes Panel Discussion. Haines Public Library, Alaska, 29 January 2010.

Smith, Jenny Lynn. Discussion with author. Haines Sheldon Museum and Culture
Center, Alaska, 20 July 2009.
Strong, Kim. Correspondence with author. Klukwan, Alaska, 30 January 2007.
———. Public Speaking class. University of Alaska Southeast. Klukwan, Alaska.
Warren Sr., Edward. Conversation with author. Klukwan History Day, Alaska, 19 April
2011.

Government Documents

Alaska Boundary Tribunal. *Case of the United States before the Tribunal Convened at
London under the Provisions of the Treaty between the United States of American and
Great Britain concluded January 24, 1903.* Part 2 of *Proceedings of the Alaska Boundary
Tribunal: Convened at London, under the Treaty between the United States of America
and Great Britain. . . .* Washington, D.C.: Government Printing Office, 1903.
Hanks, Henry G. [California State Mining Bureau]. *Fourth Annual Report of the State
Mineralogist for the Year Ending May 15, 1884.* Sacramento: California Division of
Mines and Geology, 1884.
Scidmore, Eliza Ruhamah. "The First District from Prince William Sound to Yakutat
Bay." United States. Census Office. *Report on Population and Resources of Alaska at
the Eleventh Census, 1890.* Washington, D.C.: U.S. Bureau of the Census, 1893.
National Archives Records Administration, Washington, D.C. Record Group 29.
Records of the Bureau of the Census. National Archives Microfilm Publications.
Microcopy No. T-623. Twelfth Census of the United States, 1900. Alaska Federal
Population Census Schedules, Southern District. Microfilm. Reel 1831.
U.S. House. *Papers Relating to Cession of Alaska to United States.* 40th Cong., 2d sess.,
1868–1869. H. Ex. Doc. No. 177. Ser. No. 1339.

Books

Aristotle. *The Rhetoric of Aristotle.* Trans. and intro. Lane Cooper. 1932. Reprint,
Englewood Cliffs, N.J.: Prentice-Hall, 1960.
Badè, William Frederic, ed. The *Life and Letters of John Muir.* 2 vols. Boston: Houghton
Mifflin, 1924.
Blaisdell, Bob, ed. *Great Speeches by Native Americans.* Mineola, N.Y.: Dover
Publications, 2000.
Dauenhauer, Nora Marks, Richard Dauenhauer, and Lydia T. Black, eds., *Anóoshi Lingít
Aaní Ká / Russians in Tlingit America: The Battles of Sitka, 1802 and 1804.* Seattle:
University of Washington Press, 2008.
Davidson, George. *Pacific Coast: Coast Pilot of Alaska, First Part, from Southern
Boundary to Cook's Inlet.* Washington, D.C.: Government Printing Office, 1869.
———. *The Alaska Boundary.* San Francisco: Alaska Packers Association, 1903.
Davis, May Lee. *We Are Alaskans.* Ill. Olaus Johan Murie. Boston: W. A. Wilde, 1931.
Emerson, Ralph Waldo. *Nature.* Cambridge, Mass.: James Munroe and Company, 1836.
Emmons, George Thornton. *The Tlingit Indians.* Ed. Frederica de Laguna with Jean
Low. Seattle: University of Washington Press; New York: American Museum of
Natural History, 1991.
Engberg, Robert, ed. *John Muir Summering in the Sierra.* Madison: University of
Wisconsin Press, 1984.

London, Jack. *The Children of the Frost.* New York: Regency Press, 1902.

Giesel, Bonnie, ed. *Kindred and Related Spirits: The Letters of John Muir and Jeanne C. Carr.* Salt Lake City: University of Utah Press, 2001.

Howard, O. O. *My Life and Experiences among Our Hostile Indians: A Record of Personal Observations, Adventures, and Campaigns among the Indians of the Great West. . . .* Hartford, Conn.: A. D. Worthington, 1907.

Jackson, Rev. Sheldon. *Alaska, and Missions on the North Pacific Coast.* New York: Dodd, Mead and Company, 1880 [1884?].

Krause, Aurel. *The Tlingit Indians: Results of a Trip to the Northwest Coast of America and the Bering Straits.* 1885. Reprint, trans. and ed. by Erna Gunther. Seattle: University of Washington Press, 1979.

Lindsley, A[aron] L. *Sketches of an Excursion to Southern Alaska.* Portland, Ore.: First Presbyterian Church, 1881.

Menzies, Archibald. *The Alaska Travel Journal of Archibald Menzies.* Ed. and annot. Wallace M. Olson. Fairbanks: University of Alaska Press, 1993.

Muir, John. *John of the Mountains: The Unpublished Journals of John Muir.* Ed. Linnie Marsh Wolfe. 2d ed. Madison: University of Wisconsin Press, 1979.

———. *Letters from Alaska.* Ed. Robert Engberg and Bruce Merrell. Madison: University of Wisconsin Press, 1993.

———. *Steep Trails.* New York: Houghton Mifflin, 1918.

———. *The Cruise of the* Corwin. Ed. and intro. William Frederic Badè. 1917. Reprint, with a foreword by Roderick Nash, San Francisco: Sierra Club Books, 1993.

———. *The Story of My Boyhood and Youth.* 1913. Reprint, San Francisco: Sierra Club, 1988.

———. *The Yosemite.* Natural History Library. 1912. Reprint, New York: Doubleday, 1962.

Olson, Wallace M., ed. *Through Spanish Eyes: Spanish Voyages to Alaska, 1774–1792.* Auke Bay, Alaska: Heritage Research, 2002.

Scidmore, Eliza Ruhamah. *Alaska: Its Southern Coast and the Sitkan Archipelago.* Boston: D. Lathrop, 1885.

Seward, Frederick W. *Seward at Washington as Senator and Secretary of State, 1861–1872.* New York: Derby and Miller, 1891.

Teale, Edwin Way, ed. *The Wilderness World of John Muir.* New York: Houghton Mifflin, 1954.

Willard, Mrs. Eugene S. [Caroline]. *Life in Alaska: Letters of Mrs. Eugene S. Willard.* Ed. Mrs. Eva McClintock. Philadelphia: Presbyterian Board of Publication, 1884.

———. *Kin-da-shon's Wife.* 3d ed. New York: Fleming H. Revell, 1892.

Yelverton, Therese. *Zanita: A Tale of the Yo-Semite.* 1872. Reprint, with an introduction by Margaret Sanborn, Berkeley, Calif.: Ten Speed Press, 1991.

Young, S. Hall. *Alaska Days with John Muir.* 1915. Reprint, introduction by Richard Fleck, Salt Lake City, Utah: Peregrine Smith Books, 1991.

———. *Hall Young of Alaska, "The Mushing Parson": The Autobiography of S. Hall Young.* New York: Fleming Revell, 1927.

Articles and Pamphlets

Anderson, Melville B. "The Conversation of John Muir." *American Museum Journal* 15 (March 1915).

Avery, Benjamin P. "Summering in the Sierra, No. 1." *Overland Monthly*, January 1874.

Chief Joseph. Speech. In Blaisdale, *Great Speeches by Native Americans*.

Davidson, George. "Abrasions of the North-Western Coast." *Overland Monthly*, January 1874.

———. "Explanation of an Indian Map of the Rivers, Lakes, Trails, and Mountains from the Chilkaht to the Yukon Drawn by the Chilkaht Chief, Koh'klux, in 1869." *Mazama*, April 1901. Reprinted in Koh'klux (Chilkat Chief), *The Koh'klux Map*. Whitehorse: Yukon Historical and Museums Association, 1995.

Emerson, Ralph Waldo. "The Oversoul." *First Texts* (1841), http://www.emersoncentral.com/oversoul.htm

Emmons, George Thornton. "The Whale House of Chilkat." *Raven's Bones*. Ed. Andrew Hope III. Sitka, Alaska: Sitka Community Association, 1982.

Glave, Edward. "Pioneer Packhorses in Alaska: The Advance." *The Century Magazine*, September 1892.

Howard, O. O. "Glaciers in Alaska." *Morning (Portland) Oregonian*, 24 January 1880.

Jackson, Sheldon. "Witchcraft among the Chilkats." *The Sitka (Alaska) North Star*, August 1888. Clipping in Haines Sheldon Museum and Cultural Center Archives, Alaska.

Moores, Merrill. "Recollections of John Muir as a Young Man." In Badè Papers. Muir Collections.

"Mountain Sculpture." *Sunday School Journal for Teachers and Young People*, September 1879.

Muir, John. "A Perilous Night on Shasta's Summit." In Engberg, *John Muir Summering in the Sierra*.

———. "Alaska Glaciers: An Ounalaska Yosemite: Glacial Theology and Sermons in Ice: The Rocks, Plants, and Trees of Alaska." *San Francisco Daily Evening Bulletin*, 23 September 1879. Clipping in Muir Papers

———. "By-Ways of Yosemite Travel." *Overland Monthly*, September 1874.

———. "Pathless Treasure Fields of the Frozen Northlands." *San Francisco Examiner*, 23 August 1897. Clipping in Muir Papers

———. "Shasta in Winter." In Engberg, *John Muir Summering in the Sierra*.

———. "The Creation of Yosemite National Park." *Sierra Club Bulletin* 29 (October 1944).

———. "The Treasures of the Yosemite." *The Century Magazine*, August 1890. Copy in Muir Papers.

———. "Trails of the Gold Hunters on Northern Seas and in Mountain Passes." *San Francisco Examiner*, 11 October 1897. Clipping in Muir Papers.

———. "Wanderings in Alaska: A Lovely Sail—Majestic Mountain View." *San Francisco Daily Evening Bulletin*, 1 November 1879. Clipping on Muir Papers.

———. "Washington and Puget Sound." In Muir, *Picturesque California and the Region West of the Rocky Mountains*.

———. "Wild Wool." *Overland Monthly*, April 1875.

Ned, Annie. "Old-Style Words Are Just Like School." *Life Lived Like a Story: Life Stories of Three Yukon Native Elders*. Julie Cruikshank. Lincoln: University of Nebraska, 1990.

Piseco [Lester A. Beardslee]. "Chilcat and Chilcoot." *Forest and Stream*, 25 November 1880.

Seward, Frederick W. "Eclipse at Chilkat." *The Alaska Journal* 2 (winter 1972).

Seward, William H. *Alaska: Speech Delivered at Sitka, 12 August 1869*. Washington, D.C.:
Philip and Solomons, 1869.

Shotridge, Louis. "A Visit to the Tsimshian Indians." Parts 1 and 2. *The Museum Journal*
10, nos. 1-3 (March/June–September 1919).

———. "Ghost of Courageous Adventurer." Reprinted in Nora Marks Dauenhauer and
Richard Dauenhauer, eds. "Louis Shotridge and Indigenous Tlingit Ethnography:
Then and Now." *Constructing Cultures Then and Now: Celebrating Franz Boas and the
Jesup North Pacific Expedition*. Ed. Lauren Kendall and Igor Krupnik. Contributions
to Circumpolar Anthropology, no. 4. Washington, D.C.: Arctic Studies Center,
National Museum of Natural History, Smithsonian Institution, 2003.

Stone, E. L. "Literary Institute, Lecture by Dr. A. L. Stone." *Sacramento (Calif.) Daily
Union,* 12 January 1876.

"The Pacific Excursion." *Sunday School Journal for Teachers and Young People,*
September 1879.

Thoreau, Henry David . "Hymn to the August Morn." *The American Transcendentalists.*
Ed. Perry Miller. New York: Doubleday, 1957.

"Withdrawal of the Federal Bayonets from Alaska," *New York Tribune*. Reprinted in
Harper's Weekly, 21 April 1877.

Newspapers

Anchorage Alaska Dispatch News, 2016.

Boise Idaho Statesman, 2014.

Chicago Tribune, 1879.

Chilkat Valley (Haines, Alaska) News, 1985, 1999, 2007.

Juneau (Alaska) Empire, 2003.

Morning (Portland) Oregonian, 1880.

New York Times, 1873, 1909.

Sacramento (Calif.) Daily Union, 1876, 1879-1880.

Sacramento (Calif.) Record-Union, 1879.

San Francisco Chronicle, 1877–1878.

San Francisco Daily Alta, 1869.

San Francisco Daily Evening Bulletin, 1876, 1879.

San Francisco Examiner, 1897.

Sitka Alaska Times, 1869.

The Sitka (Alaska) North Star, 1888.

Miscellaneous

Hotch, Marsha. *Tlingit Time*. KHNS-FM. Haines, Alaska. Radio.

Howser, I. B. Howser's Café menu. 1950. Haines, Alaska. Author's collection.

Kawaky, Joseph, prod. *Haa Shagoon*. Haines, Alaska: The Association, 1983. Film.

Our Language, Our Stories, Our Life. Juneau, Alaska: Joel Bennett Productions, 2008.
Film.

SECONDARY SOURCES

Books

Austin, Richard Cartwright. *Baptized into Wilderness: A Christian Perspective on John Muir*. Atlanta: John Knox Press, 1987.

Boyd, Robert. *The Coming of the Spirit of Pestilence: Introduced Infectious Diseases and Pestilence among Northwest Coast Indians, 1774–1884*. Seattle: University of Washington Press, 1999.

Brown, Dee. *Bury My Heart at Wounded Knee: An Indian History of the American West*. New York: Holt, Rinehart and Winston, 1970.

Burke, Kenneth. *A Rhetoric of Motives*. Berkeley: University of California Press, 1969.

Carlton, Rosemary. *Sheldon Jackson, the Collector*. Juneau: Alaska State Museums, 1999.

Burroughs, John. *The Art of Seeing Things: Essays*. Ed. Charlotte Zoe Walker. Syracuse, N.Y.: Syracuse University Press, 2001.

Connell Szasz, Margaret, ed. *Between Indian and White Worlds: The Cultural Broker*. Norman: University of Oklahoma Press, 1994.

Cruikshank, Julie. *Do Glaciers Listen? Local Knowledge, Colonial Encounters, and Social Imagination*. Vancouver: UBC Press; Seattle: University of Washington Press, 2005.

Dauenhauer, Nora, and Richard Dauenhauer, *Haa Kusteeyí, Our Culture: Tlingit Life Stories*. Seattle: University of Washington; Juneau: Sealaska Heritage Foundation, 1994.

———. *Haa Shuká, Our Ancestors: Tlingit Oral Narratives*. Seattle: University of Washington Press; Juneau: Sealaska Heritage Foundation, 1987.

———. *Haa Tuwunaagu Yís, for Healing Our Spirit: Tlingit Oratory*. Seattle: University of Washington, 1990.

De Armond, Robert. *Early Visitors to Southeastern Alaska*. Anchorage: Alaska Northwest Publishing, 1978.

De Laguna, Frederica. *The Story of a Tlingit Community: A Problem in the Relationship between Archeological, Ethnological, and Historic Methods*. Washington, D.C.: U.S. Government Printing Office, 1960.

Dowie, Mark. *Conservation Refugees: The Hundred-Year Conflict between Global Conservation and Native Peoples*. Cambridge, Mass.: MIT Press, 2009.

Eastman, Charles A. *Indian Heroes and Great Chieftains*. Boston: Little, Brown, 1918.

Faris, John T. *The Alaskan Pathfinder*. New York: Fleming Revell, 1913.

Fleck, Richard F. *Henry Thoreau and John Muir among the Indians*. Hamden, Conn.: Archon, 1985.

Furtwangler, Albert. *Answering Chief Seattle*. Seattle: University of Washington Press, 1997.

Goodwin, Doris Kearns. *Team of Rivals: The Political Genius of Abraham Lincoln*. New York: Simon and Schuster, 2005.

Grinev, Andrei Val'Terovich. *The Tlingit Indians in Russian America, 1741–1867*. Trans. Richard L. Bland and Katerina G. Solovjova. Lincoln: University of Nebraska Press, 2005.

Gwynne, S. C. *Empire of the Summer Moon: Quanah Parker and the Rise and Fall of the Comanches, the Most Powerful Indian Tribe in American History*. New York: Scribner, 2010.

Hinckley, Ted C. *The Canoe Rocks: Alaska's Tlingit and the Euramerican Frontier, 1800–1912.* Lanham, Pa.: University Press of America, 1996.

Howard, Helen Addison. *Saga of Chief Joseph.* Caldwell, Idaho: Caxton Printers, 1965.

Jones, Holway R. *John Muir and the Sierra Club; the Battle for Yosemite.* San Francisco: Sierra Club Books, 1965.

Kan, Sergei. *Memory Eternal: Tlingit Culture and Russian Orthodox Christianity through Two Centuries.* Seattle: University of Washington, 1999.

———. *Symbolic Immortality: The Tlingit Potlatch of the Nineteenth Century.* Washington, D.C.: Smithsonian Institution Press, 1989.

Kirchoff, M. J. *Dyea, Alaska: Rise and Fall of a Klondike Gold Rush Town.* Juneau: Alaska Cedar Press, 2012.

Kurtz, Rick S. *Glacier Bay National Park and Preserve Historical Resources Study.* Anchorage: National Park Service, Alaska System Support Office, 1995.

Lazell, J. Arthur. *Alaskan Apostle: The Life Story of Sheldon Jackson.* New York: Harper and Brothers, 1960.

Lewis, Oscar. *George Davidson: Pioneer West Coast Scientist.* Berkeley: University of California Press, 1954.

Limbaugh, Ronald. *John Muir's "Stickeen" and the Lessons of Nature.* Fairbanks: University of Alaska Press, 1996.

Limerick, Patricia Nelson. *The Legacy of Conquest: The Unbroken Past of the American West.* New York: Norton, 1987.

Litwin, Thomas S., ed. *The Harriman Alaska Expedition Retraced: A Century of Change, 1899-2001.* New Brunswick, N.J.: Rutgers University Press, 2005.

Marks, Paula Mitchell. *In a Barren Land: American Indian Dispossession and Survival.* New York: Quill/William Morrow, 1998.

Miller, Sally M., ed. *John Muir: Life and Legacy.* Stockton, Calif.: University of the Pacific for the Holt-Atherton Pacific Center for Western Studies, 1985.

Miller, Sally M., and Daryl Morrison, eds. *John Muir: Family, Friends, and Adventures.* Albuquerque: University of New Mexico Press, 2005.

Nabokov, Peter. *A Forest of Time: American Indian Ways of History.* New York: Cambridge University Press, 2002.

Olson, Ronald L. *Social Structure and Social Life of the Tlingit in Alaska.* University of California Publications. Anthropological Records, vol. 26. [Berkeley]: [University of California Press], [1967]).

Olson, Wallace M. *The Tlingit: An Introduction to Their Culture and History.* 3d ed. Juneau, Alaska: Heritage Research, 1997.

Pierre, Berton. *The Klondike Fever: The Life and Death of the Last Great Gold Rush.* 1958. Reprint, New York: Carroll and Graf, 1985.

Riddle, Jefferson C. Davis. *The Indian History of the Modoc War.* 1914. Reprint, with an introduction by Peter Cozzens, Mechanicsburg, Pa.: Stackpole Books, 2004.

Sackett, Russell. *The Chilkat Tlingit: A General Overview.* Fairbanks: Anthropology and Historic Preservation, University of Alaska Cooperative Park Studies Unit, 1979.

Scharnhorst, Gary. *Bret Harte: Opening the American Literary West.* The Oklahoma Western Biographies. Norman: University of Oklahoma Press, 2000.

Spence, Mark David. *Dispossessing the Wilderness: Indian Removal and the Making of the National Parks.* New York: Oxford University Press, 1999.

Thornton, Thomas F. *Klondike Gold Rush National Historical Park Ethnographic*

Overview and Assessment. Skagway, Alaska: National Park Service, Alaska Regional
 Office, 2004.

Turner, Frederick. *Rediscovering America: John Muir in His Time and Ours*. San
 Francisco: Sierra Club Books, 1985.

Turner, Frederick Jackson. *The Frontier in American History*. 1920. Reprint, Tucson:
 University of Arizona 1994.

Utley, Robert M. *The Indian Frontier of the American West, 1846-1890*. Albuquerque:
 University of New Mexico Press, 1984.

Williams, Dennis C. *God's Wilds: John Muir's Vision of Nature*. College Station: Texas
 A&M University Press, 2002.

Wilson, Clifford. *Campbell of the Yukon*. Toronto: Macmillan of Canada, 1970.

Wolfe, Linnie Marsh. *Son of the Wilderness: The Life of John Muir*. New York: Alfred A.
 Knopf, 1945.

Worster, Donald. *A Passion for Nature: The Life of John Muir*. New York: Oxford University
 Press, 2008.

Articles and Chapters

Brown, Steven B. "A Tale of Two Carvers." *American Indian Art*, autumn 2005.

Burkher, Pauline V. "Amanda McFarland: Mother of Protestant Missions in Alaska."
 http://www.yukonpresbytery.com/history/Interviews/amanda.htm.

Buske, Frank. "John Muir's Alaska Experience." In Miller, *Life and Legacy*.

Cloud, John. "Benjamin Peirce and the 'Science of Necessary Conclusions.'" http://
 www.lib.noaa.gov/noaainfo/heritage/coastandgeodeticsurvey/Peircechapter.pdf.

———. "George Davidson and Native Peoples," *California Coast & Ocean* 23, no. 2 (2007).

———. "George Davidson and the Point of the Beginning: 'Once Seen, It Will Never Be
 Forgotten.'" *California Coast and Ocean* 23, no. 2 (2007).

Connor, Cathy, et al. "The Neoglacial Landscape and Human History of Glacier Bay,
 Glacier Bay National Park and Preserve, Southeast Alaska, USA." *The Holocene* 19, no.
 3 (May 2009): 381–93.

Cowan, Ellen A., et al. "Fjords as Temporary Sediment Traps: History of Glacial Erosion
 and Deposition in Muir Inlet, Glacier Bay National Park, Southeastern Alaska."
 Geological Society of America Bulletin 122, nos. 7–8 (July 2010): 1067–80.

De Laguna, Frederica. "Tlingit." *Northwest Coast*. Ed. Wayne P. Suttles. Vol. 7 of
 Handbook of North American Indians. Ed. William Sturtevant. Washington, D.C.:
 Smithsonian Institution, 1990.

Engberg, Robert. "On John Muir: Letters from Alaska." *John Muir Newsletter*, winter
 1992.

Fisher, Asst. Chief Ranger Don C., and John E. Doerr Jr. "Outline of Events in the
 History of the Modoc War." *Park Naturalist Nature Notes from Crater Lake* 10, no.
 1 (June 1937). http://www.craterlakeinstitute.com/online-library/nature-notes/
 vol10no1-modoc-war.htm.

Henry, Daniel Lee. "Wild Line." *Community College Moment*. Vol. 16. Eugene, Ore.: Lane
 Community College, Spring 2016.

Herem, Barry. "The Curse of the Tlingit Treasures: The Struggle for Possession of the
 Secret Masterworks of North American Art." *Connoisseur*, March 1991.

James, Susie. "Glacier Bay." In N. M. and R. Dauenhauer, *Haa Shuká, Our Ancestors*.

Johnson, Linda. "The Day the Sun Was Sick." *Yukon Indian News,* summer 1984.

Langdon, Steven J. "Unreciprocated 'Reverence': 'Papers,' Political Recognition, and Tlingit Engagement with US Governmentality in the late 19th Century." *Ethnohistory* 60, no. 3 (July 2013).

Lehman, Richard L. "The 1879 National Sunday School Assembly Convention in Yosemite Valley." *Yosemite Nature Notes*, January 1957.

Limbaugh, Ronald. "California's Kindred Spirits: John Muir and William Keith." In Miller and Morrison, *John Muir.*

Linsley, Earle G. "A Description of Meteorites Available for Public Inspection in the San Francisco Bay Region." Notes from the Society for Research on Meteorites. *Popular Astronomy* 42 (1934).

McClellan, Andrea Verplank. "The Evolution of Tlingit Daggers." *Sharing Our Knowledge: The Tlingit and Their Coastal Neighbors.* Ed. Sergei Kan with Steve Henrikson. Lincoln: University of Nebraska Press, 2015.

Merrell, Bruce. "A Muir Letter." *John Muir Newsletter,* spring 1991.

———. "A Wild, Discouraging Mess: John Muir Reports on the Klondike Gold Rush." *Alaska History* 7 (fall 1992).

Miraglia, Rita. "Yindastuki and Chilkoot Village: The Fates of Two Chilkat Tlingit Villages Claimed under ANCSA 14 (h) (1)." *Chasing the Dark: Perspectives on Place, History and Alaska Native Land Claims.* Ed. Kenneth L. Pratt. Shadowlands series, vol. 1. Anchorage, Alaska: United States Department of the Interior, Bureau of Indian Affairs, Alaska Region, Division of Environmental and Cultural Resources Management, ANCSA Office, 2009.

Morrison, Daryl. "John Muir and the Bains." In Miller and Morrison, *John Muir.*

Pauly, Steve. "The Importance of John Muir's First Public Lecture, Sacramento, 1876." *John Muir Newsletter,* winter 1998–1999.

Sanborn, Margaret. Introduction to Yelverton, *Zanita.*

Sherwood, Morgan B. "A Pioneer Scientist in the Far North: George Davidson and the Development of Alaska." *The Pacific Northwest Quarterly* 53 (April 1962).

Sutter, Ruth E. "John Muir and the John Swett Family." In Miller and Morrison, *John Muir.*

Wells, Daniel A. "Mark Twain in the 'Overland Monthly' (1868–1900): An Annotated List of Citations." *American Literary Realism, 1870–1910* 20, no. 2 (winter 1988).

Wilkerson, Laura. "General vs. General and a Horrible Betrayal of Slave Refugees." http://open.salon.com/blog/laura_wilkerson.

Worl, Rosita. "Standing with Spirits, Waiting." In Litwin, *The Harriman Alaska Expedition Retraced.*

Wyatt, Victoria . "Female Native Teachers in Southeast Alaska: Sarah Dickinson, Tillie Paul, and Frances Willard." In Connell Szasz, *Between White and Indian Worlds.*

Yale, Charles G. "Brief Sketch of the Public Services of George Davidson." *Mining and Scientific Press,* August 1885. http://www.history.noaa.gov/.

Reference Works

Edwards, Keri. *Dictionary of Tlingit.* Juneau, Alaska: Sealaska Heritage Institute, 2009.

Grun, Bernard. *The Timetables of History.* 3d ed. New York: Simon and Schuster, 1991.

Oxford Encyclopedia Dictionary.

Parrinder, Geoffrey, ed. *World Religions: From Ancient History to the Present.* New York: Facts on File, 1971.

Thian, Ralph P., comp. *Notes Illustrating the Military Geography of the United States, 1813–1880.* Ed. John M. Carroll. 1881. Reprint, with a foreword by Robert M. Utley, Austin: University of Texas Press, 1979.

Warner, Ezra J. *Generals in Blue: Lives of the Union Commanders.* Baton Rouge: Louisiana State University Press, 1964.

Theses, Dissertations, and Unpublished Papers and Essays

Higgs, Andrew. "Encounters with Kohklux: Historical Images of the Charismatic Chilkat Chief Shotridge." Paper presented at the Annual Meeting of the Alaska Historical Society, Haines, Alaska, 23 September 2003.

Hopper, Harold. "The First Alaska Day Celebration." Speech delivered in Haines on Alaska Day, 18 October 1991. Manuscript in Haines Sheldon Museum and Cultural Center Archives, Alaska.

Hotch, Lani. "Yanwaa Sháa." Unpublished essay. March 2011. Copy in Chilkat Indian Village Archives, Alaska.

Smith Sr., Norman L. "To the Mouth of the Chilkaht." Paper presented at the Alaska Historical Society, Haines, 4 October 2006.

Miscellaneous

"Sitka Charlie." Tlingit, Haida, and Tsimshian Genealogy of Alaska, http://wc.rootsweb.ancestry.com/cgi-bin/igm.cgi.

"Sitka Jack." Genealogy. http://wc.rootsweb.ancestry.com/cgi-bin/igm.cgi?op=GET&db=klea&id=I35871.

Index

Page numbers with an *f* refer to a figure; *n* refers to an endnote. Subject headings with (fict) refer to fictitious situations. Some personal names are glossed to distinguish them from place names or to indicate rank within the Tlingit social structure.

Armed with a masters degree in rhetoric and communication, Daniel Lee Henry settled in rural Alaska in the early 1980s aiming to immerse himself in the study of "frontier rhetoric," or the manner in which rural residents try to persuade each other about land and natural resources.

The author was drawn to Haines (pop. 2500) for its scrappy, smart culture; his work as a newspaper reporter, public radio program director, oral historian, and high school English teacher allowed him to make gains on his passion. In 1991 he received a Teacher-Scholar Award from the National Endowment for the Humanities which, along with four more awards from the Alaska Humanities Forum in the 1990s, allowed the author to build a research base for this book. In 2003 Henry's efforts were recognized with the Governor's Award for Civic Advocacy.

From these experiences flowed over 60 published articles, essays, and academic papers, including a 2000 Pushcart winner and a Pushcart special mention in 2004. His work appears in 8 anthologies, including *Pushcart Book of Essays: The Best of a Quarter Century of Pushcart, Book of the Tongass,* and *Travelers Tales Alaska.* Much of this book was presented as papers at the semi-annual Tlingit Clan Conference in Juneau and Sitka. Henry is a co-founder and program director of North Words Writers Symposium in Skagway, Alaska, featuring premier writers like Mary Roach, Brian Doyle, Howard Blum, and Paul Theroux.

In a decade of teaching communication for University of Alaska, Henry coached UA debaters to a national championship and founded the Alaska Native Oratory Society, a statewide program geared toward reviving oral traditions in the rural villages. Henry is a fulltime communication instructor at Lane Community College in Eugene, Oregon, where he lives with his wife, Robin Grace. They maintain a summer residence on a remote shore near Haines.